EXILE IN COLONIAL ASIA

Perspectives on the Global Past

Jerry H. Bentley and Anand A. Yang
SERIES EDITORS

Interactions: Transregional Perspectives on World History
Edited by Jerry H. Bentley, Renate Bridenthal, and Anand A. Yang

Contact and Exchange in the Ancient World
Edited by Victor H. Mair

Seascapes: Maritime Histories, Littoral Cultures, and Transoceanic Exchanges
Edited by Jerry H. Bentley, Renate Bridenthal, and Kären Wigen

Anthropology's Global Histories: The Ethnographic Frontier in German New Guinea, 1870–1935
Rainer F. Buschmann

Creating the New Man: From Enlightenment Ideals to Socialist Realities
Yinghong Cheng

Glamour in the Pacific: Cultural Internationalism and Race Politics in the Women's Pan-Pacific
Fiona Paisley

The Qing Opening to the Ocean: Chinese Maritime Policies, 1684–1757
Gang Zhao

Navigating the Spanish Lake: The Pacific in the Iberian World, 1521–1898
Rainer F. Buschmann, Edward R. Slack Jr., and James B. Tueller

Sea Rovers, Silver, and Samurai: Maritime East Asia in Global History, 1550–1700
Edited by Tonio Andrade and Xing Hang

Exile in Colonial Asia

Kings, Convicts, Commemoration

Edited by
Ronit Ricci

University of Hawai'i Press
Honolulu

Printed in the United States of America

25 24 23 22 21 20   6 5 4 3 2 1

Library of Congress Cataloging-in-Publication Data

Names: Ricci, Ronit, editor.
Title: Exile in colonial Asia : kings, convicts, commemoration / Ronit Ricci.
Other titles: Perspectives on the global past.
Description: Honolulu : University of Hawai'i Press, [2016] | Series: Perspectives on the
  global past | Includes bibliographical references and index.
Identifiers: LCCN 2015044544 | ISBN 9780824853747 cloth : alk. paper
Subjects: LCSH: Exiles—Asia—History. | Great Britain—Colonies—Asia. |
  Netherlands—Colonies—Asia. | France—Colonies—Asia.
Classification: LCC DS33.1 .E93 2016 | DDC 305.9/0691405—dc23 LC record
  available at http://lccn.loc.gov/2015044544

ISBN 978-0-8248-8314-0 (pbk.)

University of Hawai'i Press books are printed on acid-free
paper and meet the guidelines for permanence and
durability of the Council on Library Resources.

Contents

Acknowledgments

This volume has its origins in a workshop held at the Australian National University in Canberra in July 2013. I thank all participants, whether their contribution is included in this volume or not, for sharing their research and for stimulating conversations that allowed us to consider exile in colonial Asia and Australia in a comparative light.

Special thanks go to Robert Cribb for generously preparing the maps, to Carolyn Ferrick for meticulous copyediting and, at the University of Hawaiʻi Press, to Masako Ikeda and Debbie Tang for their support and patience and for seeing this volume through to publication. I am grateful to the two anonymous readers whose comments and suggestions on the manuscript were invaluable. My biggest debt of gratitude is to Maria Myutel for her assistance in organizing the workshop from its earliest stages and in preparing the manuscript for print. Her dedication, reliability, and insight made these tasks a pleasure. Funding for the workshop and the follow-up editorial work was generously provided by the School of Culture, History and Language, College of Asia and the Pacific, the Australian National University. The workshop was an offshoot of a larger project funded by a DECRA grant (DE120102604), awarded by the Australia Research Council.

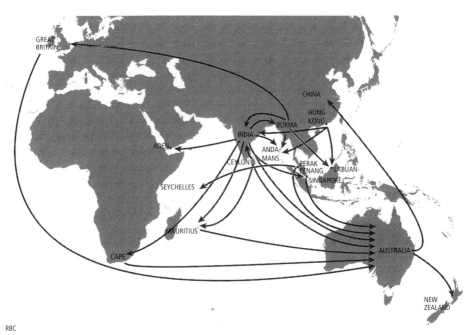

British colonial exile routes. (©Robert Cribb)

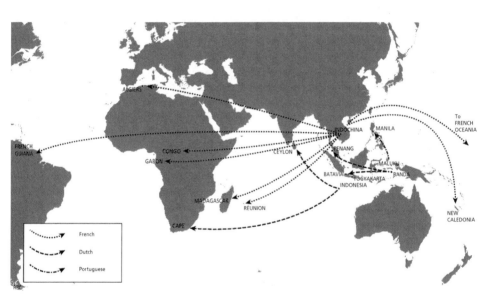

Dutch, French, and Portuguese colonial exile routes. (©Robert Cribb)

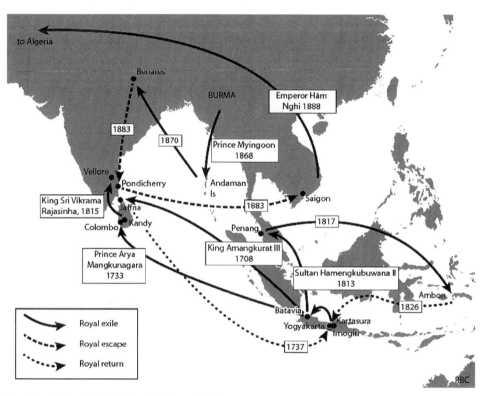

Royal exile in colonial Asia. (©Robert Cribb)

Exile in Colonial Asia
Kings, Convicts, Commemoration

Ronit Ricci

E xile was a potent form of punishment and a catalyst for change in colonial Asia. Through vast networks of forced migration, labor was supplied to emerging colonial settlements while individuals threatening social stability and European rule were shipped to faraway destinations, with the lines that separated exiled prince, convict laborer, and slave often blurred in the process. The temporal, spatial, and conceptual breadth of this theme means that studying exile's various manifestations, meanings, and implications in colonial Asia is as challenging as it is intriguing.

The workshop where this volume had its origin, convened at the Australian National University in Canberra in July 2013, constituted an attempt to begin to sort through a range of questions and comparisons related to exile in colonial Asia and think collaboratively about new approaches and methodologies with which to address them. Temporally the workshop's focus was on the seventeenth through nineteenth centuries, prior to the height of national struggles that in many cases involved banishment of high-profile leaders, and the subsequent cases of punitive exile in postcolonial Asian states. In terms of disciplinary breadth and regional expertise, participants came from the fields of history, anthropology, literature, and Asian, Australian, and Pacific Studies.

The case studies presented in this volume cover myriad contexts, from Colombo to Cape Town, from New Caledonia to New South Wales, from Burma to Banda; French, British, and Dutch policies toward and practices of banishment; various categories of people whose lives were touched or shaped by exile in the colonial period, among them royalty, slaves, convicts, rebels, soldiers, and officials; and the condition of exile and the ways it was remembered, reconfigured, and commemorated after the fact. These case studies allow us to see both a big picture of mobility, circulation, and displacement and some of the details it is made up of, as well as commonalities and differences in the experience of exile across colonial Asia. There is value in viewing these cases not in isolation but within a broad framework, beginning with the very wide, almost catchall idea of "colonial Asia"—acknowledging its constructed nature and its great internal diversity in terms of ruling imperial powers, colonial policies, and local circumstances—and moving toward the regional, personal, and particular.

"Colonial" in this volume is limited to the consideration of Europeans as colonizers and imperial rulers and excludes cases of intra-Asian colonization. The term as used in the following chapters encompasses both the era of powerful European trade companies gradually gaining control in the region and the subsequent era of colonial states. Although there were important differences between these two stages of European intervention, they also lie on a continuum, and when considering questions of banishment and forced migration, clear-cut distinctions are not always possible. Profit, legal authority, and the control of territory and lives were often inextricably linked. For example, as Kerry Ward claims, the Dutch East India Company's network of forced migration "was based on an extension of Dutch sovereignty that constituted an imperial domain in which the Company could impose its laws to run its business and turn a profit."[1] Finally, "Asia" in this volume is in some ways only a heuristic, as the movement of people depicted in its chapters spans Africa, the Pacific islands, Europe, and Australia, highlighting the global dimensions of colonial exile and the interconnectivity of the numerous sites, routes, and trajectories it encompassed.

This comparative approach is the reason why—in addition to the workshop's location in Australia, to whose fascinating history exile and banishment are central—transportation to Australia is included in this endeavor. Considering what transpired in Australia during the same period, and the ways in which European colonial powers thought of political offenses, crime, and punishment of their own citizens vis-à-vis those of people they colonized in Asia, helps put the events and processes of our "Asian examples" in a broader context and does the same for Australia.[2]

KINGS, CONVICTS, COMMEMORATION

The subtitle of this volume reflects three elements that are central to thinking about the condition of exile in colonial Asia and that are explored in detail in the pages that follow. "Kings" is used here as shorthand for members of royal families—kings, queens, princes, heirs to the throne, and their relatives—who were removed from power by Europeans, often at the request of a rival local ruler who promised support or territorial concessions in return. In other cases exile was a way to place a more compliant ruler on the throne or abolish a dynasty. Royalty and various officials of kingdoms and sultanates were considered political prisoners. Although they never constituted more than a minuscule minority within the large flows of convicts and slaves, the significance of their removal, both political and symbolic, far exceeded their numbers.

In chapter 2, "Out of Ceylon," Aldrich offers a brief survey that shows clearly the contours and extent of royal banishment: "Among other hereditary rulers sent into exile by the British were Maharaja Dalip Singh (the last Sikh ruler), a Zanzabari sultan, a Zulu king, a Malay sultan, and an Ashanti chief. The French deposed and banished no fewer than three Vietnamese emperors—and several princes in the Indochinese countries were also forced into exile—as well as West African rulers, the last queen of Madagascar, a sultan of the Comoros Islands, and several sultans of Morocco. The Dutch continued to send rulers whom they wished to punish into internal exile in the East Indies. The Portuguese in the early 1600s had exiled the last monarch of Jaffna, the Tamil kingdom in northern Ceylon, to India."

The dramatic exile of kings reverberated in the societies left behind and had profound consequences for the exiled themselves, who in many cases spent years pleading for return, often to no avail. Sometimes, as in the case of Prince Myngoon of Burma, which Penny Edwards explores in chapter 10, "Watching the Detectives," such figures evaded capture for long periods and crisscrossed colonial territories while consistently confounding their pursuers, raising doubts about the efficiency and subtlety of those in power. In other cases, including that of Yogyakarta's ruler Hamengkubuwana II and his family, Sri Margana's subject in chapter 5, "Caught between Empires," exile meant a life of confinement and longing combined peculiarly with attendance at dinners, dances, and performances and mingling with European colonial society. In two of the cases discussed in this volume (Ronit Ricci, chapter 4, "From Java to Jaffna," and Aldrich's chapter 2), it is not only kings and their retinues who were sent away but also their regalia—in the Javanese case taken along to Ceylon, and in the case of Kandy shipped to London. The regalia, which were considered important to the king's capacity to rule and to the well-being of his kingdom, were material and spiritual objects that, once removed from the palace, contained and symbolized the power, as well as the helplessness, of a defeated monarch. Their divergent appearances in indigenous and European accounts of royal exile offer a concrete representation of both.

Convicts and others on whom migration was imposed in the colonial period, whether as slaves, soldiers, indentured laborers, or rebels, made up the vast majority of those whose lives are explored in this book. They came from diverse backgrounds and places across Asia and contended with personal and communal challenges of many kinds, as Anderson (chapter 1, "A Global History of Exile in Asia"), Gelman Taylor (chapter 7, "Belongings and Belonging"), Liston (chapter 8, "An Exile's Lamentations?"), Paterson (chapter 9, "Prisoners from Indochina in the Nineteenth-Century French Colonial World"), and Yang (chapter 3, "'Near China beyond the Seas Far Far Distant from Juggernnath'") deftly show. In different ways these authors engage with the social hierarchies of convict life, including hierarchies of gender, race, and class, that shaped individual destinies. They also address the hardships as well as the opportunities arising from labor, resettlement, and distance, and the emotional states of people thrust into novel circumstances where identities and attachments were renegotiated and recast. The separation between the categories of kings and convicts in the subtitle, however, should not be taken to imply that these categories were mutually exclusive at all times. Rather, as Anderson argues in chapter 1, "the lines between the treatment of political prisoners and the treatment of ordinary convicts were at once both distinct and indistinct," and, certainly in the case of British colonialism in India, where caste played a role, but also elsewhere, caste notwithstanding, "the nature of their punishment was determined out of particular constellations of status, caste, and gender, rather than the offense for which they were transported."

Commemoration, finally, is here broadly defined and refers to the myriad ways in which exile and its aftermaths were considered and remembered by those left behind when family members, friends, gurus, or leaders were banished; by the exiled themselves, who wrote letters, poems, and songs that recounted their experiences of loss and adjustment and who built monuments often reminiscent of home; by colonial officials, clergy, and scholars, who documented proceedings and events from their own perspective; and by subsequent generations of descendants, devotees, pilgrims, scribes, historians, novelists, and politicians, who recast and re-created the exilic experiences of colonial Asia in various forms and contexts. The authors contributing to this volume form no exception, as we continue, through our research and writing, to engage with the topic from diverse geographic and disciplinary vantage points into the twenty-first century. That memory of exile is a site of contestation is evident in many of the chapters that follow but perhaps nowhere more powerfully than in Timo Kaartinen's discussion of the conflicting views of Dutch sources and Bandanese narrative traditions on the forced displacement of the Banda people from their home in the early seventeenth century (chapter 6, "Exile, Colonial Space, and Deterritorialized People in Eastern Indonesian History"). In songs passed down through the generations and recounting their collective history, the Bandanese stress their armed resistance and explicitly deny a condition of exile.

The Study of Forced Migration

There has been growing interest in recent years, especially among historians but also among scholars of literature, migration, law, diaspora studies, and anthropology, in investigating, reframing, and offering fresh perspectives on some of the inherited truths about penal transportation and convict labor in the colonial period. Central to recent work on the topic has been a de-emphasizing of the assumed hardened-criminal character of those transported and the bringing into focus of the utilitarian aspect of these mass movements of people for the sake of empire building, expansion, and settlement.[3] This shift, pioneered in the revisionist scholarship on Australian convict history and extended to research on additional regions, is reflected in a changing vo-cabulary that includes the term "convict workers." Its use, as Anand Yang has written, "is intended to underscore [the convicts'] roles as productive labourers and to shift attention away from their criminal pasts, which previ-ously misled considerations of their potential and effectiveness as workers."[4]

In addition to distancing itself from criminalizing notions, recent scholarship is choosing to closely consider, in as much detail as often-limited archival sources allow, the social and personal lives of banished individuals, the families and communities they created overseas, their memories, struggles, and hopes. An exemplary case of such work is Clare Anderson's exploration of subaltern biographies in the Indian Ocean world. Her excavation of the lives of marginalized men and women under British colonialism "proposes a biographical approach to penal transportation as a means of opening up a different perspective on colonialism, and working through critical questions of power, resistance and identity."[5] To this emphasis on how the personal and particular attests to larger histories of banishment and expansion can be added a growing concern with the histories of diasporas that grew out of exile, military recruitment, and other forms of labor under colonialism, as evident in the work of B. A. Hussainmiya, Brian Keith Axel, Sunil Amrith, and Ato Quayson and Girish Daswani, among others.[6] Two journals have also dedicated issues to related themes in recent years: the Journal of World History to "free and unfree labor migration, 1600–1900," and the Journal of Social History to "marginal centers: writing life histories in the Indian Ocean world."[7] The present volume builds on and continues such investiga-tions while highlighting in particular the exilic dimension of diverse contexts and experiences.

A word on the choice of "exile" is therefore warranted. Although "exile" is just one among several terms—including "banishment," "transportation," "enslavement," "forced migration"—employed in the following chapters to depict and define policies, processes, and experiences of sending people away from their homes and communities—words that overlap and diverge from "exile" in their emphasis, tone, and particular contextual meaning—the poignant potency of "exile" is one I did not wish to neglect or omit. "Exile" allows for the lived trajectories examined by the authors to be framed, in part, by the emotive forcefulness and historical echoes the word carries with it, thus bringing to life the experiences of those faraway moments and places, the reality of vast distances not easily traversed and discrepancies that are difficult for us to grasp—the king in his majestic garments boarding a ship, never to return to his kingdom; the prince confined to a fort; agony-filled letters that never reached their destination—the emphasis on the longings, dislocation, and pain of exilic life representing not a retrospective, anachronistic view, but one reflected in numerous ways in the testimonies available to us and presented in this volume's chapters.[8]

Difficult and isolating as exile and displacement often were, however, in many cases they gave rise over time to circumstances that were unintended by their planners and executors and set in motion processes that had profound consequences. As the chapters show in a recurring theme, colonial power over exiles and sites of banishment was never complete or total: not even the heavy gates of forts and prisons in Batavia, Jaffna, or Calcutta were hermetically sealed; no island (and certainly not a continent-size one like Australia) was completely isolated; no full control was exercised over forms of human expression in writing and speech. The cracks and loopholes emerge in this volume in Paterson's account of subversive poems by an exiled anti-French fighter slipping back into Vietnam despite government censorship; in Anderson's discussion of the ongoing flow of information to the supposedly isolated Andamans; in Liston's depiction of the vast British territories in Australia and convicts' freedom to set up their own living arrangements; and in Edwards' journey in the footsteps of an exiled Burmese prince who crossed between two empires' lands while evading colonial detectives. The de facto permeability of exile sites helped encourage and sustain the circulation of information, the creation of political and religious networks, and the potential for escape and resistance.

Thus when considering exile we should examine its various goals and manifestations in their own right but also think of exile as a step toward or a building block of new social opportunities both private and collective. As several chapters show, life away from home opened up opportunities for new forms of marriage and child rearing, employment, accumulation of property, religious affiliation, and attachment to place, and it allowed for the renegotiating of social hierarchies, gender roles, and one's perspective on both the past and the future.

For example, Jean Gelman Taylor's study of slaves of Indonesian origin in South Africa allows us to establish that "ex-slaves, like ex-convicts, found opportunity in foreign environments and capacity in themselves to rise above miserable circumstances and succeed in ways they could never have done in the lands of their birth." The inventories of possessions that constitute the main source for this study foster an appreciation of the accomplishments of individuals who began life in Indonesian villages, were transported to Africa, labored for others, established small businesses, and provided for the next generation, whose future and identity were locally based. In the Australian case, Liston argues that although transportation to New South Wales removed people from their families and communities, this exile to the antipodes was neither as remote nor as foreign as it might at first seem. The convicts, despite experiencing a radical break from their familiar environment, came to a settlement where the ethnicity, religion, and skills of the population were not greatly different from those of their communities at home. The combination of a new, remote environment and familiar cultural affiliations encouraged novel social and political developments. Kaartinen shows in chapter 6 how the eighteenth-century Dutch policies of forced migration in Eastern Indonesia resulted in the emergence of new forms of deterritorialized identity among the Bandanese.

Exile thus produced a range of unintended consequences both during the colonial period and in retrospect: in the ways events, people, and processes have been remembered and forgotten. Temporally, exile was bound up with past customs, with events in the present, and with future reimaginings.

EXILE: CONTINUITY AND MEMORY

Exile in colonial Asia was strongly connected with, and continued, precolonial practices of forced migration and the removal of political rivals. As Markus Vink has shown in his pioneering study of "the world's oldest trade," in the seventeenth century the Dutch mapped their slave trade in the Indian Ocean on older indigenous routes of slave trade and commerce.[9] The removal of political rivals and vanquished leaders also continued precolonial practices of local rulers. When applied by Europeans it was not a policy reserved exclusively for the colonies. As Robert Aldrich notes in chapter 2, just five months before the last king of Kandy, Sri Vikrama Rajasinha, set sail in 1816 for exile from Colombo, Napoleon was dispatched from Portsmouth to Saint Helena. The penal system in India had clear continuities with that of England, and the one employed in Indochina with that of France.[10] In some cases, however, European discourse claimed a sharp, morally driven distinction between the assumed brutality of precolonial punishment (including that favored by "harsh Islamic laws") and the development of transportation as a penalty that, although severe, inflicted a "just measure of pain" and was merciful in comparison to its antecedents.[11]

The question of how exiles—first and foremost political exiles, including royalty and military and religious leaders—would be remembered into the future was one that concerned colonial officials already in "real time" as they debated potential punishments and sites of banishment. Exile was often viewed as an appropriate substitute for execution, in a conscious effort to avoid the creation of martyrs.[12] While an executed king or sheikh might be seen as a hero whose death at the hands of foreigners would be memorialized through ritual, literature, song, and the commitment of subsequent generations to the cause he represented, exile offered the possibility of such figures withering away in confinement, forlorn and forgotten. Spatially, a geographical hierarchy of banishment posited that the more dangerous or threatening the culprit, the farther away the site of exile. Thus, as Yang writes in chapter 3, British authorities in India concluded that the Sikh rebel Nihal Singh could under no circumstances remain in the country, so potent were his leadership and spiritual sway over the masses. Sheikh Yusuf of Makassar, a political and religious leader exiled by the Dutch to Ceylon in 1684, was ten years later exiled farther afield to South Africa, despite his advanced age, still viewed as a threat to be contained via distance and its hoped-for consequence of irrelevancy.[13]

Needless to say, such strategies were not always successful and, at times, once more, had unintended results that subverted their original intentions. In contemporary and later sources the same people criminalized by the colonial state and its historiography were celebrated and championed for kingly qualities and anticolonial rebellions in the colonized society and postcolonial state.[14] Nihal Singh's shrine is today visited by Tamils, Muslims, and Sikhs, all of whom believe that great merit is earned by praying there for the intercession of this powerful, divinely touched saint; Sheikh Yusuf is credited by some as bringing Islam to South Africa, and his tomb at the Cape of Good Hope is an important pilgrimage site. Moreover, Nelson Mandela claimed him as a forefather of the liberation struggle against apartheid, and then President Suharto enshrined him as a national Indonesian hero in 1995.[15]

Colonial authorities attempted to anticipate and shape the afterlives of exile with varying degrees of success. It is worth briefly addressing a certain continuum apparent in the revealed and in the silenced as regards exile in colonial Asia across time. In an insightful article, Kerry Ward discusses a letter she found by chance in the Indonesian National Archives, written in 1816 by three Madurese princes serving in the Bugis Corps and addressed to the governor-general of India, Lord Minto. In it the princes stake a claim to the throne of Madura based on the exile of their grandfather, Cakraningrat IV, by the Dutch East India Company to the Cape of Good Hope in the 1740s.[16] Acknowledging the almost complete marginalization of royal exiles in national histories of Indonesia, Ward writes that in bringing to the forefront the story of the Madurese princes and their genealogy, she is suggesting that there are other paths and other stories to be told that shed light on the processes of constructing national histories rather than naturalizing a single narrative through the stories of the victors.

Ward rightly claims that "marginalization is a process and not a historical fact" and that writing other kinds of history from the perspective of marginalized persons and events "helps bring these processes into sharp relief instead of fading into the background of historical obscurity." The present volume, although it does not engage explicitly with the silencing of exile in postcolonial national histories across Asia, is suggestive of the approach put forth by Ward and seeks, more broadly, to ask how histories of exile in colonial Asia continue to be rethought, reshaped, and ignored in the present.

We might consider, for example, nomenclature practices that emerged over time in exilic sites and which reflected the shifting identities of those who had been forcibly relocated to elsewhere: the use of "Malay" as an ethnic category in Ceylon and later Sri Lanka, a homogenizing term that masked the diverse roots of its forefathers in numerous sites across the archipelago now known as "Indonesia"; or convicts and indentured laborers in late-eighteenth-century Bengkulen or the Straits Settlements who "increasingly defined themselves as part of an 'Indian' community that emerged in these outposts of empire as a result of the mixing and melding of different groups of people from the South Asian subcontinent."[17] Kaartinen offers another case in point in his discussion of the ongoing use of "Banda" for a community that was almost wiped out by early Dutch conquests in Eastern Indonesia in 1621, then dispersed and displaced, but that retained its language, oral traditions, and adherence to Islam.

We might also wish to imagine the communities that "could have been" had the rules of exilic movement been determined differently, in less racialized ways: as Yang notes in chapter 3, in the initial years of transporting convicts from South Asia to Southeast Asia, a few Europeans, mostly Portuguese, were transported along with Indians, although they were typically treated differently, housed separately, and placed as overseers. Generally, however, Europeans convicted of transportable offenses were sent from British colonies to Australia, which early on the authorities in London decided to preserve as a place for Europeans, and so, for the most part, they refrained from sending Indian convicts there (for exceptional cases of Asians sent to

Australia, see Liston's chapter 8). Would Australia differ, and how, had thousands of Indians been transported to its shores? What character would Malaya, Singapore, and Bengkulen possess had a diverse mix of Europeans been sent there for imprisonment, labor, and settlement in the early nineteenth century? These are some of the "shadows," or unrealized potentialities, of communities created by exile and forced labor migration in Ceylon, South Africa, the Andamans, the Straits Settlements, and Australia.

NOTE ON METHODOLOGY AND SOURCES

Methodologically, the study of exile in colonial Asia is highly challenging, first and foremost due to the globality of the relevant archives, spread across continents and states. Exiled individuals often came from one place and were sent to another, which was administered from a third. Records pertaining to practices of exile by the Dutch East India Company, for example, are housed today across three continents in Indonesia, Sri Lanka, India, South Africa, and the Netherlands. The volume of colonial records is vast, and archival collections differ markedly in their levels of organization, preservation, and accessibility.

But no less challenging and problematic is the circumscribed nature of archival documents available for study. Whereas convicts, by virtue of their exposure to state surveillance, were typically better documented than any other nonelite group in colonized societies, European documentation offers a very particular perspective on such individuals, which—important as it is—rarely represents their thoughts and voices. Anderson, following Stoler, stresses the ways in which archives' structure and content "refract relations of power as much as they inscribe them."[18] One way to counter the reliance on circumscribed colonial collections, to overcome it, however partially, and to open up spaces for other kinds of testimony and commemoration, is to look to non-European, local chronicles that engage with the same events but from a (sometimes radically) different perspective.

For example, the eighteenth-century Javanese *Babad Giyanti* recalls the weekly arrival in Ceylon of tempeh and other delicacies from faraway Java. The familiar food is intended to offer solace to a group of homesick exiles gathered around their Muslim guru and emerges from the sleeve of his gown after Friday prayers.[19] In what we might call, paraphrasing A. L. Becker, a "silence across histories,"[20] the account says not a word about the exiles' whereabouts in Ceylon, about the lives they led and the reasons for their banishment, all practical details prone to appear in Dutch contemporary records; yet the *Babad Giyanti* account conveys much about the longing, solidarity, religious networks, and memories that filled people's lives in a strange land, revealing sentiments and elements of cultural resilience that are altogether absent from the colonial archive but allow for the writing of a different kind of history.[21] Also written in the *babad* genre, the *Babad Mang-kudiningratan*, discussed by Sri Margana, reveals a remarkable contemporary depiction of the lives of royal exiles in the early nineteenth century, down to the details of their meals, social pastimes, sorrows, and loves. This rare glimpse into the realm of the personal and intimate removes the story of exile from the colonial office and places it squarely back into its local, immediate context, where it is perceived very differently even after two centuries have passed.[22]

Considering the *babad* genre leads to the broader theme of written documents, mentioned repeatedly in the various accounts of exile. Letters, above all, play a prominent role in the studies presented here, and in others, as a means of communication between exiles and their families, friends, and communities, and as a major source for historians. Many of the surviving letters are available only in translation into English and Dutch; most personal letters passed through government agencies and forms of censorship, especially after the mid-nineteenth century; and letters from exiles were often concerned more with old places and with people left behind than with recounting their new lives, thus contributing to the tendency of the archive to produce subaltern biographies that are consistently partial, fragmentary, and fleeting. And yet with all their limitations, letters still reveal a great deal about lives lived in exile, especially the trials and challenges they entailed and the longing that accompanied them.[23]

Petitions were a subcategory of letters that were especially widespread and have been relatively well preserved and that, contrary to the official document one might expect upon hearing the word "petition," contained moving personal accounts that were often the only firsthand testimony of the exiles' lives. For example, in an 1814 petition to the British government in Penang asking to return to India, Aundoo Konda Vunnam Tinnevelly, who had been transported with a group of Poligar rebels when he was just sixteen, wrote that the two years he was confined in Madras plus the thirteen years in Penang had caused him "very extensive distress . . . [from] the want of relatives and friends. . . . Torn from parents, possessions, and ease in his childhood, doomed to pass his youth in exile."[24] Many petitions included a request for added funds, a raise in allowances granted to royal exiles and their descendants, who were not expected to work. Thus in an 1807 letter sent from Ceylon by Siti Hapipa, widow of the exiled king of Gowa to the Dutch government in Batavia, she recounted her suffering since her husband's death and begged the governor-general to increase her payment so she could support her children and grandchildren. She also promised that if allowed to return to the Indies she would repay her debt by serving the governor in any possible way.[25] Although many letters contained such requests and pleadings, some, like the one written by the Madura princes mentioned earlier, bear testimony to claims of power and a right to rule. Letters home written by convicts in Australia, explored in Liston's chapter 8, revealed "people caught between interest in the new opportunities and sorrow at the loss of family and friends."

In the cases where original letters have been preserved alongside translations, there is scope for studying the translations as sites of intercultural exchange, mistranslation, and doubt. The range of languages in which letters were written and the ways in which languages and scripts were employed and deployed constitute another aspect worth studying and one that places language, writing practices, and cultural traditions at the fore of understanding the exilic condition. The use of literary language, with its reliance on cultural repositories, the knowledge of prior texts, and particular forms of training, is especially intriguing when found in exilic contexts.

Paterson in chapter 9 offers the example of a poem attributed to Nguyễn Hữu Huân, a Vietnamese prisoner sent to New Caledonia in 1864 after participating in a battle against the French. The poem, written in classical Chinese, attests to the author's grounding in that tradition and to his ability to employ its tropes and allusions to write about his experience of estrangement in exile, evoking images of departure and grief. The significance of the metaphorical language is said to have eluded the French censor, as the poem was transmitted back to Vietnam, where it became a rallying point for anti-French sentiments. In a reminiscent example from the Andamans, Anderson cites in chapter 1 the moving Persian-language poetry of two convicts who depicted exile as seen through the social, cultural, and political ruptures of transportation: Fazl-i-Haq Khairabadi (1797–1861), an Awadhi scholar who was alleged to have joined the 1857 revolt, described himself as "a heart-broken and suffering prisoner" and detailed his personal circumstances; Lucknow poet Mohammed Ismail Hussain ("Munir") Shikohabadi (1819–1881) wrote more broadly of crossing the "black waters" into exile and the anguish and dread of transportation.

Exile in Context

This volume presents ten case studies of exile in colonial Asia and Australia. It opens with Clare Anderson's broad yet richly detailed overview of the history of exile in colonial Asia circa 1700–1900 as seen from a global perspective. In chapter 1 Anderson considers how banishment and transportation became bound up with larger imperial agendas of labor extraction, colonization, and frontier expansion, and explores the eruption of contradictions between punishment and political economy. In unpacking the suggestion that caste and status were of key importance in the organization and management of political *and* criminal convicts, a central focus of the chapter is on how the exiled, banished, and transported experienced their sentence within the larger penal context. It shows how many ordinary prisoners, convicts, and their families felt keenly the social, cultural, and religious impacts of their forced shipment overseas, and centered "exile" in later accounts of their transportation or in expressions of their familial loss. Importantly, Anderson's account is located both within and beyond Asia, its underlying contention that exile in Asia can be understood only through an appreciation of the inter- and transcolonial networks of which the continent was a part.

In chapter 2 Robert Aldrich examines the journey of the last king of Kandy, Sri Vikrama Rajasinha, from Ceylon to India in 1815 and his subsequent, lifelong exile in Vellore as an example of the British practice of exiling indigenous Asian rulers. He shows how the study of this practice opens a window onto life stories of empire, the human drama of men and women born to power who ended their lives in captivity. The chapter highlights the transnational, intercolonial contexts in which exile took place and the challenges it created for colonial authorities; and it points to how, though physically eliminated as a force of resistance, exiled rulers could pose a threat—both in their lifetimes and in their legacies—as a rallying point for anticolonialism.

Anand Yang's contribution dwells on the exile experience of the Sikh rebel Nihal Singh and of his disciple Kharak Singh, in Singapore in the mid-nineteenth century. Chapter 3 tracks their journey from Punjab to Calcutta to Singapore to highlight the lived experiences of exiled political prisoners, especially in relation to those of the transmarine convicts who lived alongside them in very different circumstances in the outposts of the British empire in Southeast Asia. Yang's analysis shows how Nihal Singh's experience of exile was shaped by his high status, which induced great anxiety in his captors. It guaranteed his living conditions and saved him from execution—for fear that he would become a martyr to his followers—*and* determined his stay in closed quarters with severely restricted freedom of movement and communication.

In chapter 4 Ronit Ricci explores the topic of political exile from and within the Indonesian archipelago under the Dutch East India Company. Drawing on evidence from eighteenth- and nineteenth-century Javanese manuscripts relating the exile of members of royal families, court officials, and their accompanying retinues from Java to Ceylon in the first half of the eighteenth century, she highlights the potential these often brief but instructive and moving depictions have to convey a perspective of a very different texture, content, and tone than those of Dutch- and English-language records in colonial archives. Her analysis also emphasizes the Javanese chronicles' ability to shed light on what remains a vague but formative episode in the larger history of exile in colonial Asia as well as specifically Indonesian and Sri Lankan understandings of the past.

Sri Margana's chapter discusses the fate of Sultan Hamengkubuwana II of Yogyakarta and his family, exiled to Penang by the British during their brief interregnum on Java, and later exiled again to Batavia and Ambon. Chapter 5 makes use of a rare Javanese manuscript, the *Babad Mangkudining-ratan*, written in exile by Mangkudiningrat, the sultan's son, or by another person close to the family and accompanying it into exile and depicting in great detail the experiences of exilic life, including its personal and emotional dimensions. The *Babad Mangkudiningratan* also expounds on shifting politi-cal circumstances, which, as Margana shows, meant that the king and his family were caught between two empires, the British and Dutch, with shifting loyalties and dramatically altered circumstances shaping their prospects of returning home or ending their lives in exile. The *Babad Mangkudiningratan*'s richness of detail contrasts sharply with the *babads* explored in Ricci's chapter, with their dearth of information on exilic life, raising questions about the range of references to colonial exile contained within the Javanese historical tradition.

Timo Kaartinen's study is based on long-term fieldwork in the islands of Maluku in Eastern Indonesia, where he explored how the Bandanese employ exile as a trope to understand their past and present conditions. More broadly, in chapter 6 Kaartinen discusses the relationship of exile to other deterritorializing effects of colonialism in the region and asks what impact it had on the creation of colonial space and on the dynamics of power set in motion by the Dutch colonial presence in the East Indies between 1600 and 1880. In this emerging colonial context, exile appears as a means for the conscious political manipulation of the indigenous society, but also as a fix for unexpected crises of legitimacy and anticolonial resistance. The chapter's comparison of the colonial government's language about identity and place with that of the community of exiles provides insight into two diverging conceptualizations of a process that continues to shape Bandanese understandings of the foreign and familiar, home and away, stranger and kin, into the present.

Jean Gelman Taylor's study in chapter 7 of forced migration focuses on slaves from the Indonesian archipelago who were shipped to the Dutch East India Company settlement at the Cape of Good Hope. In attempting to sketch a view "from below," she examines inventories and wills drawn up in

Cape Town in the eighteenth century by European settlers, Dutch East India Company officials, and freed slaves of Indonesian origin. Employing an innovative methodology that views such inventories and wills as sources for reconstructing the lives of the slaves, their possessions, bequests, names, occupations, and relationships, she shows the wealth of information available within these rarely scrutinized documents and their potential contribution to our understanding of the large-scale involuntary circulation of peoples across the Indian Ocean and their lives in new places that became their homes.

In chapter 8, Carol Liston offers an analysis of exile from the perspective of Australian history. The British legal system enforced exile, or "transportation," as a punishment for criminal offenses. In the sixteenth and seventeenth centuries, exiles were sent to Ireland; in the eighteenth century they were sent to the North American colonies; and from 1788 they were sent to a new colony established specifically for transported felons: Botany Bay. Recent opinion shifts among Australian academics and the general public toward the origins of white settlement in the country have meant that, especially when compared to the availability of sources on exile in its Asian neighbors, Australia possesses a wealth of evidence collected by social historians, genealogists, and archaeologists that provides insight into the personal space of its convict experience. The chapter considers a sample of men and women transported from their homeland and explores their attitudes toward exile, community building, life in a new land, and the gradual creation of a new society that offered many an ex-convict unprecedented freedoms and opportunities.

In chapter 9 Lorraine Paterson shifts our gaze to French colonial approaches to exile, providing an important counterexample to British and Dutch policies, which are explored at greater length in the volume. From French Equatorial Africa to the penal colony of Guiana, the French administration of Indochina used various territories within the expanse of the French colonial world as sites of exile for political prisoners. However, as Paterson's research shows, the French penal colony of New Caledonia was the initial location of exile for Vietnamese political prisoners, even before the Federation of Indochina itself was formed. Exiled in the early 1860s, these male political prisoners served ten-year sentences of hard labor in the nickel mines of this Pacific island. Once released, they were forbidden to return to Indochina and instead received land plots from the government and were obliged to enter into arranged marriages with recently freed French prisoners, a policy that, as Paterson notes, would seem "utterly fantastical" to prisoners in Vietnam itself. She examines the unique mestizo community that arose from these unions and the forms of transcolonial social life among exiles that left important traces both in the French penal colony of New Caledonia and in the southern Vietnamese communities the deportees had left behind.

Chapter 10, by Penny Edwards, interrogates the limits of colonial surveillance through an examination of the life in exile of Prince Myngoon of Burma, who traveled across Rangoon, Benares, Pondicherry, and Saigon from the 1860s to 1920s, crossing from British to French territory and back, thus testing the limits of patience, trust, and anxiety between the two powers. In exploring Myngoon's histories of subterfuge and evasion, Edwards questions "the uniform applicability to colonial states of the Foucauldian trope of the panopticon and the Scottian notion of the colonial state as an entity which left its subjects nowhere to hide," showing that the colonial states that surveilled Myngoon were often outwitted, feeling helpless and frustrated at the complexity of their task. Central to the concern of colonial authorities beguiled by Myngoon was the figure of the imposter or trickster. The chapter examines three instances of colonial confusion over suspected trickery—two in British India and one in French Indochina—and through this exploration asks what kind of sources are generated by, and generative of, histories of exile.

Notes

I thank Jesse H. Grayman and Jean Gelman Taylor for kindly reading, and commenting on, an earlier version of this introduction.

1. Kerry Ward, *Networks of Empire: Forced Migration in the Dutch East India Company* (Cambridge: Cambridge University Press, 2009), 11.

2. Clearly, current debates raging in Australia and in its Asian and Pacific neighbors about those now referred to, depending on one's point of view, as "asylum seekers," "boat people," or "economic migrants" also echo with the stories of people in this part of the world forced to leave their homes, families, and countries in the past.

3. On the use of convict labor to consolidate and develop colonial settlements and alleviate labor shortages in the British Empire, see Anand Yang, "Bandits and Kings: Moral Authority and Resistance in Early Colonial India," *Journal of Asian Studies* 66, no. 4 (2007): 888.

4. Anand Yang, "Indian Convict Workers in Southeast Asia in the Late Eighteenth and Early Nineteenth Century," *Journal of World History* 14, no. 2 (2003): 181.

5. Clare Anderson, *Subaltern Lives: Biographies of Colonialism in the Indian Ocean World, 1790–1920* (Cambridge: Cambridge University Press, 2012), 12.

6. B. A. Hussainmiya, *Orang Rejimen: The Malays of the Ceylon Rifle Regiment* (Bangi: Universiti Kebangsaan Malaysia, 1990); Brian Keith Axel, "The Diasporic Imaginary," *Public Culture* 14, no. 2 (2002): 411–428; Sunil Amrith, *Migration and Diaspora in Modern Asia* (Cambridge: Cambridge University Press, 2011); Ato Quayson and Girish Daswani, eds., *A Companion to Diaspora and Transnationalism* (Chichester: Wiley-Blackwell, 2013), especially "Part II: Backgrounds and Perspectives," 161–230.

7. See, respectively, *Journal of World History* 14, no. 2 (June 2003), and *Journal of Social History* 45, no. 2 (Winter 2011).

8. Although the studies presented in this volume do not explicitly dwell on vocabularies of exile and the exiled in the different contexts and languages, such words—especially when examined comparatively—are important to understanding the experience and its images: the neutral practicality of "transportation"; the site specificity of *disailanaken* (to be "Ceyloned" in Javanese); or the emphasis on difference and alienation of *diasingkan* (to be "foreigned" in Malay). Banished men and women were known as "convicts" in court records in England but as "government servants" once arrived in Australia; Javanese honorific titles like *pangèran, tumenggung,* and *adipati* continued to be employed in Dutch records to refer to those who carried them previously; under Dutch rule in Ceylon, groups of exiles, slaves, and soldiers continued to be referred to based on their regional identity in the archipelago, e.g., Ambonese, Javanese, Makassarese, but later came to be known collectively as "Malays" under British rule.

9. Markus Vink, "'The World's Oldest Trade': Dutch Slavery and Slave Trade in the Indian Ocean in the Seventeenth Century," *Journal of World History* 14, no. 2 (2003): 131–177. For a pioneering analysis of the history of slavery in Southeast Asia, including during the colonial period, see Anthony Reid, "Introduction," in *Slavery, Bondage and Dependency in Southeast Asia,* ed. Anthony Reid (St. Lucia: University of Queensland Press, 1983), 1–43.

10. On the continuities with England, Yang writes, "From the outset transportation was also developed as a punishment in India—as it had been in England—to serve economic objectives as well." Yang, "Indian Convict Workers," 190. On French policies see Lorraine Paterson, chapter 9, "Prisoners from Indochina in the Nineteenth-Century French Colonial World," in this volume.

11. Yang, "Bandits and Kings," 884.

12. For some of the convicts sent to Australia, a death sentence had been commuted to transportation; see Carol Liston, chapter 8, "An Exile's Lamentations?," in this volume.

13. Abu Hamid, *Syekh Yusuf Makassar: Seorang Sufi, Ulama dan Penjuang* (Jakarta: Yayasan Obor Indonesia, 1994).

14. For an example of this phenomenon in South India, centered on the Poligar rebel Kattabomman, see Yang, "Bandits and Kings."

15. On Singh's shrine, see Anand Yang, chapter 3, "'Near China beyond the Seas Far Far Distant from Juggernath,'" in this volume; on Sheikh Yusuf's stature in modern South Africa and Indonesia and the invocation of his biography in contemporary political contexts, see Ward, *Networks of Empire,* 1–3.

16. Kerry Ward, "Blood Ties: Exile, Family, and Inheritance across the Indian Ocean," *Journal of Social History* 45, no. 2 (2011): 449.

17. Yang, "Indian Convict Workers," 183–184.

18. Anderson, *Subaltern Lives,* 11. Anderson cites Stoler's 2009 work on "arrested histories."

19. Radèn Ngabehi Yasadipura, *Babad Giyanti,* 21 vols. (Batavia Sentrum: Balai Pustaka, 1937–1939), vol. 21, 85.

20. A. L. Becker, "Silence across Languages," in *Beyond Translation: Essays toward a Modern Philology* (Ann Arbor: University of Michigan Press, 1995), 283–294.

21. For a discussion of the importance of, and challenges inherent in, revealing the perceptions and attitudes of those exiled, forced to migrate and labor, see David Northrup, "Free and Unfree Labor Migration, 1600–1900: An Introduction," *Journal of World History* 14,

no. 2 (2003): 129–130. On a late-nineteenth-century Sri Lankan Malay text that indicates an ongoing engagement with the history of their ancestors' homeland, see Ronit Ricci, "Remembering Java's Islamization: A View from Sri Lanka," in *Global Muslims in the Age of Steam and Print,* ed. James Gelvin and Nile Green (Los Angeles: University of California Press, 2013), 185–203.

22. The explorations of Javanese *babads* in this volume, mining them as they do for information and insight on exile, invite research into additional writing traditions across the region, which may contain similar depictions or perspectives on exile.

23. For an illuminating example of such documents as providing important evidence and perspective on the penal colony, see Anderson's presentation and analysis of the diary and letters of Edwin Forbes, an American convict guard stationed in the Andaman Islands from 1861 to 1864. Anderson, *Subaltern Lives,* 157–186.

24. Yang, "Bandits and Kings," 890.

25. Suryadi, "Sepucuk surat dari seorang bangsawan Gowa di tanah pembuangan (Ceylon)," *Wacana: Jurnal ilmu pengetahuan budaya* 10, no. 2 (2008): 214–243.

BIBLIOGRAPHY

Amrith, Sunil. *Migration and Diaspora in Modern Asia.* Cambridge: Cambridge University Press, 2011.

Anderson, Clare. "Introduction to Marginal Centers: Writing Life Histories in the Indian Ocean World." *Journal of Social History* 45, no. 2 (2011): 335–344.

———. *Subaltern Lives: Biographies of Colonialism in the Indian Ocean World, 1790–1920.* Cambridge: Cambridge University Press, 2012.

Axel, Brian Keith. "The Diasporic Imaginary." *Public Culture* 14, no. 2 (2002): 411–428.

Becker, A. L. "Silence across Languages." In *Beyond Translation: Essays toward a Modern Philology,* 283–294. Ann Arbor: University of Michigan Press, 1995.

Hamid, Abu. *Syekh Yusuf Makassar: Seorang sufi, ulama dan penjuang.* Jakarta: Yayasan Obor Indonesia, 1994.

Hussainmiya, B. A. *Orang Rejimen: The Malays of the Ceylon Rifle Regiment.* Bangi: Universiti Kebangsaan Malaysia, 1990.

Northrup, David. "Free and Unfree Labor Migration, 1600–1900: An Introduction." *Journal of World History* 14, no. 2 (2003): 129–130.

Quayson, Ato, and Girish Daswani. *A Companion to Diaspora and Transnationalism.* Chichester: Wiley-Blackwell, 2013.

Reid, Anthony. "Introduction." In *Slavery, Bondage and Dependency in Southeast Asia,* edited by Anthony Reid, 1–43. St. Lucia: University of Queensland Press, 1983.

Ricci, Ronit. "Remembering Java's Islamization: A View from Sri Lanka." In *Global Muslims in the Age of Steam and Print,* edited by James Gelvin and Nile Green, 185–203. Los Angeles: University of California Press, 2013.

Suryadi. "Sepucuk surat dari seorang bangsawan Gowa di tanah pembuangan (Ceylon)." *Wacana: Jurnal ilmu pengetahuan budaya* 10, no. 2 (2008): 214–243.

Vink, Markus. "'The World's Oldest Trade': Dutch Slavery and Slave Trade in the Indian Ocean in the Seventeenth Century." *Journal of World History* 14, no. 2 (2003): 131–177.

Ward, Kerry. "Blood Ties: Exile, Family, and Inheritance across the Indian Ocean." *Journal of Social History* 45, no. 2 (2011): 436–452.

———. *Networks of Empire: Forced Migration in the Dutch East India Company.* Cambridge: Cambridge University Press, 2009.

Yang, Anand. "Bandits and Kings: Moral Authority and Resistance in Early Colonial India." *Journal of Asian Studies* 66, no. 4 (2007): 881–896.

———. "Indian Convict Workers in Southeast Asia in the Late Eighteenth and Early Nineteenth Century." *Journal of World History* 14, no. 2 (2003): 179–208.

Yasadipura, Radèn Ngabehi. *Babad Giyanti.* 21 vols. Batawi Sentrum: Balai Pustaka, 1937–1939.

ONE

A Global History of Exile in Asia, c. 1700–1900

Clare Anderson

This chapter explores banishment, exile, and penal transportation within and between South and Southeast Asia and the Indian Ocean during the period circa 1700–1900.[1] Banishment and exile were important elements of the penal repertoire of precolonial states and polities, with prisoners cast out of their home district or city and refused the right of return. From the end of the eighteenth century, as the East India Company monopolized trade and so expanded its legal authority across large areas of India, Burma, and the Malay Peninsula, and the British Crown colonized islands including Ceylon, Labuan, and Mauritius, the British continued to use such punishments, but they altered their character in significant ways. Like previous rulers, they removed political prisoners from areas under their control, but rather than refusing them the right of return, they confined them in forts, barracks, and camps or shipped them to distant locations. Coalescing with the confinement and transportation of these political prisoners was perhaps the most significant British penal innovation of all in Asia and the Indian Ocean: the establishment of overseas penal settlements and colonies for ordinary criminal offenders. Convicts were transported to and from locations across India, the Bay of Bengal, and beyond, where they were put to forced work for life or a term of years. In this way, the banishment of political prisoners became intertwined with the flow of ordinary convicts into penal transportation and hard labor.

This chapter opens with an examination of continuity and change in the precolonial and colonial use of banishment, specifying in particular the way in which the British invoked their understanding of the importance of culture and religion in India in order to create what they viewed as a peculiarly deterrent new punishment: transportation. I move on to argue that transportation was more than a penal sanction, though, and that it underpinned a larger imperial agenda of forced migration and labor extraction for the purpose of colonization and frontier expansion. Within this broad penal, social, and economic framework, the foci of my argument are on some unintended consequences of transportation as well as on how exiled, banished, and transported people experienced the geographical, religious, and cultural dislocations that were perceived as so important for their effective punishment. Necessarily, then, my account is located both within and beyond Asia and the history of punishment, for I seek to bring together the penal history of exile, banishment, and transportation with a larger global history of cultural production, subaltern experience, and coerced labor. In this respect, my underlying contention is that exile in Asia can be understood only through an appreciation of the inter- and transcolonial networks of which the continent was a part.

Before I begin, it is valuable to note who constituted these flows of "political" and "criminal" convicts, the large majority of whom were men, and to define the geographical scope of the chapter. The convicts whom I refer to as "political" were usually elite rebels, and the British generally referred to them either by name or by community. "Criminal" convicts were transported for ordinary offenses. Though political offenders constituted only a small minority of overall transportees, the lines between who was a "political" and who was a "criminal" convict were sometimes blurred. This was because elites were often tried in specially constituted or summary courts, but peasant rebels usually appeared before ordinary criminal judges, and sentences of banishment or penal transportation were awarded to them without explicit reference to what we might view as their "political" crimes. In addition, after removal to penal settlements and colonies, convict treatment hinged on status rather than offense. Social elites were usually lodged separately and exempted from hard labor, while peasant rebels were accommodated and worked together with ordinary convicts. For the small minority of female convicts in the settlements and colonies (never more than 10 percent), gender trumped altogether crime and status in organization and management. In transportation, subaltern rebels and women alike were, in many ways, rendered politically and socially invisible.[2]

As for their crimes, ordinary convicts were predominantly convicted of murder, *dacoity* (gang robbery), or violence against the person and were sentenced to terms of seven or fourteen years or life. According to the regulations, any Indian prisoner, including those serving sentences of imprisonment, could apply for the commutation of his sentence to transportation, and a few did just that. There was, then, some room for agency and maneuver, even in the most unpromising of circumstances.[3] In terms of where they were sent, Indian convicts were transported to penal settlements and colonies including in the Andaman Islands; Bencoolen; Amboyna; Arakan and Tenasserim

(Burma); Singapore, Penang, and Malacca (Straits Settlements); and farther afield to Aden and Mauritius. Chinese, Malay, and Indians from the Straits Settlements, Burma, and Hong Kong were transported to the Andamans, Labuan, or mainland Indian jails. Overseas transportation operated multidirectionally, then, and with its networking of East India Company and British Crown (and occasionally other European) territories, it also connected Asia to a much larger imperial agenda of colonization and expansion.

BANISHMENT, IMPRISONMENT, AND TRANSPORTATION

In those areas of precolonial South Asia that later constituted Britain's Indian Empire and now form a significant part of the Indian republic, banishment and exile were viewed as particularly useful punishments for high-caste Hindu Brahmins. This was because, for cultural and religious reasons, their flogging or execution was taboo. Thus punishments included confinement within the limits of a city or subjection to public exposure, seated backward on a donkey, with a blackened face.[4] As it gradually expanded its territorial control during the late eighteenth and first half of the nineteenth centuries, the East India Company continued to use banishment, expelling offenders from their homes, sometimes keeping them in forts, and forbidding them to return. As in precolonial regimes, the British saw it as especially useful for high-caste offenders, the harsh punishment of whom risked social approbation.[5] Increasingly, as its jail building program gained momentum during the first half of the nineteenth century, Company courts sentenced criminals to imprisonment in banishment, and ordered prisoners to large central jails like Alipore, in the suburbs of Calcutta. Banishment was also used to punish prisoners for further offenses committed in jail, and men and women who became riotous or refractory could be sent to prisons in other districts. The Indian presidencies stretched across such huge distances that as well as attempting to break links with family and community outside the jail walls, important elements of this punishment were the linguistic and other cultural crossings of removal and confinement over large distances, including in social association but also in food, climate, clothing, religion, and religious practice.[6]

The East India Company also sometimes used banishment as a means of extracting labor from jail inmates, for it saw work as a means of both reforming prisoners and compensating the state for their crimes. Indeed, sentences of simple imprisonment—that is to say, without labor—were rare. As early as 1797, the governor of Bombay wrote that hard labor restrained prisoners from "habits of idleness and dissipation" and reduced the strain on the public purse that incarceration implied.[7] For the next three decades those male prisoners fit to work were employed in three ways: on the station roads, on the district roads, or on the main roads, notably by the mid-1830s the New Delhi–to–Calcutta trunk road. As the Bengal Committee of Convict Labour put it in 1837, it was of the utmost importance to trade and the movement of troops that roads were kept open and in a good state of repair.[8] In Bengal, in 1838, a staggering average of thirteen thousand prisoners was employed in this way.[9] Some district officers reported that the geographical removal associated with working on the roads was greatly disliked by inmates. As one East India Company surgeon wrote in 1836, "Being sent to the New Road they consider a banishment and have the utmost abhorrence of it."[10] Despite its apparent value as a deterrent, in 1838, the Prison Discipline Committee (which was by then considering larger questions of imprisonment and transportation) recommended an end to road labor. This ought to have closed off one main stream of subcontinental banishment, though in practice prisoners continued to work outdoors.[11] Colonial administrators in India were far more attached to this important source of labor exploitation than were their counterparts in Britain. There, outdoor work was gradually abolished on the grounds that truly penal labor ought to promote self-reflection and rehabilitation rather than underpin productivity or profit. Separate, cellular confinement and the turning of the crank handle or treadwheel were, therefore, ideal types of penal work. The prolonged employment of Indian prisoners on the roads was an important line of distinction in this respect, with colonial labor preferences overriding metropolitan ideas about the purpose and ideal practice of incarceration. Indeed, as Satadru Sen has shown in a study of the penal colony in the Andaman Islands during the second half of the nineteenth century, convict labor was linked to broader attempts to mold Indians into rational, useful, and orderly political subjects. But there was a fundamental contradiction here, for productive forms of work were supposed to both demean *and* reform convicts.[12] It was this contradiction that the British were never able to resolve.

Though it clearly changed the nature of precolonial banishment, to incorporate incarceration and outdoor public works labor, without doubt the East India Company's greatest penal innovation was the introduction of convict transportation. This had the same intent as overland banishment with respect to physical removal and displacement, but because it necessitated travel overseas, which they believed to be culturally degrading, the British perceived it as a particularly deterrent punishment in the Indian context. In its deliberations of 1837–1838, the Prison Discipline Committee concluded that the large majority of Hindus had a horror of sea journeys, over what they called the *kala pani* (black waters), because their common chaining and sharing of cooking pots, water pumps, and latrines compromised their caste.

Thus the actual journey into transportation was a key part of the entire punishment.[13] Despite these closely held views, it is important to appreciate that although in India some convicts were outcaste by the voyage over the *kala pani*, this was not always the case (or they could perform particular ceremonies to wipe out the effects of it), and so there was never universal antipathy to it. There was dissent even within the deliberations of the Prison Discipline Committee, when official witnesses made distinctions between the various attitudes of city dwellers, seafarers, high-caste Hindus, low-caste Hindus, and Muslims to crossing the ocean.[14]

Besides the sea journey, the other main difference between banishment and transportation was the latter's explicit connection with the East India Company's desire to secure a cheap and malleable labor force for the purpose of territorial expansion. In this respect, transportation was something more than punishment or forced labor, for it constituted a form of coerced migration. Convicts were highly mobile, convict flows were often circulatory, and Asian penal settlements and colonies were interconnected in significant ways to the timeframe and geography of other forms of bondage, including enslavement, servitude, and indenture.[15] There were significant parallels also between British and other European colonial powers, and important comparisons to be made, with respect to the penal and labor intentions of transportation in Asia and its geographically dynamic and networked character. Earlier, the Dutch East India Company had transported considerable numbers of convicts between the East Indies and the Cape of Good Hope (1602–1799).[16] Portugal transported convicts between its Indian and African colonies, including Goa and Mozambique, over a long period from the eighteenth to the twentieth century.[17] Following an early disaster in the establishment of a penal colony in French Guiana, in the late eighteenth century, when most of the convicts died of fevers and other diseases, *bagnards* (convicts) were transported from France to Guiana and *Communards* (convicted in the wake of the uprising of the Paris Commune in 1871) to the Pacific colony of New Caledonia. Receiving convicts from French colonies in Africa and Indochina, French Guiana remained open until 1952.[18] Other Asian polities also incorporated penal transportation into their judicial process. Mid-Qing China used convict exile for colonization purposes from the mid-eighteenth to the nineteenth century. Convicts were moved over huge overland distances.[19] Feudal Japan exiled prisoners offshore, and when it passed a new penal code in 1880, the Meiji Restoration systematized island *tokei* (servitude) and *rukei* (exile), to set up penal colonies in newly secured northern Hokkaido.[20] But beyond these *parallel practices* was the *intertwining* of empires. This was particularly the case in those parts of Southeast Asia that were transferred between Dutch and

British rule at the turn of the nineteenth century. In Ceylon, for example, immediately after the British takeover, sentences of banishment were passed under Dutch law.[21] In the western Indian Ocean in the first half of the nineteenth century, the British colonial state even sent transported Indian convicts from South Asia on to Madagascar, their subsequent servitude constituting part of British diplomatic negotiations with the Merina empire.[22]

The East India Company banished or transported a small number of convicts for treason, rebellion, and other political crimes, though in sum never more than 5 percent of the total. The British faced endemic resistance to their colonization of South Asia, and they used banishment and penal transportation as a symbol of their political power, as a warning against revolt, and as a means of punishing rebels. Such convicts were sometimes sentenced by courts-martial and included various individuals and communities. Following the ceding of Malabar to the East India Company in 1792, leaders of the Poligar rebellion of 1799–1802 were, for instance, banished from their home districts[23] or sent to Penang. All were permitted to return home in 1814, though initially those returning from overseas remained banished from the districts of Coimbatore, Tinnevelley, and Madura and were only later allowed to return to what the superintendent of police in the Madras Presidency described as "their country."[24] In the aftermath of the Anglo-Sikh wars of the 1840s, Sikh officers and their followers were sent long distances, including to Allahabad jail, Calcutta's Fort William, and Benares' Fort Chunar. They were also transported to the Straits Settlements and Burma.[25] There are many other such examples. The founding convicts of the Andamans settlement in 1858 were mutineer sepoys (soldiers) and rebels, sentenced to transportation by special tribunal for offenses committed during the Great Indian Revolt of 1857–1858.[26] They were followed in the 1860s by Wahabis (at the time called Muslim "fanatics"), in the 1870s by Kukas (Namdhari noncooperation movement), and beyond the scope of this chapter, in the early twentieth century by Mapilahs from Kerala and Indian nationalists. We might consider all of them political prisoners or freedom fighters.[27] There is evidence that for at least some of these convicts transportation was chosen over execution because it was seen as a more severe punishment. Wahabi Maulana Muhammad Ja'far Thanesari, who was transported to the Andamans in 1866 for conspiring to smuggle funds to Afghan mujahideen,[28] served nearly eighteen years in the colony and subsequently wrote a quite lengthy autobiography.[29] He recalled that the judge had addressed him thus:

> You seem to be very eager to get hanged and consider it as martyrdom. Therefore, the government will not give you the punishment that you are

looking forward to. Your capital punishment has been converted into exile for life.[30]

The best-known exiles were undoubtedly members of deposed royal families who, like the rulers and monarchs discussed by Aldrich, Margana, Paterson, and Ricci in this volume (chapters 2, 5, 9, and 4, respectively), were sent away from their home districts and confined in colonial towns, islands, and enclaves. Wajid Ali Shah, the deposed king of Awadh, was detained in Garden Reach in Calcutta from 1856 to 1859, for example. The Mughal emperor of Delhi and his entourage were sent to Rangoon in the aftermath of 1857–1858, and the Nawab of Farrukhabad was exiled in Aden in 1859.[31] Following the Anglo-Manipur War (Assam), in 1871 members of the Manipuri royal family were shipped to the Andamans, where they were kept separately from the transportation convicts in the cool climes of Mount Harriet. In 1877, Sultan Abdullah of Perak was deposed and exiled in the Seychelles after he was accused of involvement in the murder of British resident James Birch.[32] King Thibaw and Queen Supayalat were forced into exile in South India at the end of the third Anglo-Burmese war (1885).

Other British colonial (as opposed to East India Company or Indian Empire) territories became imbricated in this regional network of political, aristocratic punishment. Groups of Kandyan rebels were, for example, sent from Ceylon to Tanjore, Trichinopoly, and Vellore in the Madras Presidency, and to the island of Mauritius, after the Great Rebellion of 1817–1818. Some were directed to be removed in what Governor Robert Brownrigg described as "the public interests of this island," some had been sentenced to banishment in courts of law, and some had had sentences of execution commuted to banishment.[33] Another group of a dozen Kandyans was sent to Mauritius in 1823, each convicted of high treason.[34] As I have argued elsewhere, "Sentences of transportation and banishment were often viewed as more appropriate than capital punishment because they ruptured networks of political 'intrigue' without risking the elevation of rebels to heroic status."[35]

The British transported other rebels overseas too, but many of them have been hidden from history, for they were convicted under *ordinary* criminal law. They were usually from peasant or tribal (*adivasi*, or indigenous) communities. Unlike all the social elites mentioned previously, these convicts were not at the time always described as "political" offenders. However, their recorded offenses can be mapped against the district in which they were convicted to produce a startling portrait of the widespread penal transportation of subaltern rebels. Tribal Khonds from central Orissa in the Bengal Presidency were transported to Moulmein after military campaigns against their rebellion in 1835, for example.[36] Some of the first transportation convicts to Mauritius (1815) were rebels from the tribal areas of Midnapur, another Bengal district that was in open revolt against the British, during the Chuar Rebellion (1797–1800) and Naik Revolt (1806–1816). Most were convicted not of political offenses per se, but of crimes such as violence, joining bandit groups, or armed extortion; some had been in prison for a decade before they were embarked across the Indian Ocean.[37] Another good example of the flow of rebels into transportation was the shipment of Santals, India's largest tribal group, to Akyab in the aftermath of their 1855 *hul* (rebellion).[38] But for all these groups, despite the context of their transportation, unlike their high-status compatriots, these convicts were ordinary men and women who were treated no differently from other convicts, but with them became absorbed into the general body of convict workers.

The transportation regime was underpinned by the use of convicts as labor at the frontiers of empire, and officials stressed continually the public advantages of transportation. For this reason, rather than the judicial departments of the Indian presidencies, it was the penal settlements themselves that drove supply, and they became anxious about interruptions to it.[39] Once the immediate needs of newly settled territories had been met, with land cleared and basic infrastructure established, convicts were sent to other locations, and eventually the character of their work expanded to include digging ditches, building and repairing roads and bridges, working in sawmills, with kilns, and on looms, and laboring as brass founders, brick and tile makers, servants, grooms, blacksmiths, boatmen, cart drivers, or grass cutters. Convicts were also engaged in experimental industry and agriculture, including, in Burma, tin mining, and in Mauritius, silk and cotton production and sugar and coffee cultivation.[40] Women—never more than 10 percent of the total number of convicts—were largely kept at "domestic" work in the barracks. This inattention to convict women's status in the allocation of work was part of a larger colonial "de-casteing" of women, though it shared much with comparable convict regimes in the convict colonies of Australia, with respect to the production of a gendered distinction between the nature of work and domesticity in "public" and "private" space.[41]

For men, class-based systems operated in the penal settlements and colonies through the threat of punishment and the promise of reward, and convicts were able to rise through the ranks until they enjoyed relative freedom. Sixth-class "incorrigible" convicts were kept in a chain gang, and first-class convicts were employed as overseers (*tindals*), so that eventually prisoners became their own warders. A convict's goal was the acquisition of a ticket of leave, with permission to live outside the barracks and take paid employment.[42] In early Bencoolen, ticket-of-leave convicts were even given land, seeds, livestock, and their families the right of inheritance.[43] Such incentives coexisted with the threat of severe punishment. I have noted elsewhere that convict resistance was endemic in all penal settlements and colonies, and it included feigning sickness, downing tools, desertion, attacks on overseers, and escape. Convicts could be punished with demotion down the penal classes, or subjection to fetters, flogging, imprisonment, execution, or retransportation to either Robben Island in the Cape of Good Hope, or even the Australian penal colony at Van Diemen's Land.[44] This serves to underline the relationship between Indian Ocean penal settlements and other spaces of confinement and punishment, like the jail, the road gang, or the gallows, and their place within a larger geography of empire and convict transportation.

Although some company officials believed that transportation destroyed caste, somewhat in contradistinction, it is evident that administrators used it as a basis to organize the penal settlements. Administrators sought *mehtas* (sweepers), *dhobis* (washermen), and barbers from among convicts of the relevant caste. In this way, high-caste convicts were able to avoid particular types of "degrading" work. We see this from an example dated August 1835, when Goberdhone Baboo, a Bengali convict who had been shipped from Calcutta to Tenasserim (Burma) for a seven-year term in December 1834, petitioned Calcutta's supreme court. Begging for the removal of his fetters and a transfer to either Singapore or Penang, he wrote:

> I am suffering the troubles and labours as follows.
>
> From 6 O[']Clock in the morning till 9 I labour by taking one and half mounds of stone upon my head and go and come about 3 miles with the same every day, and sometimes by taking woods &c.
>
> The time for my eating only half an hour after the 9. Again after half past nine I engage in the above several works by the order of the head man of the jail till half past 4—Sometimes I am forced by the head man to clear the dirties of the place Moarny. Sometimes if the merchants inhabitants of the place require me and other prisoners the head man of the jail orders me and them immediately to accompany them who pays the head man of the jail for my labour and other prisoners and take work from me and others more than the others.
>
> I engage in the above labours with iron chain on my legs and at the night when I lay in bed with a large iron chain put and bind my legs with other prisoners whereupon I am unable to turn my back on my side and no order to go into privy at the night should I feel unwell myself, I sheet [shit] in the bed and clear the dirty myself in the next morning.[45]

The petition was enclosed in a further appeal from his father, Chadiloll Baboo, from which it emerged that Goberdhone was a wealthy man from the Burra Bazaar neighborhood of Calcutta and "a higher class of people amongst the Hindoo nation." If his living and working conditions did not change, his father pleaded, his son would be dead within six months.[46] The supreme court referred the petition to the Bengal judicial department; if the claims were true, it said, they would take action to alleviate the man's condition. When the court contacted the Burmese authorities, they, however, dismissed it, writing that this convict in fact worked far less than other convicts and was one of the healthiest men in the jail.[47] The petition perhaps reveals something of one high-caste man's feelings about some of the hardships and indignities of transportation and hard labor. But the response to it suggests that transportation convicts were subject to differential treatment on status grounds.

The exchange of letters regarding just one of many tens of thousands of transportees also throws into sharp relief one of the problems facing penal administrators in colonial Asia: how to equalize punishment between prisoners from a wide range of social backgrounds, especially those of high caste. In short, if high-caste Hindus felt the deprivations of transportation more acutely than those of the lower castes, should they be made subject to the same treatment, or was transportation in and of itself a severe penal sanction? As one sessions judge put it during the Prison Discipline Committee's consultations in the 1830s, high-caste prisoners suffered a "double punishment . . . by being placed in compulsory juxta-position with persons who, and things which, are his abomination."[48] This issue also blew up regarding the treatment of Anglo-Indian (Eurasian) convicts transported from India to Southeast Asia during the first half of the nineteenth century. In the Tenasserim Provinces, in 1844, a new commissioner, George Broadfoot, introduced measures that put them to the same work, and issued them with the same clothing and rations, as Indians. In numerous petitions to the government, these convicts complained of what they saw as a gross injustice, and it was not long before the measures were rescinded and the separation of Indian and Anglo-Indian convicts was once again enforced.[49] As it was, white convicts convicted in South Asia (mainly court-martialed soldiers) were sent not to the Indian penal settlements of Southeast Asia but to mainly white Australia. Race, then, was also an organizing principle in India's penal settlements, as well as in Britain's larger carceral empire.[50]

Beyond caste and race, the politics of "offense for which transported" was relevant to penal management. As I described earlier, in many penal settlements and colonies, political convicts were subject to quite distinct treatment. The Kandyans transported to Mauritius in 1818 lived at quite a distance from the convict headquarters at Grand River, in a place called Powder Mills, and some of the Bengal transportation convicts even worked as their servants. Indeed, the instructions issued to William Stewart, the overseer who accompanied them into exile and then took charge of them, noted, "[I]t is expected that you will conduct yourself towards the Prisoners, with as much humanity, gentleness, and condescension to their wants, under circumstances foreign to their established habits, as lies in your power."[51] They directed him to supply the Kandyans with the same kind of food that they had eaten in Ceylon, as well as betel leaf and tobacco, and to attend to their medical needs. Though Stewart himself was fluent in Singhalese, the government also employed an interpreter.

Such special treatment does not mean that the prisoners did not feel confined or suffer from the deprivations of their situation. Indeed, the Kandyans were prolific petitioners of the Ceylon, Mauritius, and Madras Presidency governments. One collective petition in 1820 pleaded,

> [W]e are placed in a situation the most trying and distressing, imprisoned in a country where we do not understand the language of the people, deprived of our wives and children, and our property—when we cast a melancholy glance on the number of dreary years of a miserable existence that are perceptibly before us, we desire to die.[52]

In another example, from 1828, one of the Kandyan exiles, Mallendeya Ganetteya, petitioned Governor William Nicolay in a vernacular that the government translator represented thus:

> The government has dignified me with the Title of "Raja," or "King"—and made me a Prisoner—but no Allowance whatever equal to my high title has been conferred on me, and they will not allow me even to return back to my native country—therefore I hope your Excellency will give me the value of a good piece of Cloth, and a Handkerchief, which I beg for the sake of the great King of England and the Seven Churches.[53]

Money and other allowances loomed large in such pleas. Indeed, after numerous Kandyan complaints about their inability to marry off their daughters in Madras (in Tanjore), the British even agreed to fund their lavish weddings.[54]

Sikhs transported in the aftermath of the Anglo-Sikh wars in the 1840s were not put to hard labor in the Straits Settlements and Burma, either. "Saint soldier" Bhai Maharaj Singh and his disciple Khurruck Sing lived quite separately in Singapore, apparently revered by many ordinary convicts and townspeople.[55] One Sikh rebel, Narain Singh, eventually became the head jailer of Moulmein prison in Burma, an extraordinary position for a transported convict to achieve.[56] The first sepoys sent to the Andamans in 1858 were even used to oversee ordinary peasant rebel convicts, whom they apparently viewed with contempt because they found them so socially inferior.[57] There are many other such examples. But low-caste and in particular tribal convicts, even when transported for what we might consider "political" offenses (rebellion or revolt), enjoyed no special treatment but were massed together with their ordinary criminal compatriots. Just as women were de-casted in transportation, low-caste and tribal convicts were de-politicized.

Transportation and Cultural Production

In the preceding discussion of convict labor, distinction, and privilege, I have suggested the importance of taking a multipronged approach to understanding the social production of penal settlements and colonies as spaces where status, caste, race, gender, and politics intersected to produce variegated outcomes and experiences. I would like to expand this point a little more, by examining some of the unintended consequences of transportation with respect to its formation of new cultural forms and connections. When the Andamans became a penal colony following the Great Indian Revolt of 1857–1858, the other Southeast Asian settlements were closed to new convict arrivals. The Andamans were very different from the earlier penal settlements because the only people living on the islands at the time were indigenous people, who were often hostile to the penal colony. There were no other free residents, settlers, or migrants. Like penal settlements in the Straits Settlements and Burma, the Andamans introduced a class system and worked the convicts at productive labor. But the islands were different because they also encouraged family emigration, convict marriage, and permanent settlement.[58] Ultimately, with no free population to merge into, as was the case in places like Singapore, Mauritius, and Burma, ex-convicts and their descendants forged an altogether new kind of society. Though convicts in the other settlements married into free communities and were occasionally joined by their mainland families, the outcome of the penal colonization of the Andamans was the emergence of a culturally distinct place where religion, caste, gender relations, and language were all transformed. By the end of the nineteenth century the growing convict-descended community had a clear social identity as "local-born." In this we see that transportation and its implied exile were not necessarily destructive—of communities, families, and kinship ties—as the colonial administration intended, but could be socially *creative*, too, of new modes of living, marrying, worshipping, and speaking. The Andamans today are celebrated as "Mini India," a place of "unity in diversity" that is a model for the entire nation.[59]

"Arracan [Arakan] 14th Febry [1849] Kyook Phoo (Kyaukpyu) Ghat & Prisoners carrying water in Buckets, Isle of Ramree." (Watercolor by Clementina Benthall. Benthall Papers, Centre of South Asian Studies, University of Cambridge.)

In relation to this idea of exile as creative, recently Uma Kothari has suggested that, across a range of colonial sites in the Indian Ocean, though political exile was supposed to break political associations and isolate political threats, in important ways it enhanced and deepened anticolonial networks, too. This was because exiles carried ideologies of resistance with them and inspired political agitation in their host localities.[60] We can locate a similar process for colonial Asia and its links to other colonial nodes of rebellion. In 1845, for instance, a group of rebel convicts transported from Kohlapur to Aden for "insurrection and bearing arms" inspired a violent attempt to escape from their chains after they arrived in port.[61] Sikhs shipped from the Punjab to Burma in 1854, following the Anglo-Sikh wars, led a transportation ship mutiny of such catastrophic (for the British) proportions that it produced the largest criminal trial the Bengal Presidency had ever seen. The men had killed many of the ship's crew, grounded the ship on a Burmese beach, and marched inland in the mistaken belief that they could offer themselves for the anticolonial army of an as yet imperially unincorporated rajah. Unfortunately, they were two years too late.[62] North Indian sepoys and mutineers sent to the Andamans in 1858 escaped en masse in the belief that they could join forces with a sympathetic rajah living in the islands or find a road to Burma where they could serve a king against the

East India Company, work for double pay, and, in the words of one British officer, return and destroy "the handful of English on the Settlement."[63]

Later, the transportation of Wahabis, who were so literate that they were almost immediately elevated to clerkships, from North India to the Andamans facilitated the flow of news and information between the colony and the mainland. This both compromised the penal intent of the colony and produced networked resistance. Indeed, Shere Ali, the famous assassin of the viceroy of India, the Earl of Mayo, during his visit to Port Blair in 1872, was said to have read out loud a letter from his *bhai* (brother) giving news of the murder of Justice Norman on the steps of Calcutta's supreme court, the night before he killed the viceroy.[64] It is clear, then, that neither banishment nor transportation produced "total" exile. Colonial officers noted the detailed knowledge mainland prisoners and transported convicts had about conditions in the settlements: they often petitioned for transfer depending on what they knew about particular destinations. Officials also complained about the difficulty of preventing communication between convicts and their kin.[65] And penal settlements and colonies could become imbricated in the political contests that played out in widespread resistance to British authority in nineteenth-century India.

EXPERIENCES OF EXILE

So far, this chapter has described banishment, exile, and penal transportation within and beyond Asia to make four points about colonial punishment: first, that beliefs about the social and cultural ruptures of forced movement across large distances of land or sea were central to the appeal of banishment and—especially—transportation as penal sentences in the region; second, that convict labor exploitation was absolutely critical to the expansion of imperial frontiers; third, that particular knots of gender, race, caste, status, and sentence were important in the organization and management of work in jails or penal settlements and colonies, whether prisoners and convicts had been banished or transported; and fourth, that whatever its intended aims as a penal sentence, convict transportation could and did extend or generate political resistance as well as new social formations. Though we have already glimpsed snapshots of prisoner and convict perspective in the chapter so far, next I would like to turn to other unintended outcomes of transportation, through a more explicit analysis of how prisoners and convicts imagined, represented, or remembered transportation. The kernel of my argument is this: that at least some convicts experienced transportation as "exile" and felt acutely their distance from family and kin, as intended by the colonial judicial process, at least as they expressed it in the largely English-language petitions that they presented to the government.

During a tour of Arakan in 1856, Bengal inspector general of jails, F. J. Mouat, wrote of how he had heard one convict speak "very feelingly of his wife and family," noting, "[B]anishment is much dreaded by the Natives of Hindustan."[66] His sentiments resonate in colonial archives across Asia and its penal satellites, where we can read numerous petitions in which convicts center exile in their expressions of anomie and loss. "Your Excellency's humble Petitioner most respectfully, begs leave," convict John Herman Maas wrote in 1828, "to submit his unfortunate and sad circumstances for Your Excellency[']s serious consideration." Of Dutch-Singhalese parentage, but able to articulate his feelings in English, Maas elaborated his transportation from Ceylon to Mauritius and lamented a recent sentence of retransportation from Mauritius to New South Wales for a further offense. Maas' biography is one of many convict lives that present a kaleidoscope view of networked colonial cultures and societies in the Indian Ocean in the early nineteenth century, including his eventual fate as one of the last men to be executed for forgery in colonial Australia.[67] What I am interested in here is the language of exile, incarceration, and family dislocation that he used in two 1828 petitions against his shipment to Sydney. He had, he wrote in his own hand, already been "banished from his native land":[68]

> Banishment from his native Country to this remote distance for these Thirty Nine Months in exile from the bosom of his Family, and the Imprisonment for these Twenty Three Months in being deprived of his Liberty is no small punishments for Him to repent for what he has done.[69]

There is a remarkable number of surviving petitions presented by convicts or ex-convicts seeking permission to return to what they or their petition writers usually described as their "native country," sometimes after several decades of transportation and, often, after their liberation. Political prisoners, including Sikh general Narain Singh, whom I mentioned earlier, presented some of them. Singh ended the first of many such petitions, in 1863, with a plea to the viceroy of India to "close his long exile by a gracious permission to return to his native land."[70] A group of eighty Bombay convicts awaiting liberation in Mauritius invoked the language of exile too, writing in 1855 of their anxiety to go home after almost twenty years of penal servitude on the island.[71] Kunnuck Mistree had been transported to Bencoolen in 1818, and after its transfer to the Dutch in 1825 he was moved to Singapore. In 1858 he petitioned for return home, the petition noting that he had suffered thirty-eight years of "banishment." He would, he said, like to spend his last years in his native country:

> [T]o a Hindoo the punishment of Transportation is more terrible than death itself and the only consolation left to a Hindoo under such circumstances is the hope of returning . . . to die on the Banks of his beloved Ganges.[72]

In 1865, after fifteen years of liberation, and an astonishing thirty-five years after his original transportation to Mauritius, fakir convict Munsha Bin Baboosh presented a document that elaborated how

> your petitioner is now more than sixty years of age, and is most desirous, before he departs this life, to revisit his own country and to see his brothers and sisters still living . . . he is old, infirm, and has but a short time to live . . . his return to his country after thirty five year's exile, cannot, possibly, prove of the slightest inconvenience.[73]

One major concern of these men seems to have been the proper conduct of funeral rites by their families. Ironically, then, for some convicts the passing of time in transportation did not promote the forgetting of kin or lessen their feelings of "exile," as the British hoped in rendering them potential permanent settlers, but enhanced them. There are important parallels here with convict transportation from Southeast Asia and Hong Kong, where the British thought that Malay and Chinese convicts especially feared transportation because after their death their families would not be able to carry out the burial rites necessary for their support in the afterlife.[74] For this reason, they chose "distant and strange" destinations on the Indian mainland for transportation convicts, rather than penal settlements in the Straits Settlements and Burma, which were closer and more culturally familiar.[75]

Though it is unlikely that all of the English-language petitions discussed were written by the convicts who presented them, we have two examples of Andaman convicts writing Persian poetry in which they foregrounded the experience of exile, especially as experienced through the social, cultural, and political ruptures of transportation. Fazl-i-Haq Khairabadi (1797–1861), an Awadhi scholar who was alleged to have joined the 1857 revolt, proclaimed his loyalty to Bahadur Shah, and drawn up the constitution of liberated Delhi, wrote a poignant description of his feelings about transportation, circa 1858–1861. He described himself as "a heart-broken and suffering prisoner." He detailed his deprivations, separation from family, and yearning for them:

He is dejected, lonely and forlorn and subjected to drudgery; he has been exiled from his country and town. He is distressed, afflicted, and in banishment; he has been made to suffer, and separated from his family and children. . . . The tyrant oppresses him and maltreats him and has kept his family and neighbours away from him.[76]

In a remarkably complex and skillful *qasida* poem, Lucknow poet Mohammed Ismail Hussain ("Munir") Shikohabadi (1819–1881) wrote more generally of the cultural effects of convicts' sea crossing and the misery and terror of transportation:

When they had to leave India and come to this island
The prisoners' evil fate made the water black [*kala pani*][77]
From the time they [the convicts] left home, thousands of
    demons and djinn appeared
In the darkness of the evening of exile, they were granted the
    kohl of Solomon[78]
A dark night, terrifying waves and so fearful a whirlpool
Crowds of physical suffering, abundance of mental distress
How do those lightly laden ones upon the shore know of the state
    we are in?
Or in what ocean of torment the ship of our existence is tossed?
On the day that death dived into the sea and reached this island
It does not emerge, being so frightened when it sees the water.[79]

The very existence of these lyrical and sophisticated Andaman narratives makes them far from typical, for most convicts were neither literate nor educated enough to write such poetry.[80] Moreover, they resonate with jail literature as a textual genre, for they purposefully sought to inspire solidarity between authors and readers, between those who had been incarcerated or transported and their sympathizers outside the prison walls or over the black waters. This was especially the case for Fazl-i-Haq, who is said to have smuggled his poetry out of the Andamans on pieces of torn cloth, through a released convict, who passed it on to Fazl-i-Haq's son.[81] It is in this sense that such narratives simultaneously *expressed* the social and geographical dislocations of transportation and positioned them within, *and potentially expanded,* larger political networks of anti-imperial resistance.

We cannot be entirely sure of the precise translations of words such as "banishment" and "exile," but the distress and longing for home described by these convict petitioners and poets find resonance in several contemporary medical reports on transportation. Its "depressing effects" usually began on board ship, it was said, when Hindu convicts usually refused cooked food. In the words of the superintendent of Alipore jail, "The ill effects of improper diet are in many cases aggravated by the despondency which a first sea voyage and banishment from their native country must produce."[82] An 1859 report on the Andamans noted that the elderly "felt the depressing effects of banishment and separation from family and friends far more keenly than younger men."[83] I quote an extract from this report at length:

> No one can expect that a new Penal Settlement can enjoy the same state
> of health as a new colony, where the settlers have left their homes to
> better their condition, and to secure an independence for themselves and
> children. . . . All natives of India look with horror at the idea of crossing the
> black water, and would rather face death than the ocean; and not one of the
> convicts now toiling in these islands can entertain a hope of seeing their
> daily toils become a benefit to their families, from whom at first the
> separation must have been considered eternal, and in many cases those
> dependent on them were reduced to poverty or to the bounty of their
> relatives.[84]

The social reduction of those who were left behind is certainly more than evident. Later on in the nineteenth century, two high-caste women wrote of the enormous impact of their *zemindar* (landlord) husband's transportation on a charge of *dacoity:*

> The banishment of the Zemindar is a standing stigma on their family, and
> many are the social difficulties in the way of giving away their daughter,
> or getting a bride for their son (now under the Court of Wards) from the
> Royal Family of Pudukotah or from other Zemindar Families. . . . They
> have a mother-in-law, now aged 65, who while she raves for her only son in
> a distant land, merely heightens their sorrow.[85]

In the meantime, the transportation of men of ordinary means often left their families in abject poverty. When the Andamans administration wrote to India regarding the release of a man named Mamoo in 1882, for example, the district magistrate of South Canara (Madras Presidency) went to his home-place and discovered the existence of a stepbrother, three stepsisters, and a female cousin. They were all living in extreme poverty, he reported.[86]

Of further interest in this respect is that sometimes convicts who escaped or returned to India at the expiration of their sentence could not overcome its long-term effects. One extraordinary petition to the government, from an escaped Bombay convict who had returned to Gujarat, articulated how he had since lived in the mountains and jungles and suffered hugely: "The punishment I have been already subjected to is greater than death itself. I am in great distress."[87] In such cases, ex-convicts were often so old that it was nearly impossible for them to provide for themselves without the support of their brothers, sons, and nephews.[88] But such convicts often found their families gone, their land occupied, or their property stolen, and with few life options those of greater youth decided to sign contracts of indenture and sail into the unknown once again, to find work on the sugar plantations of Mauritius and the Caribbean.[89]

This chapter has developed a framework for understanding the history of exile in British colonial Asia. It has invited us to consider the continuities between precolonial and colonial penal forms, particularly with respect to the banishment of elite offenders; the introduction of transportation in the context of its perceived strength as a cultural punishment, for some administrators believed that it was peculiarly appropriate for Indians because of their horror of sea voyages; and the significance of British penal innovations in the use of transportation convicts as extractive labor. Further, it has suggested that exile in British Asia can be situated within a narrative of penal transportation by other European empires, and China and Japan, and in some instances within histories of imperial interconnectedness. It is notable also that the lines between the treatment of political prisoners and the treatment of ordinary convicts were at once both distinct and indistinct, and that the nature of their punishment was the product of particular constellations of status, caste, and gender, rather than the offenses for which they were transported. Thus peasant rebels became ordinary convict workers, while royal exiles were separated from them and made subject to different treatment.

Further, the chapter has noted that notwithstanding great differences of opinion about the caste degradations of crossing the *kala pani*, transportation had some significant if unintended consequences. These included the production of new forms of identity, particularly in the previously uncolonized Andaman Islands, as well as the spread of knowledge about transportation, and anticolonial sentiment more broadly. Moreover, the cutting of ties with family and home in the penal settlements impacted deeply on at least some convicts, particularly older men who left families behind, and who especially as they aged expressed in petitions and other writings their aching to see home again before they died. Here, one should not forget the profound impact of transportation on families left behind, bringing shame to the wealthy and destitution to the poor. Placing exile in Asia within the larger history of punishment as well as the history of labor migration enables us to appreciate its character in these respects and to connect it to the opportunity that migration to the sugar colonies seemed to present to some ex-convicts. Moreover, in situating convict mobility in this broader sense within punishment, labor, and colonial expansion, a focus on penal settlements opens out to view a larger history of connectedness within and beyond Asia.

NOTES

1. The research leading to these results has received funding from the European Research Council under the European Union's Seventh Framework Programme (FP/2007–2013) / ERC Grant Agreement 312542. It is based on archival research in the India Office Records of the British Library (IOR), the National Archives, London (TNA), National Archives of India (NAI), National Archives of Mauritius (NAM), and Tamil Nadu State Archives (TNSA).

2. This resonates with the arguments of Ranajit Guha in his *Elementary Aspects of Peasant Insurgency in Colonial India* (New Delhi: Oxford University Press, 1983).

3. IOR P.139.66 Bengal judicial consultations (hereafter cited as BJC) 1 February 1831: J. Master, Superintendent Alipore jail, to J. Thomason, Deputy Secretary to Government Bengal, 21 January 1831; Thomason to Master, 1 February 1831; IOR P.139.66 BJC 15 February 1831: Thomason to Master, 14 February 1831.

4. For an overview of East India Company legal and penal innovation, see Tapas Kumar Banerjee, *Background to Indian Criminal Law* (Calcutta: R. Cambray and Co., 1990); Radhika Singha, *A Despotism of Law: Crime and Justice in Early Colonial India* (New Delhi: Oxford University Press, 1998). Also note the contemporary text Frederick John Shore, *Notes on Indian Affairs*, vol. 2 (London: John W. Parker, 1837), 307–345.

5. Singha, *Despotism of Law*, 98, 101–102.

6. On the broader disciplinary context of incarceration, see David Arnold, *Colonizing the Body: State Medicine and Epidemic Disease in Nineteenth-Century India* (Berkeley: University of California Press, 1993).

7. IOR P.128.34 BJC 1 September 1797: John Shore, Governor of Bombay, 23 July 1797.

8. IOR P.141.9 BJC 14 March 1837: Second and Concluding Report of the Committee of Convict Labour, 28 January 1837 (hereafter cited as Second Report CCL).

9. IOR V.26.170.1: *Report of the Committee on Prison Discipline, 8 January 1838* (Calcutta: Baptist Mission Press, 1838) (hereafter cited as PDC), 61.

10. IOR P.141.9 Second Report CCL, Appendix: J. Macrae, Civil Assistant Surgeon Monghyr, to W. Adam, Secretary to the CCL, 10 June 1836.

11. IOR P.141.40 BJC 29 October 1839: F. J. Halliday, Secretary to Government Bengal, to F. C. Smith, Superintendent Police Lower Provinces, 29 October 1839 (order no. 1156, 2 October 1838). On Indian convict road labor generally, see Chitra Joshi, "Fettered Bodies: Labouring on Public Works in Nineteenth-Century India," in *Labour Matters: Towards Global Histories*, ed. Marcel van der Linden and Prabhu P. Mohapatra (New Delhi: Tulika, 2009), 3–21.

12. Satadru Sen, *Disciplining Punishment: Colonialism and Convict Society in the Andaman Islands* (New Delhi: Oxford University Press, 2000), chap. 3.

13. Clare Anderson, "The Politics of Convict Space: Indian Penal Settlements and the Andamans," in *Isolation: Places and Practices of Exclusion*, ed. Alison Bashford and Carolyn Strange (London: Routledge, 2003), 41–45.

14. PDC, Paper C.

15. Clare Anderson, "After Emancipation: Empires and Imperial Formations," in *Emancipation and the Remaking of the British Imperial World,* ed. Catherine Hall, Nicholas Draper, and Keith McClelland (Manchester: Manchester University Press, 2014), 113–127.

16. Kerry Ward, *Networks of Empire: Forced Migration in the Dutch East India Company* (Cambridge: Cambridge University Press, 2009).

17. Timothy J. Coates, *Forced Labor in the Portuguese Empire, 1740–1932* (Leiden: Brill, 2013).

18. Isabelle Merle, *Expériences Coloniales: La Nouvelle-Calédonie, 1853–1920* (Paris: Belin, 1995); Peter Redfield, *Space in the Tropics: From Convicts to Rockets in French Guiana* (Berkeley: University of California Press, 2000); Alice Bullard, *Exile to Paradise: Savagery and Civilization in Paris and the South Pacific* (Stanford, CA: Stanford University Press, 2000); Miranda F. Spieler, *Empire and Underworld: Captivity in French Guiana* (Cambridge, MA: Harvard University Press, 2012); Stephen A. Toth, *Beyond Papillon: The French Overseas Penal Colonies, 1854–1952* (Lincoln: University of Nebraska Press, 2006).

19. Joanna Waley-Cohen, *Exile in Mid-Qing China: Banishment to Xinjiang, 1758–1820* (New Haven, CT: Yale University Press, 1991).

20. Daniel V. Botsman, *Punishment and Power in the Making of Modern Japan* (Princeton, NJ: Princeton University Press, 2005); Hideki Hatakeyama, "Convict Labor at the Sumitomo Besshi Copper Mine in Japan," *International Journal of Social Economics* 25, nos. 2–4 (1998): 365–369; Osamu Tanaka, "The Labour Form of the Initial Stage of Capitalism in Hokkaido: With a Focus on Convict Labour" [*Shihonshugi kakuritsuki Hokkaido ni okeru rodo keitai: Shujin rodo o chushin toshite*], *Keizaironshu* (March 1955): 67–112.

21. IOR F.4.421 Transportation of persons banished from Ceylon to certain parts of the Company's dominions: Extract of Bengal political consultations, 21 May 1813, R. Brownrigg, Governor of Ceylon, to Lord Minto, Governor General in Council Fort William, 19 April 1813.

22. Clare Anderson, *Convicts in the Indian Ocean: Transportation from South Asia to Mauritius, 1815–53* (Basingstoke: Macmillan, 2000), 48–49.

23. TNSA Madras judicial consultations (hereafter cited as MJC) vol. 152A: W. Ormsby, Superintendent of Police Madras, to D. Hill, Secretary to Government Madras, 25 September 1820; Hill to Ormsby, 27 October 1820.

24. TNSA MJC 152A: Ormsby to Hill, 25 September 1820. For a detailed account, see Anand A. Yang, "Bandits and Kings: Moral Authority and Resistance in Early Colonial India," *Journal of Asian Studies* 66 (2007): 881–896.

25. *Documents relating to Bhai Maharaj Singh [Died as State Prisoner on 5th July, 1856, at Singapur], by Nahar Singh, with an introduction by M. L. Ahluwalia* (Gurdwara Karamsar, Distt. Ludhiana: Sikh History Source Material Search Association, 1968), xxxi; IOR F.4.2527: H. P. Burn, town major Calcutta, to C. Allen, officiating secretary to Government of India, 16 May 1853; minute of the Governor-General of India, 4 July 1853. IOR P.143.45 BJC 24 April 1850 names the "Sikh sirdars" confined in Calcutta and Benares as Chuttar Sing, Shere Sing, Ootar Sing, Hakim Bal, Kishn Kano, Korjun Sing, Lal Sing, Mushtah Sing, Oomed Sing, and Juggut Chund—List of convicts embarked per *Enterprize,* 10 April 1850. For detailed accounts of the Sikh prisoners, see Clare Anderson, "The Transportation of Narain Sing: Punishment, Honour and Identity from the Anglo–Sikh Wars to the Great Revolt," *Modern Asian Studies* 44, no. 5 (2007): 1115–1145; Clare Anderson, *Subaltern Lives: Biographies of Colonialism in the Indian Ocean World, 1790–1920* (Cambridge: Cambridge University Press, 2012), chap. 4; Anoma Pieris, "The 'Other' Side of Labor Reform: Accounts

of Incarceration and Resistance in the Straits Settlements Penal System, 1825–1873," *Journal of Social History* 45, no. 2 (2011): 453–479.

26. Clare Anderson, *The Indian Uprising of 1857–8: Prisons, Prisoners and Rebellion* (New Delhi: Anthem, 2007, repr., 2012), chap. 5.

27. Clare Anderson, Madhumita Mazumdar and Vishvajit Pandya, *New Histories of the Andaman Islands: Landscape, Place and Identity in the Bay of Bengal, 1790–2012* (Cambridge: Cambridge University Press, 2015); Sen, *Disciplining Punishment*, 264–272.

28. Literally "strugglers for Islam."

29. Sen, "Contexts, Representation and the Colonized Convict: Maulana Thanesari in the Andaman Islands," *Crime, History and Societies* 8, no. 2 (2004): 117–139.

30. Maulana Jafer Thanesari, *In Exile (A Strange Story)*, English translation by Satadru Sen, n.p. I extend my deep gratitude to Satadru Sen for sharing his translation of the text with me.

31. Abu Muhammad Sahar, ed. *Intikhab-e qasa'id-e urdu* [Selection of Urdu qasidas] (Lakhnao: Nasim Book Depot, 1975), 358.

32. Uma Kothari, "Contesting Colonial Rule: Politics of Exile in the Indian Ocean," *Geoforum* 43 (2012), 700–703; NAM RA2525: correspondence Straits Settlements and Mauritius, May–November 1880.

33. NAM RA54: Governor Robert Brownrigg to Major-General Hall, Acting Governor of Mauritius, 18 May 1818; TNA CO54/73: Brownrigg to Colonial Secretary Lord Bathurst, 8 January 1819. See also IOR F.4.421 Transportation of persons banished from Ceylon to certain parts of the Company's dominions [1813]; IOR F.4.1594 Proceedings relating to the Kandyan prisoners [1836].

34. NAM RA229: Chief Secretary to Government Ceylon to Chief Secretary to Government Mauritius, 16 August 1823.

35. Anderson, *Subaltern Lives*, 108.

36. TNSA MJC vol. 304B: H. G. A. Taylor, Commander Northern Division, to H. Chamier, Secretary to Government Madras, 26 January 1836.

37. Anderson, *Convicts in the Indian Ocean*, 31–32.

38. Clare Anderson, "'The Wisdom of the Barbarian': Rebellion, Incarceration, and the Santal Body Politic," *South Asia: Journal of South Asian Studies* 31, no. 2 (2008): 223–240.

39. For instance, IOR P.133.22 BJC 10 March 1818: W. A. Clubley, Secretary to Government Bengal, to A. Trotter, Acting Secretary to Government Bengal, 2 January 1818.

40. IOR P.141.18 BJC 5 December 1837: E. A. Blundell, Commissioner Tenasserim Provinces, to R. D. Mangles, Secretary to Government Bengal, 17 September 1836; IOR P.141.66 BJC 9 July 1842: Blundell to G. A. Bushby, Secretary to Government of India, 22 June 1842; Anderson, *Convicts in the Indian Ocean*, 46–48.

41. Some of the key theoretical issues concerning gender and subaltern history are laid out in Kamala Visweswaran, "Small Speeches, Subaltern Gender: Nationalist Ideology and Its Historiography," in *Subaltern Studies IX*, ed. Shahid Amin and Dipesh Chakrabarty (New Delhi: Oxford University Press, 1996), 83–125. Also see Clare Anderson, "Gender, Subalternity and Silence: Recovering Women's Experiences from Histories of Transportation," in *Behind the Veil: Resistance, Women and the Everyday in Colonial South Asia*, ed. Anindita Ghosh (Basingstoke: Palgrave, 2007), 145–166; Satadru Sen, "Rationing Sex: Female Convicts in the Andamans," *South Asia* 30, no. 1 (1999): 29–59.

42. IOR P.129.32 BJC 1 January 1807: Rules for the management of convicts in Bencoolen, 18 June 1800; A regulation for the management of the convicts transported

from Bengal to Fort Marlborough, 5 August 1806; IOR P.136.66 BJC 19 May 1825: Minute on the Management of Convicts at Prince of Wales' Island (Penang), 8 March 1825; IOR P.142.37 BJC 17 September 1845: Regulations for Convict Management Singapore, 23 June 1825 (revised 1 December 1825). For a contemporary summary of the convict system in Bencoolen and the Straits Settlements, see J. F. A. McNair, *Prisoners Their Own Warders: A Record of the Convict Prison at Singapore in the Straits Settlements Established 1825, Discontinued 1873, Together with a Cursory History of the Convict Establishments at Bencoolen, Penang and Malacca from the Year 1797* (Westminster: Archibald Constable and Co., 1899).

43. IOR P.129.32 BJC 1 January 1807: A regulation for the management of the convicts transported from Bengal to Fort Marlborough, 5 August 1806.

44. For more details of secondary punishments, see especially Clare Anderson, "The Execution of Rughobursing: The Political Economy of Convict Transportation and Penal Labour in Early Colonial Mauritius," *Studies in History* 19, no. 2 (2003): 185–197.

45. IOR P.140.70 BJC 25 August 1835: A. Holroyd, Clerk of the Crown, to Mangles, 15 August 1835, enclosing abstract translation of the Bengal letter of Goherdhone Baboo, n.d.

46. IOR P.140.70 BJC 25 August 1835: Petition of the Defendant above named and now a prisoner of the Jail of Moarny Island, n.d.

47. IOR P.140.73 BJC 15 December 1835: H. Macfarquhar, Officiating Commissioner in the Tenasserim Provinces, to J. P. Grant, Secretary to Government Bengal, 10 November 1835.

48. PDC Appendix IV: J. S. Shaw, Sessions Judge Conkan.

49. IOR P.142.13 BJC 20 February 1844: Petition of the East Indian convicts at Moulmein, 12 January 1844; IOR P.143.8 BJC 27 October 1847: Commissioner J. R. Colvin to F. J. Halliday, 22 September 1847.

50. Anderson, *Subaltern Lives,* chap. 3.

51. TNA CO54/73: Brownrigg to Bathurst, 8 January 1819, enclosure. Instructions to Lieutenant William Stewart of His Majesty's 2nd Ceylon Regiment, proceeding in charge of the Kandyan Prisoners to the Mauritius, 21 February 1819.

52. TNA CO54/77: Barnes to Bathurst, 18 August 1820, enc. Petition of Kandyans in Mauritius, n.d.

53. NAM RD3: Petition of Mallendeya Ganetteya, translated by Don Bastian, the Modiliar interpreter, enclosed in letter from Henry Bates, Superintendent of Kandyan Prisoners, 12 September 1828. "Seven Churches" refers to the seven churches of the New Testament's book of Revelation. I thank Sujit Sivasundaram for arranging a modern (2013) translation of the original document, which reads, "I am lost and miserable. I am writing to Your Lordship to ask for some money to buy some cloth and a handkerchief and some food. I do not spend money in vain, and therefore only need some money, for my clothes are worn out. I do not travel overseas, and am in need of simply surviving my life. I beg Your Lordship and the Great King of England to give me some money, which is a great charity." One might choose to interpret the difference in tone between the two documents as evidence of the nineteenth-century translator's sympathy for the plight of his regal charge.

54. IOR F.4.1594 Proceedings relating to the Kandyan prisoners: Extract Political General Letter from Fort St George, 16 August 1836.

55. Anderson, *Subaltern Lives,* chap. 4; Pieris, "The 'Other' Side of Labor Reform."

56. Anderson, "The Transportation of Narain Singh."

57. Anderson, *The Indian Uprising of 1857–8,* 152–154.

58. Sen, "Rationing Sex."

59. Anderson, Mazumdar and Pandya, *New Histories of the Andaman Islands*. There are important parallels here with patterns of creolization in former sugar colonies like Mauritius and Trinidad, which received large numbers of Indian and Chinese indentured workers during the British colonial period. For a theoretically innovative interpretation of identity formation, see Marina Carter and Khal Torabully, *Coolitude: An Anthology of the Indian Labour Diaspora* (London: Anthem, 2002).

60. Kothari, "Contesting Colonial Rule."

61. IOR P.403.47 Bombay judicial consultations (hereafter cited as BomJC) 13 August 1845: Political Agent Aden to W. Escombe, Secretary to Government Bombay, 27 June 1845.

62. Clare Anderson, "'The Ferringees Are Flying—The Ship Is Ours!': The Convict Middle Passage in Colonial South and Southeast Asia, 1790–1860," *Indian Economic and Social History Review* 41, no. 3 (2005): 143–186.

63. IOR P.206.61 India judicial proceedings (hereafter cited as IJP) 29 July 1859: Dr Browne's report on the sanitary state of the Andamans, n.d. July 1859.

64. Cambridge University Library, Department of Manuscripts, Add. Ms 7490 Mayo Papers: 94: Events of assassination, 8–13 February 1872: notes from verbal and written statements made by Major General Stewart, superintendent of Port Blair, 10 February 1872. *Bhai* indicates close social kin, not necessarily a blood sibling. For a detailed life history of another convict Wahabi, Liaquat Ali, in the Andamans, see Anderson, *Subaltern Lives*, chap. 5.

65. NAI Home (Port Blair) A Proceedings, February 1876, nos. 53–55: Note of C. A. Barwell, 18 November 1875.

66. F. J. Mouat, *Reports on Jails Visited and Inspected in Bengal, Bihar and Arracan* (Calcutta: F. Carbery, Military Orphan Press, 1856), 185.

67. Anderson, *Subaltern Lives*, 44–46.

68. NAM RA377: The humble petition of John Herman Maas, a Native of the Island of Ceylon [to Governor Charles Colville], Civil Prisons, 23 June 1828.

69. NAM RA376: The humble petition of John Herman Maas, a Native of the Island of Ceylon [to Colville], Civil Prisons, 31 July 1828.

70. IOR P.205.44 Foreign judicial proceedings, December 1863, no. 59: Petition of Narain Sing, formerly a sikh sirdar now a prisoner in Moulmein jail prays for remission of sentence and permission to return to native land.

71. NAM RA1182: To His Excellency James Macaulley Higginson Esquire C. B. Governor and Commander in Chief of Mauritius and Dependencies &c. &c. &c. The humb[l]e petition of Seewarpar, Sidjide, Tarabapoo, Tookarom, Nottoo, Abdallah, Harry Bapojee, Bymah, Harry Norasa, Diaroom, Mahomed Khan, Sucarom Singh, Pondoo, Rana, Bapoo, Ynapah, Sacoo, Sheik Munsur, Peratapoo, Mossoo Mytil, Bogarne and others in all 80 [Bombay convicts], 24 February 1852.

72. IOR P.146.12B BJC 14 Jan. 1858: The humble petition of Kunnuck Mistree a convict now undergoing his sentence of transportation in the settlement of Singapore, n.d.

73. NAM RA1792: To His Excellency The Governor of the Bombay Presidency. The humble petition of Munsha Bin Baboosha, Faqueer of the District of Grand Port in the Island of Mauritius, 18 June 1865.

74. Christopher Munn, "The Transportation of Chinese Convicts from Hong Kong, 1844–1858," *Canadian Historical Association* 8, no. 1 (1997): 113–145; IOR P.142.38 BJC 1 October 1845: J. Davis, secretary to government of Hong Kong, to Lord Stanley, colonial secretary, 29 January 1845.

75. IOR P.404.3 BomJC 11 August 1846: W. A. Bruce, colonial secretary Hong Kong, to Bushby, 30 April 1846; Bushby to Bruce, 11 July 1846.

76. Moinul Haq, "The Story of the War of Independence, 1857–8 (being an English translation of Allamah Fadl-i-Haqq's Risalah on the War)," *Journal of the Pakistan Historical Society* 5, no. 1 (1957): 26–27. An early, annotated draft of this article is located in the P. C. Joshi Collection of JNU Library. I thank Deborah Sutton for locating and copying this file.

77. The literal translation of "evil fate" is "black-fatedness," black waters = *kala pani*.

78. Solomon's kohl allowed the unseen world to be seen.

79. "A Prisoner's Appeal" (*firyad-e zindani*). I am enormously grateful to Chris Shackle, who uniquely in the UK had the skills to translate Munir's complex and sophisticated *qasida* poetry and was generous enough to share his translations with me. See Christopher Shackle, "Munir Shikohabadi: On His Imprisonment," in *Nationalism in the Vernacular: Hindi, Urdu, and the Literature of Indian Freedom*, ed. Shobna Nijhawan (New Delhi: Permanent Black, 2009), 235–250.

80. Sen, "Contexts," 118–119.

81. Jamal Malik, "Letters, Prison Sketches and Autobiographical Literature: The Case of Fadl-e Haqq Khairabadi in the Andaman Penal Colony," *Indian Economic and Social History Review* 43, no. 1 (2006): 77–100; Haq, "Story of the War of Independence," 23n1; Mahdi Husain, *Bahadur Shah II and the War of 1857 in Delhi with Its Unforgettable Scenes* (New Delhi: M. N. Publishers, 1987), 298, 372–392.

82. IOR P.434.25 IJP 9 July: State of certain convicts per SS *Scotia*: J. Fawcus, Superintendent Alipore Jail, to Mouat, 25 April 1870.

83. IOR P.206.61 29 July 1859: Report by Dr. G. G. Brown on the sanitary state of the Andamans, n.d. March 1859 (hereafter cited as Brown's report).

84. Brown's report.

85. TNSA MJP 28 April 1887, no. 927: J. P. Hewett to the secretary to Government Madras, 13 April 1887, enc. To the Earl of Dufferin, Viceroy and Governor-General of India. The humble Memorial of Ayiammal Ayiar and Nallamuthalakammal Ayiar, wives of Atchutha Pandarathar, Zemindar of Ghandharvakotai, Tanjore District, 4 December 1886.

86. TNSA MJP 14 December 1882, nos. 2135–2136: J. Sturrock, Acting District Magistrate of South Canara, to C. G. Master, Chief Secretary to Government Madras, 24 November 1882.

87. NAM RA1616: Chief Secretary to Government Bombay to Chief Secretary to Government Mauritius, 22 February 1861, enc. Substance of a petition from Thakore Bhugtajee Jalumjee, 21 August 1860.

88. TNSA MJP, 4 February 1884, no. 300: N. A. Roupell, District Magistrate of Anantapur, to Chief Secretary to Government Madras, 26 January 1884.

89. Clare Anderson, "Convicts and Coolies: Rethinking Indentured Labour in the Nineteenth Century," *Slavery and Abolition* 30, no. 1 (2009): 100.

BIBLIOGRAPHY

Ahluwalia, M. L. *Sant Nihal Singh Alias Bhai Maharaj Singh: A Saint-Revolutionary of the 19th Century Punjab*. Patiala: Punjabi University, 1972.

Anderson, Clare. "After Emancipation: Empires and Imperial Formations." In *Emancipation and the Remaking of the British Imperial World*, edited by Catherine Hall, Nicholas Draper, and Keith McClelland, 113–127. Manchester: Manchester University Press, 2014.

———. "Convicts and Coolies: Rethinking Indentured Labour in the Nineteenth Century." *Slavery and Abolition* 30, no. 1 (2009): 93–109.

———. *Convicts in the Indian Ocean: Transportation from South Asia to Mauritius, 1815–53.* Basingstoke: Macmillan, 2000.

———. "The Execution of Rughobursing: The Political Economy of Convict Transportation and Penal Labour in Early Colonial Mauritius." *Studies in History* 19, no. 2 (2003): 185–197.

———. "'The Ferringees Are Flying—The Ship Is Ours!': The Convict Middle Passage in Colonial South and Southeast Asia, 1790–1860." *Indian Economic and Social History Review* 41, no. 3 (2005): 143–186.

———. "Gender, Subalternity and Silence: Recovering Women's Experiences from Histories of Transportation." In *Behind the Veil: Resistance, Women and the Everyday in Colonial South Asia,* edited by Anindita Ghosh, 145–166. Basingstoke: Palgrave, 2007.

———. *The Indian Uprising of 1857–8: Prisons, Prisoners and Rebellion.* New Delhi: Anthem, 2007. Reprint, 2012.

———. "The Politics of Convict Space: Indian Penal Settlements and the Andamans." In *Isolation: Places and Practices of Exclusion,* edited by Alison Bashford and Carolyn Strange, 40–55. London: Routledge, 2003.

———. "Sepoys, Servants and Settlers: Convict Transportation in the Indian Ocean, 1787–1945." In *Cultures of Confinement: A History of the Prison in Africa, Asia and Latin America,* edited by Ian Brown and Frank Dikötter, 185–220. London: Christopher Hurst, 2007.

———. *Subaltern Lives: Biographies of Colonialism in the Indian Ocean World, 1790–1920.* Cambridge: Cambridge University Press, 2012.

———. "The Transportation of Narain Sing: Punishment, Honour and Identity from the Anglo–Sikh Wars to the Great Revolt." *Modern Asian Studies* 44, no. 5 (2007): 1115–1145.

———. "'The Wisdom of the Barbarian': Rebellion, Incarceration, and the Santal Body Politic." *South Asia: Journal of South Asian Studies* 31, no. 2 (2008): 223–240.

Anderson, Clare, Madhumita Mazumdar, and Vishvajit Pandya. *New Histories of the Andaman Islands: Landscape, Place and Identity in the Bay of Bengal, 1790–2012.* Cambridge: Cambridge University Press, 2015.

Appuhamy, Millewa Adikarange Durand. *The Kandyans' Last Stand against the British.* Colombo: Gunasena, 1995.

———. *Rebels, Outlaws and Enemies to the British.* Colombo: Gunasena, 1990.

Arnold, David. "The Colonial Prison: Power, Knowledge and Penology in Nineteenth-Century India." In *Subaltern Studies VIII: Essays in Honour of Ranajit Guha,* edited by David Arnold and David Hardiman, 148–187. New Delhi: Oxford University Press, 1994.

———. *Colonizing the Body: State Medicine and Epidemic Disease in Nineteenth-Century India.* Berkeley: University of California Press, 1993.

Banerjee, Tapas Kumar. *Background to Indian Criminal Law.* Calcutta: R. Cambray and Co., 1990.

Baxi, Upendra. "'The State's Emissary': The Place of Law in Subaltern Studies." In *Subaltern Studies VII: Writings on South Asian History and Society,* edited by Partha Chatterjee and Gyanendra Pandey, 247–264. New Delhi: Oxford University Press, 1994.

Botsman, Daniel V. *Punishment and Power in the Making of Modern Japan.* Princeton, NJ: Princeton University Press, 2005.

Bullard, Alice. *Exile to Paradise: Savagery and Civilization in Paris and the South Pacific.* Stanford, CA: Stanford University Press, 2000.

Carter, Marina. *Voices from Indenture: Experiences of Indian Migrants in the British Empire.* London: Leicester University Press, 1996.

Carter, Marina, and Khal Torabully. *Coolitude: An Anthology of the Indian Labour Diaspora.* London: Anthem, 2002.

Coates, Timothy J. *Forced Labor in the Portuguese Empire, 1740–1932.* Leiden: Brill, 2013.

Cohn, Bernard S. *Colonialism and Its Forms of Knowledge: The British in India.* Oxford: Oxford University Press, 1997.

Dalrymple, William. *The Last Mughal: The Fall of a Dynasty, Delhi, 1857.* London: Bloomsbury, 2006.

Guha, Ranajit. *Elementary Aspects of Peasant Insurgency in Colonial India.* New Delhi: Oxford University Press, 1983.

Haq, Moinul. "The Story of the War of Independence, 1857–8 (being an English translation of Allamah Fadl-i-Haqq's Risalah on the War)." *Journal of the Pakistan Historical Society* 5, no. 1 (1957): 23–57.

Hatakeyama, Hideki. "Convict Labor at the Sumitomo Besshi Copper Mine in Japan." *International Journal of Social Economics* 25, nos. 2–4 (1998): 365–369.

Husain, Mahdi. *Bahadur Shah II and the War of 1857 in Delhi with Its Unforgettable Scenes.* New Delhi: M. N. Publishers, 1987.

Joshi, Chitra. "Fettered Bodies: Labouring on Public Works in Nineteenth-Century India." In *Labour Matters: Towards Global Histories,* edited by Marcel van der Linden and Prabhu P. Mohapatra, 3–21. New Delhi: Tulika, 2009.

Kolsky, Elizabeth. *Colonial Justice in British India: White Violence and the Rule of Law.* Cambridge: Cambridge University Press, 2010.

Kothari, Uma. "Contesting Colonial Rule: Politics of Exile in the Indian Ocean." *Geoforum* 43 (2012): 697–706.

Malik, Jamal. "Letters, Prison Sketches and Autobiographical Literature: The Case of Fadl-e Haqq Khairabadi in the Andaman Penal Colony." *Indian Economic and Social History Review* 43, no. 1 (2006): 77–100.

McNair, J. F. A. *Prisoners Their Own Warders: A Record of the Convict Prison at Singapore in the Straits Settlements Established 1825, Discontinued 1873, Together with a Cursory History of the Convict Establishments at Bencoolen, Penang and Malacca from the Year 1797.* Westminster: Archibald Constable and Co., 1899.

Merle, Isabelle. *Expériences coloniales: La Nouvelle-Calédonie, 1853–1920.* Paris: Belin, 1995.

Mouat, F. J. *Reports on Jails Visited and Inspected in Bengal, Bihar and Arracan.* Calcutta: F. Carbery, Military Orphan Press, 1856.

Munn, Christopher. "The Transportation of Chinese Convicts from Hong Kong, 1844–1858." *Canadian Historical Association* 8, no. 1 (1997): 113–145.

Pieris, Anoma. *Hidden Hands and Divided Landscapes: A Penal History of Singapore's Plural Society.* Honolulu: University of Hawai'i Press, 2009.

———. "The 'Other' Side of Labor Reform: Accounts of Incarceration and Resistance in the Straits Settlements Penal System, 1825–1873." *Journal of Social History* 45, no. 2 (2011): 453–479.

Rai, Rajesh. "Sepoys, Convicts and the 'Bazaar' Contingent: The Emergence and Exclusion of 'Hindustani' Pioneers at the Singapore Frontier." *Journal of Southeast Asian Studies* 35, no. 1 (2004): 1–19.

Redfield, Peter. *Space in the Tropics: From Convicts to Rockets in French Guiana.* Berkeley: University of California Press, 2000.

Sahar, Abu Muhammad, ed. *Intikhab-e qasa'id-e urdu* [Selection of Urdu qasidas]. Lakhnao: Nasim Book Depot, 1975.

Sen, Satadru. "Contexts, Representation and the Colonized Convict: Maulana Thanesari in the Andaman Islands." *Crime, History and Societies* 8, no. 2 (2004): 117–139.

———. *Disciplining Punishment: Colonialism and Convict Society in the Andaman Islands.* New Delhi: Oxford University Press, 2000.

———. "Rationing Sex: Female Convicts in the Andamans." *South Asia* 30, no. 1 (1999): 29–59.

Shackle, Christopher. "Munir Shikohabadi: On His Imprisonment." In *Nationalism in the Vernacular: Hindi, Urdu, and the Literature of Indian Freedom,* edited by Shobna Nijhawan, 235–250. New Delhi: Permanent Black, 2009.

Sherman, Taylor C. "From Hell to Paradise? Voluntary Transfer of Convicts to the Andaman Islands, 1921–1940." *Modern Asian Studies* 43, no. 2 (2009): 367–388.

Shore, Frederick John. *Notes on Indian Affairs.* Vol. 2. London: John W. Parker, 1837.

Singha, Radhika. *A Despotism of Law: Crime and Justice in Early Colonial India.* New Delhi: Oxford University Press, 1998.

Spieler, Miranda F. *Empire and Underworld: Captivity in French Guiana.* Cambridge, MA: Harvard University Press, 2012.

Tanaka, Osamu. "The Labour Form of the Initial Stage of Capitalism in Hokkaido: With a Focus on Convict Labour" [*Shihonshugi kakuritsuki Hokkaido ni okeru rodo keitai: Shujin rodo o chushin toshite*]. *Keizaironshu* (March 1955): 67–112.

Toth, Stephen A. *Beyond Papillon: The French Overseas Penal Colonies, 1854–1952.* Lincoln: University of Nebraska Press, 2006.

Turnbull, C. M. "Convicts in the Straits Settlements, 1826–27." *Journal of the Malay Branch of the Royal Asiatic Society* 43, no. 1 (1970): 87–103.

Visweswaran, Kamala. "Small Speeches, Subaltern Gender: Nationalist Ideology and Its Historiography." In *Subaltern Studies IX,* edited by Shahid Amin and Dipesh Chakrabarty, 83–125. New Delhi: Oxford University Press, 1996.

Waley-Cohen, Joanna. *Exile in Mid-Qing China: Banishment to Xinjiang, 1758–1820.* New Haven, CT: Yale University Press, 1991.

Ward, Kerry. *Networks of Empire: Forced Migration in the Dutch East India Company.* Cambridge: Cambridge University Press, 2009.

Yang, Anand A. "Bandits and Kings: Moral Authority and Resistance in Early Colonial India." *Journal of Asian Studies* 66 (2007): 881–896.

Two

Out of Ceylon
The Exile of the Last King of Kandy

Robert Aldrich

On the afternoon of 24 January 1816, HMS *Cornwallis*, armed with seventy-eight guns and conveying six hundred crew and passengers, set sail from Colombo in Ceylon bound for Madras in India. Among those on board was Sri Vikrama Rajasinha,[1] king of Kandy (*Kanda uda rata*), the last reigning monarch on the island before he was captured by the British and deposed. The thirty-five-year-old former king was now headed for exile, accompanied by his four wives and a retinue of sixty persons, including a woman described as his court jester. The royal party had been escorted to the harbor, riding in the open carriage of Governor Robert Brownrigg, watched by a "crowd of natives, all eager to witness the embarkation," in the words of William Granville, the captor's minder, who kept a detailed diary during the journey to India.[2] Even deprived of his throne, Sri Vikrama Rajasinha demanded that the procession momentarily halt so that spectators gathered on an archway under which his carriage passed could descend, since he found it improper for subjects to stand higher than the royal personage. He had dressed in finery, "attired in a red silk cloth wrought with gold thread, and his purple silk trousers, which were baggy, were secured to his ankle with ribbons. He wore an embroidered jacket, and over the jacket a very fine white upper dress with innumerable frills or pleats, and over it he had a green silk mantle edged with gold lace; and a magnificent turban completed the toilette of Rajasingha."

The voyage from Colombo to Madras took a month. At first, the British and the Ceylonese warily kept their distance from each other, but gradually Granville and Sri Vikrama Rajasinha engaged in cordial conversation (mediated by interpreters). The king brushed aside questions about his alleged brutalities and complained that he had not been given an opportunity to talk to the British governor about hidden royal treasures. Granville listened sympathetically while he solicitously attended to the needs of the king. He formed an opinion of Sri Vikrama Rajasinha as intelligent in thought and regal in bearing, though sometimes moody in temperament: on one occasion the king hacked at a royal daybed desecrated because a servant had sat on it. The captive enjoyed watching the officers dine in their mess—they rose courteously when he arrived and drank a toast to him after their meal—and he invited Granville, the captain, and other senior officers to a feast of Ceylonese specialties prepared by his own cooks. Granville, otherwise rather sweet natured, wrote ungraciously that "the greasy slops, and other nausea spread before us, almost overcame me, and produced divers sensations of a tendency which I need not expatiate upon."

When the ship docked in Madras, where thousands of people turned out to see the arrival of the former monarch, Sri Vikrama Rajasinha again dressed in royal apparel before disembarking. Soon he was taken to an old fort in Vellore—ironically, the place where some of the family of Tippu Sultan had been confined after his defeat by the British, but also the site of one of the first mutinies in the East India Company army. There he would live, in relative comfort, and die in 1832.[3]

Forty-two years after the banishment of Sri Vikrama Rajasinha, another royal ruler dethroned by the British would be sent into exile, the last Mughal emperor, Bahadur Shah Zafar, who finished his life in Burma. When the British annexed Awadh in 1856, they exiled King Wajid Ali Shah to Calcutta. In 1885, completing their conquest of Burma, the British exiled its last monarch, King Thibaw, to India. And while playing the Great Game, the British were involved in the exile and return to Kabul of Emir Dost Mohammed Khan and Shah Shuja in Afghanistan.[4] Such were the niceties of imperial conquest.

Banishment of political rivals or vanquished leaders was not a new tactic of victors; the tradition went back to antiquity.[5] Nor was it a policy applied just in the colonies; just five months before Sri Vikrama Rajasinha set sail for exile from Colombo, Napoleon was dispatched from Portsmouth to Saint Helena. Banishing a deposed ruler provided a way for the triumphant to get rid of the defeated, and in the empire, for colonial masters to substitute a more pliable occupant on the throne or, as the British did in Ceylon, India, and Burma, to abolish a dynasty altogether. Such action removed a figure, and sometimes a family, who might become a rallying point for resistance, while avoiding making the deposed a martyr through execution. The tactic often proved successful in the short term, though opposition to the colonizers inevitably metamorphosed from support for a monarchy in the style of the old regime to other forms of anticolonialism and nationalism.

Deposition and banishment of indigenous rulers, and of many others considered dangerous to new rulers (both native and foreign), was not uncommon, and indeed had long preceded the exile of the last king of Kandy. Several chapters in this volume evidence a tradition of royal exile in colonized Asia. In the late 1600s and early 1700s, as Ronit Ricci (chapter 4) and Jean Gelman Taylor (chapter 7) show, the Dutch banished contrary religious and political figures from the East Indies to the Cape Colony and Ceylon, still Dutch outposts. The Dutch East India Company, in other cases studied by Timo Kaartinen (chapter 6), also sent rebellious princes into internal exile in the East Indies, a territory so vast and culturally diverse that they were effectively banished to foreign lands. The Dutch thus hoped not only to enthrone docile successors, but also to disrupt old social networks and hierarchies and to secure political, commercial, and land rights for themselves. Sri Margana (chapter 5) follows the exile of another particularly ill-fated figure from the East Indies, Hamengkubuwana II. In their brief rule of the Dutch East Indies during the Napoleonic wars, the British exiled this sultan of Yogyakarta to their colony of Penang; when the Dutch resumed control, they allowed the sultan to return, but later sent him into exile once again, this time to Ambon. Perhaps the British learned some lessons from these experiences in the East Indies.

Among other hereditary rulers later sent into exile by the British were Maharaja Dalip Singh (the last Sikh ruler), a Zanzabari sultan, a Zulu king, a Malay sultan, and an Ashanti chief.[6] The French deposed and banished no fewer than three Vietnamese emperors—and several princes in the Indochinese countries were also forced into exile—as well as West African rulers, the last queen of Madagascar, a sultan of the Comoros Islands, and several sultans of Morocco.[7] The Dutch continued to send East Indian rulers whom they wished to punish into internal exile. The Portuguese in the early 1600s had exiled the last monarch of Jaffna, the Tamil kingdom in northern Ceylon, to India; though he then converted to Christianity, he was beheaded and his female relatives were sent into religious orders so there would be no further heirs to his throne.[8] Such exiles totaled only a minuscule proportion of the vast numbers of unfree migrants displaced in the colonial age—Clare Anderson in this volume (chapter 1) and in her other works writes, for instance, about the varieties of exile to the Andaman Islands, Mauritius, and other parts of the Indian Ocean—but they represent a unique intersection between old and new hierarchies, institutions, and uses of power.

Research on the practice by colonial conquerors of dethroning and exiling rulers opens a window onto life stories of empire, the human drama of men and women born to power who ended their lives in captivity. Not all of the exiles command admiration for their deeds, but they do offer biographies full of human interest, as readers will know from two excellent novels, Amitav Ghosh's *The Glass Palace*, which concerns the fate of King Thibaw, and Romesh Gunesekera's *The Prisoner of Paradise*, which centers on a Sinhalese figure who collaborated in the British overthrow of Sri Vikrama Rajasinha, with probable hopes of becoming king himself, but was later implicated in a rebellion and exiled to Mauritius—more on him presently.[9] In addition to personal stories of dispossession, a study of these rulers charts some of the pathways of empire, with links, for example, connecting Ceylon and India and Mauritius, and even the Straits Settlements, since another pretender to the Kandyan throne was exiled to Malacca in 1848.[10] The theme also sheds light on the dynamics of conquest: conflicts within indigenous elites, the contracting of alliances against or sometimes with the colonizers, the various strategies the colonialists used to entrench their authority, the persistence of support for an ancien régime institution displaced by conquest.[11] This history of the last Kandyan king tells us about imperial policy, about territoriality and the trajectories of empire, about the artifacts of exile (a subject also discussed in this volume by Ricci and Taylor), and the emotional history of imperial exile, the sentiments that one can glean, for instance, from William Granville's account of his voyage with Sri Vikrama Rajasinha.

For the remainder of this chapter, I focus on the events that took place in the island the Europeans called Ceylon, looking at the context of the deposition and exile of the king of Kandy, then briefly at some aspects of the legacy left by the abolition of the dynasty, and finally at the fate of the royals and their regalia.

The circumstances that produced the deposition of Sri Vikrama Rajasinha were both local and global. In Ceylon, the kingdom of Kandy— several other kingdoms had disappeared in the wake of the Portuguese invasion—was a Buddhist polity that traced its ancestry back for two and a half millennia on an island with a rich cultural past evidenced by the archaeological sites at the earlier capitals of Anuradhapura and Polonnaruwa. The king combined secular power with a semidivine status; in the words of H. L. Seneviratne, "The king was an embryo Buddha, a *Bodhisattva*, who would one day be Buddha; and he was also an approximation to the ideal monarch of Sinhalese thought, *cakravarti* or Universal Ruler."[12] Two features, according to Vernon L. B. Mendis, symbolized the power and the duty of the king: the temple and the tank.[13] There existed an intimate link between the Kandyan king and the *sangha*, or religious community, as the king was the protector of Buddhism and the guardian of the sacred Tooth Relic, believed by many to be a relic of the Buddha himself, at the Dalada Maligawa temple in Kandy.[14] The king was also the builder of tanks, the artificial lakes and reservoirs that gathered monsoonal rain so vital in the dry season. The king

"Sri Wickrama Raja Sinha, Last King of Kandy, 1798–1815." (Tuck's postcard, produced for the British Empire Exhibition, 1924–1925. Collection of the author.)

was surrounded by an elite of Sinhalese aristocrats (from the Radala segment of the Govigama caste), whom historians often label the Kandyan chiefs; they served as provincial governors (*dissaves*) and held other offices with administrative and tax-collecting duties (and gained income from taxes). At the apex of the bureaucracy were two ministers (*adigars*) who served at the king's pleasure.

The system worked efficiently, though not without problems. Succession to the throne did not follow the rules of primogeniture, and male relatives of the king vied for power; these included not only his sons, often numerous because of multiple marriages, but also nephews and brothers-in-law, since there was a tradition of Kandyan rulers seeking brides from the Kshatriya caste in southern India because there were not suitable spouses from the "solar" caste in Kandy. Thus, the history of the Kandyan rulers extended to familial and cultural links with southern India, ties that sometimes provoked discontent among Sinhalese chiefs possessive of their own privileges and culture. The other problem was factionalism among the chiefs, who regularly jousted for power with each other but also bucked up against the authoritarian powers of the king. There was, for instance, a rebellion against Narendra Rajasinha in 1732 after his appointment of a Tamil to a high office. As the anthropologist Stanley Tambiah has put it, Kandyan politics alternated between tyranny and oligarchy.[15] The ordinary people played little role in high politics, where the main actors were the king and his relations, the Radala chiefs, and the upper echelons of the Buddhist monastic community.

In 1739, the last Sinhalese king of Kandy died without an heir; the new king, Vijaya Rajasinha, his brother-in-law, began the Nayakkar dynasty. The Nayaks originally came from Madurai, in southern India, and there is considerable historiographical debate about the degree to which the new rulers were indigenized in Kandy.[16] They spoke Telugu or Tamil rather than Sinhala; they were by origin Saivite Hindus rather than Buddhists, though they fulfilled their key responsibilities as defenders of the Buddhist faith. In 1760, another insurrection broke out, led by Sinhalese chiefs and the *bhikkhus* (monks) with whom they were allied, against Kirti Sri Rajasinha, accused of engaging in the Saivite practice, unacceptable to Buddhists, of ceremonially spreading ash on his forehead, though ironically it was under his reign that Buddhism was significantly revitalized in the Kandyan kingdom.[17]

On the death of his successor, Rajadhi Rajasinha, in 1798, another succession problem presented itself, as Rajadhi Rajasinha had produced no heir with his senior queen, and a probable successor, Muttusamy, was the son of a lesser spouse. The chief minister (*maha adikaram*) had the effective power of choosing the king, and Pilima Talawe selected an eighteen-year-old protégé who was the king's nephew and of southern Indian background.[18] He was enthroned as Sri Vikrama Rajasinha, and over the next few years he gave Pilima Talawe free rein in governing the country. Historians differ on whether the chief minister simply wished to amass influence as the power behind the throne, or whether he actually hoped in due course to depose the Nayakkar king and reestablish a native Sinhalese dynasty. From the early years of the 1800s, however, the king asserted his authority against Pilima Talawe and the other Radala notables, whose discontent steadily mounted.

The global situation was not propitious for the Kandyan dynasty.[19] Foreigners had steadily whittled away at the maritime areas of Ceylon, with the Dutch having taken and then enlarged the Portuguese holdings on the littoral from the 1630s.[20] After another war with the Kandyans, the Dutch in 1766 imposed a harsh treaty through which they gained control of the entire coast of Ceylon, leaving Kandy a reduced and landlocked kingdom. Ceylon had long attracted the interest of foreigners for its gemstones and spices, for its strategic position at the crossroads of the Indian Ocean, and for its fine protected harbors, especially in Jaffna and Trincomalee. Ceylon was a great prize in the imperial scramble of the seventeenth and eighteenth centuries, and so it would remain. In the early 1790s, during the revolutionary wars in Europe, when the French occupied the United Provinces, the Dutch ruler had taken refuge in Britain, where he was persuaded to relinquish the Dutch colonies, in principle as a temporary measure, to the British in their struggle against the French. The British navy, after having taken the Cape Colony, occupied Trincomalee and the remaining Dutch territory in Ceylon in 1796, though temporary occupation turned into permanent possession with the Treaty of Amiens in 1802.

Relations between the British and the Kandyans were initially cordial enough, though it was clear that the successors to the Dutch regarded the kingdom as an obstacle in their desires to gain easier access to Kandyan resources and to have free passage from one coast to another across Kandyan land. In 1803, an inconclusive war took place between the British and the Kandyans. The British, rather disingenuously, had tried to depose the king, acknowledging as monarch Muttusamy, the leading alternative candidate for the crown in 1798; in their retreat, as much because of disease as from defeat, they shamefully then abandoned Muttusamy to Sri Vikrama Rajasinha, who promptly had him executed. Subsequently an uneasy stand-off prevailed between the two states cohabiting on the island.[21] Napoleon was still menacing the British and was said to harbor dreams of reconquering an Indian empire; the British had soundly trounced the French on the subcontinent in the late eighteenth century, though the French maintained a few small enclaves there. The British remembered that the Bourbons had briefly occupied Trincomalee in 1782, and rumors circulated that the king of

Kandy had made contact with the Bonapartists. For the British, takeover of the Kandyan state thus promised distinct geopolitical benefits. Alicia Frederika Schrikker has emphasized that the British moreover wanted to secure land for coffee plantations to diversify the economy in order to make the colony fiscally self-sufficient; there was a significant economic imperative to further expansion as well as a political concern.[22] Though the Colonial Office remained very cautious about intervention, Lieutenant-General Sir Robert Brownrigg, who took up his gubernatorial post in 1812, made no secret of his hopes of extending British sovereignty over the whole island.

Meanwhile, dramatic events had taken place in Kandy. In 1811, Pilima Talawe had hatched a plot to assassinate Sri Vikrama Rajasinha, his erstwhile protégé; the plot was uncovered and Pilima Talawe was executed, his place as chief minister taken by another senior nobleman, Ehelepola, who was also his nephew. Sri Vikrama Rajasinha had already alienated many of the Sinhalese chiefs, limiting their powers and the revenues they received, while the influence of his "Malabar" relatives had grown ever greater at court. The sangha had also been offended by royal actions, including plans to shift several temples and their monastic communities outside Kandy, urbanistic projects seen as an effort architecturally to "Hinduize" the capital. Incidents that violated Buddhist precepts, such as the slaughter of goats in the vicinity of the Dalada Maligawa, also caused offense. Popular discontent grew because of use of corvée labor (*rajakariya*) in the king's building program. Soon Ehelepola, like his predecessor, began conspiring against the king and collaborating with the British, informing them of various injustices and cruelties meted out by Sri Vikrama Rajasinha. A fine strategist, Ehelepola convinced the British of the need to intervene for what we would now call humanitarian reasons, and these accorded well with the desiderata of Brownrigg. Ehelepola was also the man who would be king, hoping to use the British to depose Sri Vikrama Rajasinha, gain the throne for himself under British auspices, and then dispense with his European allies.

Ehelepola first masterminded a direct plot to assassinate the king. This plot, too, was discovered, and although Ehelepola managed to flee over the border into British territory, the king took his revenge with the killing of Ehelepola's wife and three children, including an infant. The particularly gruesome manner of their execution, along with reports of mutilation of prisoners, darkened the king's reputation to the deepest shades of black; British observers branded the king barbarous, drunken, and unfit to rule. Soon the British found a casus belli, and thus began the Second Kandyan War. It took only forty days for the British troops (reinforced with Indian soldiers) to occupy Kandy.[23] They arrived to find that the king had fled his capital, but soon they captured him not far away. Hidden in a village house with two of his queens, he was taken captive on 18 February 1815 by a group of Ceylonese, led by one of the rebel noblemen, with only a minor scuffle—the queens suffered some injury when their earrings were torn off by irregulars, though the king faced the distinct possibility of greater harm, as he was bound with vines and dragged across a meadow. Senior British figures propitiously arrived and tried to restore order; they gave some Madeira to the king and claret to the queens to lift their spirits.[24] The central British official on the campaign, John D'Oyly, took charge of the royals; one of the most interesting characters in British imperial history, he had worked in Ceylon since 1801, was almost unique among the British in having mastered Sinhala, and made it a point of honor that the king be treated with dignity.[25] Nevertheless, this represented an ignominious end to a reign, a dynasty, and a kingdom.

D'Oyly looked after the king and the two queens who had been in hiding with him, and he had the king's other two queens and the king's mother brought to join them. After a week in rest houses in the vicinity of Kandy, the royal party was taken by palanquin to Colombo, where they remained for almost a year while the British authorities discussed their future. Their exile had been determined as a matter of course by the British, but East India Company officials in Madras bickered about where to house them.

Within days of the king's capture, D'Oyly had also composed an agreement, the Kandyan Convention, signed by the British governor and the Kandyan chiefs, with Ehelepola as primus inter pares. It declared British sovereignty over the kingdom but preserved the rights and privileges of the Kandyan nobles. It forbade "Malabar" heirs of Sri Vikrama Rajasinha to enter Ceylon or to make claims on the throne. Most important, a clause promised British protection of an inviolate Buddhism.[26] Soon D'Oyly also managed to have returned to the Dalada Maligawa the sacred Tooth Relic, which had been spirited out of the city when the king fled, and he persuaded Ehelepola to hand over items of the kingdom's regalia, which had come into his possession no doubt with his hope that he would soon don the trappings of monarchy. The British thus gained the palladium of the kingdom, to which D'Oyly paid reverence at the Dalada Maligawa, as well as the symbols of the Kandyan monarchy. The king's crown and throne were taken by the governor's son to England and presented to the prince regent; they were then housed at Windsor Castle until they were returned to Ceylon in 1934.

Ehelepola's dream of becoming king was thwarted; the British saw no advantage in crowning a new Kandyan monarch, no matter how trusty a vassal he might be. Ehelepola took retirement rather than accept a nonregal position, compensated with the title "Friend of the British," a gift of money, and, rather pointedly, a cameo of the Prince Regent, the future king of England. Neither he nor the other Kandyan chiefs, however, were long resigned to the new regime. In 1817, a rebellion, or attempted war of emancipation from the point of view of the colonized, broke out, led by the Radala chief Keppetipola.[27] A pretender to the throne had just emerged in a remote province, a shadowy figure named Vibave, and he was installed as king by some of the rebel leaders, though Keppetipola had already learned that he was an imposter in his claims to be a Nayak prince. Vibave, and the idea of a monarchical restoration, nonetheless served to recruit support. The insurrection spread around the country and encompassed chiefs, monks, and Veddas (considered the aboriginal people of Ceylon by many Europeans), with guerrilla warfare waged by the rebels. The British responded with terror tactics and a scorched-earth policy, torching entire villages, destroying rice paddies, and felling fruit trees.

The British suppressed the rebellion, and Keppetipola, along with another of the leading noblemen, was captured, tried, convicted, and executed by decapitation, his skull sent off to the Edinburgh Phrenological Society (and only returned in 1954). Several dozen of the others who had fought against the British were deported to Mauritius, where the last prisoners remained until the early 1830s. Ehelepola, Britain's earlier ally, had not directly taken part in the rebellion, though Keppetipola let it be known that he had thrown his support behind the pretender. In the midst of the insurrection, the British had taken Ehelepola into custody and moved him to Colombo. He remained in detention there until 1824, six years after the rebellion had ended, when he, too, was deported to Mauritius, though with no indictment, trial, or conviction. Treated with more consideration than the earlier exiles to Mauritius, he had a translator, Ceylonese servants, and "Government Blacks" (enslaved Africans) assigned to him as labor. He lived in relatively pleasant conditions and enjoyed minor celebrity status in Mauritius, as Gunesekera's novel dramatizes, though disgruntled at what he saw as British ingratitude, until his death from natural causes in 1829.[28]

A British declaration in 1818, when the resistance movement had been put down in Ceylon, reaffirmed British sovereignty, "the source alone from which all Power emanates, [and] to which obedience is due."[29] The people of Ceylon were required to acknowledge their new British king by bowing before his portrait in the old Kandyan royal audience hall, and to clear away from the middle of the road when any British officer, civilian or military, passed. The 1815 statement of protection of Buddhism was significantly diluted in the new proclamation. The victory did not, however, secure the peace, and a series of rebellions of greater or lesser magnitude troubled the British over the next thirty years. According to Kumari Jayawardena, they brought together Sinhalese noblemen, *bhikkhus,* and peasants disaffected with taxation, labor demands, and other impositions, alongside Veddas, and the rebels often grouped symbolically around a pretender to the throne. Over the years until 1848, at least eight pretenders appeared, men with dubious royal credentials, if any at all, and they failed to galvanize support.[30] The British apprehended most of the claimants, imprisoning some, flogging others, and exiling still others; Vibave, the 1817 pretender, had gone into hiding in the jungle, however, not captured by the British until 1830, and then released as harmless.

The deposition and exile of the last legitimate king left a complex legacy in Ceylon, in addition to the persistence for several decades of monarchist sentiment (though never with demands for the restoration of Sri Vikrama Rajasinha himself). According to Nira Wickramasinghe, the British continued to regard the Kandyans—as the Kandyans saw themselves—as the "authentic" Sinhalese, repositories of the historical culture of Ceylon confirmed by the survival of the Kandyan kingdom for several centuries after the European conquest of the maritime provinces. This affirmation of Kandyan identity perpetuated a long conflict with the low-country Sinhalese population (and its secular and monastic elite) that was still visible in the early twentieth century.[31] Other historians, such as Michael Roberts, have explored the way in which Kandyan traditions entered into the construction of a more general Sinhalese identity and the emergence of an avowedly Sinhalese and Buddhist nationalism in Ceylon.[32] Ananda Coomaraswamy, premier historian of medieval Sinhalese art, identified another effect of the deposition; the removal of the king ended the royal patronage and aristocratic commissions that sustained both an artisan class and the vitality of indigenous arts and crafts.[33]

Having dispensed with the Kandyan king and dynasty, the British moved in the apparatus of their own monarchy. This added extra luster to the British crown with the addition of another country over which the sovereign ruled. Along with other new possessions taken over at this time and later, the conquest of Ceylon reinforced the British throne as a truly international monarchy, indeed one with global reach. Meanwhile, as Sujit Sivasundaram has put it, the "British could appear as inheritors of the tradition of the Buddhist kings."[34] The 1818 declaration explicitly prescribed obeisance to the king and his representatives—the governor, on vice-regal progress around the island, "shall be attended by all the persons in office belonging to each province in manner as they attended the former Kings of Kandy." The power that possessed the Tooth Relic held the right to govern, as Brownrigg and D'Oyly well recognized at the time, and as later historians such as Sivasundaram have underlined.[35] When the British oversaw the recovery of the palladium and protected its tabernacle in the Dalada Maligawa, they assured themselves of de facto sovereignty.

"Palais de Kandy (Ceylon)." The building is in fact the Sri Dalada Maligawa (Temple of the Tooth). (From Ernest Breton, *Monuments de Tous les Peuples,* Paris, 1843.)

Sivasundaram has identified the multiple and profound ways in which the British "recycled" (as he puts it) the institution of the Kandyan monarchy, especially in the first decades of their suzerainty over the island. Indeed, "all of the structures of Kandy were kept intact, and a British board of governance was superimposed on them in place of the king." The British took on the Kandyan king's role as protector of Buddhism. Officials interested in Pali and Sanskrit, and Buddhist traditions, such as D'Oyly and Alexander Johnston, the chief justice, served as patrons for scholarship and translation, as had the kings. British attention to archaeological sites, especially at the medieval royal capital of Anuradhapura, represented a clear continuity with the Nayakkar kings' interest in the site. Although in 1831 the British abolished the system of corvée labor owed to the Kandyan king, seventeen years later they instituted a system of mandatory labor for road building that essentially revived the old system. The Ceylonese could also perceive the British as successors to the Kandyan rulers; when the poet Gajaman Nona addressed verses to D'Oyly, she wrote them as earlier petitioners would have addressed the king, and a Sanskrit blessing for King George IV took the form of a traditional glorification of the Kandyan king. Local people could view British visits to the holy mountain of Sri Pada (Adam's Peak) as the practice of traditional pilgrimages. For Sivasundaram, "This idea of the British as new kings of the island, and as doers of righteous acts like the Buddhist kings of the past, only went into abeyance as the state disassociated itself from the official patronage of Buddhism in the mid-nineteenth century."[36]

A tradition of the "stranger king" in Ceylon dated back to the origin myths of rulership on the island, and according to Alan Strathern, later rulers with Indian antecedents, including those of the Nayakkar dynasty, subsequently assumed real and sacral powers. It might be suggested that the British followed suit, establishing what Strathern calls "outsider kingship."[37] Even through later years, the panoply of the Britannic monarchy—gubernatorial protocol, tours by Prince Alfred in the 1870s and other royals afterward, the celebrations of Queen Victoria's jubilees, the awarding of imperial decorations and knighthoods, as well as the erection of grand imperial buildings—affirmed that the British monarch both reigned and ruled in place of the deposed dynasty of Kandy.[38]

Meanwhile, the ci-devant Nayakkar king lived on in exile with his family members in Vellore, themselves only some of at least two hundred "Malabars" from Kandy whom the British banished to India in 1815 and 1816. Any hopes of return faded, if he had ever, unrealistically, nursed such aspirations. He celebrated the coming-of-age of his daughters and the birth of a son, mourned the death of his mother, quarreled with his relatives, and entreated the British for various comforts. The British responded positively to some requests, though they refused to accommodate one that gold in his possession be fashioned into a crown-like headdress, considering it inappropriate that he should own such an evident symbol of royalty.

The king's only son outlived Sri Vikrama Rajasinha, still residing in Vellore Fort after the monarch's death, for only eleven years. In 1834, the British allowed most of those exiled to Vellore to return to Ceylon, though not close relatives of the former king. Those who remained continued to send petitions for various benefits to the British for many years.[39] In 1889, after a visit to southern India, the Ceylonese public servant (and budding nationalist) Ponnambalam Arunachalam wrote to his friend Edward Carpenter that "here also, but in far greater and pitiable destitution [than survivors of the Mahrattas], are the descendants of the last native dynasty of Ceylon. A good deal of the time of the royal folks is spent in building castles in the air and scheming for increased allowances and restoration of the throne."[40] The British colonial government of Ceylon, then the government of independent Ceylon, continued paying a pension to Sri Vikrama Rajasinha's descendants until 1965. A Sri Lankan journalist who visited the king's tomb in Vellore in 2007 met a fifth-generation descendant who bemoaned the end of the pension and his own impecunious state, though little else is known about the king's descendants.[41]

If the Sinhalese nobles rebelled against their last king, and the British displaced the Nayakkar dynasty, that did not mean that the Kandyan monarchy was effaced in the collective memory, the historical narrative, or the material heritage of the island's people.[42] The early and medieval Sinhalese kings continue to be lauded for their achievements as builders, guardians of Buddhism, and defenders of the homeland.[43] Even the Nayakkar monarchs receive some credit: Kirti Sri Rajasinha for the revival of Buddhism; his successor, Rajadhi Rajasinha, for his gifts as a poet; Sri Vikrama Rajasinha for building a lake in Kandy. The rebel Keppetipola, however, finds a more honorable place in the national pantheon than does the last king, evidenced by a monument to the executed leader standing on the esplanade of the lake in Kandy. The only real monument to that last Nayakkar king is a largely forgotten stele erected by the British in 1908 near Medamahanuwara, the place of his capture. Other material traces of the king do remain: the elegant octagonal pavilion he constructed at the Dalada Maligawa, artifacts in the Kandy museum (housed in the old queens' palace), a tiny building purporting to stand on the site of the house where he was held in detention in Colombo, and his tomb and a small display in Vellore.

More important, however, are the treasures in the National Museum of Colombo, including portraits of the king and one of his queens, his gold watch, and his crown and throne. The splendid throne, presented to the king by the Dutch around 1693, is made of wood covered in gold sheeting, ornamented with hundreds of gemstones, its arms lions couchant representing the Sinhalese (the "lion people"), its back displaying a radiant solar image showing the power of the monarch. Many royal possessions were taken by the British as booty and ended up being auctioned in London in 1820, despite D'Oyly's promise that they would be safeguarded with as much care as the regalia of the British monarch. The throne, crown, scepter, and royal sword were preserved, however, and returned to Ceylon in the 1930s or at the time of independence.[44] In the 1948 ceremonial opening of the parliament of the Dominion of Ceylon, the throne of the king was placed on the dais, standing on a platform behind and above the chairs reserved for the Ceylonese dignitaries and the Duke of Gloucester, representing King George VI, whose dynasty reigned over the island until 1972.[45]

The deposition and banishment of Sri Vikrama Rajasinha bears comparison with several other cases of royal exile analyzed in this volume. Similar to the cases of the eighteenth-century Javanese king Amangkurat III and Pangéran Arya Mangkunagara, discussed by Ronit Ricci (chapter 4 in this volume), and that of the nineteenth-century sultan Hamengkubuwana II, covered by Sri Margana (chapter 5), the fate of the Kandyan king was determined by both court intrigues and colonial imperatives.[46] All were eventually exiled to distant enough locations to keep them from being a nuisance. In the cases of the Javanese, the exiles were generally sent to places—Ceylon, Penang, and Ambon—with which they had no family connections, though the Ceylonese were banished to the ancestral country of the Nayakkar dynasty in southern India. They were accompanied by family members and courtiers, and there is a parallel between the eventual exile of court adviser Patih Danureja Penang, who had played a role in Pangéran Arya Mangkunagara's downfall but then had himself fallen out with the colonial overlords, and the exile of Ceylon's Ehelepola. The exiles seem to have pined to return home and dreamed of regaining their thrones. Only Hamengkubuwana II, however, was able to do so, though Amangkurat III's body was repatriated and buried in the royal necropolis. There was similar concern among both the royals and the colonials about the heirs to the deposed monarchs and the fate of the royal regalia. Several of the Kartasura *pusaka* (treasures) were returned to Java with the king's remains, whereas the Kandyan regalia, as noted, ended up in Britain, only some of it returned more than a century after the exile of Sri Vikrama Rajasinha. In Kartasura (and later Surakarto) and Yogyakarta, unlike Kandy, the dynasties endured, and indeed the sultan of Yogyakarta retains his traditional status and, in a unique arrangement in Indonesia, is the hereditary governor of the province.

The history of the last king of Kandy shows the importance of monarchy in the anciens régimes displaced by colonial overlordship, and the confrontation between two hierarchical and hereditary systems during colonial encounters. In the case of the British Empire, it underlines the connection between Crown and colonies that formed one of the foundations of imperial rule. It shows how one power, and in this case, one monarchy, replaced another, and the way real and ceremonial power was exercised and contested. Both Sri Vikrama Rajasinha and the British forces under Governor Brownrigg, were their actions undertaken today, might well be accused of crimes of war or even crimes against humanity. The exiled Nayakkar king and the banished Sinhalese chief who fomented a conspiracy against him and against the British might well make convincing legal arguments against unjust imprisonment. The colonial age did not allow such legal initiatives.

Ultimately, the exile of Sri Vikrama Rajasinha in 1815 proved less important in securing British dominion over the Kandyan kingdom than the execution or exile of the Kandyan chiefs from the 1817–1818 rebellion. The first banishment rid the country of an unpopular and compromised king who had become dispensable even to some of the Sinhalese, leaving royal slippers that the British sovereign metaphorically attempted to fill. The execution of Keppetipola and one of his rebel colleagues, and the exile of Ehelepola and a host of other noblemen and supporters, however, meant that the Kandyan chiefs who remained unreconciled, at least to some degree, to British overlordship were eliminated as a menacing opposition. During the first decades of the British presence, those who may have been the most convincing, or most aspirational, of the candidates to replace Sri Vikrama Rajasinha disappeared—Muttusamy abandoned by the British, Pilima Talawe Sr. executed by the king (with his son exiled by the British), and Ehelepola thwarted in his ambitions by the colonialists, sidelined, and then effectively transported to Mauritius for the term of his natural life. Out of sight and out of mind, they posed no threat to the British imperium, and by the time the exiled survivors died, in Mauritius or in India, in some cases after more than a decade in a foreign country, they were of little real consequence to the British. The experiment in controlling resistance by an indigenous elite through banishment of a king, noblemen, and commoners, however, had proved successful in British eyes, providing a valuable precedent to be used again in other conquered lands.

Notes

1. There are differing transliterations of names from Sinhala into English: Wikrama or Vikrama, Rajasinha or Rajasimha, and other variations, for example. The present chapter forms part of a larger research project on the exile of indigenous rulers by the British and French colonial authorities in the nineteenth and twentieth centuries, which includes a more extensive treatment of the Ceylonese case. I would like to acknowledge the funding for the research provided by a grant from the Australian Research Council.

2. William Granville, "Journal of Reminiscences Relating to the Late King of Kandy When on His Voyage from Colombo to Madras in 1816, a Prisoner-of-War on Board His Majesty's Ship 'Cornwallis.'" The journal was published as "Deportation of Sri Vikrama Rajasinha," in two parts: *Ceylon Literary Register* 3, no. 11 (1936): 487–504; 3, no. 12 (1936): 543–550, from which the quotations are taken.

3. K. M. de Silva, *A History of Sri Lanka* (Colombo: Vijitha Yapa Publications, 2008), is the standard history of the island. Nira Wickramasinghe, *Sri Lanka in the Modern Age: A History of Contested Identities* (London: Hurst & Company, 2006), provides an insight with perspectives drawn from cultural studies and the "new imperial history." John Clifford Holt, ed., *The Sri Lanka Reader: History, Culture, Politics* (Durham, NC: Duke University Press, 2011), offers a valuable collection of documents and excerpts. On the period of the British takeover of Ceylon, the classic historical work is P. E. Pieris, *Tri Sinhala: The Last Phase, 1796–1815* (New Delhi: Asian Educational Services, 2001), supplemented with a particular emphasis on military engagements, by Geoffrey Powell, *The Kandyan Wars* (London: Leo Cooper, 1973). See also Colvin R. de Silva, *Ceylon under the British Occupation, 1795–1833* (New Delhi: Navrang, 1995); and Upali C. Wickremeratne, *Hearsay & Versions in British Relations with the Kingdom of Kandy, 1796–1818* (Colombo: Vijitha Yapa Publications,

2012). There is no full-scale biography of Sri Vikrama Rajasinha, but stories about the king and his reign, including popular beliefs, are collected in Punchibandara Dolapihilla, *In the Days of Sri Wickramarajasingha*, 2nd ed. (Ratmalana: Vishva Lekha, 2006).

4. William Dalrymple, *The Last Mughal: The Fall of a Dynasty, Delhi, 1857* (London: Bloomsbury, 2006), chap. 12; Rosie Llewellyn-Jones, *The Last King in India: Wajid Ali Shah* (London: Hurst & Company, 2014); Sudha Shah, *The King in Exile: The Fall of the Royal Family of Burma* (New Delhi: HarperCollins, 2012); William Dalrymple, *Return of a King: The Battle for Afghanistan* (London: Bloomsbury, 2013).

5. On European royal exiles, voluntary or otherwise, see Philip Mansel and Torsten Riotte, eds., *Monarchy and Exile: The Politics of Legitimacy from Marie de Medicis to Wilhelm II* (London: Palgrave Macmillan, 2011).

6. Tony Ballantyne, "Maharajah Dalip Singh, Memory, and the Negotiations of Sikh Identity," in *Between Colonialism and Diaspora: Sikh Cultural Formations in an Imperial World*, ed. Tony Ballantyne (Durham, NC: Duke University Press, 2006), 86–120; Fiona Groenhout, "Loyal Feudatories or Depraved Despots? The Deposition of Princes in the Central India Agency, c. 1880–1947," in *India's Princely States: People, Princes and Colonialism*, ed. Waltraud Ernst and Biswamoy Pati (Abingdon: Routledge, 2007), 99–117; Uma Kothari, "Contesting Colonial Rule: Politics of Exile in the Indian Ocean," *Geoforum* 43, no. 3 (2012).

7. Robert Aldrich, "French Colonisers and Vietnamese Emperors," in *French History and Civilization: Papers from the George Rudé Seminar* (H-France.net, 2014). On other Vietnamese and Cambodian exiles, see, respectively, Tran My-Van, *A Vietnamese Royal Exile in Japan: Prince Cuong De (1882–1951)* (London: Routledge, 2005); and Pierre Lamant, *L'Affaire Yukanthor: autopsie d'un scandale colonial* (Paris: Société Française d'Histoire d'Outre-Mer, 1989). On the Madagascar case, see Marie-France Barrier, *Ranavalo, dernière reine de Madagascar* (Paris: Balland, 1996).

8. De Silva, *History of Sri Lanka*, 166–168.

9. Amitav Ghosh, *The Glass Palace* (London: HarperCollins, 2000); and Romesh Gunesekera, *The Prisoner of Paradise* (London: Bloomsbury, 2012).

10. Anoma Pieris, "The 'Other' Side of Labor Reform: Accounts of Incarceration and Resistance in the Straits Settlements Penal System, 1825–1873," *Journal of Social History* 45, no. 2 (2011): 453–479.

11. Nicholas B. Dirks, *The Hollow Crown: Ethnohistory of an Indian Kingdom* (Ann Arbor: University of Michigan Press, 1993), presents a well-known analysis of how the British transformed native princes into puppets, but its conclusions have been disputed by, among others, Sujit Sivasundaram, "Ethnicity, Indigeneity, and Migration in the Advent of British Rule to Sri Lanka," *American Historical Review* 115, no. 2 (2010): 428–452.

12. H. L. Seneviratne, *Rituals of the Kandyan State* (Cambridge: Cambridge University Press, 1978), 2.

13. Vernon L. B. Mendis, *The Rulers of Sri Lanka* (Colombo: S. Godage & Brothers, 2000), 194.

14. On this connection, see Kitsiri Malalgoda, *Buddhism in Sinhalese Society, 1750–1900: A Study of Religious Revival and Change* (Berkeley: University of California Press, 1976), esp. chap. 2.

15. Stanley Jeyaraja Tambiah, *Buddhism Betrayed? Religion, Politics, and Violence in Sri Lanka* (Chicago: University of Chicago Press, 1992).

16. Among other works, see K. N. O. Dharmadahsa, "The Sinhala Buddhist Identity and the Nayakkar Dynasty in the Politics of the Kandyan Kingdom, 1739–1815," in *Sri*

Lanka: Collective Identities Revisited, ed. Michael Roberts (Colombo: Marga Institute, 1997), 79–104; R. A. L. H. Gunawardana, "Colonialism, Ethnicity and the Construction of the Past: The Changing 'Ethnic Identity' of the Last Four Kings of the Kandyan Kingdom," in *Pivot Politics: Changing Cultural Identities in Early State Formation Processes,* ed. Martin van Bakel, Renée Hagesteijn, and Pieter van de Velde (Amsterdam: Het Spinhuis, 1994), 197–221; and S. Gopalakrishnan, *The Nayaks of Sri Lanka, 1739–1815: Political Relations with the British in South India* (Madras: New Era Publications, 1988).

17. See John Clifford Holt, *The Religious World of Kirti Sri: Buddhism, Art, and Politics in Late Medieval Sri Lanka* (New York: Oxford University Press, 1996).

18. There is biographical information on Pilima Talawe and other chiefs in Ananda S. Pilimatalavuva, *The Chieftains in the Last Phase of the Kandyan Kingdom (Sinhalé),* 2nd ed. (Pannipitiya: Stamford Lake, 2008), and *The Pilimatalavuvas in the Last Phase of the Kandyan Kingdom,* 2nd ed. (Pannipitiya: Stamford Lake, 2008).

19. The geopolitics of British colonialism are well covered in C. A. Bayly, *Imperial Meridian: The British Empire and the World, 1780–1830* (Harlow: Longman, 1989); while several volumes provide overviews of the setting of the Indian Ocean, including most recently Michael Pearson, *The Indian Ocean* (London: Routledge, 2003); and Sugata Bose, *A Hundred Horizons: The Indian Ocean in the Age of Global Empire* (Cambridge: Cambridge University Press, 2006).

20. See Alan Strathern, *Kingship and Conversion in Sixteenth-Century Sri Lanka: Portuguese Imperialism in a Buddhist Land* (Cambridge: Cambridge University Press, 2010); and S. Arasaratnam, *Ceylon and the Dutch, 1600–1800: External Influence and Internal Change in Early Modern Sri Lanka* (Brookfield, VT: Variorum, 1996).

21. The permutations in relations between the Kandyans and the British is charted through letters to and from Governor Brownrigg and the Kandyan chief minister, edited by Tennakoon Vimalananda: *Sri Wickrema, Brownrigg and Ehelepola, Being Letters Addressed to the Home Government from 1811–1815 by Major General John Wilson and Lieut-General John Brownrigg, Governor of Ceylon* (Colombo: Gunasena, 1984); and in John D'Oyly's diary, H. W. Codrington, ed., *Diary of Mr. John D'Oyly* (New Delhi: Navrang, 1995).

22. Alicia Frederika Schrikker, *Dutch and British Intervention in Sri Lanka c. 1780–1815: Expansion and Reform* (Leiden: Brill, 2007).

23. Channa Wickremesekera, *Kandy at War: Indigenous Military Resistance to European Expansion in Sri Lanka, 1594–1818* (New Delhi: Manohar, 2004), covers the long history of conflicts culminating in this period.

24. William Adrian Dias Bandaranayaka, "How the Last King of Kandy was Captured by the British: An Eye-witness's Account, Rendered from the Sinhalese," *Journal of the Royal Asiatic Society (Ceylon)* 14, no. 47 (1896), from which this account is taken.

25. Brendon Gooneratne and Yasmine Gooneratne, *This Inscrutable Englishman: Sir John D'Oyly (1774–1824)* (London: Cassell, 1999).

26. The convention is reproduced in various works, including G. C. Mendis, ed., *The Colebrooke-Cameron Papers* (Oxford: Oxford University Press, 1956).

27. The classic account by a Sri Lankan historian is P. E. Pieris, *Sinhale and the Patriots, 1815–1818* (Colombo: Colombo Apothecaries Co., 1950).

28. On the exiles to Mauritius, see M. A. D. Appuhamy, *The Rebels, Outlaws and Enemies to the British* (Colombo: Gunasena, 1990); and Raja C. Bandaranayake, *Betwixt Isles: The Story of the Kandyan Prisoners in Mauritius* (Colombo: Vijitha Yapa Publications, 2006). See also Sheila Ward, *Prisoners in Paradise* (Rose Hill, Mauritius: Éditions de l'Océan Indien, 1986).

29. The declaration is also reproduced in Mendis, *Colebrooke-Cameron Papers*.

30. Kumari Jayawardena, *Perpetual Ferment: Popular Revolts in Sri Lanka in the 18th and 19th Centuries* (Colombo: Social Scientists' Association, 2010).

31. Nira Wickramasinghe, "The Return of Keppetipola's Cranium: Authenticity in a New Nation," *Economic and Political Weekly* (26 July 1997): 85–92.

32. Michael Roberts, *Sinhala Consciousness in the Kandyan Period, 1590s to 1815* (Colombo: Vijitha Yapa Publications, 2004).

33. Ananda K. Coomaraswamy, *Mediaeval Sinhalese Art*, rev. ed. (New York: Pantheon Books, 1956).

34. Sujit Sivasundaram, "Buddhist Kingship, British Archaeology and Historical Narratives in Sri Lanka, c. 1750–1850," *Past and Present*, 197 (2007): 114.

35. Ibid., 130.

36. Sujit Sivasundaram, *Islanded: Britain, Sri Lanka and the Bounds of an Indian Ocean Colony* (Chicago: University of Chicago Press, 2013), 125, 7.

37. Alan Strathern, "The Vijaya Origin Myth of Sri Lanka and the Strangeness of Kingship," *Past and Present* 203 (2009): 3–28, and "Vijaya and Romulus: Interpreting the Origin Myths of Sri Lanka and Rome," *Journal of the Royal Asiatic Society* 24, no. 1 (2014): 51–73.

38. On the remodeling of the landscape, see Anoma Pieris, *Architecture and Nationalism in Sri Lanka: The Trouser under the Cloth* (London: Routledge, 2013); and James L. A. Webb Jr., *Tropical Pioneers: Human Agency and Ecological Change in the Highlands of Sri Lanka, 1800–1900* (Athens: Ohio University Press, 2002).

39. Sujit Sivasundaram, "Ethnicity, Indigeneity, and Migration in the Advent of British Rule to Sri Lanka," *American Historical Review* 115, no. 2 (2010), 444.

40. Ponnambalam Arunachalam, *Light from the East, Being Letters on Gnanam, the Divine Knowledge*, ed. Edward Carpenter (London: Allen & Unwin, 1927), 33–34.

41. Kausalya Santhanam, "Lankan Legacy," *The Hindu*, 6 May 2007. See also Satharathilaka Banda Atugoda, "The Last King of Kanda Udarata," *The Island (Colombo)*, reprinted as "Tomb of King Wickrama Rajasinhe in Vellore—India" on the website amazinglanka .com, n.d.; and Ajith Amarasinghe, "Rediscovering the Tomb of Our Last King," *Sunday Times (Colombo)*, 11 March 2012, http://sundaytimes.lk/120311/Plus/plus_01.html.

42. Steven Kemper, *The Presence of the Past: Chronicles, Politics, and Culture in Sinhala Life* (Ithaca, NY: Cornell University Press, 1991), offers insight into the role of Sinhalese history in colonial and postcolonial ideology.

43. See, e.g., J. B. Disanayaka, *Lanka: The Land of Kings* (Nugegoda: Sumitha, 2007).

44. Wikramasinghe, *Sri Lanka in the Modern Age*, 106–111.

45. Robert Aldrich, "The Abolition of a Monarchy and the Fate of Its Regalia: The Kandyan Kingdom and the British Colonial State," in *Crowns and Colonies: Monarchies and Overseas Empires*, ed. Robert Aldrich and Cindy McCreery (Manchester: Manchester University Press, 2016).

46. Comparisons could also be made with such other East Indian royal figures as Diponegoro and the last rajah of Karangasem. See Peter Carey, *Destiny: The Life of Prince Diponegoro of Yogyakarta, 1785–1855* (Oxford: Peter Lang, 2014); and A. A. A. Dewi Girindrawardani, Adrian Vickers, and Rodney Holt, *The Last Rajah of Karangasem: The Life and Times of Anak Agung Agung Anglurah Karangasem (1887–1966)* (Denpasar: Saritaksu Editions, 2014).

Bibliography

Aldrich, Robert. "The Abolition of a Monarchy and the Fate of Its Regalia: The Kandyan Kingdom and the British Colonial State." In *Crowns and Colonies: European Monarchies and Overseas Empires*, edited by Robert Aldrich and Cindy McCreery. Manchester: Manchester University Press, 2016.

———. "French Colonisers and Vietnamese Emperors." In *French History and Civilization: Papers from the George Rudé Seminar*, Vol. 5, H-France.net, 2014.

———. "Imperial Banishment: French Colonizers and the Exile of Vietnamese Emperors." In *French History and Civilization: Papers from the George Rudé Seminar*. Vol. 5, 123–133. H-France.net, 2014.

Amarasinghe, Ajith. "Rediscovering the Tomb of Our Last King." *Sunday Times (Colombo)*, 11 March 2012. http://sundaytimes.lk/120311/Plus/plus_01.html.

Appuhamy, M. A. D. *The Rebels, Outlaws and Enemies to the British*. Colombo: Gunasena, 1990.

Arasaratnam, S. *Ceylon and the Dutch, 1600–1800: External Influence and Internal Change in Early Modern Sri Lanka*. Brookfield, VT: Variorum, 1996.

Arunachalam, Ponnambalam. *Light from the East, Being Letters on Gnanam, the Divine Knowledge*, edited by Edward Carpenter. London: Allen & Unwin, 1927.

Atugoda, Satharathilaka Banda. "The Last King of Kanda Udarata." *The Island (Colombo)*, reprinted as "Tomb of King Wickrama Rajasinhe in Vellore—India," amazinglanka.com, n.d.

Ballantyne, Tony. "Maharajah Dalip Singh, Memory, and the Negotiations of Sikh Identity." In *Between Colonialism and Diaspora: Sikh Cultural Formations in an Imperial World*, edited by Tony Ballantyne, 86–120. Durham, NC: Duke University Press, 2006.

Bandaranayaka, William Adrian Dias. "How the Last King of Kandy was Captured by the British: An Eye-witness's Account, Rendered from the Sinhalese." *Journal of the Royal Asiatic Society (Ceylon)* 14, no. 47 (1896): 107–116.

Bandaranayake, Raja C. *Betwixt Isles: The Story of the Kandyan Prisoners in Mauritius*. Colombo: Vijitha Yapa Publications, 2006.

Barrier, Marie-France. *Ranavalo, dernière reine de Madagascar*. Paris: Balland, 1996.

Bayly, C. A. *Imperial Meridian: The British Empire and the World, 1780–1830*. Harlow: Longman, 1989.

Bose, Sugata. *A Hundred Horizons: The Indian Ocean in the Age of Global Empire*. Cambridge: Cambridge University Press, 2006.

Carey, Peter. *Destiny: The Life of Prince Diponegoro of Yogyakarta, 1785–1855*. Oxford: Peter Lang, 2014.

Codrington, H. W., ed. *Diary of Mr. John D'Oyly*. New Delhi: Navrang, 1995.

Coomaraswamy, Ananda K. *Mediaeval Sinhalese Art*. Rev. ed. New York: Pantheon Books, 1956.

Dalrymple, William. *The Last Mughal: The Fall of a Dynasty, Delhi, 1857*. London: Bloomsbury, 2006.

———. *Return of a King: The Battle for Afghanistan*. London: Bloomsbury, 2013.

De Silva, Colvin R. *Ceylon under the British Occupation, 1795–1833*. New Delhi: Navrang, 1995.

De Silva, K. M. *A History of Sri Lanka*. Colombo: Vijitha Yapa Publications, 2008.

Dharmadahsa, K. N. O. "The Sinhala Buddhist Identity and the Nayakkar Dynasty in the Politics of the Kandyan Kingdom, 1739–1815." In *Sri Lanka: Collective Identities Revisited,* edited by Michael Roberts, 79–104. Colombo: Marga Institute, 1997.

Dirks, Nicholas B. *The Hollow Crown: Ethnohistory of an Indian Kingdom.* Ann Arbor: University of Michigan Press, 1993.

Disanayaka, J. B. *Lanka: The Land of Kings.* Nugegoda: Sumitha, 2007.

Dolapihilla, Punchibandara. *In the Days of Sri Wickramarajasingha.* 2nd ed. Ratmalana: Vishva Lekha, 2006.

Ghosh, Amitav. *The Glass Palace.* London: HarperCollins, 2000.

Girindrawardani, A. A. A. Dewi, Adrian Vickers, and Rodney Holt. *The Last Rajah of Karangasem: The Life and Times of Anak Agung Agung Anglurah Karangasem (1887–1966).* Denpasar: Saritaksu Editions, 2014.

Gooneratne, Brendon, and Yasmine Gooneratne. *This Inscrutable Englishman: Sir John D'Oyly (1774–1824).* London: Cassell, 1999.

Gopalakrishnan, S. *The Nayaks of Sri Lanka, 1739–1815: Political Relations with the British in South India.* Madras: New Era Publications, 1988.

Granville, William. "Journal of Reminiscences Relating to the Late King of Kandy When on His Voyage from Colombo to Madras in 1816, a Prisoner-of-War on Board His Majesty's Ship 'Cornwallis,'" published as "Deportation of Sri Vikrama Rajasinha." Pts. 1 and 2. *Ceylon Literary Register* 3, no. 11 (1936): 487–504; 3, no. 12 (1936): 543–550.

Groenhout, Fiona. "Loyal Feudatories or Depraved Despots? The Deposition of Princes in the Central India Agency, c. 1880–1947." In *India's Princely States: People, Princes and Colonialism,* edited by Waltraud Ernst and Biswamoy Pati, 99–117. Abingdon: Routledge, 2007.

Gunawardana, R. A. L. H. "Colonialism, Ethnicity and the Construction of the Past: The Changing 'Ethnic Identity' of the Last Four Kings of the Kandyan Kingdom." In *Pivot Politics: Changing Cultural Identities in Early State Formation Processes,* edited by Martin van Bakel, Renée Hagesteijn, and Pieter van de Velde, 197–221. Amsterdam: Het Spinhuis, 1994.

Gunesekera, Romesh. *The Prisoner of Paradise.* London: Bloomsbury, 2012.

Holt, John Clifford. *The Religious World of Kirti Sri: Buddhism, Art, and Politics in Late Medieval Sri Lanka.* New York: Oxford University Press, 1996.

———, ed. *The Sri Lanka Reader: History, Culture, Politics.* Durham, NC: Duke University Press, 2011.

Jayawardena, Kumari. *Perpetual Ferment: Popular Revolts in Sri Lanka in the 18th and 19th Centuries.* Colombo: Social Scientists' Association, 2010.

Kemper, Steven. *The Presence of the Past: Chronicles, Politics, and Culture in Sinhala Life.* Ithaca, NY: Cornell University Press, 1991.

Kothari, Uma. "Contesting Colonial Rule: Politics of Exile in the Indian Ocean." *Geoforum* 43, no. 3 (2012): 697–706.

Lamant, Pierre. *L'Affaire Yukanthor: autopsie d'un scandale colonial.* Paris: Société Française d'Histoire d'Outre-Mer, 1989.

Llewellyn-Jones, Rosie. *The Last King in India: Wajid Ali Shah.* London: Hurst & Company, 2014.

Malalgoda, Kitsiri. *Buddhism in Sinhalese Society, 1750–1900: A Study of Religious Revival and Change.* Berkeley: University of California Press, 1976.

Mansel, Philip, and Torsten Riotte, eds. *Monarchy and Exile: The Politics of Legitimacy from Marie de Medicis to Wilhelm II.* London: Palgrave Macmillan, 2011.

Mendis, G. C., ed. *The Colebrooke-Cameron Papers*. Oxford: Oxford University Press, 1956.

Mendis, Vernon L. B. *The Rulers of Sri Lanka*. Colombo: S. Godage & Brothers, 2000.

My-Van, Tran. *A Vietnamese Royal Exile in Japan: Prince Cuong De (1882–1951)*. London: Routledge, 2005.

Pearson, Michael. *The Indian Ocean*. London: Routledge, 2003.

Pieris, Anoma. *Architecture and Nationalism in Sri Lanka: The Trouser under the Cloth*. London: Routledge, 2013.

———. "The 'Other' Side of Labor Reform: Accounts of Incarceration and Resistance in the Straits Settlements Penal System, 1825–1873." *Journal of Social History* 45, no. 2 (2011): 453–479.

Pieris, P. E. *Sinhale and the Patriots, 1815–1818*. Colombo: Colombo Apothecaries Co., 1950.

———. *Tri Sinhala: The Last Phase, 1796–1815*. New Delhi: Asian Educational Services, 2001.

Pilimatalavuva, Ananda S. *The Chieftains in the Last Phase of the Kandyan Kingdom (Sinhalé)*. 2nd ed. Pannipitiya: Stamford Lake, 2008.

———. *The Pilimatalavuvas in the Last Phase of the Kandyan Kingdom*. 2nd ed. Pannipitiya: Stamford Lake, 2008.

Powell, Geoffrey. *The Kandyan Wars*. London: Leo Cooper, 1973.

Roberts, Michael. *Sinhala Consciousness in the Kandyan Period, 1590s to 1815*. Colombo: Vijitha Yapa Publications, 2004.

Santhanam, Kausalya. "Lankan Legacy." *The Hindu*, 6 May 2007.

Schrikker, Alicia Frederika. *Dutch and British Intervention in Sri Lanka c. 1780–1815: Expansion and Reform*. Leiden: Brill, 2007.

Seneviratne, H. L. *Rituals of the Kandyan State*. Cambridge: Cambridge University Press, 1978.

Shah, Sudha. *The King in Exile: The Fall of the Royal Family of Burma*. New Delhi: Harper-Collins, 2012.

Sivasundaram, Sujit. "Buddhist Kingship, British Archaeology and Historical Narratives in Sri Lanka, c. 1750–1850." *Past and Present* 197 (2007): 111–142.

———. "Ethnicity, Indigeneity, and Migration in the Advent of British Rule to Sri Lanka." *American Historical Review* 115, no. 2 (2010): 428–452.

———. *Islanded: Britain, Sri Lanka and the Bounds of an Indian Ocean Colony*. Chicago: University of Chicago Press, 2013.

Strathern, Alan. *Kingship and Conversion in Sixteenth-Century Sri Lanka: Portuguese Imperialism in a Buddhist Land*. Cambridge: Cambridge University Press, 2010.

———. "The Vijaya Origin Myth of Sri Lanka and the Strangeness of Kingship." *Past and Present* 203 (2009): 3–28.

———. "Vijaya and Romulus: Interpreting the Origin Myths of Sri Lanka and Rome." *Journal of the Royal Asiatic Society* 24, no. 1 (2014): 51–73.

Tambiah, Stanley Jeyaraja. *Buddhism Betrayed? Religion, Politics, and Violence in Sri Lanka*. Chicago: University of Chicago Press, 1992.

Vimalananda, Tennakoon, ed. *Sri Wickrema, Brownrigg and Ehelepola, Being Letters Addressed to the Home Government from 1811–1815 by Major General John Wilson and Lieut-General John Brownrigg, Governor of Ceylon*. Colombo: Gunasena, 1984.

Ward, Sheila. *Prisoners in Paradise*. Rose Hill, Mauritius: Éditions de l'Océan Indien, 1986.

Webb, James L. A., Jr. *Tropical Pioneers: Human Agency and Ecological Change in the Highlands of Sri Lanka, 1800–1900*. Athens: Ohio University Press, 2002.

Wickramasinghe, Nira. "The Return of Keppetipola's Cranium: Authenticity in a New Nation." *Economic and Political Weekly,* 26 July 1997.

———. *Sri Lanka in the Modern Age: A History of Contested Identities.* London: Hurst & Company, 2006.

Wickremeratne, Upali C. *Hearsay & Versions in British Relations with the Kingdom of Kandy, 1796–1818.* Colombo: Vijitha Yapa Publications, 2012.

Wickremesekera, Channa. *Kandy at War: Indigenous Military Resistance to European Expansion in Sri Lanka, 1594–1818.* New Delhi: Manohar, 2004.

THREE

"Near China beyond the Seas Far Far Distant from Juggernath"

The Mid-Nineteenth-Century Exile of Bhai Maharaj Singh in Singapore

Anand A. Yang

> Guru Bhaie Maharaj Sing has been captured in the Jullundur Doab. . . . [S]o mischievous and so bold a traitor should be at once brought to trial, and, if convicted should be subjected to the heaviest penalty which public law can inflict. In deference to . . . the local authorities . . . the Bhaie should be . . . at once removed to Allahabad. The disciple who is stated to have been taken with him should be sent with him. . . . [F]urnish a guard sufficient to convey the prisoners . . . [and] take advantage of the escort provided . . . to guard the Bhaie to Allahabad, whence he will be conveyed to Calcutta.
>
> —"Minute by the Most Noble the Governor-General"

Exile is strangely compelling to think about but terrible to experience." That striking opening line from Edward Said's "Reflections on Exile"[1] serves well as an epigraph for this meditation about a Sikh named Nihal Singh, aka Guru Bhai Maharaj Singh, who was banished to Singapore for his tenacious military campaign against the British after their takeover of the north Indian kingdom of Maharaja Ranjit Singh. Colonial authorities extended control over Punjab first as a protectorate in early 1846 and then followed up with its outright annexation in March 1849, when his youngest son, eleven-year-old Maharaja Dalip Singh, was deposed and the Sikh army disbanded. Eventually captured in Jalandhar (Jullundur) District in December 1849, Nihal Singh was quickly whisked out of Punjab under armed guard and sent to the headquarters town of Allahabad in the neighboring North-Western Provinces, from where he was taken to Calcutta to be transported overseas on the first available ship.

This chapter dwells on the "terrible" experience of Nihal Singh's exile in Singapore, which can be recounted in some detail, including in his own words and those of his "disciple" Kharak Singh. Such firsthand accounts of men and women incarcerated in penal colonies or colonial jails in the nineteenth century are rare, even for "state prisoners," who were much more likely to leave behind paper trails because a greater proportion of them were literate, of elite backgrounds, and more closely surveilled by the colonial state than the rank-and-file convicts. My interest in his story is not only to document the subjective experience of physical and mental pain associated with exiles who are typically "cut off from their roots, their land, their past," as Said has rightly emphasized,[2] but also because I wish to consider the lived experiences of political prisoners in relation to those of the transmarine convicts who resided alongside them but in very different circumstances. For the latter were transported to Southeast Asia from India and, to a lesser extent, from Sri Lanka, to service the projects of the emerging British Empire in the region, in effect becoming "convict workers," as were prisoners in many penal colonies around the world.[3]

I begin by narrating the events that led to Bhai Maharaj Singh's banishment, namely, his activities as a rebel against colonial rule, which prompted the authorities to condemn him as a "traitor" deserving of the most severe punishment legally permissible. For his fiercely subaltern career as a political, military, and religious leader explains why he was designated a "state prisoner" who had to be executed or expelled and, once the decision was made to banish him, "closely and carefully watched" in captivity. This chapter then traces his journey out of Punjab to Calcutta to highlight the experiences of prisoners sentenced to transportation in north India who were removed from the interior and remanded into the custody of Alipur Jail in Calcutta—and in western and southern India to Bombay and Madras, respectively—from where they were shipped overseas. It closes out the narrative by recounting Singh's exile experiences in Singapore, from the time of his arrival on 9 June 1850 to his demise on 5 July 1856, a period during which its population of transmarine convicts increased from 1,402 to a little over 1,500.

I begin with Nihal Singh and why he was forcibly removed from India. He was banished because he was deemed a major threat to the consolidation of colonial rule in Punjab: he had joined forces with many of the leaders who opposed the British and remained on the battlefield long after most of them had laid down their arms. Furthermore, he enjoyed considerable support in the region, not only because he continued to beat the drums of war but also because he was highly respected as a religious leader. His role in the resistance to the British occupation became conspicuous in the wake of the First Anglo-Sikh War of 1845–1846 when he participated in the so-called Prema Conspiracy of 1847, hatched to restore the power of Rani Jindan, the youngest wife of Ranjit Singh, and her son, the minor king Dalip Singh, by assassinating the chiefs, who vied with them for control of the *darbar* (royal court, executive government) in Lahore, and the British Resident, who had become the effective power in the Sikh kingdom.[4]

A resident of Ludhiana, Nihal Singh rose to prominence as a disciple of a highly respected leader named Bhai Bir Singh, a warrior ascetic who made a name for himself by establishing a gurdwara (place of worship and assembly) in Naurangabad near Amritsar, where hundreds of pilgrims were fed, and by mobilizing Sikh soldiers to side with the princes who sought to inherit the throne in 1839 following the death of their father, Ranjit Singh. He assumed Bir Singh's mantle after the latter's death in 1844 and was thereafter "held in as great esteem as his predecessor by the peasantry and nobility."[5]

A price of one thousand rupees on his head—eventually the reward was raised to the princely sum of ten thousand rupees—and the local authorities in pursuit following the exposure of the Prema Conspiracy, Maharaj Singh fled, periodically surfacing in the central Punjab area known as the *manjha, or doab*, to rally people to the cause of the *khalsa* (Sikh militant order) against the *feringhis* (foreigners, the British).[6]

British attempts to seize him led to raids on his *dera* (encampment or dwelling place of a religious teacher) at Amritsar and Naurangabad and confiscation of his property but not his arrest.[7] When an uprising broke out in Multan—more than two hundred miles to the southwest—led by its *diwan* (governor), Mul Raj, in April 1848, he joined the revolt, accompanied by several thousand men he had recruited in the *manjha*. In the ensuing Second Anglo-Sikh War, the "rebels" were completely routed, thus bringing to an end resistance in the Punjab and the Khalsa Raj, and extending British rule over the entire region.[8]

While most leaders in Punjab capitulated, Maharaj Singh continued campaigning against the British, briefly fleeing to Jammu in the north to evade capture. Back in Punjab toward the end of 1849, he was finally captured near Jalandhar on 28 December, apparently in the midst of planning attacks on British troops stationed in nearby cantonments and the kidnapping of Henry Vansittart, the deputy commissioner of Jalandhar.[9]

By then, Nihal Singh was a celebrated military and religious leader. He was better known as *maharaj,* or king, a name he had acquired, along with the honorific *bhai,* meaning brother.[10] "Sikh elites and masses recognized," as one scholar has remarked, that he possessed "the major characteristics of a bhai: the ability to expound on gurbani [i.e., the teachings of the Sikh gurus as recorded in the Adi Granth and Dasam Granth texts], piety, and a demonstrated capacity to work miracles. These features confirmed for his followers that Maharaj Singh was a holy man, and those who supported his mission to check British expansion in Punjab were sure to earn religious merit."[11] "Such fully realized men," Harjot Oberoi adds, "were sometimes also honoured with the appellation Baba, and more rarely Guru."[12] He was "much venerated" as well "by the women of the manjha," many of whom were the wives and mothers of the Sikh elite.[13]

Nihal Singh accrued these marks of distinction through his military and religious activities. His considerable local standing issued in part from his military exploits, which included "giving away swords" to his followers and mobilizing people to take up arms against the British. In the eyes of the colonial authorities, he was an "outlaw," a man who became "a leader" by virtue of his striking presence on the battlefield astride a black mare and seemingly omnipresent because he would turn up in Amritsar one day and Lahore, some fifty kilometers away, the next. Increasingly, he "appeared at the head of large armed parties . . . possessing command of sums of money sufficient for lavish distribution to the poor and to those who came for service." And he had a knack for evading arrest, supported as he was by local inhabitants who were unwilling to betray a leader they "respected for religious and political reasons,"[14] notwithstanding the sizable reward offered for his capture.

Indeed, Maharaj Singh was their *bhai* and guru. He was known for his "incantations at Umritsar [Amritsar]," the religious and historical center of Sikhs. He was also acknowledged as a "miracle worker" whom people followed because of his religious teachings and prophecies and his remarkable ability to feed and provision them. He had acquired this latter reputation when he was in the *dera* of his guru, Bir Singh—he ran his master's *langar* (free kitchen) and made sure that it never ran out of food. And once he took over from his guru, Maharaj Singh became even more renowned for possessing the gift of giving: always providing for his followers in times of need, whether they numbered a handful or several hundred. As the testimonies of his captured followers reveal, he devoted considerable attention and effort to securing "stores of grain" and other supplies for his entourage. No wonder the British government considered him a formidable opponent who had to be stopped: he had the religious, military, and political capital to wage "a people's rising against the British political domination over the land of the five rivers and the Sikh gurus."[15]

Perhaps nothing better illustrates his standing in the region than the hero's reception he was accorded by the local population when he was finally taken prisoner. As his captor, Deputy Commissioner Vansittart, noted in his dramatic eyewitness account of the moment that his famous prisoner was ushered into the local jail in Jalandhar, even the guards acknowledged his authority and influence:

When Maharaj Sing and his companions were led into the Jail, some of the Seikh [Sikh] Guard bowed themselves down. During the whole day numbers of Hindoos had been gathering round the Jail with the view of casting their eyes on the building in which he was confined. . . .

When to this I add the fact . . . that seldom a day passed that hundreds of devotees did not worship him—that his presence in the Doab was well known to all the villages around . . . When all this is established . . . I assert that the Jalundhur is no safe place of custody for the Gooroo.[16]

As Vansittart's testimony indicates, the authorities were not confident about their ability to keep their famous prisoner under lock and key in the local jail. He was "not an ordinary man," the deputy commissioner insisted, underlining his point with an analogy that his superiors found highly offensive. What specifically upset them was Vansittart's claim that Maharaj Singh

is to the natives what Jesus Christ is to the most zealous of Christians. His miracles were seen by tens of thousands, and are more implicitly relied on, than those worked by the ancient prophets.

But now the man has been captured, that vast power by which the whole Seikh [Sikh] mind from Pateela [Patiala] to Pesawur [Peshawar] is swayed is rapidly passing away. This man who was a God, is in our hands (unless he eludes our vigilance). An ordinary mortal and his schemes, already in part organized, are forever overthrown.[17]

Understandably, Maharaj Singh's exalted position in the community made the local authorities uneasy about the reliability of the local guards and the possibility of a jailbreak. Moreover, because he was not "an ordinary captive," Vansittart deemed it appropriate not to secure him in leg irons or body chains, choosing instead to bind his right hand "at night to the left hand of a determined Mussulman [Muslim]."[18] In the deputy commissioner's eyes, this arrangement presumably militated against escape because he considered Sikhs and Muslims to be at loggerheads, which they were at times, although not always, as the shifting alliances among different groups during the Prema Conspiracy indicate.[19] Part of the British concern about him also stemmed from the fact that their military victories did not ensure control of the region. As Charles Napier, the commander in chief of the British forces, noted, they had occupied the territory militarily but not conquered it as yet, because there were still large numbers of Sikh soldiers present who could rise against the government.[20]

The famous rebel added to the deputy commissioner's anxieties by maintaining a "sullen silence." Briefly, he also alarmed local officials by refusing to eat, a decision that Vansittart construed as an attempt at self-starvation and martyrdom. Once he broke his fast, their next worry was that he would escape with the help of supporters both inside and outside the jail. As a precaution, Vansittart transferred him to the nearby cantonment, where he could be more securely guarded by the military.

There was little, if any, discussion among colonial administrators about their high-profile prisoner's alleged suicide attempt. No doubt there was not because Maharaj Singh seemed to have entertained that option for less than forty-eight hours, not nearly long enough for authorities in Jalandhar and Calcutta, let alone Jalandhar, Calcutta, and London, to communicate with one another. The deputy commissioner, however, was unequivocal about not allowing his adversary to become "an unperishable name amongst his followers." Better to have him live on and "pass the remainder of his days, whatever may be the time allotted him by government or by god, . . . [in] ignominy," Vanittart noted. "It would be a misfortune," he added, "if the man now a miserable captive should . . . die by starvation, and . . . have, after his death, a name, to be cherished by all posterity—a name, which if he be kept safe captive for 2 years, will die away and be half forgotten."[21] Nothing in the colonial archives suggests that anyone recognized the irony in a situation where a "miracle worker," renowned for his resourcefulness in provisioning his followers, considered terminating his life by refusing sustenance willingly supplied by his enemies.

Much more deliberate were the calculations that went into determining an appropriate and efficacious punishment for Maharaj Singh. For the most part, Punjab authorities sought his immediate and complete removal from his territorial base of support, not just the region but all of India, with an eye to diminishing his fame, if not casting him outright into oblivion. In other words, they were intent on ensuring that his present and future would have no connection to his past, either substantively or spatially, and thus his removal from his roots and his territorial base. Relocation was all the more imperative because they considered him one of the few remaining stumbling blocks to their consolidation of control over the entire region and military recruitment efforts among Sikhs, who had more than proven their mettle as fighting men in the two Anglo-Sikh wars. For him, there was to be no trial as there was for one of his fellow rebels, Mul Raj.

At the highest level of government, Governor-General Dalhousie in particular, initially wanted to hang the "pestilent vagabond," as he termed Maharaj Singh, so that he would "meet with his long-standing deserts."[22] But he subsequently backed away from insisting on "the heaviest penalty which public law can inflict" and agreed that it was better to banish him than make a martyr out of him by executing him. "In deference to . . . the local authorities," as he put it, "the Bhaie should be . . . at once removed to Allahabad. The disciple who is stated to have been taken with him should be sent with him." He also insisted on "a guard sufficient to convey the prisoners . . . [and on] tak[ing] advantage of the escort provided . . . to guard the Bhaie to Allahabad, whence he will be conveyed to Calcutta."[23]

Legal justification for exiling Maharaj Singh entailed issuing a "warrant of commitment" under Regulation III of 1818, which allowed the government to "place under personal restraint individuals against whom there may not be sufficient ground to institute any judicial proceedings, or when such proceedings may not be adapted to the nature of the case, or may for other reasons be unadvisable or improper." Such a warrant was authorized for "reasons of state" having to do with the "due maintenance of the alliances formed by the British Government with foreign powers, the preservation of tranquillity in the territories entitled to its protection and the security of the British dominions from foreign hostility and from internal commotion."[24]

In invoking the "Regulation for the Confinement of State Prisoners," the governor-general sided with Punjab officials who sought Singh's displacement "from the jurisdiction . . . and from among his own people; with a view to avoid the excitement and prolonged uncertainty which the delay necessarily attendant on a trial would create."[25] Colonial administrators at all levels agreed, in other words, not to risk convening a trial in Lahore that would in all likelihood inflame and mobilize his supporters.

They also concurred that "personal restraint" in the case of Maharaj Singh meant banishment "at once beyond seas" and not merely expulsion from Punjab to "Hindustan" or north India, a punishment imposed on many of the other prominent Sikh rebels.[26] The lone objection to this interpretation of Regulation III came not from within the ranks of the government in India but from an official in Singapore, and then only after the prisoners had already arrived there. Apparently the local sheriff, with the support of legal counsel, challenged the guru's internment in the Singapore jail. Although he eventually relented, his reaction led local officials to scramble to find other venues. For a while, they entertained the possibility of transferring the "state prisoners" to nearby Fort Cornwallis in Penang, where the men would have been under military and not civil jurisdiction.[27]

As these deliberations leading up to the decision to exile Maharaj Singh indicate, colonial authorities perceived him as a significant threat to the consolidation of their rule in Punjab. Banishment was the only recourse once they had decided not to execute him, not only because it was considered second only to capital punishment in severity but also because it expelled him not only from his home base but also from all of India—almost as if the only way to extirpate a larger-than-life figure with political, military, and religious standing was to erase his presence and, in the long run, any memory of him, or at least that was the intention behind removing him from Indian soil as expeditiously as possible and dumping him in faraway Southeast Asia. For him internal exile was not an option, no keeping under lock and key beyond Punjab, as was the punishment meted out to many of his fellow rebels. Overseas exile for the rest of his natural life was the most promising solution because it combined distance and time into a potent brew that offered the possibility of making his many followers forget him, of casting him into oblivion.

Convicts from India, by contrast, were routinely dispatched to Singapore and to the other penal colonies in Southeast Asia because they had been specifically sentenced to transportation for their "heinous offences." They had been going to Singapore since 1825, and to Bengkulu in west Sumatra, Penang in present-day Malaysia, and other penal colonies in the region since the late eighteenth century. Such punishments were meted out either by the supreme court in the presidencies of Bengal, Bombay, and Madras or by the courts at the local level. Most offenders were sentenced to transportation for life, others for terms ranging from seven to fourteen years. At different times in the early nineteenth century, transportation was substituted in lieu of long-term sentences of imprisonment, at the behest of either the authorities or prisoners who chose banishment over the prison.[28]

For Maharaj Singh and Kharak Singh—the latter characterized in some colonial documents as the former's "servant"—the journey seaward began on 3 January 1850. Under armed escort, they traveled first to the cantonment town of Ambala, a little over a hundred miles away. At the end of March, they were sent to Allahabad, almost five hundred miles away, where a contingent of Sikh rebels had arrived earlier in the month and were under lock and key in the Mughal fort. From Allahabad, located at the confluence of the Jamuna and Ganges Rivers, the prisoners traveled to Calcutta by steamer in April, a distance of another five hundred miles, as did their Multan co-conspirator, Diwan Mul Raj. By late April, all three men reached Calcutta and were consigned to the garrison barracks at Fort William, which they entered in *palkis* (palanquins) escorted by an armed guard.[29] Every step of the way, the two Singhs traveled under a "warrant of commitment" that underlined their treatment as requiring "personal restraint."

Once they were in Calcutta, the orders from Governor-General Dalhousie were that the "Bhaee and his disciple should be dispatched to Singapore" right away. As for Mul Raj, whom Dalhousie had met earlier in Lahore and found "in a state of bodily and mental prostration" and seemingly unable to "survive long enough to reach Calcutta," he postponed his banishment indefinitely because he did not believe that the *diwan* would "reach Singapore, alive." In his estimation "the distress on religious grounds, the agitation, the want of ordinary food, and the sea, would kill him." And *that* the governor-general did not want to see happen, because his "death under such circumstances would receive the sympathy with which he was regarded, and would give for him the pity and admiration which attach to martyrdom of any kind." About Maharaj Singh, however, he did not have any health concerns: he characterized the former as "strong and would not be endangered by the voyage."[30]

Indeed, there is very little of the rhetoric of mercy present in the colonial discourse about the Bhai, not only in comparison to statements made about his coconspirator Mul Raj but also in relation to other cases of political exiles. In sentencing political prisoners to transportation, the colonial government often made a point of emphasizing its quality of mercy by underlining its preference for inflicting more civilized and less sanguinary punishments than those allowable by its own laws as well those imposed by previous Indian regimes. In fact, such language and logic informed its development of transportation as a punishment that inflicted a "just measure of pain," severe but not sanguinary the way precolonial punishments were, as the British were wont to emphasize.[31]

On 19 April 1850, Maharaj Singh and Kharak Singh were handed over to Fort William. They were lodged, as was Mul Raj, in cells described as clean, with "plenty of space for air, and perfectly secure." That is, they were under the watchful eyes of European guards, in Maharaj Singh's case, of a European sergeant and, at night, European soldiers.

Less than a month later, on 15 May, the two Singhs were placed on board the bark *Mahomed Shaw,* destined for China with a stopover in Singapore. They were remanded into the custody of a British military detail consisting of a sergeant, a corporal, and six privates and housed in a "good cabin," while their guards were assigned "space between decks." The sergeant's orders were to keep the prisoners in "irons" until the vessel was at sea, and to ensure that they were turned over to the Singapore authorities "without irons."[32] There were also careful instructions about their food and water on board the ship, as there generally were for convicts and soldiers traveling overseas. However, as "state prisoners," they were treated much more leniently than were convicts, for whom the very experience of reaching their penal destinations was much more varied and involved.[33]

As "state prisoners," Maharaj Singh and Kharak Singh were handed over to the Singapore authorities with the same guidelines about being "placed under personal restraint" and "closely and carefully watched" that had been in effect on their journey across north India. As before, "great importance" was attached to their "safe custody" and to their not being "treated with any unnecessary rigor." In fact, the governor-general, who had visited Singapore earlier that year, specifically directed its officials to confine the state prisoners in the "upper rooms of the new gaol, as being both healthy and secure." He also urged them "for some time to come, to have a special military guard set over the prisoners" consisting of "some trustworthy non-commissioned European officer, or government servant of some class. . . . No one should be admitted to the apartment occupied by the prisoners except with the knowledge of this officer, and he should himself see the prisoners at least twice every day."[34] Lieutenant-Colonel Messiter, in charge of the troops in Singapore, carried out this order by informing the civilian authorities that no one would be permitted to enter their chambers except for the sheriff, the assistant resident, and the surgeon of the jail.[35]

State prisoners were treated both more and less severely than transmarine convicts. They were much more "carefully watched," as is suggested by the "personal restraint" under which the two Singhs were held in Singapore and the extraordinary precautions taken en route to Calcutta, on board the transportation ship, and in the penal colony, including by ensuring that they were always in the custody of European guards. Such close supervision stands in sharp contrast to the practices developed for the discipline and surveillance of convicts. In fact, by the time the Singhs arrived in Singapore in 1850, prisoners served as "their own warders," to quote a phrase bandied about by local authorities to characterize the system of self-discipline in practice there and appropriated by Major J. F. A. McNair, the comptroller of Indian convicts in the Straits Settlements between 1857 and 1877, as the title of his book on that subject.[36]

The special status of the Singhs also came with tangible benefits, notably access to better rations. Their diet consisted of rice, flour, ghee (clarified butter), dal (lentils), sugar, salt, coffee, curry spices, onions, chilies, vegetables, dry dates, dry milk, and firewood, many more items than allocated to the rank-and-file convicts, as the senior administrator in Singapore noted in characterizing their allowance as "liberal." Maharaj Singh and Kharak Singh did not, however, consider their allowances sufficient. They asked for more; they requested and received a small stipend to hire a cook because the latter did not wish to fill that role. Less successful was Kharak Singh's attempt to add a small quantity of bhang (marijuana) to his list of dietary needs.[37]

Maharaj Singh and Kharak Singh were also treated differently in that they did not have to engage in manual labor, which convicts from India were routinely charged with doing in Singapore and elsewhere in Southeast Asia. In fact, the transportation of convicts in the early nineteenth century was as much about mobilizing their bodies for building the infrastructure of the rising British Empire in the region as it was about punishing offenders by removing them from their homes and compelling them to cross the *kala pani*, or black waters.[38]

Consider the lot of the fourteen hundred or so convicts, predominantly men, who were stationed in Singapore when the two Singhs arrived there. Much of the colonial discourse about this population revolved around their disciplining, about the techniques developed to manage and organize them in order to transform them into productive workers at minimal cost to the government. Consequently, parts of the annual reports on Indian convicts read as if they are balance sheets, with convicts constituting assets whose numbers were always in flux because of additions resulting from new arrivals and subtractions stemming from manumissions, deaths, or escapes; investments and the returns on them, denoted in terms of the roads, canals, bridges, buildings, and other work done, and their labor value in cash equivalents; liabilities made up by the costs incurred for feeding and sheltering the convicts; and the equity expressed as the surplus that the local authorities received from having convicts support their own keep and from freeing the local government from the costs of hiring paid labor.

State prisoners, by contrast, as the biannual reports mandated by Regulation III suggest, were not consigned to lives of labor. Not that Maharaj Singh and Kharak Singh considered themselves better off than the convict workers. As their jailers consistently noted, both men continued to resist in their own way, Maharaj Singh by persisting in his silence; he barely spoke when he was first captured in Punjab and remained reticent throughout much of his captivity in Singapore. As his British visitors observed, he was quiet, seldom speaking "when spoken to" or "even when questioned by the visiting officer."

Kharak Singh, on the other hand, was rarely bashful about expressing himself, even lashing out frequently. Whether he played this part because he was the mouthpiece for both men cannot be ascertained from the colonial archives. However, his master was certainly aware of his behavior because much of it was enacted in his presence. Their jailer bore the brunt of his verbal assaults. These apparently became so disrespectful that a senior administrator intervened and met with him in January 1851, some seven months into their first year in exile. As this official recounted, he went to "the very comfortable apartment allotted to the state prisoners . . . and found Kurruck Sing on his bed." He took up "a chair close to him" and then proceeded to explain to the latter that he had been "sent to Singapore for safe custody by the government of India, [and] that . . . the Governor-General was anxious he should have every reasonable indulgence, [and] that it was unbecoming on his part to use violence towards or be angry with the jailor, as he merely obeys orders." Rather than heed the advice, Kharak Singh, as the Singapore Resident recounted, "interrupted . . . several times in a most disrespectful manner and when asked what he really wanted replied proper food" and "1000 rupees a day." His demeanor "throughout was most violent, [and] he made use of terms extremely offensive in the presence of the sepoys which to me was particularly galling[;] it appears to me that the conduct of KS is, and has been such as to render coercive measures indispensable."[39]

In 1852, Maharaj Singh's health began to fail, a change duly recorded in the official reports. Increasingly described as "emaciated," he was no longer only portrayed as silent, although he continued to be taciturn. Kharak Singh, however, remained a study in contrast: a picture of "good health," somewhat better behaved, but still "occasionally verging on disrespect."[40]

The following year, Maharaj Singh's condition worsened, his list of ailments including "continued fever, cataract and irritation of stomach and bowels."[41] Later that year, the local medical officer found him in ill health, complaining "of pain and swelling of his feet and ankles, and . . . now all but blind from milky cataract in both eyes, he is able to distinguish black from white, but cannot guide himself from one place to another, his health in other respects is good, he eats well and is generally cheerful."[42]

His declining health prompted the resident councillor, the senior local official in Singapore, to write the governor of the Straits Settlements for "some trifling degree of relaxation" in the regimen of "personal restraint." Noting that Singh had been in confinement since June 1850 and that escape was highly improbable, he proposed that the two state prisoners be permitted to have "an airing twice a week in a palankeen [palanquin], accompanied, of course, by the European in charge, and a responsible peon."[43] The request was promptly denied.

What was granted in mid-1853, three years into their exile in Singapore, was an opportunity to send messages home. Maharaj Singh and Kharak Singh penned their letters in Gurmukhi (Punjabi script), dated them "Asadha," or the Hindu calendar month of June/July, to indicate when they were written, and addressed them to their *dera* at Naurangabad. They assured the Singapore authorities—none of whom were in any position to decipher the language—that their missives referred exclusively "to their present situation and family matters."[44] Singapore sent their correspondence on to Calcutta, from where it was forwarded to the chief commissioner in Punjab, who translated the letters into English before delivering them to Amritsar. Presumably he had them translated by one of his Punjabi subordinates or, more likely, by the one or two missionaries from the American Presbyterian Mission who were known to be the only Europeans with any fluency in the language.[45] Not finding the letters objectionable, the commissioner relayed them forward, although he ruled against anymore correspondence, a decision that the Calcutta government agreed with wholeheartedly, particularly as it adjudged them censurable. As the governor-general put it, the letters did not even mention "a word about 'family affairs.'"[46]

Actually they did, but only in the sense that their authors conceived of their religious brotherhood (*sadh sangat*) at their *dera* in Naurangabad as family. Furthermore, their letters were very much about their "situation," which they clearly found to be abominable. Indeed, as their contents indicate, they are the only first-person expressions of the reflections and feelings of the Singhs in exile. Without such letters, as the examples discussed by Aldrich (chapter 2), Anderson (chapter 1), Margana (chapter 5), Paterson (chapter 9), and Ricci (chapter 4) in this volume also reveal, historians would know far less about the emotional state of exiles.

In part an appeal, in part testimony, and in part lament, Maharaj Singh's letter, which deserves to be quoted at length, opens by referring to its author by both his original and acquired names, as if its intention was to detail the bleak life in captivity of both the individual and the religious and political leader he had become in the course of the wars against the foreigners:

> Let the affairs of Nehal Sing and Maharaj Sing be made known to Guru Juswunt Sing Sahib, let him learn the particulars of his slaves. I drank neem three years, my eyes cannot see. Kurrug Sing continually forbade me to drink neem but I did not leave it off.
>
> You have told me that a dog even will not befriend me. So not a single dog has been of any service to me. I had no idea then that what you said was true. I have now become well aware of it. Now kindly allow me to enjoy the company of your feet which are like the lotus.
>
> Many were friends in prosperity but no one befriends in adversity. Meditate oh my heart says Nanak our god that he may assist thee in the end. We oh lord always forget thee, but thou art beneficent and the forgiver of sins. Who ever goes to see thee, is relieved of all worldly cares and troubles. Come to my aid. Oh lord now that I am on the eve of destruction. Oh true guide, the hope of the hopeless. I who am utterly hopeless adore you. I am the dust of your feet.
>
> Deprived of all power placed in confinement, there is no remedy for me. Rughoo Nath is the only supporter who vouchsafes assistance in time. Power is restored I am set free every remedy is at hand. All blessings I received at your hand the moment you come to my assistance.[47]

His health deteriorating with each passing month, Maharaj Singh understandably thought that his life verged on the "eve of destruction." He had been drinking neem[48] consistently for three years—imbibing neem literally as well as metaphorically (i.e., drinking the cup of bitterness)—and that had turned him blind. In exile, he lamented, he had no followers; in confinement, he had been stripped of all his powers. Once he commanded *sardars* and subalterns alike; now, as he put it, he did not even have a dog "befriend" him, let alone be "of any service." "Many were friends in prosperity but no one befriends in adversity," he intoned. He regretted that there appeared to be no "remedy" for his predicament, which presumably was a reference to both his medical and incarcerated condition. The only hopeful chords he struck are when he invoked Guru Nanak, the founder of his Sikh religion, and expressed faith in the solace that comes from surrendering to his power and goodness. These lines, too, are highly suggestive, in that his allusions seem to be as much about seeking physical and spiritual release as they are about securing liberation from his "worldly cares and troubles." If only he—the First Sikh Guru or Maharaj Singh's family of gurus and disciples—could come to his "aid."

Kharak Singh's letter sounded many of the same notes struck by his master, but more overtly, thus seemingly paralleling the public roles they had played in exile. To begin with, he titled his missive a "petition" and then proceeded to affix an address to it as if to furnish a geographical grid of his location. In his words, he was lodged "at Singapore near China beyond the seas far far distant from Juggernath."

Clearly, what his plea underlined in part by alluding to China was his physical distance and remoteness from Naurangabad. He was almost in China, far removed from Jagannath, which is a very long way from Punjab. After all, he had traveled to Singapore on board the ship *Mahomed Shaw,* headed for China. Furthermore, the Singhs were in Singapore, a predominantly Chinese settlement—more than half of its sixty thousand inhabitants were Chinese at the beginning of 1850. Indeed, to many a visitor the Chinese presence in Singapore was noticeable from the time they approached its harbor and saw that many ships "going to, or coming from, China . . . call at this port for news or supplies," and from the many boats including "Chinese junks" always at the port.[49]

That Kharak Singh invoked Jagannath to triangulate his location seems puzzling at first blush, but perhaps not entirely, because it refers, of course, to that well-known pilgrimage site in the coastal town of Puri, in the eastern province of Orissa, where a temple bearing the name of Jagannath, an avatar of Vishnu, has long been revered as a sacred site. A famous Hindu pilgrimage destination, it is also celebrated by Sikhs as one of the venues that Guru Nanak is believed to have visited during his peregrinations. Perhaps Jagannath also came to mind because its principal festival, the Ratha Jatra, to which pilgrims flock from all over the country, is always held in Asadh, the very same month in which the two Singhs wrote their letters. Conceivable as well—although not verifiable—is the possibility that the allusion to the famous temple was made in the same vein that migrants did later in the century when they equated whatever ship they boarded with Jagannath, thus nullifying the ritual transgressions that necessarily resulted from crossing the *kala pani,* or black waters, and in the company of people of other castes and religions, with whom food and drink transactions were likely to be polluting.[50]

As did his master, Kharak Singh, too, entreated the gods in his missive not to forsake him. But he also brazenly proclaimed, "we," that is, master and disciple, "will present ourselves before you." Furthermore, right after the address—and, intriguingly, the letter is addressed to Bhai Bir Singh (presumably Maharaj Singh's guru, who had died in 1844) and the religious community at the Naurangabad *dera* that Maharaj Singh had taken over from his master—are the words "we will come within one year." A sketch of two figures then followed, one ostensibly representing a ship and the other the island of Singapore. "Not a word in the letter about family affairs," concluded one colonial official, seemingly oblivious to the fact that both letters, on the contrary, were about precisely such matters in that they sought to reestablish communication with their religious brotherhood organized around their *dera,* the community that they considered their "relations and friends."[51]

Meanwhile, Kharak Singh opened another front in his ongoing struggles with the local authorities. While the letters were in transit, he expressed a desire to become a Christian. As John William Ganno, the keeper of the Singapore jail, informed his superiors, he often found books on Singh's table that the latter said were the scriptures in Hindustani. Singh also engaged him in conversation, apparently in Hindustani, about Moses and Jesus Christ and pointed to the similarities between Christianity and the Sikh faith. However, before these conversations could lead to a visit from the chaplain, Governor-General Dalhousie, who was regularly apprised about the "state prisoners" by the Singapore authorities, intervened. In his estimation, Kharak Singh's interest in Christianity was "a very shallow desire" to seek a release, and while he was willing to allow a visit from a chaplain, he wanted the prisoner to know in no uncertain terms "that if he is playing a part and hopes to obtain liberty, by adopting Christianity, he is deluding himself and that, Christian or Sikh, he will equally remain in Singapore gaol."[52]

The letters never reached their destination—apparently no one was at the *dera* when the one and only attempt was made to deliver them. As for

Kharak Singh's flirtation with Christianity, that did not last long, and there are no subsequent mentions of it in the colonial records. While there is ample reason to doubt his desire for conversion, it is not something completely out of the realm of possibility. After all, Dalip Singh, the maharaja he and his master had championed, converted to Christianity in 1853, with the approval of Dalhousie, after first expressing interest in Christianity as early as 1850. News of this dramatic event, no doubt, was widely disseminated.[53]

More than likely it reached the ears of the two Singhs in Singapore because they were joined by a number of Sikhs in 1853 who came as the newest batch of convicts. Perhaps not coincidentally, "a serious outbreak" occurred among these new prisoners in July 1853. Whether Maharaj Singh or Kharak Singh had a hand in it cannot be discerned from the extant records. The Singhs and the convicts would certainly have been familiar with each other's presence on the island, although their paths were not likely to cross routinely, and not often, if ever, because of the different disciplinary regimens under which state prisoners and convicts were kept.[54]

Thereafter, the story of Maharaj Singh, stitched together from government reports, describes a person in increasingly poor health—his deteriorating condition at times eliciting sympathy in official quarters in Singapore and even in Calcutta. The January 1854 medical report indicating that he was "quite blind" from his cataracts, with "cure by operation" impossible, prompted the government in India to urge "everything . . . be done with a view to effect a cure."[55] No wonder his request for reading materials was approved. The books purchased for him arrived in Singapore in January 1855 and included a "Bible Hindoo in 2 volumes, new testatment 1 volume" and other items; for example, a 115-year-old manuscript copy of the granth [presumably the Guru Granth Sahib, or the principal scriptural text of the Sikhs] that cost Rs. 30–8, was procured in Lahore and then conveyed by bullock train to Calcutta from where it was shipped.[56]

After the medical officer pronounced him "perfectly blind and incapable of moving about unaided" in early 1856, Singapore proposed allowing him a *gharry* (horse-drawn cab) so that he could ride a few miles into the country twice or thrice a week under the escort of a "steady and trustworthy official of the jail," whose job was to prevent "all strangers from having access to him."[57] On 5 July 1856, three days after the *gharry* order was issued, Bhai Maharaj Singh was dead. Thus his Singapore exile story ended, seemingly in obscurity, far, far away and without his becoming "an unperishable name" and "cherished by all posterity," as per the wishes of British officials. Exile seemingly had not only severed him from his roots and his past but shut down his memory and history so that his life of rebellion would have no future.

His "disciple," however, was not done quite yet. In the aftermath of his master's death, Kharak Singh was allowed to remain in the jail under police surveillance and granted an allowance of sixty rupees per month. By February 1857 he was permitted to reside wherever he chose to as long as he did not leave the island. Never one to refrain from speaking up, he right away asked for but was denied an increase in his allowance.[58]

Nor did he contain himself for long in other ways. In August 1857 he was accused of having "formed association[s] with and obtained influence over the convicts at Singapore." According to two prisoners who visited him, Singh proposed attacking and massacring the European community in Singapore while they were at church—a plan that resembled what had occurred at the outbreak of the Mutiny/Rebellion in the northern Indian town of Meerut in May 1857. When confronted by the Singapore authorities, Singh pleaded innocence: he proclaimed his loyalty to the British government and offered his "services" against the mutineers. Calcutta chose not to entertain his offer, noting instead that he was a "disciple of the Guru Maharaj," wielded "considerable influence" among Sikhs, and was unlikely to use his "influence" for anything other than acts of "hostility to the British government." Best to ship him off to Fort Cornwallis in Penang, where he would become "a perfect stranger" and "unable to perpetrate any mischief should he feel so inclined." There he was to be kept, moreover, under "strict and rigorous confinement." None of this placated Penang officials worried about having a dangerous "state prisoner"[59] on their island.

The change of address did not slow down Kharak Singh, who continued to press for special dispensations. In May 1858 he asked for permission to send a letter to his "friends in India." His request was denied on grounds that state prisoners were forbidden to send letters. Convicts in the Straits Settlements were permitted to receive letters, but only after their review by the superintendent of convicts.[60] The last reference to Kharak Singh I have been able to locate is when he surfaced again in the colonial records in 1861, when he petitioned for his family to join him in Penang. Although the local administration was willing to accede to his request, Calcutta was not.[61]

As for Bhai Maharaj Singh, I have no evidence as yet that his memory was preserved in the immediate aftermath of his death either by the local Indian community in Singapore or by his fellow Punjabis in India. To my knowledge, no obituaries appeared in any published account in English or South Asian languages. The colonial records are also largely silent—no triumphalist account of his death in captivity and obscurity, in contrast to the exultation with which his capture in 1849 was reported. The official correspondence in Singapore and between the Straits Settlements and Calcutta takes note of his passing but says little else; his presence in Singapore is not even mentioned in the extended history of the penal colony of Singapore written by the former superintendent of convicts, J. F. A. McNair.[62] Nor do I have documentation to show that the arrival of Sikhs as policemen in Singapore in the 1880s—some two decades after their countrymen came as convicts in the early 1850s—followed by the in-migration of other members of the community ensured his memory and history on the island in the late nineteenth century. According to Choor Singh Sidhu (1911–2009), a judge of the Supreme Court of Singapore and a historian of Sikhism, he was informed by Sikh policemen in 1922 that the tombstone in the General Hospital grounds had once been at Outram Road, where Singh's prison was located and where he was believed to have been cremated just outside the prison. That suggests that local people were familiar with the famous rebel who once lived among them. After World War II, Tamils began to place flowers at the foot of the tombstone. Sikhs followed suit, as did Muslims in the belief that it was a saint's shrine (*kramat*). At some point local Sikhs built a structure over the tombstone, installed the Granth Sahib, and built a gurdwara, all of which was moved to Silat Road in 1966. Today his shrine, the Memorial Gurdwara of Bhai Maharaj Singh, adjoins the main place of devotion known as Silat Road Gurdwara Sahib. Before visiting the main gurdwara, worshippers typically visit his shrine first, which is held "in great reverence . . . [because it] earns the devotee great merit. It is believed that prayers recited sincerely from the heart are answered and vows have been fulfilled when a devotee worships at this shrine. This is the only Gurdwara Sahib in Singapore where *langar* is prepared and served everyday round the clock if necessary."[63] As in his heyday, he is revered today as a "miracle" *bhai*. Maharaj Singh also lives on in regional and nationalist historiography, celebrated in Punjab and India since the 1960s as a "saint-revolutionary," a "rebel," and an early nationalist, as well as by Sikh communities everywhere. Exile was but a momentary rupture in the life and history of Bhai Maharaj Singh.

NOTES

Epigraph. "Minute by the Most Noble the Governor-General," Document No. 26, in Bhai Nahar Singh and Bhai Kirpal Singh, eds., *Rebels Against the British Raj: Bhai Maharaj Singh (1810–1857)* (New Delhi: Atlantic Publishers, 1989), 90–91. Doab refers to the river basin or land between two confluent or converging rivers.

1. Edward Said, "Reflections on Exile," *Reflections on Exile and Other Essays* (Cambridge, MA: Harvard University Press, 2000), 173. See also Anderson's chapter 1, "A Global History of Exile in Asia, c. 1700–1900," in this volume.

2. Said, "Reflections," 140.

3. See Anand A. Yang, "Indian Convict Workers in Southeast Asia in the Late Eighteenth and Early Nineteenth Centuries," *Journal of World History* 14, no. 2 (2003):

179–208. See also Anoma Pieris, "The 'Other' Side of Labor Reform: Accounts of Incarceration and Resistance in the Straits Settlements Penal System, 1825–1873," *Journal of Social History* 45, no. 2 (2011): 453–479; and Anoma Pieris, *Hidden Hands and Divided Landscapes: A Penal History of Singapore's Plural Society* (Honolulu: University of Hawai'i Press, 2009), regarding Bhai Maharaj Singh.

4. Punjab Record Office, *Political Diaries of the Agent to the Governor-General, North-West Frontier and Resident at Lahore*, vol. 3 (Allahabad: Pioneer Press, 1909), 175–176.

5. Khushwant Singh, *A History of the Sikhs*, vol. 2, *1839–1964* (Princeton, NJ: Princeton University Press, 1966), 64; Andrew J. Major, *Return to Empire: Punjab under the Sikhs and British in the Mid-Nineteenth Century* (New Delhi: Sterling Publishers, 1996), 40–124.

6. *Manjha*, or *doab*, refers to a tract between two rivers, in this case, to the area in Lahore and Amritsar Districts between the Beas/Sutlej and Ravi Rivers. It became one of the prime recruitment areas for the colonial military.

7. Punjab Government, "Political Diary," 25 June 1847 and 30 June 1847, in *Political Diaries of Lieutenant Reynell G. Taylor, Mr. P. Sandy Melvill, Pandit Kunahya Lal, Mr. P. A. Vans Agnew, Lieutenant J. Nicholson, Mr. L. Bowring and Mr. A. H. Cocks, 1847–1849* (Allahabad: Pioneer Press, 1915), 188, 201. Maharaj Singh's confiscated property in Amritsar, which included fifty-five head of cow and buffalo, was sold for six thousand rupees.

8. M. L. Ahluwalia, *Sant Nihal Singh alias Bhai Maharaj Singh: A Saint-Revolutionary of the 19th Century Punjab* (Patiala: Punjabi University, 1972), 13–22; Singh, *History of the Sikhs*, 85–97; Major, *Return to Empire*, 81–124.

9. Ahluwalia, *Sant Nihal Singh*, 48–61.

10. W. H. McLeod, "The Meaning of 'Sant' in Sikh Usage," in *The Sants: Studies in a Devotional Tradition of India*, ed. Karine Schomer and W. H. McLeod (Delhi: Motilal Banarasidass, 1987), 257–260.

11. Harjot Oberoi, *The Construction of Religious Boundaries: Culture, Identity, and Diversity in the Sikh Tradition* (Chicago: University of Chicago Press, 1994), 122–123. The term *bhai* was used in "early Sikh tradition . . . as an honorific for the holy men of the Panth. To qualify for this title a person had to demonstrate a capacity to interpret the Adi Granth [Sikh scriptures], communicate the wisdom of the gurus it enshrined, and be publicly recognised for his piety. If in addition he could work miracles, heal the sick and give succour to the distressed, he was sure to occupy a position of considerable reverence and influence within the community." See also Ricci's chapter 4 in this volume for another example of a religious leader who provided his followers miraculously with food and sustenance.

12. Ibid., 118.

13. Punjab Government, "Political Diary," 22 June 1847, in *Political Diaries of Taylor*, 182.

14. Edwin Arnold, *The Marquis of Dalhousie's Administration of British India*, vol. 1 (London: Saunders, Otley, & Co., 1862), 97–98.

15. Nahar Singh, *Documents Relating to Bhai Maharaj Singh* (Ludhiana: Sikh History Source Material Search Association, 1968), 6, 61–62, 265; Ahluwalia, *Sant Nihal Singh*, 8–9. See also the testimony of a military officer who believed that Maharaj Singh was someone the "[Sikh] army are anxious to canonize." "Diary of Captain James Abbott, Assistant Resident, on Deputation to Huzara, 9 June 1848," in *Political Diaries of Taylor*, vol. 4, 182.

16. H. Vansittart, Deputy Commissioner, Jalandhur, to D. F. McLeod, Commissioner and Suptd, 30 December 1849, in Singh, *Documents*, 91.

17. Ibid., 92.

18. Ibid., 93.

19. J. Royal Roseberry III, *Imperial Rule in Punjab: The Conquest and Administration of Multan* (New Delhi: Manohar, 1987), 67–87.

20. Farina Mir, *The Social Space of Language: Vernacular Culture in British Colonial Punjab* (Berkeley: University of California Press, 2010), 50. Mir also notes that Urdu rather than Punjabi was made the official language because of government fears that the designation of the latter would have heightened Sikh political aspirations.

21. Vansittart to McLeod, 30 December 1849, in Singh, *Documents*, 92–93.

22. Dalhousie, 15 December 1849, in J. G. A. Baird, ed., *Private Letters of the Marquess of Dalhousie* (Edinburgh: William Blackwood & Sons, 1910), 105, 195.

23. Minute by Governor-General Dalhousie, 13 January 1850, in *Rebels Against the Raj*, ed. Bhai Nahar Singh and Bhai Kirpal Singh (New Delhi: Atlantic Publishers, 1989), 90–91.

24. C. D. Field, ed., *The Regulations of the Bengal Code* (Calcutta: Thacker, Spink & Co., 1875), 464.

25. P. Melvill, Secretary to the Board, to Sir H. M. Elliot, Secty, to government, 5 January 1850, in Singh, *Documents*, 100. Diwan Mul Raj, by contrast, was tried in court and convicted, his death sentence transmuted to transportation. See Sita Ram Kohli, *Trial of Diwan Mul Raj* (Patiala: Languages Department, Punjab, 1971).

26. Melvill to Elliot, 5 January 1850, in Singh, *Documents*, 100.

27. Resident Councillor (R.C.) to Governor, 18 June 1850, Singapore: Letters to Governor, January 1850–December 1850.

28. See Yang, "Indian Convict Workers."

29. *Allen's Indian Mail, and Register of Intelligence for British and Foreign India, China,* vol. 8, January–December 1850, 349.

30. Governor-General Dalhousie, 22 March 1850, in Singh, *Documents*, 142–143.

31. Anand A. Yang, "Bandits and Kings: Moral Authority and Resistance in Early Colonial India," *Journal of Asian Studies* 66, no. 4 (2007): 881–896; Yang, "Indian Convict Workers."

32. Singh, *Documents*, 152–159; *Allen's Indian Mail*, 378.

33. Yang, "Indian Convict Workers."

34. Offg. Secretary, Fort William, Foreign Dept., to Govt of Straits Settlements, no. 1227, 7 May 1850, in Singh, *Documents*, 158–159.

35. Lt. Col. E. Messiter, Commanding, Singapore, to R.C., 11 June 1850, Singapore: Letters to Governor, January–December 1850.

36. See Anand Yang, "Mobilizing Convict Bodies: Indian Convict Workers in Southeast Asia in the Early Nineteenth Century," in *The Hidden History of Crime, Corruption, and States*, ed. Renate Bridenthal (New York: Berghahn Books, 2013).

37. R.C. to Governor, Singapore: Letters to Governor, 25 June 1850, January–December 1850.

38. See Yang, "Mobilizing Convict Bodies," for a discussion of the multiple reasons for developing transportation as a punishment in colonial India.

39. R.C. to Governor, 22 January 1851, Singapore: Letters to Governor, May 1850–May 1852; R.C. to Governor, 28 August 1852, Singapore: Letters to Governor, July–December 1852. Some scholars have speculated that Kharak Singh may have been whipped for his "offensive" behavior.

40. To Officiating Governor, Prince of Wales Island (POWI), Singapore (S), and Malacca (M) 28 August 1852, India Judicial Proceedings, 27 August–22 December 1852, 24 September, nos. 15–43.

41. Offg. Governor of POWI to Secty, Government of India (GOI), Home, 15 January 1853, India Judicial Proceedings, 7 January to 24 June 1853, 16 February, no. 3.

42. Jas. Cowper, Resident Assistant Surgeon, to T. Church, R.C., 1 July 1853, in Singh, *Documents*, 193–194.

43. J. Church, to Secty to Governor of Straits Settlements, 1 July 1853, 193.

44. Church to Secty, Straits Settlements, 2 August 1853, 196. See also Paterson's chapter 9 in this volume for a discussion of the linguistic challenges colonial authorities faced with letters written by Vietnamese exiles in classical Chinese or in the Vietnamese-based character system rather than in Romanized form, which they were better positioned to translate.

45. Mir, *Social Space of Language*, 58–61. Persian and Urdu were the administrative languages of the region until 1854, when Urdu was designated the sole official language of the colonial government in Punjab. Although local officials were aware that Punjabi was the colloquial language of the majority, few were familiar with it in the 1850s and 1860s.

46. India, Board's Collection, F/4/2570, 1853–1854.

47. Translation of Letter from Maharaj Singh to Bhai Jaswant Sing, Naurangabad, near Bhgyrowal, pargana Tarn Taran, Amritsar, Asadh 1853, in ibid.

48. Neem, or *Azadirachta indica*, is a tree whose leaves and flowers are bitter but consumed in various ways for their medicinal properties.

49. L. S. Jackson, Assistant Resident, Singapore, to R.C., 25 January 1850, Singapore: Letters to Governor, January–December 1850; W. Tyrone Power, *Recollections of a Three Years' Resident in China* (London: Richard Bentley, 1853), 93; John Cameron, *Our Tropical Possessions in Malayan India: Being a Descriptive Account of Singapore, Penang, Province Wellesley, and Malacca; Their Peoples, Products, Commerce, and Government* (London: Smith, Elder & Co., 1865), chaps. 3, 5, 8.

50. On the historical significance of Orissa to Sikhs, see Himadri Banerjee, *The Other Sikhs: A View from Eastern India*, vol. 1 (New Delhi: Manohar, 2003), 73–119.

51. See Anand A. Yang, "The Long and Short of Bihari Peasant Migration" (paper presented at the Association for Asian Studies, Toronto, 15–18 March 2012).

52. "Kurruck Sing at Singapore," Minute by Governor-General, 14 October 1853; and S. Garling, Asst. Resident, to T. Church, R.C., 31 August 1853; in India, Board's Collections, 1853–1854.

53. Dalhousie to Sir George Couper, 3 March 1851, in Bikrama Jit Hasrat, ed., *The Punjab Papers: Selections from the Private Papers of Lord Auckland, Lord Ellenborough, Viscount Hardinge, and the Marquis of Dalhousie, 1836–1849 on the Sikhs* (Hoshiarpur, Punjab: V. V. Research Institute Press, 1970), 246.

54. Letter from R.C., Singapore, 7 July 1853, no. 122, India Home Miscellaneous Proceedings, vol. 530, 1853. The newly arrived Sikh prisoners were thereafter divided up: some sent to Malacca, others to Penang, and the rest confined in special cells in Singapore.

55. Singapore, Governor's Diary, Foreign and Military, 1852–1856, 14 January and April 1854.

56. R. Cox, Offg. Secty., Penang, to R.C., 20 January 1855, and Cox to Governor, 29 January 1855, Singapore: Letters from Governor, 1855.

57. R. Church, secty., to R.C., no 247, 2 July 1856, Singapore: Letters from Governor, 1854, 1856.

58. Secty. GOI to Governor, 28 April 1857, Singapore: Letters from Governor, 1857–1858.

59. "Narrative of the Proceedings of the Government of the Straits during the Second Half of 1857," Home Miscellaneous, vol. 528, 1856–1859; R. B. Chapman, Offg. Undersecty., GOI, to Blundell, Governor, 30 September 1857, Singapore, Governor's Letters from Bengal, 1857; Blundell to R.C., Penang, 8 August 1857, Singapore: Governor's Letters to Resident Councillors, 1856–1857.

60. F. L. Playfair, Acting Secretary, to R.C., Penang, 13 July 1858 and 1 October 1858, Letters to Resident Councillors, 1857–1859.

61. Governor to Secty., GOI, 1 September 1861, Governor's Letters to Bengal, 1860–1861.

62. J. F. A McNair (assisted by W. D. Bayliss), *Prisoners Their Own Warders: A Record of the Convict Prison at Singapore in the Straits Settlements Established 1825* (London: Westminster, 1899).

63. His importance in Singapore is commemorated in Central Sikh Gurdwara Board, *Bhai Maharaj Singh Ji 150th Anniversary 2006* (Singapore: Central Sikh Gurdwara Board, 2006), which includes a chapter (chap. 2) adapted from Choor Singh Sidhu's book, *Bhai Maharaj Singh Ji, Martyr of the Sikh Faith.*

BIBLIOGRAPHY

Ahluwalia, M. L. *Sant Nihal Singh alias Bhai Maharaj Singh: A Saint-Revolutionary of the 19th Century Punjab.* Patiala: Punjabi University, 1972.

Allen's Indian Mail, and Register of Intelligence for British and Foreign India, China. Vol. 8, January–December 1850.

Arnold, Edwin. *The Marquis of Dalhousie's Administration of British India.* Vol. 1. London: Saunders, Otley, & Co., 1862.

Baird, J. G. A., ed. *Private Letters of the Marquess of Dalhousie.* Edinburgh: William Blackwood & Sons, 1910.

Banerjee, Himadri. *The Other Sikhs: A View from Eastern India.* Vol 1. New Delhi: Manohar, 2003.

Cameron, John. *Our Tropical Possessions in Malayan India: Being a Descriptive Account of Singapore, Penang, Province Wellesley, and Malacca; Their Peoples, Products, Commerce, and Government.* London: Smith, Elder & Co., 1865.

Central Sikh Gurdwara Board. *Bhai Maharaj Singh Ji 150th Anniversary 2006.* Singapore: Central Sikh Gurdwara Board, 2006.

Field, C. D., ed. *The Regulations of the Bengal Code.* Calcutta: Thacker, Spink & Co., 1875.

Hasrat, Bikrama Jit, ed. *The Punjab Papers: Selections from the Private Papers of Lord Auckland, Lord Ellenborough, Viscount Hardinge, and the Marquis of Dalhousie, 1836–1849 on the Sikhs.* Hoshiarpur, Punjab: V. V. Research Institute Press, 1970.

India. Board's Collections, 1853–1854, F/4/2570, British Library.

India Home Miscellaneous Proceedings, 1853; 1856–1859, British Library.

India Judicial Proceedings, 1852, 1853, British Library.

Kohli, Sita Ram. *Trial of Diwan Mul Raj.* Patiala: Languages Department, Punjab, 1971.

Major, Andrew J. *Return to Empire: Punjab under the Sikhs and British in the Mid-Nineteenth Century.* New Delhi: Sterling Publishers, 1996.

McLeod, W. H. "The Meaning of 'Sant' in Sikh Usage." In *The Sants: Studies in a Devotional Tradition of India,* edited by Karine Schomer and W. H. McLeod, 251–263. Delhi: Motilal Banarsidass, 1987.

McNair, J. F. A. (assisted by W. D. Bayliss). *Prisoners Their Own Warders: A Record of the Convict Prison at Singapore in the Straits Settlements Established 1825*. London: Westminster, 1899.

Mir, Farina. *The Social Space of Language: Vernacular Culture in British Colonial Punjab*. Berkeley: University of California Press, 2010.

Oberoi, Harjot. *The Construction of Religious Boundaries: Culture, Identity, and Diversity in the Sikh Tradition*. Chicago: University of Chicago Press, 1994.

Pieris, Anoma. *Hidden Hands and Divided Landscapes: A Penal History of Singapore's Plural Society*. Honolulu: University of Hawai'i Press, 2009.

———. "The 'Other' Side of Labor Reform: Accounts of Incarceration and Resistance in the Straits Settlements Penal System, 1825–1873." *Journal of Social History* 45, no. 2 (2011): 453–479.

Power, W. Tyrone. *Recollections of a Three Years' Resident in China*. London: Richard Bentley, 1853.

Punjab Government. *Political Diaries of Lieutenant Reynell G. Taylor, Mr. P. Sandy Melvill, Pandit Kunahya Lal, Mr. P. A. Vans Agnew, Lieutenant J. Nicholson, Mr. L. Bowring and Mr. A. H. Cocks, 1847–1849*. Allahabad: Pioneer Press, 1915.

Punjab Record Office. *Political Diaries of the Agent to the Governor-General, North-West Frontier and Resident at Lahore*. Vol. 3. Allahabad: Pioneer Press, 1909.

Roseberry, J. Royal, III. *Imperial Rule in Punjab: The Conquest and Administration of Multan*. New Delhi: Manohar, 1987.

Said, Edward. *Reflections on Exile and Other Essays*. Cambridge, MA: Harvard University Press, 2000.

Singapore: Governor's Letters from Bengal, 1857, National Library, Singapore.

Singapore: Governor's Letters to Bengal, 1860–1861, National Library, Singapore.

Singapore: Governor's Letters to Resident Councillors, 1856–1857, 1857–1859, National Library, Singapore.

Singapore: Letters from Governor, 1854, 1855, 1856, National Library, Singapore.

Singapore: Letters to Governor, January 1850–December 1850, May 1850–May 1852, July–December 1852, National Library, Singapore.

Singh, Bhai Nahar, and Bhai Kirpal Singh, eds. *Rebels against the British Raj: Bhai Maharaj Singh (1810–1857)*. New Delhi: Atlantic Publishers, 1989.

Singh, Khushwant. *A History of the Sikhs*. Vol. 2, *1839–1964*. Princeton, NJ: Princeton University Press, 1966.

Singh, Nahar. *Documents Relating to Bhai Maharaj Singh*. Ludhiana: Sikh History Source Material Search Association, 1968.

Yang, Anand A. "Bandits and Kings: Moral Authority and Resistance in Early Colonial India." *Journal of Asian Studies* 66, no. 4 (2007): 881–896.

———. "Indian Convict Workers in Southeast Asia in the Late Eighteenth and Early Nineteenth Centuries." *Journal of World History* 14, no. 2 (2003): 179–208.

———. "The Long and Short of Bihari Peasant Migration." Paper presented at the Association for Asian Studies, Toronto, 15–18 March 2012.

———. "Mobilizing Convict Bodies: Indian Convict Workers in Southeast Asia in the Early Nineteenth Century." In *The Hidden History of Crime, Corruption, and States*, edited by Renate Bridenthal. New York: Berghahn Books, 2013.

FOUR

From Java to Jaffna
Exile and Return in Dutch Asia
in the Eighteenth Century

Ronit Ricci

The topic of political exile from and within the Indonesian archipelago under the United Dutch East India Company (VOC) remains understudied. Especially limited is our understanding of exile to territories outside the Indies yet under VOC control during the seventeenth and eighteenth centuries, among them Ceylon. Dutch archives in the Netherlands, Indonesia, Sri Lanka, and South Africa contain detailed lists of those exiled and their retinues, comments on why particular individuals were sent away, the names of the ships that carried them, and the monthly allowances of rice and cash provided in new settings. These sources, although important and revealing, tell only part of the story. One way to gain better insight into the exilic experience—for those exiled and those left behind—is to move beyond the colonial archive and explore indigenous chronicles.

In this chapter I examine preliminary evidence from eighteenth- and nineteenth-century Javanese manuscripts relating experiences of exile and return of members of royal families, court officials, and their accompanying retinues from Java to Ceylon (and back again) in the first half of the eighteenth century. These typically very brief depictions have the potential to offer information and perspective, however fragmentary, on what remains a vague but dramatic and significant chapter in the larger history of exile in colonial Asia as well as specifically Indonesian and Sri Lankan understandings of the past.

My exploration of these sources has so far yielded only a handful of depictions of exile and its aftermath. I consider these textual depictions, and the more common silence surrounding exile in these chronicles, for what both the inclusion and the exclusion of exilic histories may reveal.

In her important book, *Networks of Empire: Forced Migration in the Dutch East India Company,* Kerry Ward examines the Dutch East India Company's network of forced migration as one among several types of networks that constituted the Company's empire (1602–1799). She notes how the High Government's diplomatic relations with indigenous polities, formalized in the signing of contracts, were underpinned by the systematic use of exile: "Batavia created a network of exile sites throughout its empire that enabled it to choose specific places of banishment according to the High Government's perceptions of the dangers of particular prisoners." Moreover, "Batavia used the nature of its far flung domain to help consolidate its interest within particular archipelagic polities, and, most especially, at the center of the Company empire in Java."[1] These twin aspects of exile—the distance of particular exile sites, in this case Ceylon, and the complex politics of decisions made about exiles and returns—are manifested in the Javanese sources discussed in this chapter. The point about distance and a penal hierarchical logic by which the greater the crime or perceived threat to indigenous rulers or Europeans, the farther away the site of banishment, reminds us that to understand exile in Dutch Asia means to consider a vast domain and the movements within it, a domain that today traverses nation-states and continents: exile to a city like Batavia on Java, to Indonesian islands like Sulawesi or Ternate, across the Indian Ocean to Ceylon, or half a world away to South Africa formed a continuum that was contained within a single imperial realm.

BACKGROUND: THE SRI LANKAN MALAYS, COLONIAL CEYLON, AND EXILED ROYALTY

The materials and questions discussed in this chapter form a part of a larger study that explores the history and literary culture of a community known as the Sri Lankan Malays. Numbering approximately fifty thousand at present, this community is descended from individuals from across the Indonesian-Malay world sent to colonial Ceylon in various capacities beginning in the mid-seventeenth century.[2] Some arrived in Ceylon as servants or craftsmen, some joined the VOC army and helped secure the Dutch takeover of the island, while others were convicts serving their terms there. An additional constituency, one that is the focus of this chapter and to which I return in the following sections, is that of royal exiles.

Studying the Sri Lankan Malays' past and their writing traditions, especially handwritten manuscripts and letters from the late eighteenth century to the early twentieth, opens many venues of inquiry. The manuscripts are written for the most part in Malay, with sections large and small in Arabic, while Tamil (written in the Arabic script), the language of the majority of Sri Lankan Muslims, figures in some. A poem and a few brief sections in Javanese have also recently come to light in an 1803 manuscript, attesting to the preservation, at least to some degree, of a non-Malay Indonesian language into the nineteenth century.[3] Many of the texts appearing in these volumes are known from across the Malay-speaking regions of Southeast Asia and can be found there in private collections as well as libraries in Jakarta, Kuala Lumpur, Leiden, and London. Among them are *hikayats*, works on Islamic ritual and theology, poems composed in the genres of *syair* and *pantun*, tales of the prophets, biographies of the Prophet Muhammad, and legal treatises. In addition to such "conventional" Malay literature there are also works that portray, often employing the same poetic genres, events of significance in the life of the local Malay community and reflections on its past and present standing. Considering Malay writing in Sri Lanka is not limited to handwritten materials but also encompasses books printed in Malay beginning in the second half of the nineteenth century as well as the *Alamat Langkapuri*, a pioneering Malay newspaper published in Colombo, 1869–1870.[4]

In searching for and reading some of this fascinating material, it is easy to drown in an ocean of Malay and forget that, in fact, at least some of the ancestors of those composing and copying texts throughout the nineteenth century (to which date most of the manuscripts extant today) likely did not speak Malay as their first language, if at all. It is true that Malay was a lingua franca of trade and widely known in Southeast Asia for several centuries, certainly along the coasts, and yet the islands known as Indonesia today were and still are among the world's most linguistically diverse regions, and the early arrivals to Ceylon must have spoken a wide range of tongues. How and why Malay came to constitute such a dominant and unifying force remains an intriguing question, but one that will not be pursued here. Instead, my goal is to go back in time and space and consider the "other side of the coin" of Sri Lankan Malay history—not from the shores of Ceylon but from those of Java, home to many of the eighteenth-century exiles banished by the Dutch. How was the early history of a diverse, multilingual community adhering to the Malay language and Islam portrayed in the lands whence came some of the community's founding members?

Answering this question, however tentatively, poses many methodological challenges. Secondary sources that touch on exile while basing themselves on indigenous sources are few, and even in these exile does not typically constitute the main focus. Notable exceptions include the work of Merle Ricklefs on eighteenth-century Javanese history and especially his research on the "missing *pusaka*" of Kartasura, discussed later in this chapter; Nancy

Florida's study of the *Babad Jaka Tingkir,* inscribed by the Surakarta ruler Pakubuwana VI, who was exiled to Ambon after the Java War; Peter Carey's monumental study of Prince Dipanagara, who was exiled to Manado and then Makassar; and Muridan Widjojo's recent book on Prince Nuku of Tidore, which discusses cases of exile from the islands of eastern Indonesia in the late eighteenth century.[5] While all these works, and several others, have contributed significantly to an understanding of exile's history in the islands of today's Indonesia, attempts to reconstruct the map and legend of exilic movement under the VOC, however partially, still encounter considerable difficulties.

More crucial than the dearth of secondary sources is the question of access to primary ones, including the vast number of potentially relevant manuscripts in Javanese, many but not all catalogued, housed in archival collections across the world. Even for those catalogued, to researchers' great advantage, detailed information needed to assess content in depth is often lacking. Javanese historical chronicles—*babad*—can be hundreds of pages long and contain a wealth of details that cannot be easily summarized in a catalogue entry. For example, in the twenty-one volumes of the *Babad Giyanti,* a mere few pages are dedicated to a rare and highly significant passage about exilic life in Ceylon.

Yet despite the challenges, this kind of search is worthwhile for several reasons. For one, Java (and especially central Java) in the eighteenth century was home to many of the most prominent among those exiled to Ceylon. In part due to their elevated status, such persons were not sent into exile alone but rather were accompanied by wives, children, additional relatives, and retinues of servants, thus expanding the numbers of those departing Java's shores. Studying exile from Java during this period sheds light on its very complex internal familial politics (as exile was often a solution to rivalries among brothers or cousins competing for the throne), as well as on the evolving dynamics of Javanese-European entanglements (with the Dutch intervening to the benefit of one contender, whose loyalty to them was then secured, along with economic and political concessions that gradually limited indigenous power). At a more practical level, which often determines what can and cannot be studied, Java's rich and long-standing literary tradition going back at least to the ninth century and Javanese scribes' tendency toward producing long historical chronicles enhance the possibility of finding written testimonies to events related to exile that would not be as likely in a less literate society. Finally, Java is still remembered today as the land of origin of several prominent Malay families in Sri Lanka; thus a better understanding of its role in the history of exile could prove significant in both personal and collective ways.

The search for Javanese accounts of exile to Ceylon goes on, but for now, four brief examples will suffice. I view these as glimpses of the complex picture that may yet emerge when additional texts that depict exile, its experiences, and its aftermath come to light. The first instance portrays a Javanese king being captured and banished; the second is a scene of travel by sea on the way to exile; the third recounts a return from exile to Java; and the fourth, also a post-repatriation scene, presents memories of exilic life that combine the ordinary and the fantastic.

THE EXILE OF KING AMANGKURAT III

In 1703 the reigning king of Kartasura in central Java passed away and his son was crowned and bestowed the title Amangkurat III. Not long after this event the new monarch's uncle, Pangéran Puger, brother of the deceased king, rebelled against his nephew and claimed to be rightful heir to the throne. Amangkurat III took flight from the palace in 1705. For the next three years this king, known also as *Sunan* Mas, lived and fought in the mountains of east Java, allying himself with various parties, most famous among them the Balinese rebel, fugitive, and legendary leader Surapati.[6] In this struggle, known as the First Javanese War of Succession (1704–1708), the Dutch supported Pangéran Puger, who, under their protection and at the price of great territorial and political concessions, ascended to the throne in 1704 with the title Pakubuwana I.[7]

When Amangkurat III concluded that his struggle was hopeless, he decided to contact the Dutch commander of Surabaya, Govert Knol. His sense of desperation was especially keen after his troops were said to have been smitten by a terrible disease that left those ill in the afternoon dead by morning.[8] He sent an emissary to Commander Knol outlining his conditions for surrender and was promised that they would be honored. Reality, however, was different, and Amangkurat III was betrayed by his captors, imprisoned, and sent to Batavia and later Ceylon. Based on fleeting but significant evidence, I believe that he was resettled in the far north of the island, in Jaffna.[9]

Following are a few verses from the *Babad Kartasura*, a history of Java during the early to mid-eighteenth century, depicting these events:

> Exceedingly happy was the king
> Upon hearing the Company's message
> Along with his officials
> Not realizing they were victims of deceit.

King Amangkurat III, in his pre-exile days, looks on as one of his wives, a daughter of Pangéran Puger, Radèn Ayu Lembah, and her illicit lover, Radèn Sukra, are strangled at court. Her female attendants are thrown into the tigers' cage. Another rebel son of Pangéran Puger, Radèn Soco Kusuma, is displayed in a cage on the palace grounds. The work is titled "Soenan Mas verlustigt zich in de aanschouwing der door hem bevolen strafen en wreedheden, 1703." (Anonymous painting, c. 1890. Courtesy Leiden University Library.)

The next few lines depict an exchange between Amangkurat III and his supporter Pangéran Blitar, then:

> Other matters will now be discussed.
> Susunan Mas was quickly brought
> Aboard the ship,
> Followed by many soldiers
> And family members,
> And the *pusaka* were carried too
> aboard the ship.[10]

The main point I wish to emphasize here is that the scene, even in the context of portrayals of exile, which are often brief and fleeting, is especially concise and laconic. Since Amangkurat III was the first Javanese king to be exiled by the VOC, the fact that the text devotes so few words to the event merits some consideration. Another point to note is mention of the royal heirlooms, the *pusaka,* made in the final lines cited above. In Java such objects, which included particular spears, gongs, daggers (*keris*), garments, saddles, and additional items belonging to the royal house, were considered vital to a king's authority and ability to rule and overcome the many obstacles he might face, such as war, rebellion, famine, and powerful supernatural forces and beings. The loss of the Kartasura *pusaka* with Amangkurat III's flight and later exile caused great consternation in the court, driving several attempts to regain them in the years both before and following his banishment, all of which were unsuccessful. Despite the brevity of the exile scene as depicted in the *Babad,* mention of the *pusaka* is not omitted, foreshadowing the relatively plentiful allusions to them yet to come, on which more later in the chapter.[11]

THE JOURNEY TO CEYLON

The next example of a Javanese source addressing exile to Ceylon depicts an unlikely meeting at sea. In 1728 Pangéran Arya Mangkunagara, older brother of the ruling king of Kartasura, Pakubuwana II (both were grandsons of the aforementioned Pakubuwana I), was exiled on charges that he had an affair with one of the king's women, an intractable historical claim no doubt, but one the Dutch did not apparently believe.[12] What is quite clear, however, is that the king's powerful chief councilor, Patih Danureja, was deeply implicated in the move to rid the court of Pangéran Arya Mangkunagara. The latter was arrested by the Dutch and sent to Batavia, where he remained for several years. Despite Pakubuwana II's recurring requests that he be exiled further, this did not transpire until 1733, when he boarded a ship to Ceylon. Meanwhile, also in 1733, Patih Danureja himself fell out of favor with the king and was turned over to the Dutch authorities, to be exiled as well.

Pangéran Arya Mangkunagara was traveling by ship when, after a month had passed, he was surprised when the ship anchored unexpectedly in midsea. Not long afterward, a smaller boat crashed into the ship, and he, along with the captain, rushed on deck to see what happened:

> Deeply startled he looked on
> Pangéran Arya Mangkunagara
> Astonished he pinched his chest:
> "Uncle Danureja
> How did you come to this,

Experiencing misery
Akin to my own hardship?"
Boarding the ship
He was startled to meet Pangéran Arya
On that boat[13]

The Patih hurried, running
To bow deeply at the feet of Pangéran Arya[14]
His weeping increasingly louder.
Pangéran Arya spoke softly:
"Why did you follow me here
O Patih what happened,
What did you do?"
He replied, gasping:
"O son I now receive my share
For committing treason against you.

I beg your forgiveness truly."[15]

Patih Danureja asks forgiveness within earshot of the shocked ship captain, who is astounded to witness the meeting of a fallen court official and the prince he betrayed, now both on a ship bound for Ceylon, sharing a fate. Pangéran Arya Mangkunagara's anger toward Danureja had subsided over the years and the two spent time together, perhaps conversing of home on the long journey. In the final section depicting the two, Patih Danureja offers Pangéran Arya Mangkunagara a vision of the future based on prophecies he had heard from the astrologers (*alul nujum*) back in Java:

Your son Radèn Mas Said
Adept at ruling as king
And enduring great battles,
His excellence famed far and wide.
When he shall die, Radèn Mas Said,
The livelihood of Java
Will be gone rice and paddy,
Livelihoods [found only] across the seas.
For among the people of Java not one will have food
That was the first[16]

To be included in the prophecy and
Your younger brother Mas Sujana
His powers renowned,

Babad Kartasura, composed by Mas Ngabéhi Rangga Panambangan III, MS. MN 185, 32–33 (Surakarta, 1852). The passage depicts the meeting at sea of Pangéran Arya Mangkunagara and Patih Danureja. (Courtesy Reksa Pustaka Library, Mangkunaragan Palace, Surakarta.)

> Exceptional noble king
> Bearing his troops' burden.
> When he shall die
> In Java then
> Not one shall be clothed.
> Yes, those are the two noblemen to be cherished
> As garments and food.[17]

After the presentation of this prophecy, Patih Danureja and Pangéran Arya Mangkunagara are said to have smiled, grasping in their hearts that which had been spoken, just as the boat was to dock at the shores of Ceylon. At this moment, when the destination of their long journey and the exilic life they would lead there became a reality, the disgraced official offered the betrayed prince a sense of comfort and hope. Patih Danureja's words implied that although Pangéran Arya Mangkunagara himself was doomed to a life far away from his land and people, the future held great things for his son and younger brother, both of whom would indeed become rulers of newly established Javanese courts.[18] Exile in this case did not signal the end of his line: his close kin were, claimed the prophecy, the very livelihood of Java, concretely depicted as its nourishment and clothing, more figuratively as its sustenance and protection.

What can a story like this tell us? It can be taken at face value, as describing a perhaps unlikely but not impossible coincidence. Dutch sources, which could have definitively corroborated or negated its occurrence, are not entirely clear on whether Pangéran Arya Mangkunagara and Patih Danureja were on a single ship bound for Ceylon. They seem to suggest the two arrived on the same day yet on board different ships.[19] But regardless of its factual validity, the story can be read as striving to put to rest some of the tensions tearing away at the fabric of the Kartasura court in the 1720s and that continued to reverberate for many years; it may be an attempt to absolve Pangéran Arya Mangkunagara through Patih Danureja's admitting his treachery or vindicate the *patih* by portraying his anguish and remorse. The narrative could also constitute an endeavor to retroactively explain the rise of two of Pangéran Arya Mangkunagara's family members to powerful positions of authority despite his exile, or even with his exile as the particular background against which their success would unfold. In the case of these speculative scenarios, the story could have been a later addition that was inserted to provide context and reason for events either past or future and as such raises questions of how exile was recounted and remembered, relevant across the texts I explore.[20]

Exiles No More—A Scene of Return

King Amangkurat III, whose capture and exile in 1708 were discussed briefly earlier in this chapter, lived out the rest of his life in Ceylon. When word of his death reached Batavia in 1734, Pakubuwana II received a letter from the governor general informing him that the deposed king had passed away in exile, that his body had not yet been buried, and that the Dutch were awaiting Pakubuwana II's preference regarding Amangkurat III's postmortem repatriation.[21] The *Babad Kartasura* recounts how Pakubuwana II, upon reading the letter, which had been brought by a messenger, was astounded. The Javanese word *ngungun* (astonished, dumbfounded, amazed) is repeated three times in this short passage, as the king assembles his close advisers and relatives to ask for their thoughts on the matter. Despite his repeated attempts to elicit an opinion about what he should do, all those present avoid voicing one and defer to him (*anyumanggaken ing karsa naréndra*), perhaps because of the issue's great sensitivity, Pakubuwana II's grandfather having had usurped the throne from the legitimate line of his brother and nephew, whose return, even posthumously, might give rise to competing claims to authority. It seems the Dutch were also not eager to weigh in and so the decision was left squarely in Pakubuwana's hands. Increasingly bewildered of heart (*èmenginirèng galih*) the king lost himself in thought for a long time, finally emerging to announce that he wished for Amangkurat III to be buried in the royal cemetery in Imogiri; that he would allow his surviving sons and families to return; and, importantly, that all the missing regalia that had disappeared with Amangkurat III's flight in 1705 shall be returned to the court.[22] It seems the desire to reclaim those sacred objects played a major role in his decision.

What most concerns me here, however, are not the *pusaka* but the question of how Javanese chronicles depicted the return of the group of exiles, which included, besides the deceased king's body, approximately two hundred of his relatives and members of his retinue, some of whom were surely born in Ceylon during the years of banishment.[23] Upon receiving Pakubuwana II's decision, the governor general sent a message to two of Amangkurat III's sons in Ceylon, Pangéran Mangkunagara[24] and Pangéran Pakuningrat, to prepare for accompanying their father's body back to Java and for their own return along with their wives, children, and retinues. They arrived in Batavia (the journey home is not recounted) with their families and the heirlooms in tow, were greeted with eleven military canon salutes, and boarded a boat to travel by sea, along Java's north coast, to Semarang:

> Then they all came ashore. The commander got word that Sunan Mangkurat Mas' sons had arrived at the mouth of the river, accompanying their late father's body. Displaying respect the commander came to welcome them along with all the Kartasura court officials.
>
> As they arrived at the mouth of the river they bowed to those two princes. When the two princes saw Radèn Pringgalaya and Radèn Natakusuma their hearts were filled with emotion and they wept, [and] both Radèn Pringgalaya and Radèn Natakusuma wept along with them.
>
> They embraced each other in turns for some time, then emerged from the river mouth and headed toward the commander's house for the night, and left Semarang in the morning to the sound of eleven cannon salutes.[25]

A section from another *Babad Kartasura* volume highlights additional aspects of this particular return: in it Amangkurat III's four sons are mentioned; thus, in addition to Pangéran Mangkunagara and Pangéran Mangkuningrat, Pangéran Jayakusuma and the youngest son, Pangéran Emas, also appear. Collectively all four are referred to in the text as "the Ceylon princes"

(Pangéran Selong), while their father is referred to as Sunan Kendhang, "the Exiled King."[26]

Immediately after the returning family is mentioned, the heirlooms make an appearance:

> Returned as the King had hoped,
> Heirlooms of the land of Java,
> All returned to Java:
> Spears, kerisses and garments,
> The small gong Kyai Becak,
> Carried to Ceylon in the past,
> By Sunan Mangkurat Mas.
> In the year Alip,
> The month of Rabingulakir,
> On the eighth day of the month,
> A Thursday,
> They were brought along,
> All those previously taken,
> Had now been returned.[27]

Clearly a triumphant, proud, and relieved tone can be detected in this passage, as the return of the *pusaka* was probably a (the?) major goal of allowing Amangkurat's descendants to return to Java despite a certain anxiety that they might try to reclaim their earlier, pre-exile status. Another depiction of the same return draws attention to the human dimension of repatriation, after many years during which there was little hope of ever returning:

> All reached Betawi,
> The members of the House of Mangkurat
> Who had lived in Ceylon:
> Pangéran Mangkunagara,
> Pangéran Mangkuningrat,
> Radèn Jayakusuma
> And the youngest, Pangéran Emas.
> Along with their households, men and women
> Great and small, yes everyone
> Two hundred in total
> Were met by the Patih.
> Like the dead meeting the living
> Great was their happiness
> No more need be said.[28]

The return of the Ceylon princes is also narrated in *Babad Jawi Karta-sura*, where the description of events is quite similar, yet less joyful sentiments also emerge: those awaiting the princes in Kartasura are said to be weighed down with sorrow as they watch the Ceylon princes arrive;[29] when the princes come before King Pakubuwana II they feel heartbroken;[30] in this source, as in the others I have cited, the princes are bestowed with new names upon their return to Java and are given tracts of land by the king.[31]

When these references are considered together, a contradiction seems to emerge between the level of detail in passages relating the return of Amangkurat III's sons, depicted in several chronicles and presenting different emphases, and the brevity of description related to their father's exile, about which the texts have little to say. The *Babad Kartasura*'s depiction of the arrival of the princes' retinues in Betawi, for example, continues as they travel onward toward Kartasura and the palace. Their journey home, which began when they departed the shores of distant Ceylon, took them across the sea to Java, first landing in Betawi, then traveling by boat to Semarang and continuing to Kartasura. Once there, they were taken first to the hall of the king's chief councilor (*kepatihan*), then to the palace (*pura*), and finally to the royal audience hall (*panangkilan*). This and other examples of attentiveness to detail suggest that this exilic return marked an event considered highly significant, and one that these texts, often passing over emotions in near silence, could not refrain from depicting in touching and emotive words.

Last but not least I explore a scene in which a Javanese woman recently returned from Ceylon recalls some events of exilic life.

REMEMBERING LIFE IN CEYLON

At present this account, appearing in the *Babad Giyanti*, is by far the most detailed and insightful one I have come across in terms of recalling the exiles' lives in Ceylon. The speaker is the wife of Pangéran Juru (previously known as Pangéran Natakusuma), who was chief councilor to Pakubuwana II until accused of leading a pro-Chinese court faction and exiled to Ceylon in 1742. In 1758 Sultan Hamengkubuwana I of Yogyakarta (brother of the late Pakubuwana II) petitioned the Dutch, requesting that Pangéran Natakusuma be returned to Java. The request was granted and Natakusuma was renamed Pangéran Juru and was appointed adviser to the sultan of Yogyakarta. In the *Babad Giyanti* scene, he and his wife, Radèn Ayu Juru, are visiting Pakubuwana III, ruler of Surakarta, whose father had sent them into exile. As they met,

> With open arms they embraced, weeping:
> They never imagined they would meet again.

It felt like a dream come true
Long they all wept.[32]

The body language and sounds of the moment come through, as does the silencing of words at this emotional and unexpected reunion. Then Radèn Ayu Juru portrays the Ceylon experiences. She includes no "objective" indications illuminating where the exiles lived, what conditions they endured, or what their surroundings were like. The emphasis of the passage is on the emergence of a group of disciples convening around two charismatic Islamic teachers, Sayyid Musa Ngidrus and Ibrahim Asmara. Besides delving into their religious functions, the text emphasizes the difficult emotional state of exilic life and how such teachers ably assisted those afflicted with homesickness and longing. Having noticed that one of the exiles seemed deeply dejected, Ibrahim Asmara turned to him and asked about his favorite food while still back home in Java.[33] The question itself brought a smile to the man's lips, and he replied immediately:

Fish, tempeh—that's what I miss,
Yes, and the fruits:
Salak, durian and pundhung,
Jackfruit, malinjo, potatoes
Every Friday appeared
Emerging from the [guru's] jubbah.[34]

From that day onward fruit and other Javanese delicacies arrived in Ceylon from Surakarta every Friday, healing the disciple's heart, thanks to the guru's special powers (kramat), expressed through his ability to transport the foods, his keen understanding of his disciples' psychological needs, and his compassion. The desire for certain flavors, smells, textures, and sensations combines a concrete form of longing for the familiar—the basic, everyday fruits and dishes that were unavailable in a foreign land—and a broader longing for all those known objects, people, places, traditions, and habits that became inaccessible in exile and that one could not trust would one day be attainable again.[35]

The Babad Giyanti's depiction of Ibrahim Asmara and Sayyid Musa also offers a glimpse of the religiously inspired contacts and relationships that must have been significant to the exiles in their attempts to overcome the many challenges they faced. In part this was achieved by joining particular circles of disciples and thus also building and maintaining ties to larger devotional and intellectual networks in Ceylon and beyond.[36] Sayyid Musa and Ibrahim Asmara are depicted as awliya, as possessing the power to materialize any wish or thought, and as attracting a very large and diverse crowd of disciples, including ship captains from Surat and Selangor, Bengal and Hyderabad. Many of these came to "request permission" (*nyuwun idi*), and although no particular Sufi *tarekat* is mentioned, the phrase may well refer to an initiation ritual.

The passage offers a depiction of gatherings in which the exiles took part: every Friday night the disciples (*murid*) would convene to recite the Qur'an. The crowd was so large that no less than fifteen goats had to be slaughtered to accommodate all those present. The gathering took place every week and, with God's compassion, food was plentiful, surpassing what the exiles used to have in Surakarta. It was on one of these occasions that Ibrahim Asmara, who was of clear insight (*waskithèng batin*) turned to a disciple and inquired about his favorite foods. Upon hearing the recollections of these events, as related by Radèn Ayu Juru years later, the sunan of Surakarta was filled with awe.

Through these emotional personal and collective aspects of exilic life depicted in a brief passage of a Javanese historical chronicle, we glimpse the human face of exile and return: disbelief and joy at reuniting with relatives, the longing for the familiar and its power to comfort and heal, the importance of Qur'anic recitations, Friday gatherings and the devotion to teachers blessed with special powers to sustain those living in exile and unsure of their prospects of returning home. Mention of Sayyid Musa's knowledge of curing pain and sadness (*mulihken lara prihatin*) weaves together these thematic threads of an individual's challenges and the solace found in leadership and community.

The passage also evokes the intertwined experiences and histories of the exiles, the many other Malay and Muslim individuals who crossed their paths in Ceylon, and the relatives who remained on Java but listened to the tales, perhaps drawing lessons from them and trying to imagine what life was like on that island that lay across the sea from their own.

This chapter constitutes a first and fragmentary attempt to assemble and consider Javanese references to the history of exile to Ceylon in the eighteenth century. Searching for passages on exile that are few and far between is challenging but also raises an interesting question of why exile does not figure more prominently in Javanese *babads* chronicling a period during which exile was used repeatedly as a punishment and deterrent. Was it the time that elapsed between the affairs depicted and their narration that dulled the force of dramatic events and raw emotions? Perhaps, but if so the same should have been true for the many other events depicted in the *babads*, which are portrayed with greater detail and nuance. Was it the lack of information available to authors and scribes about what became of those exiled on their journeys and of the circumstances under which they lived in Ceylon? There may have been very little or no contact between those exiled and their families and officials who remained behind, although letters to the governor general and council in Batavia have survived, proving that at least some contacts were maintained.

The reasons for the brevity of depiction could have been less straightforward, relating to the exiles' position on the "losing side" of history, as in the case of Amangkurat III, and yet clearly his descendants still had some claims to power and still posed a threat, evident in Pakubuwana II's rather anxious insistence, depicted in the *Babad Kartasura*, that he was the legitimate heir to Amangkurat III, not the latter's two sons who had returned from exile; and even though Pangéran Arya Mangkunagara was not allowed to return alive, prophecies and historical developments alike bestowed his nearest of kin with royal authority.[37] The question remains open: was there a purposeful attempt to forget, to erase such figures, so they would not be kept alive in historical chronicles and popular memory?

Clearly, the diverse repository of Javanese historical materials also contains examples contrasting those I have examined here, as in the fascinating case, discussed by Sri Margana in chapter 5 in this volume, of the *Babad Mangkudiningratan*, a memoir that depicts in great detail the exilic experiences of Sultan Hamengkubuwana II and his two sons in Penang, Batavia, and Ambon in 1813–1826. But the *babads* I have cited tend to employ brief, nonemotive language and are largely descriptive. This tendency means that when they do portray events or interactions that involve feelings and a range of human reactions, these stand out and can be very moving, as in the simile likening the reunion between the returning exiles and the people in Surakarta to the dead meeting the living; Amangkurat III's despair before surrendering, not knowing where to turn; and the longing for Javanese food. Also related to language is the way the Javanese speech levels are employed in the texts. Further analysis will allow a more conclusive assessment to emerge, but it may be that using *krama inggil* (the high, very refined form of Javanese) when speaking of figures like Pangéran Arya Mangkunagara and Amangkurat III was one of the ways royal status was maintained, at least textually, even after exile.

In closing, I wish to reflect on a particular prism we might take when considering the material presented in this chapter. The story of the Javanese exiles to Ceylon can be read, in part, as a familial one, stretching from the first-ever Javanese king to be exiled by the Dutch in the early eighteenth century, through many exiles and returns during that century—a very tumultuous one in Java's history—to a letter written in the early nineteenth century and addressed to the governor general in Batavia by a descendant of the same royal family who still claimed special status and a connection to Java.[38] Writing from Colombo in 1806, almost a century to the day after Amangkurat III was exiled, one of his offspring via Pangéran Arya Mangkunagara's son Mas Kerti beseeched the Dutch authorities in Batavia for protection from Ceylon's British rulers. This letter, composed in Malay rather than Javanese, can be viewed as an early sign marking the gradual transition of identity from Javanese royals to Sri Lankan Malays.[39]

Thinking about exile in the House of Mataram allows us to consider exile across generations, experiences, and places and to explore the intertwining of genealogy, historical developments of war, ascensions to the throne, and colonial expansion and the workings of cultural memory. And in considering how the Javanese language and its literature reflected and engaged with such processes, there is perhaps no better place to begin than with the Javanese word *dipunsélongaken*—to be "Ceyloned"—which came to signify exile.

NOTES

I wholeheartedly thank Muhammad Endy Saputro and Sri Ratna Saktimulya in Yogyakarta for assisting me in locating and reading several of the Javanese manuscripts mentioned in this chapter and for insightful discussions of their content. I also thank Nadeera Rupasinghe for her invaluable assistance at the National Archives of Sri Lanka. I am grateful to Sunil Amrith, Nancy K. Florida, Jean Gelman Taylor, Merle C. Ricklefs, and Kerry Ward for their helpful comments on earlier versions of this chapter, and the Australian Research Council for generously supporting the research on which this chapter is based.

1. Kerry Ward, *Networks of Empire: Forced Migration in the Dutch East India Company* (Cambridge: Cambridge University Press, 2009), 186.

2. There were Malays residing in Ceylon prior to Dutch rule there, before and during the 150 years of Portuguese presence, but their history is beyond the scope of my discussion.

3. On this manuscript see Ronit Ricci, "The Discovery of Javanese Writing in a Sri Lankan Malay Manuscript," *Bijdragen tot de Taal-, Land- en Volkenkunde* 168, no. 4 (2012): 511–518.

4. On the history of the *Alamat Langkapuri*, see Ronit Ricci, "The Malay World, Expanded: The World's First Malay Newspaper, Colombo 1869," *Indonesia and the Malay World* 41, no. 120 (July 2013): 168–182.

5. See Merle C. Ricklefs, *Jogjakarta under Sultan Mangkubumi 1749–1792: A History of the Division of Java* (London: Oxford University Press, 1974); Merle C. Ricklefs, *Modern Javanese Historical Tradition: A Study of an Original Kartasura Chronicle and Related Materials* (London: SOAS, 1978); Merle C. Ricklefs, "The Missing Pusaka of Kartasura, 1705–37," in *Bahasa- Sastra-Budaya: Ratna Manikam Untaian Persembahan kepada Prof. Dr. P. J. Zoetmulder,* ed. Sutrisno Sulastin et al. (Yogyakarta: Gadjah Mada University Press, 1985), 601–630; Merle C. Ricklefs, *The Seen and Unseen Worlds in Java, 1726–1749: History, Litera-*

ture and Islam in the Court of Pakubuwana II (Honolulu: University of Hawai'i Press, 1998); Nancy K. Florida, *Writing the Past, Inscribing the Future: History as Prophecy in Colonial Java* (Durham, NC: Duke University Press, 1995); Peter Carey, *The Power of Prophecy: Prince Dipanagara and the End of an Old Order in Java, 1785–1855* (Leiden: KITLV, 2008); Muridan Widjojo, *The Revolt of Prince Nuku: Cross-Cultural Alliance-Making in Maluku, c. 1780–1810* (Leiden: Brill, 2008).

6. On the life and historical afterlives of Surapati, see Ann Kumar, *Surapati: Man and Legend* (Leiden: E. J. Brill, 1976). Several of Surapati's descendants were exiled to Ceylon.

7. On the agreement between Pakubuwana I and the VOC, see Ward, *Networks of Empire*, 212–213.

8. *Babad Sangkala* canto III, 64–65; see Ricklefs, *Modern Javanese Historical Tradition*, 119.

9. Travel diary of the Dutch Governor of Ceylon, 1720. SLNA 1/2723/ 85–87.

10. "*Langkung trusthanira sri bupati / amiarsa kumpeni turira / tuwin sagung pung-gawané / tan wruh yèn kenèng apus . . . Gantya ingkang winuwus / Susunan Mas binekta aglis / minggah dhateng ing kapal / kang wadya keh tumut / lan sagung ingkang Santana / tuwin sagung pusaka binekta sami / minggah dhateng ing kapal.*" Anonymous, *Babad Kartasura*, MS. MN 199, transliteration as B21d by Mulyo Hutomo, n.d., Reksapustaka Library, Mangkunagaran Palace, Surakarta, 1869, 102–103. This *babad* was copied in 1869 but the date of the original is unknown. The manuscript was commissioned by, and belonged to, Bendara Radèn Ayu Purbasumarsa; see Nancy K. Florida, *Javanese Literature in Surakarta Manuscripts: Manuscripts of the Mangkunagaran Palace*, vol. 2 (Ithaca, NY: Cornell University Press, 2000), 126. The verses are written in the *dhandhanggula* meter and intended to be sung. This scene is also depicted in *Babad Sangkala*. All punctuation here and following was added to the original.

11. By far the most in-depth study of the missing *pusaka* is Ricklefs, "Missing Pusaka of Kartasura." For an interesting comparative perspective on royal regalia in exile, see Robert Aldrich's contribution on the last king of Kandy, chapter 2 in this volume.

12. Although they did not trust the rumors, the Dutch feared that Arya Mangkunagara would rebel and be followed by many dignitaries and therefore felt compelled to exile him. Merle C. Ricklefs, *A History of Modern Indonesia since c. 1200*, 4th ed. (Stanford, CA: Stanford University Press, 2008), 108.

13. "*Langkung kagèt dènira ningali / Pangéran Arya Mangkunagara / ngungun amijet jajané / siwa Danurejèku / déné kongsi mangkéné iki / nemu papa kaliwat / kaya susah ingsun / duk prapta minggah ing kapal / kagyat Pangran Harya kang pinanggih / wonten palatar palwa.*" Anonymous, *Babad Kartasura*, MS. MN 200, transliteration as B21c by Mulyo Hutomo, n.d, 27, in *dhandhanggula*, Rektapustaka Library, Mangkunagaran Palace, Surakarta, 1844. The manuscript on which this transliteration is based, MN 200, was copied in 1844. *Amijet jajané* means to pinch, squeeze, or massage the chest, here a gesture of great surprise or consternation.

14. *Anyungkemi* refers to touching the feet of another with one's head as a sign of respect and deference.

15. "*Kiya Patih gupuh malayoni / anungkemi mring Pangéran Arya / pan sarya asru tangisé / Pangran Harya lingnya rum / yapagéné nusulirèki / wah Patih kenèng apa / mangkana tingkahmu / saurira megap-megap / adhuh angger pun uwa mangké manisi / duraka ing panduka // mangkya nuwun apunten sayekti.*" *Babad Kartasura*, B21c, 27, in *dhandhanggula*. An almost identical rendering appears in Mas Ngabéhi Rangga Panambangan III, *Babad Kartasura*,

MS. MN 185, transliteration as MN 185 TT (B21i) by Hatmo Wasito, 1981, 27–28, Reksapustaka Library, Mangkunagaran Palace, Surakarta, 1852.

16. *"Putra paduka Radèn Mas Said / tembé kuwawi adamel raja / ing prang awrat sasanggané / urageng jagat panjul / yèn sirnaa Radèn Mas Said / rejeki Tanah Jawa / sirna beras pantun / rejeki nabrang sadara / pan wong Jawa tan ana kang bisa bukti / déné ta kang satunggal."* Babad Kartasura, B21c, 28, in *dhandhanggula*.

17. *"Kang kalebet ing wirayat nenggih / rayi paduka Mas Sujana / tembé ampuh paparabé / arang satriya ratu / kang anangga wawraté jurit / yèn punika sirnaa / Tanah Jawa bésuk / tan ana kang bisa nyandhang / gih satriya kakalih kang dèn panuti / ing sandhang lawan pangan."* Babad Kartasura, B21c, 28.

18. The son, Radèn Mas Said (later bestowed the title Mangkunagara I), was to become first ruler of Surakarta's minor court, the Kadipatèn Mangkunagaran (r. 1757–1796). The brother, Mas Sujana (Pangéran Mangkubumi), was to reign as the founding sultan of the newly established Karaton Yogyakarta, Sultan Hamengkubuwana I (r. 1749–1792).

19. SLNA 1/69. Political Council Meeting of 14 November 1733, Department of National Archives, Colombo.

20. Another important issue raised by this story is the relationship between domestic politics and the implementation of exile that was enabled by European involvement.

21. I am assuming that even though the text claims the body had not yet been buried (*kang layon samangké dèrèng pinetak*), it had been interred temporarily in Ceylon but had not yet received the official burial due a Javanese king. A similar example is found in the case of Cakraningrat IV (r. 1718–1746), who died in exile at the Cape of Good Hope in South Africa and was later reburied in Madura.

22. This scene is described in Anonymous, *Babad Kartasura*, transliteration as B21j by Djayeng Susarno, 1980, 92–93, Rektapustaka Library, Mangkunagaran Palace, Surakarta, n.d. This volume was authored by Panambangan III, Mas Ngabéhi Rangga (b. 1783) in Surakarta in 1852; see Florida, *Javanese Literature*, 118.

23. Details of expanding and contracting households, especially those of royal exiles, were noted regularly in Dutch documents from Ceylon. For example, SLNA 1/3956 lists Dutch state exiles residing in Ceylon in 1788, noting those who had recently been added to an earlier list (through birth or arrival in Ceylon) or detracted from it (through death or repatriation).

24. This prince had the same name, but was not the same person, as the abovementioned Pangéran Arya Mangkunagara.

25. *"Nulya sami mentas ing baita. Ingriku kumendur wus amiyarsa lamun putrané Sunan Mangkurat Mas sampun prapta muara, sarta angiringaken layoné kang rama. Nulya komendur ngormati methuk lan sagung punggawèng Kartasura sami methuk sedaya.Yata sak praptané muwara sampun tundhuk lawan Pangéran kalih wau. Pangéran kekalih duk aningali Radèn Pringgalaya lawan Radèn Natakusuma, kathah ingkang taraosèng galih dadya sami karuna. Kalihipun Radèn Pringgalaya lawan Radèn Natakusuma sami tumut karuna.Nuntut sami rangkul rinangkul gantya, wau sareng sampun antawis dangu, lajeng budhal saking muara, anjujug wismané kumendur, among rerep sadalu, énjing gya budhal saking Semawis sarta kinurmatan mariyem saking sawelas."* Babad Kartasura, B21j, 94.

26. *Sunan* was a title applied to the ruler of Kartasura and later Surakarta. It is also applied to the *wali sanga*, the nine "saints" said to have brought Islam to Java.

27. *"Pamrihira Sri Bupati / pusaka ing Tanah Jawa / mantuka mring Jawa kabèh / waos dhuwung lan rasuka / bendhé Kiyai Becak / binektèng Sélong rumuhun / mring Sunan Mangkurat Mas // Anuju ing taun Alip / Rabingulakir kang wulan / tanggal ping wolu angkaté / marengi*

ing dina Soma / déné ta kanthènira / kang samya tumut rumuhun / winangsulaken sadaya." *Babad Kartasura*, B21c, 28, in *asmaradana* meter.

28. "*Sadaya prapta Betawi / Santana kamangkuratan / kang sami wonten ing Sélong / Pangéran Mangkunagara / Pangéran Mangkuningrat / Radèn Jayakusuma / wuragil Pangéran Emas // Sarayaté jalu èstri / geng alit nenggih sadaya / wong kalihatus cacahé / wus panggih lan Kiyai Patya / lir pejah manggih gesang / samya langsung sukanipun / mangkana sah ing bicara.*" *Babad Kartasura*, B21j, 29, in *asmaradana*.

29. "*Jibeg kang samya ningali / rawuhira Pangéran kang saking Sélan.*" Anonymous, *Babad Jawi Kartasura*, vol. 4, transliteration by Sri Soehartini (Jakarta: Department Pendidikan dan Kebudayaan Proyek Penerbitan Buku Sastra Indonesia dan Daerah, 1987), 83.

30. "*Samya sumedhot tyasira.*" Anonymous, *Babad Jawi Kartasura*, 83.

31. Anonymous, *Babad Jawi Kartasura*, 84. The practice of receiving a new name often accompanied certain life transitions, including promotion or attaining a new position within the court, recovery from illness, ascension to the throne, and various other moments that signaled a new beginning.

32. "*Ngebyaki ngrangkul karuna / tan andipé yèn papanggih / kadya ciptané supena / adangu karuna sami.*" Radèn Ngabéhi Yasadipura, *Babad Giyanti* (Batavia: Balai Pustaka, 1937–1939), 84, in *sinom* meter. The published edition contains no information about its source manuscript. However, there are grounds to believe that it was the Ned. Bijbel. Genootschap MS 29–33; see Theodore T. G. Pigeaud, *Literature of Java: Catalogue Raisonné of Javanese Manuscripts in the Library of the University of Leiden and Other Public Collections in the Netherlands*, 3 vols. (Leiden: Leiden University Press, 1967–1970), 719–720.

33. "*Dinangu kadoyanira / kala wonten Tanah Jawi.*" Yasadipura, *Babad Giyanti*, 85, in *sinom*.

34. "*Ulam témpé dèn kangeni / lawan woh wohan nenggih / salak durèn lawan pundhung / nongka malinjo kenthang / ing saben Jumuwah prapti / wedalipun saking ing rasukan jubbah.*" Yasadipura, *Babad Giyanti*, 85, in *sinom*. *Ulam* is ambiguous, as it can refer to meat, fish, or side dishes eaten with rice. However, since in a previous section in the story the Friday meal of goat meat enjoyed by the disciples is mentioned, I am assuming that it is a longing for fish that is expressed here. All the fruits listed in the verse are native to Southeast Asia except the potato (*kenthang*), which was brought to west Java around 1794, a time that postdated Pangéran Juru's return in 1755 and certainly his years in exile. The inclusion of potatoes in the list could be a change or mistake made by a copier of the particular *Babad Giyanti* manuscript or an indication that it was written retrospectively at a later period. This particular scene does not appear in several additional *Babad Giyanti* versions consulted.

35. Jean Gelman Taylor's chapter (chap. 7) in this volume, on inventories of possessions of deceased Indonesian slaves at the Cape of Good Hope in the eighteenth century, shows how the study of material belongings opens a window to understanding their owners' forms of belonging. The same innovative methodology of paying close attention to things can be applied to studying textual passages such as the one quoted on food, as well as to depictions related to the royal heirlooms.

36. The emergence of such religious networks was often an unintended result of banishment, as far as the Dutch were concerned. On the case of exiles from Indonesia contributing to Islam's spread at the Cape of Good Hope, see Ward, *Networks of Empire*, 20.

37. Pakubuwana II's explicit claim of his status as heir to Amangkurat III, presented to the latter's sons Pangéran Pakuningrat and Pangéran Mangkunagara, appears in *Babad Kartasura*, B21j, 95–96. On that same occasion Pakubuwana II also inquired about the

precise number of children fathered by Amangkurat III, both before his exile and later in Ceylon: "*Lah kakangmas samangké dipuneca wonten ingriki / sak sedané kangjeng uwa / inggih kula kangmas kang dadya gegentinipun / semana pèngetan kalih aturé anuwun / yata sang nata andangu malih / sak mangké pinten sadaya tetilaranipun kangjeng uwa / punapa malih sak laminé wonten ing Sélong / punapa sampun puputra malih.*" The recurring use of the name Amangkurat by descendants of the deceased and disgraced king may have also signaled undiminished, ongoing aspirations for the return of his line to power; see, for example, a letter written from Colombo in 1806 by Pangéran Mas Dipati Mangkurat, apparently a relative of Mas Garendi (aka Sunan Kuning), grandson of Amangkurat III (MS. Cod.Or. 2241-I/23).

38. Descendants of the House of Mataram exiled to Ceylon in the eighteenth century include Amangkurat III, his children and wives, Pangéran Arya Mangkunagara and family, Radèn Tumenggung Sosrodiningrat and Radèn Tumenggung Ronodiningrat, sons of Cakraningrat IV of Madura, whose wife, Radèn Ayu Maduretna, was the sister of Pakubuwana II, several of Pangéran Mangkubumi's brothers, and others. Also relevant to this analysis are the various exiled court officials, who were often related by marriage to the royal family.

39. MS. Cod. Or. 2241 I/24. The author refers to himself as Cucunda Radèn Tumenggung Wirakushuma ibn Mas Kerti. The use of the Arabic/Jawi letter *shīn* instead of *sīn* is common in Sri Lankan Malay writing, thus Kushuma, not Kusuma.

BIBLIOGRAPHY

Primary Sources

Anonymous. *Babad Jawi Kartasura*. Vol. 4. Transliteration by Sri Soehartini. Jakarta: Departemen Pendidikan dan Kebudayaan Proyek Penerbitan Buku Sastra Indonesia dan Daerah, 1987.

———. *Babad Kartasura*. Transliteration as B21j by Djayeng Susarno, 1980 (original manuscript unavailable). Reksapustaka Library, Mangkunagaran Palace, Surakarta.

———. *Babad Kartasura*. MS. MN 199. Transliteration as B21d by Mulyo Hutomo, n.d. Reksapustaka Library, Mangkunagaran Palace, Surakarta, 1869.

———. *Babad Kartasura*. MS. MN 200. Transliteration as B21c by Mulyo Hutomo, 1999. Reksapustaka Library, Mangkunagaran Palace, Surakarta, 1844.

Letter from Cucunda Radèn Tumenggung Wirakushuma to the Governor General in Batavia, 1792. MS. Cod. Or. 2241 I/24.

Letter from Pangéran Mas Adipati Mangkurat to the Governor General in Batavia, 1806. MS. Cod. Or. 2241-I/23.

Panambangan, Mas Ngabéhi Rangga, III. *Babad Kartasura*. MS. MN 185. Transliteration as MN 185 TT (B21i) by Hatmo Wasito, 1981. Reksapustaka Library, Mangkunagaran Palace, Surakarta, 1852.

SLNA 1/69. Political Council Meeting of 14 November 1733. Department of National Archives, Colombo.

SLNA 1/2723. Travel Diary of the Dutch Governor of Ceylon Isaac Augustin Rumpf, January 25, 1720. Department of National Archives, Colombo, 85–87.

SLNA 1/3956. Documents sent by the Central Government to the dessave of Colombo, relating to the state exiles, 1769–1792. Department of National Archives, Colombo.

Yasadipura, Radèn Ngabéhi. *Babad Giyanti*. Batavia: Balai Pustaka, 1937–1939.

Secondary Sources

Baldaeus, Phillipus. *A True and Exact Description of the Great Island of Ceylon.* 1672. Translated by Pieter Brohier. Maharagama: Ceylon Historical Journal, 1960.

Carey, Peter. *The Power of Prophecy: Prince Dipanagara and the End of an Old Order in Java, 1785–1855.* Leiden: KITLV, 2008.

Florida, Nancy K. *Javanese Literature in Surakarta Manuscripts: Manuscripts of the Mangkunagaran Palace.* Vol. 2. Ithaca, NY: Cornell University Press, 2000.

———. *Writing the Past, Inscribing the Future: History as Prophecy in Colonial Java.* Durham, NC: Duke University Press, 1995.

Hussainmiya, B. A. *Lost Cousins: The Malays of Sri Lanka.* Bangi: Universiti Kebangsaan Malaysia, 1987.

———. *Orang Rejimen. The Malays of the Ceylon Rifle Regiment.* Bangi: Universiti Kebangsaan Malaysia, 1990.

Jappie, Saarah. "Jawi dari jauh." *Indonesia and the Malay World* 40, no. 117 (2012): 143–159.

Kumar, Ann. *Surapati: Man and Legend.* Leiden: E. J. Brill, 1976.

Paranavitana, K. D., ed. *Memoir of Librecht Hooreman Commandeur of Jaffna 1748 for His Successor Jacob De Jong.* Colombo: Department of National Archives under the Sri Lanka-Netherlands Cooperation Program, 2009.

Pigeaud, Theodore T. G. *Literature of Java: Catalogue Raisonné of Javanese Manuscripts in the Library of the University of Leiden and Other Public Collections in the Netherlands.* 3 vols. Leiden: Leiden University Press, 1967–1970.

Poerwadarminta, W. J. S. *Baosastra Djawa.* Groningen: J. B. Wolters, 1939.

Ricci, Ronit. "The Discovery of Javanese Writing in a Sri Lankan Malay Manuscript." *Bijdragen tot de Taal-, Land- en Volkenkunde* 168, no. 4 (2012): 511–518.

———. "The Malay World, Expanded: The World's First Malay Newspaper, Colombo 1869." *Indonesia and the Malay World* 41, no. 120 (July 2013): 168–182.

Ricklefs, Merle C. *A History of Modern Indonesia since c. 1200.* 4th ed. Stanford, CA: Stanford University Press, 2008.

———. *Jogjakarta under Sultan Mangkubumi 1749–1792. A History of the Division of Java.* London: Oxford University Press, 1974.

———. "The Missing Pusaka of Kartasura, 1705–37." In *Bahasa- Sastra-Budaya: Ratna Manikam Untaian Persembahan kepada Prof. Dr. P. J. Zoetmulder,* edited by Sutrisno Sulastin et al., 601–630. Yogyakarta: Gadjah Mada University Press, 1985.

———. *Modern Javanese Historical Tradition: A Study of an Original Kartasura Chronicle and Related Materials.* London: SOAS, 1978.

———. *The Seen and Unseen Worlds in Java, 1726–1749: History, Literature and Islam in the Court of Pakubuwana II.* Honolulu: University of Hawai'i Press, 1998.

Ricklefs, Merle C., Petrus Voorhoeve, and Annabel Teh Gallop. *Indonesian Manuscripts in Great Britain: A Catalogue of Manuscripts in Indonesian Languages in British Public Collections.* New ed. with addenda and corrigenda. Jakarta: EFEO, 2014.

Robson, Stuart, and Singgih Wibisono. *Javanese-English Dictionary.* Singapore: Periplus, 2002.

Said, H. M. "Ceylon Malays." *Journal of the Malaysian Branch of the Royal Asiatic Society* (1926): 266–268.

Suryadi. M. A. "Sepucuk surat dari seorang bangsawan Gowa di tanah pembuangan (Ceylon)." *Wacana: Jurnal ilmu Pengetahuan Budaya* 10, no. 2 (2008): 214–243.

Ward, Kerry. "Blood Ties: Exile, Family, and Inheritance across the Indian Ocean in the Early Nineteenth Century." *Journal of Social History* 45, no. 2 (2011): 436–452.

———. *Networks of Empire: Forced Migration in the Dutch East India Company.* Cambridge: Cambridge University Press, 2009.

Widjojo, Muridan. *The Revolt of Prince Nuku: Cross-Cultural Alliance-Making in Maluku, c. 1780–1810.* Leiden: Brill, 2008.

Wieringa, E. P. *Catalogue of Malay and Minangkabau Manuscripts in the Library of Leiden University and Other Collections in the Netherlands.* Leiden: Legatum Warnerianum in the Library of the University of Leiden, 1998.

FIVE

Caught between Empires
Babad Mangkudiningratan and the Exile of Sultan Hamengkubuwana II of Yogyakarta, 1813–1826

Sri Margana

Wars and conflict between countries in Western Europe affected their overseas colonies. In 1795 France occupied Holland and Willem V fled to England and made a covenant with the British ruler concerning the fate of the Dutch colonies in Asia and Africa. Under that agreement the British began to occupy key areas of the Dutch colonies in Africa and Asia, including the East Indies. Concurrently, the French authorities in the Netherlands sent Herman Willem Daendels to Java to defend the East Indies from British attack.[1] At the time Java was undergoing a transition of power. In Yogyakarta, Sultan Hamengkubuwana II was unreceptive toward the administrative and political reforms Daendels introduced, and he opposed the British takeover of Java in 1811. The sultan's resistance to the British ruler resulted in his dethronement and exile to Penang, Batavia, and Ambon. For a few years he endured an uncertain fate in exile, caught between two empires: the British and the Dutch.

This chapter examines the fate of Sultan Hamengkubuwana II and his family at the time of their exile in Penang, during the transition period from British to Dutch administration, from 1813 to 1826. The study is based first and foremost on the *Babad Mangkudiningratan*, an early-nineteenth-century Javanese manuscript belonging to the Library of the Pakualaman court in Yogyakarta, which chronicles this royal family's exilic experience.[2] More broadly, the chapter seeks to address the question of how the study of colonial attitudes toward exile and the response of the exiled may contribute to a better understanding of life in exile, including the cultural and psychological aspects of exiles' lives.

"Exile" in everyday use evokes images of individual political dissidents sent overseas: the displacement it entails and the effect such displacement has on the exile's perception of his or her current location, the homeland, and intellectual products of exile manifested in the form of literary, artistic, and political expressions. Exile was part of colonial practice, beginning in the second half of the eighteenth century when the Dutch East India Company was establishing a stronger foothold in Java by intervening in indigenous political affairs, and continuing through the late colonial state in Indonesia. Colonial practices of exile in early modern Indonesia were peculiar, especially those involving members of indigenous royal families. Certain peculiarities were manifest in the way exiles were confined and treated and in their response to their condition. The available Javanese sources, mainly in the form of *babads,* are silent on many instances of exile from Java, while others are revealed in these historical and literary works.

Babads, or Javanese chronicles, appeared in various forms. During their early development, in the eighteenth century, *babads* were produced inside the Javanese royal courts by the court poets. They were written to glorify the king and used to legitimate his power. At a later stage, beginning in the early nineteenth century, *babads* became an integral part of royal families' intellectual activities. Many members of royal families, including the sultans of Yogyakarta and the *Sunans* of Surakarta, had *babads* ascribed to their names. Modern philologists have categorized *babad* as a traditional genre of writing history in Java, while historians of modern Indonesia have regarded *babads* as primary historical sources.[3]

In early modern Java very few *babads* were written outside the palaces of Surakarta and Yogyakarta. Some were categorized as *Babad Pasisiran,* produced along Java's northern coast, while others were written even farther afield. *Babad Mangkudiningratan* and *Babad Dipanegara* were among the few *babads* written in exile. *Babad Mangkudiningratan,* the subject of this chapter, was written in three different places—Penang, Batavia, and Ambon—in the second decade of the nineteenth century. *Babad Dipanegara,* the subject of Peter Carey's important book,[4] was written in Makassar in the first half of the nineteenth century.

Babad Mangkudiningratan shares many features with other *babads* written within the courts of Surakarta and Yogyakarta in the nineteenth century, yet it also exhibits aspects that reflect its unusual production site and writing circumstances. The existence of *Babad Mangkudiningratan* as an intellectual product of exile allows for an exploration of some common dimensions of colonial exile, including above all a consideration of the ways in which those exiled experienced their physical and cultural displacement.

The events taking place in Java, especially in central Java, during the transition period from the fall of the Dutch East India Company at the end of the eighteenth century until the first half of the nineteenth century have been extensively studied by Peter Carey.[5] This period witnessed many events beyond the Java War (1825–1830), which was its main focus, including the attack on the court of Yogyakarta by the British army in 1813 and the looting of the palace by British soldiers, the foundation of the Pakualam dynasty, and the exile of Sultan Hamengkubuwana II and his two sons, Mangkudiningrat and Mertasana, to Penang, Batavia, and Ambon.[6]

In 1795 the French invaded the Dutch Republic. They established the Batavian Republic and the Kingdom of Holland in 1806. The Kingdom of Holland was annexed to the First French Empire in 1810, and Java became a titular French colony, though it continued to be administered and defended primarily by Dutch personnel. Java remained in Dutch hands throughout the French Revolutionary and Napoleonic Wars. In 1799, the first sultan of Yogyakarta, Sultan Hamengkubuwana I, passed away. His successor, Mas Sundoro, later to be crowned Sultan Hamengkubuwana II, was, like his predecessor, anti-European. The first major political decision he made was to replace his *patih* (prime minister), Danureja II, who was very loyal to the Dutch. He also wrote a book, *Serat Surya Raja*, in which he interpreted the "end of the universe" as the end of the dual kingdoms of Java (Surakarta and Yogyakarta). This can be interpreted as an expression of his wish to unite Surakarta and Yogyakarta as one strong kingdom under his command. It was a desire that contradicted the Dutch colonial policy of weakening Javanese political power.

In 1808 Daendels, the newly appointed governor of the Dutch East Indies, introduced new rules concerning the relationship between the European and indigenous rulers. Hamengkubuwana II strongly opposed the new rules, which were viewed as undermining the dignity and social status of indigenous rulers. The conflict with Daendels continued when Sultan Hamengkubuwana II supported the rebellion of Radèn Rangga against Daendels, a move that finally cost him the throne. In 1810, Daendels removed Hamengkubuwana II from the palace for supporting the rebellion, and the crown prince was installed as his successor.

During the same period drastic political change was unfolding in Europe. The British rose as prominent actors of European overseas expansion. After the fall of the French colonies in the West Indies in 1809 and 1810, and a successful campaign against French possessions in Mauritius in 1810 and 1811, British attention turned to the Dutch East Indies. Daendels failed to defend Java against a British amphibious operation between August and September 1811 and left the country. In the same year Thomas Stamford Raffles was appointed governor of the Dutch East Indies. During the transition of power from Daendels to Raffles, Sultan Hamengkubuwana II, who had been dethroned by Daendels, took over power from his son, who was returned to his earlier position as crown prince.

In 1812 Raffles' government discovered a hidden correspondence between Sultan Hamengkubuwana II and Susuhunan Pakubuwana IV of Surakarta to rid Java of the British. The letters the kings had exchanged were leaked by an important figure inside the sultanate. Hamengkubuwana II was once again dethroned, this time by Raffles: in 1812 the British army invaded the palace of Yogyakarta and took Hamengkubuwana II and his family into custody. The crown prince was reinstalled as sultan of Yogyakarta. The success of the British invasion of Yogyakarta was owed to the collaboration of two prominent figures within the court: Natakusuma, the brother of Sultan Hamengkubuwana II, and Tan Jin Sing, the Chinese captain of Yogyakarta. As a reward for assisting the British, Natakusuma was installed as the founding ruler of Pura Pakualaman, the newly established "minor court" of Yogyakarta, and Tan Jin Sing was installed as regent.

THE *BABAD'S* STRUCTURE

Babad Mangkudiningratan, a Javanese chronicle, belongs to the Library of Pura Pakualaman in Yogyakarta (Code. 237/PP73, Bb. 20). Pura Pakualaman, founded in 1813 by the British government in Java, had as its first prince Natakusuma, later called Pakualam I (1813–1829), son of the first sultan of Yogyakarta. Natakusuma played a prominent role in helping the British army invade the sultan's palace and force Sultan Hamengkubuwana II to step down. The *Babad Mangkudiningratan*'s author is unknown, but no doubt it was written by a person who was exiled along with the sultan's family to three different places in sequence between 1813 and 1826: Penang, Batavia, and Ambon. The manuscript, which is undated, mentions that it was written in Penang, but it was likely also written in Batavia and Ambon, because it describes events in these two sites during a subsequent period. Considering the manuscript's title, it was allegedly written under the instruction of Pangéran Mangkudiningrat. Written in Javanese in both the *krama* (high) and *ngoko* (low) registers, it incorporates many Kawi (old Javanese) and Malay words. It is written in Javanese and *pegon* characters (Javanese written in the Arabic script), although the latter is used only on the first and second pages. The manuscript is composed in *tembang macapat,* Javanese traditional meters, in fifteen cantos. The meters employed include *asmarandana, durma, pangkur, dhandhanggula, sinom, mijil, maskumambang,* and *pucung*. The *Babad* narrates the experiences of the family of Hamengkubuwana II chronologically, beginning with the British attack on the palace of Yogyakarta and ending with Mangkudiningrat's fate in Ambon. It was written in the form of a journal, with the dates of the events written at the top of each page or episode. Judging from the detailed information presented in the *Babad*, the author was deeply involved with the family of Hamengkubuwana II, especially with Mangkudiningrat, whose experiences constitute the bulk of the *Babad*'s narration.

In terms of authorial perspective it is quite clear that the *Babad* was composed on behalf of Hamengkubuwana II's family, to enhance the reputation of Mangkudiningrat, who was described by the Dutch as rebellious and ambitious. In some sections of the *Babad* the author presented Mangkudiningrat's positions in the political disputes involving his father and the British; in others Mangkudiningrat is described as a loving son and a loyal family member.

SUMMARY OF THE *BABAD*

In its opening stanza the author announces that the purpose of writing the *Babad* is "to alleviate the pain." The author begins his story with a portrayal of political events in Yogyakarta in the early nineteenth century, when the sultanate was ruled by Sultan Hamengkubuwana II. The Chinese captain of Yogyakarta,[7] Tan Jin Sing, reported to Resident Crawfurd that Sultan Hamengkubuwana II was plotting rebellion against the British colonial government; he suggested that the Resident take immediate measures to dispose of the rebellious sultan. He also offered assistance should the British government launch a military campaign against Yogyakarta. British soldiers marched immediately to Yogyakarta and prepared for a massive assault on the palace. Governor Raffles wrote to the sultan suggesting resignation and the handing over of his throne to the crown prince, Pangéran Surojo, and set an ultimatum that the sultan must surrender by noon or else British troops would attack the palace. However, the sultan was determined to fight against the British rather than surrender.[8]

British soldiers attacked from the north, east, and southeast sides of the palace (*kraton*) walls, and the sultan and his soldiers failed in their defense. The British army rushed into the palace, preventing the sultan from escaping or fighting back, and demanded his surrender. The crown prince and his wife were captured but soon released when the prince was able to produce the stamp, signifying his special status, entrusted to him by Captain Tan Jin Sing. Meanwhile, the sultan and his son Mangkudiningrat were captured and brought to the resident's office by Crawfurd. The sultan's property was confiscated and much of the court was destroyed. Three sons of Hamengkubuwana II, Mangkudiningrat, Kusumayuda, and Yudadijaya were forced to pay their respects to the newly anointed Sultan Hamengkubuwana III. The next morning the new sultan paid a visit to the Chinese Captain Tan Jing Sing to thank him for his help in elevating him to the throne. Meanwhile Mangkudiningrat was brought back to the resident's house as captive and accused of sending a spy to the house of the Chinese captain.[9] After an exchange of letters with Crawfurd, Raffles decided to send Hamengkubuwana II and his family into exile. Penang was chosen as the site of exile since the British army had built a military stronghold on the island.

THE JOURNEY BEGINS: SULTAN HAMENGKUBUWANA II AND FAMILY DEPART FOR SEMARANG

The son of the regent of Semarang, Radèn Saleh, was the British envoy who was to meet Sultan Hamengkubuwana II and Mangkudiningrat before they departed for Penang. Mangkudiningrat used the meeting to explain what in fact had transpired in Yogyakarta, particularly regarding the false accusation that he had been involved in sending a spy to the Chinese quarter (*pecinan*). He reassured Radèn Saleh that the spy had not been sent by him or by his father but rather by the crown prince. The discussion turned also to the relatives of the sultan and Mangkudiningrat who would be permitted to accompany them into exile. The sultan proposed a few names, including his principal wife, Ratu Kencana, and his two daughters, Ratu Timur and Ratu Sasi. Apart from his family, four other names of those who might accompany him were mentioned: Tumenggung (ministers) Prawiranata, Wiryaduwirya, Brangtakusuma, and Sesmitaraga.[10]

Mangkudiningrat, however, decided not to take any members of his family along except his wife from Nitipuran. He said he would take all responsibility and bear all misery on his own. Through Radèn Saleh he committed to the British governor the care of his mother, Kanjeng Ratu Mas, his wife Radèn Ayu of Serang, and twenty-three other family members. On the following day Radèn Saleh returned to meet the sultan carrying gold shirt-buttons belonging to the sultan that had been stolen by British soldiers. Radèn Saleh returned these to the sultan and conveyed Raffles' promise to grant an amount of five hundred ringgit to the sultan's children and guards. The *Babad* also mentions that just before the sultan and family departed for Penang, the regent of Semarang sent his sons, Radèn Saleh and Radèn Sokur, to accompany the sultan's family on pilgrimage to Kadilangu, site of the graves of Pangéran Wijil and Radèn Ayu Batang.[11] Pangéran Wijil, otherwise known as Panembahan Hadi, was a member of the sultan of Demak's family whose genealogy reached back to the founder of the Mataram kingdom, Senapati. Radèn Ayu Batang was the first wife of the greatest sultan of Mataram, Sultan Agung, who launched a military expedition against the Dutch East India Company twice, in 1628 and 1629. In Javanese culture, pilgrimage to the graves of ancestors or holy figures is considered a pious and advisable act, believed to impart mystical benefits on the pilgrims. The spirits of these powerful ancestors would, it was hoped, assist the soon-to-be exiles with the challenges they faced.

The wealth of information found in this *Babad* might be comparable only to a similar account written by Pangéran Arya Panular in *Babad Bedhahing Ngayogyakarta*[12] and the work of the Javanese exiled prince Dipanegara, *Babad Dipanegara*. These Javanese chronicles were written where events transpired and in their immediate aftermath, whereas most other Javanese chronicles that describe exile, such as those discussed by Ronit Ricci in chapter 4, were written at a fair distance from the actual events, in terms of both place and time, and offer far less detail and nuance.

SULTAN HAMENGKUBUWANA II AND FAMILY DEPART FOR PENANG

On Thursday the sixth of Rejeb in the year Alip (1813), the ship *Pranenggya* brought the sultan and his family to Penang via Batavia. The *Babad* mentions that the son of General Lord Minto, George Elliot (twenty-eight years old at the time), was responsible for transporting the sultan and his family to Penang.[13] Finally, after two days' stopover in Batavia, the ship anchored in Penang. The exiles were welcomed with thirteen canon shots and received by Colonel Colin Mackenzie,[14] who showed them to their residence in exile. Mackenzie arranged a welcome dinner at the British lodge, where the sultan and family were introduced to Tuan Sayid Ali, the local ruler of Penang who advised the sultan to accept his destiny. The *Babad* also decribes how during dinner the conversation turned to the natural succession in England: when the king is old and frail it is right to hand over power to his successor. It seems that Sayid Ali was someone who was given a special task by the British government to persuade the exiled Sultan to accept his fate given the fact that the sultan was more than sixty years old.[15]

After several weeks in Penang, the sultan wrote to the British authorities in Java to reconsider the fate of his son Pangéran Mangkudiningrat who, he claimed, had been a victim of slander, accused of sending a spy to the *pecinan*. In his letter the sultan reassured the British that his son did not commit this act, and therefore he did not deserve to be punished by exile. The British authorities in Java never replied to the letter.[16]

After fifty five days in Penang the sultan and his family were moved to a new residence, and Governor Willem Pieter indulged the sultan by meeting all his needs.[17] Meanwhile the sultan was kept informed of the situation in Yogyakarta by the governor and the envoy of the regent of Semarang, Sayid Anwar. The newly appointed king, Sultan Hamengkubu-wana III, was now facing difficulties caused by opposition and disloyalty among the court families.[18] The sultan was also living in poverty after British forces' attack and looting of the palace. A rumor even claimed that the new sultan was forced to step down. Three months after the sultan arrived in Penang Willem Pieter paid a visit to the sultan's residence for the first time. The sultan used the opportunity to discuss his fate. As it had been promised that he would be exiled for only three months, he questioned why there was no indication from the British ruler as to when he would be brought back to Yogyakarta. The sultan was advised by the British authorities in Penang to write to those in Java. Several letters had been sent to Java but there had hitherto been no response from Raffles.[19]

Sayid Husein, like Sayid Ali, was entrusted by the British authorities in Penang with the task of persuading the sultan to remain calm in facing his fate in exile. Sayid Husein invited the sultan and his family to his residence for parties and performances of Chinese *wayang, wayang keling,* Siamese, and Kedah dances. On such occasions Sayid Husein approached the sultan and persuaded him to forget his ambition of reclaiming the throne from his son. He suggested the sultan assure the British authorities in Java of his disavowal of the throne in a written statement so that the British would allow him and his family to return to Java. The sultan followed Sayid Husein's suggestion and wrote such a letter.[20]

During their exile in Penang, the members of Sultan Hamengkubu-wana II's family were not entirely alienated from the outside world. The British gave them freedom to receive visitors, who informed the sultan and his family of developments in and around Penang, and even of those in Europe. When the sultan and his family were honored as guests at dinners held by British officials in Penang, they were told of political developments in Europe. They also received news from Java carried by Javanese pilgrims who stopped in Penang en route to Mecca.

It seems that the exile of Sultan Hamengkubuwana II in Penang came to the attention of an Acehnese Arab by the name of Sayid Muhammad, who paid a visit to the sultan to comfort him with religious advice and stories of the prophets. He also advised him to surrender his fate to God and keep praying for his salvation.[21] The old sultan also received his subject, a man named Kyai Angga, from Kedu, when he stopped in Penang on his way to Mecca. Kyai Angga came with presents and letters from the sultan's wives and family in Yogyakarta. He also updated the sultan on political developments in Yogyakarta since the time he had left the palace. He reported that Yogyakarta was in chaos and that the land of Kedu had been given to the British and the Chinese Captain Tan Jin Sing. He revealed that the sultan's wife and three of his sons remained in the palace but all the wives of Mangkudiningrat had left the palace and returned to their own parents. Radèn Ayu Serang, one of the wives of Mangkudiningrat, and her son Radèn Mas Suwija were seriously ill. Meanwhile, Radèn Ayu Anem, who was promised permission by the British to accompany Mangkudiningrat into exile, had returned to her village in Nitipuran. Kyai Angga also handed over a piece of *kain* (cloth) and *minyak kasai* (perfume) to Mangkudiningrat from his beloved mother, Ratu Mas.[22]

The *Babad* also depicted Mangkudiningrat's private life: his feelings, thoughts, and relationship with his father. The sultan was already more than sixty years old, weak and frail. During the journey from Semarang to Penang, Mangkudiningrat and other accompanying relatives had to massage his body regularly. However the sultan was still eager to take a young woman to comfort him during this time. Not long after arriving in Penang the sultan expressed his love for a young Malay girl. Mangkudiningrat did not favor the sultan's desire to marry the girl since he felt the sultan should not betray his wives who remained in Yogyakarta.[23]

Mangkudiningrat expressed his disapproval to his father and the sultan agreed. They prayed together, asking for forgiveness. Mangkudiningrat swore to remain faithful to the wives he had left behind in Yogyakarta. He prayed that he would remain strong in his faith and that all the family members who were left in Yogyakarta, especially his son and daughter Suwija and Rukmini, would remain strong and committed to him. Mangkudiningrat vowed to bear all the sorrow by himself.[24] Several months later Mangkudiningrat's loyalty to his wives was tested when a girl from Palembang, Encik Sumekar, expressed her feelings toward him. She revealed that she had fallen in love with him and she promised to devote herself to him, to serve and follow him wherever he went. Concurrently, Mangkudiningrat received a letter from his wife in Yogyakarta saying she did not dare to join him in exile. Mangkudiningrat was sad and could only respond with prayer. He invited a few local Muslim leaders to pray on behalf of the thirty-seven family members he left behind in Yogyakarta and on his own behalf.[25]

In his loneliness Mangkudiningrat always remembered his mother, Ratu Mas. He consulted with his spiritual adviser, Haji Dulgani, and shared his feelings toward his beloved mother, saying that as a good son he had paid his debt to his father by accompanying him into exile but had neglected to fulfill his obligation to his mother. He felt he had not made his mother happy. He struggled to contain his eagerness to return to Java. Mangkudiningrat asked Haji Dulgani to convey his impatience to return to Yogyakarta to his father. Responding to Mangkudiningrat's wish, Haji Dulgani took him to meet his father to convey his anxiety and eagerness. On behalf of Mangkudiningrat, Haji Dulgani told the exiled sultan that if the newly appointed sultan resigned, Mangkudiningrat would not wish to be a successor but would appeal to pass the throne to his descendant (his only son remained in Yogyakarta). By doing so he could make his mother, Ratu Mas, happy. The exiled sultan had no objection, but everything now was in Batavia's hands, and the exiled men could only await a decision.[26]

The sultan had repeatedly petitioned the British authorities in Penang and Java regarding the end of his exile. Time passed, and they had already spent more than a year in exile, but still there was no sign that they would be allowed to return to Java. To persuade the British government, they had asked two of his sons, Mangkudiningrat and Martasana, to voluntarily offer themselves as "adopted sons" (*anak pupon*)[27] of the British. The sultan also wrote yet another letter to the British authorities, requesting repatriation. In his letter the sultan personified himself as a white thread that could be colored with red or black. In other words, he was ready to be treated according to British wishes as long as he was allowed to return to Java. Replying to the sultan's request, Mackenzie said that all the letters sent were now under discussion in Batavia and that Raffles and the Dutch were still negotiating a new agreement. Therefore, the sultan should wait for good news from Batavia.[28]

In his desperation the sultan asked for Mangkudiningrat's opinion about the sultan's attitude toward the British while he was still in power. Mangkudiningrat replied that his father should be aware that he had ascended to the throne thanks to the Dutch East India Company.[29] As a subject of the Dutch East India Company, and later the British, he should have been obedient to whatever these authorities desired. If his father had accepted this reality sincerely, perhaps he would never have been exiled. And if his father still had the ambition to regain power, this would only cause him and his family additional misery.[30]

THE SULTAN AND HIS FAMILY RETURN TO JAVA

After several years in exile, the long-awaited good news finally arrived: Colonel Mackenzie announced that the sultan and family would soon be returned to Java. The colonel, however, cautioned the sultan that he should forget his desire to return to power. Replying to Makenzie's advice the sultan said that he just wanted to go home, to die and be buried in his homeland. On that occasion Mackenzie also informed the sultan that the newly appointed sultan, Hamengkubuwana III, had just passed away due to a serious illness, and that Radèn Mas Bagus Timur had been appointed as his successor. Again the sultan fully surrendered, since he knew he was now old and weak. He also showed no objection since the newly crowned king was his own grandson. The long-awaited day finally came and after the farewell party was over the sultan and his family boarded a ship under Captain Dhuri and sailed to Batavia.[31]

During his exile in Penang, Mangkudiningrat decided not to take a new wife or concubine because of his loyalty to his wives and for the sake of the happiness of the family he left in Yogyakarta. This, however, did not mean that he refrained from entertaining a close relationship with a woman. When the news about his departure to Java was announced by the British authority, there was a young girl who cried for him. Her name was Dyah Ludiyah, an Ambonese girl who lived in Penang. It seems that Mangkudiningrat had fallen in love with this girl, yet the *Babad* recounts that despite this love they remained close friends and did not marry because of his loyalty to his Yogyakarta wives. Mangkudiningrat described Dyah Ludiyah as a beautiful woman who loved to wear red *sinjang lurik* (textile decorated with vertical lines) and white *kabaya* (traditional Javanese or Malay woman's dress) with gold ornaments and who wore her hair in the Chinese bun style. He likened her to Ragil Kuning, the princess of Jenggala. The mole under her right eyelid and the smile that always shone whenever she spoke made her look exceedingly lovely.[32]

In Batavia

Sultan Hamengkubuwana II and his family arrived in Batavia from Penang but did not immediately meet Raffles, who at the time was still in Surakarta to meet Susuhunan Pakubuwana IV, ruler of Surakarta. Rumor claimed that the *susuhunan* was behind the British sepoy conspiracy.[33] It seems Raffles viewed it as a serious event and decided to leave Batavia for Surakarta. The sultan and his family were housed in the area of Kampung Jaga Monyet. In Batavia, Mangkudiningrat received word that his wife Radèn Ayu Sepuh of Serang had died of illness. Concurrently, there was news that British forces that had arrived from Bengal were to be deployed to Surakarta to attack the susuhunan. Meanwhile, the exiled sultan received the envoys of his wives Ratu Mas and Ratu Kencana, who brought a letter from his younger brother Pangéran Jayakusuma. The letter informed him of the latest situation in Yogyakarta, reporting that the sons of Hamengkubuwana II were preparing for rebellion against Sultan Hamengkubuwana IV. The exiled sultan replied to his brother that he did not agree with the plan and suggested they remain calm and keep the peace. Meanwhile, after the death of his wife Radèn Ayu Sepuh, Mangkudiningrat married Siti Jaleka, the granddaughter of Sawunggaling of Surabaya.[34]

After a few weeks in Batavia the sultan sent his envoys to Semarang carrying his letter for Raffles, but the British authorities in Semarang advised the sultan not to write any additional letters to Raffles because the British would soon be replaced by the Dutch. Another letter sent from Batavia, this time by Mangkudiningrat and Mertasana, reminded the British that according to the agreement they made in Semarang, they would both be exiled for only three months, and urged them to allow their return to Yogyakarta.[35]

The transition of power from the British to the Dutch in Batavia was about to transpire. The Dutch ship that brought John Fendal, the man charged with accepting the transfer of sovereignty from the British, had arrived in Batavia. However, the major flood that hit Batavia at that time delayed the transfer of power by several days. The *Babad* also noted that in the following days Susuhunan Pakubuwana IV of Surakarta and his family arrived in Batavia as captives. Pakubuwana IV was accused by the British government in Java of encouraging the sepoy army to rebel against Raffles. Meanwhile, Hamengkubuwana II and Mangkudiningrat wrote several more letters to the new governor of Batavia, asking about the government's intention to return them to Yogyakarta, yet not a single reply was received from the Dutch.[36]

Wouter Hendrik van Ijsseldijk was appointed to receive authority over Java from the British in 1816 following the departure of the British armies to Bengal. Godert van der Cappelen was appointed the new governor in Java, and for the first time the Dutch flag replaced the British one. The news about the arrival of Sultan Hamengkubuwana II in Batavia was heard by Tan Jin Sing, the head of the Chinese community who had assisted the British to topple the sultan. At the same time, the newly appointed governor invited four regents of Yogyakarta to discuss political developments in the sultanate.[37] The Chinese captain was anxious about the four regents communicating with the exiled sultan while visiting Batavia and therefore warned them to keep their distance from him.

Another effort made by Sultan Hamengkubuwana II to meet the Dutch authorities in Batavia failed. Engelhard, one of the Dutch officers in Batavia, informed him that the governor was still very busy. A few weeks later word came from the Dutch governor that Sultan Hamengkubuwana II and family would be sent to Ambon. Engelhard, who was in charge of telling the sultan and his family the news, explained that the Dutch authorities were still of the opinion that the sultan was considered a dangerous man who entertained too many expectations of the Dutch.[38]

In Ambon

The sultan and his family, guarded by four hundred Javanese and eighty Dutch soldiers, departed for Ambon in 1817.[39] Mangkudiningrat and his brother Mertasana were hosted in Baturapta, to the east of the house of Resident Middelkoop in Ambon.[40]

Soon after they arrived in Ambon, there was a massive rebellion led by a young man named Patimura, an Ambonese from Saparua. The rebellion was triggered by a taxation system introduced by the Dutch. According to the *Babad Mangkudiningratan*, Patimura's adviser was a Javanese, presumably a man exiled from Surakarta or Yogyakarta on account of his involvement in the war against the Dutch East India Company in the second half of the eighteenth century. The Dutch officials in Ambon were anxious about the sultan making contact with Patimura's Javanese adviser, so to prevent communication between the rebels and the sultan and his family, the Dutch decided to remove the latter from their residences to the Dutch ship.[41]

The wives of the sultan and Mangkudiningrat arrived in Ambon aboard a British ship and joined their husbands imprisoned inside the Dutch ship. A few days later Engelhard arrived in Ambon to visit the sultan. He informed him that Mangkudiningrat's fate was now under discussion. Meanwhile, Patimura's rebellion ended after hundreds of Dutch soldiers were dispatched to Ambon. After the war the sultan and his family were once more allowed on land.[42]

After peace in Ambon was attained, Sultan Hamengkubuwana II was finally allowed to return to Yogyakarta. Meanwhile, Mangkudiningrat had made several attempts to gain permission to return to Java, yet his efforts were never acknowledged by the Dutch. He remained in Ambon until his death in 1822. During his stay in Ambon, Mangkudiningrat was known as a *tabib* (traditional healer) who was skillful in curing various kinds of diseases. To the people of Ambon he was known as Panji Angon Asmoro.[43]

The *Babad* gives the impression that it is an unfinished work. Its title indicates that it would recount Mangkudiningrat's life in exile, but it concludes while he is still exiled. Two speculations can be offered regarding why the *Babad* ended abruptly once the sultan was allowed to return to Java. First, perhaps the author of the *Babad* was a man who followed the sultan upon his return to Java. However, if true, this would raise the question of why the author did not recount the sultan's homecoming. Second, perhaps this *Babad* was written by Mangkudiningrat himself, and it was brought back to Java by his father to be preserved and given to his family in Yogyakarta. This also might be an adequate explanation for why the *Babad* is now kept in the library of the Pakualam court in Yogyakarta.

MANGKUDININGRAT, THE *BABAD*, AND THE PAKUALAM DYNASTY

Before further exploring the *Babad Mangkudiningratan* as a cultural product of exilic life, it is important to consider why the *Babad* was kept at the Pakualam court and has become its intellectual property. This question can be answered by looking at the family tree of the Pakualam dynasty. Mangkudiningrat would never return to Yogyakarta, as he died in Ambon on 13 March 1822. And yet he was the man who created significant genealogical links between the Pakualam dynasty and Siti Jaleka, the woman he married in Batavia. It seems that the *Babad* was brought to Java by the author or the sultan and given to Siti Jaleka. When she passed away, the *Babad* was inherited by her daughter, Gusti Kanjeng Ratu Ayu, a woman who according to Javanese tradition was considered *andaneswari,* or endowed with *wahyu kedaton,* divine revelation or inspiration, indicating she was destined for greatness.[44] Gusti Kanjeng first married Nataningrat, the son of Pakualam II (1830–1858), and after the death of her husband was taken by Pakualam III (1858–1864) as his second main wife. Her son with her first husband was anointed Pakualam IV (1864–1878), and her daughter with Pakualam III, a second Siti Jaleka (taking her late grandmother's name), married Pakualam VI (1901–1902). The subsequent leaders of Pakualaman, Pakualam VII through Pakualam X, were their descendants. After the death of her husband Pakualam III, she married Pakualam V (1878–1890).[45]

PHYSICAL AND CULTURAL SPACES OF EXILE

There are few indications, within the limits of the narrative, to suggest that each physical site of exile brought about intellectual and mental transformations, especially to Mangkudiningrat. The *Babad* devotes abundant words to describing social and political events in exile, especially in Penang and Ambon, and it highlights the movement of armies, officials, and social activities such as dinners and meetings. There is no clear physical description of the island, the fortress, the settlement, or even the houses where the exiled were living. Perhaps the author himself was not very conscious of the place where he spent his exile since his mind was filled with longing for family and homeland. The influence of the physical spaces on the mental and intellectual lives of the exiles could be traced by examining historical books and reports about the development of Penang during the period. Andrew Barber describes Penang in the beginning of the nineteenth century as a "classic colonial port settlement" though following no preordained plan. Its development was influenced by colonial agendas, economic pressures, and the contributions of myriad settlers and migrants. It was built with a fort, government buildings, a central *padang*, or grass square, and an exclusive residential area for the mostly European commercial and elite officials.[46] Its environment contrasted sharply with that of Yogyakarta, which was an inland kingdom with open *pendapa* (the main part of a Javanese traditional house) and quiet settlements surrounded by rice fields.

The crowded and dynamic environment of the town of Penang did not offer comfort to the exiled. On the contrary, it fostered loneliness and displacement. There is no doubt that in almost every paragraph the *Babad* depicts the anxiety, sadness, loneliness and regrets of the exiles, who found two ways in which to aleviate their pain and sorrow: as mentioned in the opening sentences of the *Babad*, writing itself was healing, and writing the diary, as well as letters to their relatives and the colonial authorities, were ways to ease the sorrow and desolation; the other way, echoing the *Babad Giyanti*'s depiction, discussed in Ricci's chapter 4, was to devote more attention to religious activities, inviting religious leaders and seeking their advice and stories. Especially in Penang, the sultan and his sons often received envoys and guests from cultural and religious backgrounds similar to their own, asking them for counsel. The exiled also attended local performances including *wayang* and dances, and interacted with local elites, British officials, and society. The *Babad* itself adopts many Malay words, attesting to social interaction with local society. The old sultan, despite his age and limited power, was still attracted to a young woman. The same held true for Mangkudiningrat, who with all his promises to remain loyal to the family still fell in love with the young Ambonese girl whom he described as the princess of Jenggala. The poetic meter (*tembang*) suddenly turned to *asmaradana*—a meter associated with love and longing—when the *Babad* described the girl he very much adored.

In Batavia the exiles spent only a few weeks in unexpected physical and political conditions. Batavia was busy preparing for the transition of power. Various treaties and agreements made between the two powers had to be implemented, and the exiles' arrival constituted a minor issue. They were housed in the Kampung Jaga Monyet, which was outside the city walls, where they experienced a great flood that severely affected the city and daily life for some time. But in Batavia social life was easier, and during their weeks there the exiles had more contact with relatives, if only by way of letters and short visits. Amazingly, a wedding ceremony between Mangku-diningrat and Siti Jaleka was successfully conducted.

The period of exile in Ambon was quite extended and the conditions were completely different. There were no official parties, dancing, perfor-mances, or encounters with local people or other visitors. The exiles were confined to the Dutch ship for a few months and alienated from Ambon's social world, especially during the local rebellion led by Patimura in 1817. However, the author of the *Babad* was still well informed about the rebel-lion, descriptions of which filled the final part of the *Babad*, with only several stanzas devoted to the sultan and family. The exiles spent almost ten years in Ambon, but the author of the *Babad* dedicated only a few pages to de-picting the final years of their lives there. Presumably, after Patimura's re-bellion, political circumstances prevented the author from continuing his writing. The last stanza of the *Babad*, composed in *dhandhanggula*, contains only seven of ten expected lines and may indicate that the author was sud-denly forced to cease writing.

To what extent the content of the *Babad*, particularly the accuracy of events described by the author, can be confirmed by additional contempo-rary sources requires further research. The same is true regarding the Dutch perceptions of the exiles. In his work on the history of the outbreak of the Java War, Peter Carey describes the psychological and mental condition of the exiles based on European sources, including the impression of a Euro-pean official. Carey writes,

> As for the old sultan, he appears to have withstood both his journey into exile and his initial period of banishment in Pulau Pinang [Penang] with fortitude . . . both the exiled ruler and his party conducted themselves with "the greatest propriety and consistency." Indeed, he would live long enough to be reinstalled on the Yogya throne in August 1826 during the darkest period of the Java War. By then, however, he had lost much of his fierce energy. . . . Fourteen years of sorrow and humiliation had taken their toll. . . . Ruling as a Dutch ally until his death on 3 January 1828, his last period as ruler would not be a happy one for the sultanate. Nevertheless, his presence both in exile and in Java, would remain a living inspiration for his religious and royal supporters in the *kasepuhan* party who flocked to see him in Batavia and Surabaya between his return from Pinang [Penang] in April 1815 and his re-exile to Ambon in January 1817.[47]

In Ambon the exiles experienced a different situation altogether. They arrived in Ambon just as a local rebellion was about to break out. Worst of all, they were suspected of being involved in the rebellion and were confined to the Dutch ship for a few months. By the end of the Patimura rebellion, life in exile became normal again. They were brought back to land and returned to their exiled residence. Mangkudiningrat took the new name Panji Among Asmara, which means "young knight who fell in love." Although he took a profession as traditional healer, the name tells something more private about what he experienced in exile.

As for Sultan Hamengkubuwana II, Carey also refers to a report written by Raffles when the British governor met the deposed Yogya monarch again in Semarang after his arrival on 4 July 1813, and informed him of his more lenient sentence of temporary banishment in Penang. He reacted with great relief, as quoted by Carey:

> Even the unfortunate Sultan has been considered of late comparatively happy, for on his first apprehension he certainly expected to have been put to death. That fear removed, transportation to Banda for life appeared inevitable and as bad as a second death. On his arrival here [in Semarang] this has since been mitigated to Pinang with a promise that if all things remain quiet, he shall in a few years be permitted to return and end his days in the land of his forefathers [Java].[48]

A *babad* written in exile, especially during the period of early modern Indonesia, is a precious source for modern historians. Perhaps *Babad Mangkudiningratan* is the only *babad* devoted in large part to exilic life, since *Babad Dipanegara*, written in Makassar around a decade later and also dealing with exile, mostly describes the life of the exiled prior to the experience itself. The preciousness of this kind of historical source is not limited to the *Babad*'s content but also encompasses the *Babad*'s composition under particular political circumstances. The European colonial practice of exile in early modern Indonesia in most cases was repressive. However, there were some peculiar features to this practice as regarded exiled royal families. The life in exile of Sultan Hamengkubuwana II and his family reflects some of these features, at least until the early years of their time in Ambon: they could still enjoy life partially out of confinement; they were still involved in parties, enjoying performances, women, social encounters, religious devotion, and access to writing and literature. In exile, the sultan and his family were still entitled to accompaniment by a court poet, or *pujangga,* whose main job was to record events the royals experienced. Thus, the *Babad Mangkudiningratan* itself represents this peculiar aspect of royal exile and its documentation, recounting what may have been the most luxurious exile experienced by Javanese royal families under Dutch colonial rule.

Repressive practices of colonial exile, which kept the exiled isolated, as discussed by Anand Yang (chapter 3, on Indian exiles) and Lorraine Paterson (chapter 9, on Vietnamese exiles), constituted perhaps the main reason behind the dearth of notes or other written documents produced in exile. In addition, as claimed by Ronit Ricci in chapter 4 on Javanese sources on exile to Ceylon, historians have not sufficiently explored the indigenous sources that do survive, in order to glean from them an understanding of local perspectives on exile, however partial and fragmentary. *Babads,* with their particular generic characteristics, as well as other Javanese writing traditions, need to be examined for what they reveal about the exilic experience and political circumstances, with colonial documents mined for additional information, whether complementary or contradictory. As Jean Gelman Taylor shows in chapter 7, inventories of documents on exile in the Cape of Good Hope have already helped historians to highlight some important and unexpected elements of exilic private and communal life. Future research in this direction is likely to reveal much more that is currently still hidden from view.

The study of *Babad Mangkudiningratan* contributes to an understanding of how the physical and cultural spaces of exile brought about a sense of loss and displacement. Despite enjoying certain privileges, the exiles could never feel a sense of belonging in their new surroundings. Sadness, loneliness, and grief were repeatedly depicted by the *Babad*'s author. The angst and sorrow directed the exiles toward spiritual devotions, and Mangkudiningrat, as portrayed in the *Babad,* was eager to devote more of his life to spiritual and religious causes, leaving his political ambitions behind. In the final episode of his life he committed himself to traditional healing, helping others in order to regain his self-esteem. Exile had significantly changed Mangkudiningrat and altered his way of thinking. This, however, was not the case for his father, Sultan Hamengkubuwana II, who remained steadfast in his ambition to return to power. Soon after his return to Java, political developments allowed him to be installed as the sultan of Yogyakarta for the third time.

In fact there was a hidden conflict in the court of Yogyakarta before the British assault on the court, with several factions competing for power. Natakusuma, the brother of Hamengkubuwana II, had harbored ambitions to become sultan; Hamengkubuwana's son, Mangkudiningrat, was also described by the British as possessing a similar desire. In addition, the sultan's anti-British attitude had invited opposition from his own *patih* and from the Chinese leader of Yogyakarta, Tan Jin Sing. The latter collaborated with the crown prince and the British to achieve their goal of deposing the sultan. The hidden agendas of each faction are missing from the *Babad*'s account of events. The accusation against Mangkudiningrat of having sent a spy to murder the Chinese captain was in fact quite vague. In this case he was slandered. Therefore, on several occasions, as narrated in the *Babad*, Mangku-diningrat and his father tried to clarify his position to the British government. The sultan and his family, as victims of Yogyakarta's political turmoil, needed to clarify their position not only to the British but also to the family that they had left behind. Exile was considered a humiliation. In the earliest stanzas the author of the *Babad* claims he wrote it to alleviate the pain. Clearly, the writing could not be interpreted merely as self-amusement but as a form of healing from vague accusations, slander, and the anguish of displacement.

The main goal of colonial exile was to tame rebellious attitudes, any ideas or actions that could threaten colonial power. In many cases exile was considered successful by colonial standards but in many other instances it gave rise to paradox. The experience could turn the exiles into different individuals and transform their personalities, making them submissive, moderate, or militant. The exile of the family of Sultan Hamengkubuwana II proved this paradox: Mangkudiningrat could forget his ambition to ascend the throne as sultan and turned to a healing profession, whereas Sultan Hamengkubuwana II maintained his desire to rule and succeeded in returning to power.

NOTES

1. Daendels was an important figure who defended several cities in the Netherlands, especially Amsterdam, against the invading Prussian Army. Louis Bonaparte made him colonel general in 1806 and governor general of the Dutch East Indies one year later. In Java, Daendels initiated important administrative and political changes, including demolishing the Castle of Batavia and replacing it with a new fort at Meester Cornelis (Jatinegara); building Fort Lodewijk in Surabaya; and building a hospital and military barracks in Surabaya and Semarang. His most important achievement was the construction of the Great Post Road across northern Java from Anjer to Panarukan.

2. Anonymous, *Babad Mangkudiningratan*, MS. Bb.20, Pura Pakualaman Library, Yogyakarta, n.d.

3. Many catalogues of Javanese manuscripts have been compiled, including those by Theodore Pigeaud on Indonesian manuscripts in the Netherlands, Merle C. Ricklefs on Indonesian manuscripts in Great Britain, Nancy K. Florida on Javanese manuscripts in Surakarta, Jennifer Lindsay and Alan Feinstein on Javanese manuscripts in Yogyakarta, Titik Pujiastuti on Javanese manuscripts at the University of Indonesia, and Sri Ratna Saktimulya on Javanese manuscripts in the Pakualaman. In these catalogues *babads* are categorized as a genre of historical writing. Many historians, including Ricklefs, Carey, Kumar, and Florida, have used *babads* as their primary sources for writing history.

4. Peter Carey, *Babad Dipanegara: An Account of the Outbreak of the Java War (1825–30)* (Kuala Lumpur: Arts Printer for the Malayan Branch of the Royal Asiatic Society, 1981).

5. Peter Carey, *The Power of Prophecy: Prince Dipanegara and the End of an Old Order in Java, 1785–1855* (Leiden: KITLV Press, 2008).

6. The *Babad* does not elaborate specifically on Mertasana and his fate during exile. There are no clues as to the reason for his banishment. It seems that Sultan Hamengkubuwana

II wanted his son Mertasana to accompany him into exile, as the British colonial government allowed the sultan to appoint members of his family as companions.

7. "Captain" here refers to the leader of the Chinese community in Yogyakarta.

8. *Babad Mangkudiningratan,* canto 1: 1–13. The crown prince was eligible for protection since he was expected by the British to succeed his father on the throne. Before the attack he had been given a particular stamp by Tan Jin Sing, who had been collaborating with the British in preparing the attack on the palace.

9. Ibid., canto 3: 25–40.

10. Ibid., canto 4: 3–12.

11. Ibid., canto 4: 30–33.

12. *Babad Bedhahing Ngayogyakarta* is a Javanese diary ascribed to Pangéran Arya Panular (one of the sons of Sultan Hamengkubuwana I). It describes the British assault on the Yogyakarta palace, which is also the focus of the early part of the *Babad Mangkudiningratan.* On *Babad Bedhahing Ngayogyakarta,* see Peter Carey, *The British in Java, 1811–1815: A Javanese Account* (Oxford: Oxford University Press, 1992).

13. *Babad Mangkudiningratan,* canto 4: 33–44.

14. Colonel Colin Mackenzie (1754–1821) was a Scottish army officer in the British East India Company who later became the first surveyor general of India. He spent two years (1811–1813) in Java during the period of British occupation and led a survey on the Javanese ancient heritage sites, which was published in three volumes.

15. *Babad Mangkudiningratan,* canto 4: 65–88.

16. Ibid., canto 4: 88–95.

17. Ibid., canto 5: 18.

18. Ibid., canto 6: 1–11.

19. Ibid., canto 5: 39–46.

20. Ibid., canto 6: 1–14.

21. Ibid., canto 7: 1–19.

22. Ibid., canto 7: 82–96.

23. Ibid., canto 5: 22–26.

24. Ibid., canto 5: 27–35.

25. Ibid., canto 5: 43–51.

26. Ibid., canto 7–8: 54–89; canto 8: 1–10.

27. This was a Javanese way to make peace with others, as practiced in Java during the Dutch period. The sultan and sunan regarded themselves as adopted sons of the Dutch Resident and the grandsons of the Governor General in Batavia.

28. *Babad Mangkudiningratan,* canto 8: 25–46.

29. Since the Treaty of Giyanti of 1755, which created the political foundation for the establishment of the Sultanate of Yogyakarta, all newly appointed sultans had to be approved by the Dutch East India Company. Sultan Hamenkubuwana II was appointed by the late Sultan Hamengkubuwana I with the approval of the Dutch East India Company.

30. *Babad Mangkudiningratan,* canto 9: 26–38.

31. Ibid., canto 10: 27–35.

32. Ibid., canto 10: 86–104.

33. On the conspiracy, see Peter Carey, "The Sepoy Conspiracy of 1815 in Java," *Bijdragen tot de Taal-, Land- en Volkenkunde* 133, no. 2 (1977): 294–322.

34. *Babad Mangkudiningratan,* canto 11: 28–75; canto 12: 1–37.

35. Ibid., canto 12: 43–79.

36. Ibid., canto 12: 84–100.

37. Ibid., canto 12: 107–140.

38. The Dutch were aware of the sultan's loyalties, his charisma, and his ambition to return to power. Their anxiety was proven justified when he returned from his final exile in Ambon and regained power as sultan in Yogyakarta for the third time. See also *Babad Mangkudiningratan*, canto 13.

39. Ambon is part of the Moluccas Islands in the eastern part of the Indonesian archipelago, located approximately fifteen hundred miles (2400 kilometers) from Batavia.

40. *Babad Mangkudiningratan*, canto 13: 24–52; canto 14: 1–6.

41. Ibid., canto 14: 7–19.

42. Ibid., canto 14: 20–42.

43. Ibid., canto 15: 10–20.

44. Sudariman Poerwokoesoemo, *Kadipaten Pakualaman* (Yogyakarta: Gadjah Mada University Press, 1985), 229.

45. Anonymous, *Silsilah Keluarga Pakualam sejak Pakualam I sampai Pakualam VIII* (Yogyakarta: Yayasan Notokusuma 1987).

46. Andrew Barber, *Penang under the East India Company, 1786–1858* (Kuala Lumpur: AB & A Publisher, 2009), 127.

47. Carey, *Power of Prophecy*, 363.

48. Ibid., 364.

BIBLIOGRAPHY

Primary Source

Anonymous. *Babad Mangkudiningratan*. MS. Bb.20. Pura Pakualaman Library, Yogyakarta, n.d.

Secondary Sources

Anonymous. *Silsilah keluarga Pakualam sejak Pakualam I sampai Pakualam VIII*. Yogyakarta: Yayasan Notokusuma, 1987.

Barber, Andrew. *Penang under the East India Company, 1786–1858*. Kuala Lumpur: AB & A Publisher, 2009.

Behrend, Timothy E., and Titik Pudjiastuti. *Katalog induk naskah-naskah Nusantara jilid 3-A, 3-B: Fakultas Sastra Universitas Indonesia*. Jakarta: Yayasan Obor Indonesia and Ecole Française d'Extrême Orient, 1997.

Carey, Peter. *Babad Dipanegara: An Account of the Outbreak of the Java War (1825–30)*. Kuala Lumpur: Arts Printer for the Malayan Branch of the Royal Asiatic Society, 1981.

———. *The British in Java, 1811–1815. A Javanese Account*. Oxford: Oxford University Press, 1992.

———. *The Power of Prophecy. Prince Dipanagara and the End of an Old Order in Java, 1785–1855*. Leiden: KITLV, 2008.

———. "The Sepoy Conspiracy of 1815 in Java." *Bijdragen tot de Taal-, Land- en Volkenkunde* 133, no. 2 (1977): 294–322.

Florida, Nancy K. *Javanese Literature in Surakarta Manuscripts: Introduction and Manuscripts of the Karaton Surakarta* vol. 1. Ithaca: Cornell University Press, 1993.

———. *Javanese Literature in Surakarta Manuscripts: Manuscripts of the Mangkunegaran Palace* vol. 2. Ithaca: Cornell University Press, 2000.

Lindsay, Jennifer, R. M. Soetanto, and Alan Feinstein, ed. *Kraton Yogyakarta. Katalog induk naskah Nusantara no. 2.* Jakarta: Yayasan Obor Indonesia, 1994.

Pigeaud, Theodore. *Literature of Java.* 3 vols. The Hague: Martinus Nijhoff, 1967–1970.

Poerwokoesoemo, Sudariman. *Kadipaten Pakualaman.* Yogyakarta: Gadjah Mada University Press, 1985.

Ricklefs, Merle Calvin, P. Voorhoeve, and Annabel Teh Gallop. *Indonesian Manuscripts in Great Britain. A Catalogue of Manuscripts in Indonesian Languages in British Public Collections. New Edition with Addenda et Corrigenda.* Jakarta: Ecole Française d'Extrême-Orient, Perpustakaan Nasional Republik Indonesia, and Yayasan Pustaka Obor Indonesia, 2014.

Saktimulya, Sri Ratna. *Katalog naskah-naskah perpustakaan Pura Pakualaman.* Jakarta: Yayasan Obor Indonesia and Toyota Foundation, 2005.

Six

Exile, Colonial Space, and Deterritorialized People in Eastern Indonesian History

Timo Kaartinen

Colonial governments used exile to control their opponents, to isolate them from the social networks from which they drew their support, and to populate newly created colonial space. This diversity of purposes reflects the political complexity of early colonial situations. European captains and trading companies initially faced indigenous political powers on their own ground, but soon began to establish limited bases for their own sovereign power in order to compete more effectively with one another. This colonial space created the conditions for assembling power relations in new ways. Indigenous people were drawn into these new configurations to be transported, disciplined, mobilized, and resettled, and forced to participate in military and commercial activities.

Much of the scholarship on colonial contexts has focused on the incorporation of indigenous peoples and polities into the imperial political order. A phenomenon that has received attention only more recently is what Europeans often interpreted as disorder: chaotic maritime polities,[1] smuggling,[2] and piracy.[3] This apparent disorder is not a symptom of displacement and resistance. Some of the people responded to their incorporation into the imperial system by replicating the imperial patterns of raiding and trading. They responded to the loss of political and cultural sovereignty by turning their localized, bounded societies into mobile, commercial communities.

In this chapter I discuss the relationship of banishment and exile to other deterritorializing effects of colonialism in the Dutch East Indies. I ask what effects it had for the creation of colonial space and the broader dynamics of power that were set in motion by Dutch policies between 1600 and 1880. The emerging colonial state used banishment and exile as the means of manipulating indigenous politics and as a fix for unexpected crises of legitimacy and anticolonial resistance. The colonizing powers initially tried to turn a number of indigenous polities into surrogates of their own power. When the leaders of these polities lost their legitimacy, the colonizers were forced to coerce and displace their opponents directly. Some of them were drawn to the space controlled by Europeans, while the rest were put on other trajectories.

Owing to its diverse political contexts and rationalizations, exile risks turning into a protean concept similar to, for instance, diaspora. Did exile mean voluntary or forced displacement? Were exiles subjected to a political order imposed by an empire or state, or did their "line of flight"[4] lead away from an order of this kind? These questions lead me to compare the colonial government's language about identity and place to that of the community of exiles.

I use "exile" in reference to movement away from "home" and into the colonial space. My argument, however, is that the deterritorializing dynamic of power underlying such movement also mobilized people in other ways. Some people remained outside the European domain of control and developed territorialities of their own. These migrants affirmed their distinct identities by naming their new settlements after the villages from which they had been forcibly removed.[5] It was only in the late nineteenth century that the colonial state began to set up a bureaucratic administration focused on localities rather than ethnic groups and peoples. Exile in this context resurfaces as a punitive measure against people who resist the territoriality of this new mode of rule.

The Politics of Exile under the Dutch East India Company

My case material is drawn from the Eastern Indonesian islands of Maluku, where I conducted long-term fieldwork in the 1990s and in 2009. This area came under the influence of European colonizing powers in the early sixteenth century when the Portuguese and Spanish sought to control it through alliances with local rulers. In the early seventeenth century, the Iberian colonizers were pushed aside by the newly formed Dutch East India Company (VOC), which was in control of the archipelago for two centuries.[6] The VOC's primary goal was to limit the cultivation of nutmeg and clove to areas under its direct control. It competed with local groups of Muslim traders and sought to eliminate them by two means: by depopulating large areas and by turning local polities into its allies. The VOC organized subordinate indigenous groups into a navy, which carried out sudden raids, known as *hongis,* on the villages of competing traders and spice cultivators east of the VOC bases in Maluku. Each major village provided a prescribed number of war canoes, known as *kora-kora,* to the VOC's war machine.[7] This navy was essential for controlling those parts of the archipelago that could not be reached by the company's large sailing ships.

During the seventeenth and eighteenth centuries, the VOC operated as a quasi state. The commanders of its fleets were empowered to make contracts with indigenous polities and to deploy military force in order to monopolize spice cultivation and trade. Direct Dutch presence was limited to strategically placed fortifications and the most important ports. The VOC seized the fort in Ambon City from the Portuguese in 1605[8] and controlled the northern coast of Ambon Island through an alliance with Hitu, a trading settlement that had been the VOC's most important ally in its campaign against the Portuguese.[9] Treaties with the sultan of Ternate in 1607[10] and the sultan of Tidore in 1657[11] turned the two north Maluku kingdoms into surrogates of nominal Dutch rule in the largely unknown periphery of Maluku.[12]

Exile served several ends in this political context. It separated leaders and noblemen from indigenous political hierarchies and networks and cultivated their affinity and subordination to the company. Initially at least, such "royal exile" was distinct from the use of punitive exile against criminals, illicit traders, and the opponents of Dutch rule. The VOC saw it as a means of grooming indigenous leaders and managing the relationship between indigenous and European power.

In 1606 Matelief de Jonge, leader of the fleet that tried to conquer Malacca from the Portuguese, took with him three sons of central Maluku chiefs "in order to groom them into princes."[13] One of them, Halaene, the twenty-year-old son of Kapitan Hitu, traveled all the way to the Netherlands and returned to Ambon in 1611.[14] The Dutch hopes for Halaene's political ascendancy were realized when he received the office of *hukum*.[15] The VOC had ensured his father's loyalty by granting him title to Ambon's best clove estates and a trading license. The extensive political networks of the *kapitan* family had helped the company against the Portuguese, but by the 1630s they had become a potential threat to the VOC's own interests. Halaene became the VOC's enemy when he was denied the trading rights enjoyed by his father.[16]

In a report from 1634, Artus Gijsels—the VOC director of trade in Ambon—warned his superiors that, in spite of befriending the company, Hitu was becoming a center of Muslim opposition against it throughout central Maluku. The new Kapitan Hitu—Halaene's father's successor—was a charismatic leader whom minor chiefs "followed like a shadow." Gijsels recommended that the company support Hitu's "legal constitution"—the formal superiority of its "king." Again, exile seemed to be the best way to manage the *kapitan*. "In short," Gijsels wrote, "I wish the Kapitan Hitu were in Batavia."[17]

Dutch policy toward Hitu reveals the territorializing effect of exile. In Maluku, *kapitan* is often the title of leaders who stand for society's capacity to engage in warfare and trade. Exiling them removes this expansive potential; the authority that remains is concerned with strictly local issues such as land and matrimonial rights. Evidently Gijsels understood this. The *kapitan* stood for a deterritorializing power similar to that of the VOC, and it was essential to make him a Company man.

PUNITIVE EXILE AND THE CREATION OF SUBJECTS

The exile of leaders and royalty served a wide range of purposes: education, diplomatic pressure, political blackmail, and punishment. Colonizers deemed exile to be an effective way of bending the will of colonized elites because of its "culturally degrading" effect on the convict (see Anderson, chapter 1 in this volume). Robert Townsend Farquhar, the officer who oversaw the short British occupation of Dutch colonies in Maluku during the Napoleonic Wars, argued that native inhabitants were "strongly affected by a sense of shame, and banishment from their country and families is one of the most mortifying and exemplary punishments" for them.[18] The Dutch initially staged spectacular public executions to deter their political opponents,[19] but the VOC regulations, found and translated by Farquhar in 1796, had a separate decree for exiling indigenous leaders. They would suffer "[p]erpetual banishment, confiscation of goods and incapacity of their children or kindred to succeed to any regency" if they allowed non-VOC traders to enter their area.[20] Evidently, however, the status claims of exiled Southeast Asian nobility often survived long-distance banishment and exile, and their kinship with rulers outside their own society was a source of legitimacy that the colonizers had to reckon with.[21]

The VOC used punitive exile on ordinary people as early as 1688, when it arrested a man called Toual for his involvement in the murder of VOC's Christian allies and exiled him permanently to Ceylon.[22] Not all exile meant removing individuals to great geographic distance. The VOC's early priority was to limit indigenous spice cultivation and trade, and the most effective means for this was the forced depopulation of villages and islands it could not control. When the VOC took over the Hoamoal Peninsula of Seram in 1656, the defeated villagers were turned into the company's direct subjects.[23] Low-class people were resettled near the company fort in Luhu, and their political and religious leaders in an Ambonese neighborhood known as Batu Merah.[24] Thirty children were seized and trained into a military company at VOC service.[25] In 1657, Hoamoal's leading figures were exiled further to Batavia.[26]

The census kept by the VOC government from 1671 onward[27] reveals that indigenous Maluku society had between five thousand and seven thousand slaves, who constituted 12 to 13 percent of the population. A comparable number of slaves were owned by the VOC government.[28] In addition to the VOC's local opponents, they included captured traders and prisoners of war from Makassar, the Sulawesi kingdom that defied the company's trade monopoly in Ambon.[29] After conquering Makassar, the last entrepôt of indigenous trade, in 1669,[30] the VOC turned its attention to the manpower needs of the nutmeg and clove estates managed by its free subjects. Many company slaves were sent to work on spice farms in the Banda Islands, where they eventually integrated in a growing population of *mardijkers,* or "freed slaves."[31]

The plantation slavery typical of New World colonialism was limited to Banda.[32] In spite of attempts to ensure that planters in Banda employed the slaves "not for their own private purposes, but in attendance of the nutmeg-trees,"[33] slaves were soon integrated in their masters' household economies.[34] For indigenous people, slavery was primarily a social relationship based on patronage and debt.[35] Slaves living in cities and towns discovered many possibilities to contest and shift their positions.[36] Ultimately, the use of exile for punishment and oppression created a diverse urban population of VOC subjects.

A WAR MACHINE AND SOVEREIGNTY

Both VOC ports and Southeast Asia's precolonial trading states were organized around trade and contained a heterogeneous immigrant population. But whereas precolonial states in Maluku sought to incorporate foreign rulers and symbols in their social and cosmological relations, the VOC mobilized its local subjects and turned them into a war machine operating at sea. The company classified the population of its towns, plantations, and forts as "free citizens," "foreign Asians," "indigenous subjects," and "slaves," and it kept a careful account of the *hongi* fleets and indigenous child soldiers it needed to project power outside these areas. VOC documents rehearse the number of *kora-koras* of each subject village, and contemporary books lovingly portray them in line drawings.

Deleuze and Guattari[37] stress that numbering individuals, boats, tribal segments, and military units is essential for distributing people in space and submitting them to a state framework. Royal exile, whether it was intended to promote the exile's political career or to exclude him from power, bears a similar effect to mobilizing and transforming power.[38] In legal terms, bringing someone into exile presupposes sovereign control of territory. This was a problem, particularly for the Dutch, whose defense of the "freedom of the seas" was an argument against Portuguese, Spanish, and English colonial

DE CORA-CORA VAN TITAWAY.

The war canoe of Titaway, a village on the island of Nusa Laut (Ambon). (Valentyn, *Beschryvinge van Amboina*, 1724.)

claims. Hugo Grotius, whom the VOC enlisted to defend its right to seize Portuguese ships at open sea, argued that "[e]very nation is free to travel to every other nation and trade with it."[39] Initially, then, the VOC recognized indigenous groups as "nations" rather than territories or estates claimed by its mother country. In spite of their ruthless use of the "freedom of the seas," the Dutch put huge legal importance on their monopolistic trade contracts with local leaders. Faced with the argument that the Dutch simply claimed for themselves a trade monopoly they denied to others, Grotius argued that these treaties were made in the domain of "Municipal Laws," presumably modeled after the Dutch city-states.[40]

Exiling politically influential persons from this municipal domain, and drawing them into the naval and military sphere of VOC towns and garrisons in Ambon, Ceylon, Cape Town, and Amsterdam, was not just an exercise of sovereignty but a way of constituting it. For Grotius and other seventeenth-century scholars, the maritime space that extended between "nations" fell in the domain of natural law.[41] Arguably, however, moving indigenous leaders into the colonial space had a positive[42] legal effect: it turned them into singular markers of controlling their place of origin. In this space, the "municipal" authority of persons and contracts articulated with an abstract, state-like power that some indigenous leaders identified with their own status.

One such leader was Sultan Hamzah of Ternate. Before rising to power as an ally of the VOC in 1628, he spent more than twenty years in Spanish

Manila. Hamzah's exile years exposed him to Spanish absolutist ideas of royal power that he later exercised on his compatriots. In spite of his "mild manners,"[43] Hamzah removed several members of his royal council,[44] and when one of them refused to go he asked the VOC to help dispose of him. This leader, Kaicili Luhu, was brought to Ambon and publicly beheaded in 1643.[45]

The VOC's attempt to use Hamzah as a proxy of its interests was largely a failure. Hamzah died in 1648 and his successors could not control Hoamoal, which the VOC then conquered by force.[46] In the eighteenth century, the VOC no longer tried to turn its local allies into puppet rulers. Instead, Cakraningrat IV of Madura was exiled to the Cape of Good Hope in 1746,[47] and Kamaluddin Kaicili Asgar of Tidore to Ceylon in 1779,[48] while the company appropriated their power at home.

Kamaluddin was *raja muda*[49] under Sultan Jamaluddin, who refused to fight against rebellious subjects of Ternate straying on his territory. After deposing Jamaluddin, the VOC tried to govern Ternate through a council of five regents.[50] Kamaluddin's exile sparked off a rebellion led by Kaicili Nuku, another Tidore nobleman, who demanded that the VOC either restore Jamaluddin or appoint Kamaluddin or himself as sultan.[51]

Nuku's self-imposed exile in the eastern islands led to an accidental intertwining of the Dutch and British imperial projects, a theme also explored in Anderson's chapter 1, in this volume. After Nuku's men rescued the crew of a wrecked British ship, he sent Mohamad Saleh and another court official to Bengal to negotiate an anti-Dutch alliance with the British. The proposed alliance fell through after the British-Dutch peace treaty of 1784. The British officer charged with bringing Nuku's diplomatic mission back to Maluku left it stranded in Bengkulu, the British trading post in southwest Sumatra, in 1786.[52] Mohamed Saleh was allowed to remarry and work on a nutmeg plantation, but otherwise he shared the fate of the Indian convicts the government of Bengal began transporting to Bengkulu in 1787.[53]

The VOC presence created a space for the interaction of what Leonard Andaya[54] has called the two "worlds" of Maluku: the Christian *oecumene* of the Iberian colonizers and the cosmological polities of indigenous Maluku. Until the VOC period these worlds remained largely separate because the Portuguese and Spanish empires were content to include new lands and people in their geography of power. Short of erasing the boundary between the two worlds, the Dutch added a third element, a space of unmediated interaction between the Company and its indigenous subjects. In addition to helping populate Company space, exile provided a vector for expanding it. But this mode of assembling power also mobilized indigenous people whom the VOC could neither count nor govern. The rest of this chapter is concerned with this unintended consequence of exile.

THE CONQUEST OF THE SPICE ISLANDS

The Bandanese are arguably the most famous Indonesian group displaced by the colonization of Eastern Indonesia by the VOC. The Company conquered the Banda Islands in 1621 and massacred most of their original population. Yet, some Bandanese survived in the Kei Islands, the site of my fieldwork in 1994–1996. Unlike many other displaced groups of Maluku, the descendants of the Bandanese have maintained their distinct language, oral tradition, and Islamic faith.

Colonial sources suggest that one thousand people out of a preconquest Bandanese population of fifteen thousand survived in the hands of the company. In 1621, the VOC removed 789 persons—287 men, 256 women, and 246 children—from Banda to Batavia on a ship called *Dragon*.[55] These people were sent to Batavia to work as slaves who built canals and fortress walls.[56] The demographic composition of the exiled group suggests that the company also intended to use them to populate its new strongholds in Java and Maluku.

Not all surviving Bandanese were captured by the VOC. A substantial number survived and sought refuge in nearby Muslim communities. On 16 May 1621, after the main Dutch force had left Banda, some people pulled out their boats, which were hidden in the forest of Great Banda, and crossed the one hundred kilometers of high seas that separated them from allied Muslim villages in Seram, the largest island of central Maluku. The Dutch tried to pursue them in the sea but had to give up due to adverse weather conditions.[57] A month later another few hundred people were hauled to safety in twenty Seramese boats.[58]

The descendants of these Bandanese insist that their ancestors were not exiles but left Banda of their own will. Some settled in the coastal villages and islands of Seram. Others moved on to the Kei Islands some five hundred kilometers from their ancestral homeland. In Kei they founded two villages, Banda Eli and Banda Elat, which were the focus of my fieldwork in 1994–1996.[59]

Present-day oral tradition does not represent a "people's history" of the Bandanese. It consists of narrative songs that belong to specific clan groups and describe the sea voyages of their founding ancestors. The songs stake a claim to an ancestry in Banda but do not present a uniform picture of the Bandanese migration to the Kei Islands. Instead, their focus is on the enduring relationship between the two Bandanese villages and a large number of other places in Maluku. History, for the Bandanese, is not about singular past events but about relations that can be revived and encounters that can be repeated in the present.

My fieldwork among the Bandanese aimed at understanding their historical discourse in the context in which it was performed and contested. In 1994–1996 I worked with a number of singers who knew the ancestral songs of their families. Knowledge of the songs is passed from older to younger generations of women, and because women usually change their clan affiliations at marriage, their sung poetry circulates among groups of different ancestry. Because the songs justify men's claims to political status, men take the role of interpreting their meaning. In doing so, they develop authoritative narrative texts around the ancestral and place names in the songs and contest alternative narratives presented by competing groups. Historical discourse among the Bandanese is intensely dialogic. People recognize the existence of different interpretations within their community, and the truth of each interpretation is tested by presenting it to ethnic outsiders.

My fieldwork in Ambon in 2009 revealed several different ways in which the Bandanese presented themselves publicly as an ethnic group. They responded to the national model of local, cultural difference, but at the same time they made specific historical arguments about their shared ancestry with landowning Ambonese groups and about their indigenous status in the Banda Islands.[60] The question of indigeneity is the main context in which the Bandanese affirm the historicity of their tradition. They deny being exiles and argue that they fought for their land.

Bandanese songs are performed in two languages: the ancestral Bandanese language, called Turwandan, and the majority language of the Kei Islands, called Evav. In Bandanese-language songs, the poetic figure that comes closest to exile is "drifting," or being driven by gusts of wind along the sea. In these songs, the Bandanese leave their islands in response to the VOC's standard practice of "uprooting" the nutmeg trees of the company's opponents, but political insecurity and Dutch persecution are described only as a cosmological force.[61] The Keiese-language songs commonly describe the condition of an absent, traveling person as *marvotun*, a word with strong connotations with the social alienation of "strangers."[62] The Bandanese always explained that this word refers to someone traveling overseas in *tana dagam*, the "trade lands."[63] This phrase makes no reference to specific geographic territory, unlike the Indonesian word *asing*, often used for foreign nationals and also the root for *pengasingan*, "exile."

Bandanese narratives about early colonial events stress their armed resistance against the Dutch, which included the assassination of the Dutch commander Verhoeven by the Bandanese in 1609.[64] They also acknowledge Jan Pieterszoon Coen's massacre of numerous Bandanese on 6–7 May 1621. Secular and religious leaders of Lonthor, the most important city in Great Banda, were brought to VOC ships and executed by six Japanese mercenaries.[65]

The Dutch record singles out eight *orangkayas,* or members of the Banda-nese trade aristocracy, as the main victims of the VOC's punishment. The Bandanese associate the same event with the murder of thirty imams, or Islamic leaders of their community.

The Bandanese do not recognize that any high-ranking people were exiled by the Dutch, and they choose not to speak about the humiliating fate of the ordinary people who escaped murder only to be shipped as slave labor-ers to Batavia, where the VOC was building its new headquarters. Dutch historians state that the last Bandanese who escaped to Seram were led by several aristocrats.[66] The Bandanese, for their part, insist that the surviving ancestors had already left Banda before the war against the Dutch. By this account, the Bandanese community was already a cosmopolitan trading group spread far and wide along the trade routes of Eastern Indonesia.

The Dutch saw the Bandanese as a local society and failed to distin-guish them from other traders based in Makassar, the last independent trading state in Eastern Indonesia.[67] They were also present in East Seram, an area the Dutch never managed to properly control. After the Dutch conquest of Banda in 1621, populous islands like Seram Laut, Goram, and Keffing, near the eastern tip of Seram, took over the role of Banda as the rendezvous point for the Asian traders whose activity had been disrupted by the VOC.[68] This was also the first refuge of the Bandanese who escaped Coen's massacre in May 1621. Many clan (*etar*) names in East Seram point to the names of old Bandanese villages, and the relocated Bandanese also paid regular visits to their former homeland.[69]

By around 1630, the Dutch were aware of the Bandanese presence in the remote islands of Kei, some five hundred kilometers southeast of Banda, where they lived in two large villages: Banda Eli and Banda Elat.[70] The people of these villages have kept their Muslim faith and continued to speak their own language, called Turwandan, or Bandanese,[71] which is different from the language of the Kei Islands majority. Whereas other exiled Ban-danese merged into the larger community of Muslim traders in Eastern Indonesia, the two villages in Kei embody the continuous existence of Ban-danese as a distinct cultural group.

Cultural isolation is not the explanation for the survival of the Banda-nese language and tradition in the Kei Islands. The two Bandanese villages lie in the best harbor sites of Great Kei Island, and throughout the colonial period the Bandanese have continued to visit other coastal trading sites in their own boats. They refuse to intermarry with their Keiese neighbors and frame their relationship to distant trade partners as ancestral kinship.

Chris Gregory[72] defines territoriality as the ethnic belonging among nonlocalized mercantile groups. It refers to the spatially extended regions in which a commercial group identifies its accumulating capital as a supreme good. Capital here signifies kinship and contiguity within the community of traders, just as the inalienable farmland of an Indian farming community, under the guardianship of a particular family, is the source of social hierarchy and belonging.

The privileged relationship of the Bandanese to a wider community of traders in Maluku is an example of territoriality in Gregory's sense. Kinship with distant places demarcates the Bandanese community from other people in Kei. Territoriality is not merely about social boundaries: above all it is an ideological phenomenon. Rather than being incorporated in the indigenous elite of the Kei Islands, the Bandanese chose to pursue prestige and recognition in the trading centers near their homeland in central Maluku.

In Jonathan Friedman's[73] terms, the Bandanese long-distance trade is a strategy of cosmological mobility. This term describes situations of imperial conquest that reshape the conquered population into class structures or semi-independent societies and implies that a member of the local elite "must strive to define himself as a member of the conquering group." Under the VOC, the sign of "conquerors" was their independent trading rights. In affirming such rights, the Bandanese constructed the commercial domain as a vast kinship network. But Friedman notes that when commercially organized societies form enclaves within larger bureaucratic empires, their dynamics of commercial accumulation and cultural identity may conflict with the imperial structure.[74]

The antagonism between the Bandanese and the Dutch in the nineteenth century, long after the Bandanese ceased to be a military threat, is evidence of such conflict. The Bandanese were not just another local society colonized by the Dutch. Their territoriality and mobility are features of the very same space the VOC created through building coastal forts, populating them with indigenous people, and exiling indigenous rulers.

OVERSEAS KINSHIP AND TRADE

The special position of the Bandanese after the colonization of Maluku makes it understandable that they refuse to call themselves refugees or exiles, even if Dutch observers used such language in noting their presence in east Seram and the Kei Islands. These areas were never effectively controlled by the VOC, and the Kei Islands were hardly ever visited by Dutch officials or traders until the late nineteenth century. This was a prelude for a "new colonial age"[75] in which the Dutch East Indies government undertook to govern, tax, and develop the entire population in its territory. In the Kei Islands, the period between 1860 and 1880 is particularly interesting for observing the dynamic between elements of the older, loosely connected trade empire and those of modern state power.

These changes should not be viewed as representing a clear-cut historical transition. In his discussion of Deleuze and Guattari's opposition between the war machine and the state, Bruce Kapferer[76] argues that the two figures should not be seen as totalizing accounts of actual societies but as modalities of forming or assembling power. As I have argued, exile served more than one strategy by which the VOC tried to stabilize its territorial control. Exile recurs in the Dutch historical imagination as a figure of movement away from home and into the colonial space. In the Bandanese imagination, the space between the islands is full of trajectories to other homes, or places in which one is recognized as a relative. In the remainder of this chapter I claim that exile had a stabilizing ideological effect for *two* modes of territoriality: that of government officials and that of indigenous travelers.

In a report written after his visit to the Kei Islands in 1887, Baron van Hoëvell, a central advocate of the study of customary law, commented on the lack of a narrative historical tradition about the circumstances in which the two Bandanese-speaking villages were founded. According to van Hoëvell, "they know that they originate from there [Banda], but stories about the reason of their expulsion are no longer carried on."[77]

Van Hoëvell was clearly expecting to find a narrative that matched his territorial sense of the areas under the Dutch colonial state. Nineteenth-century Dutch observers like him were romantics who wanted to locate traces of their own history, intensely documented during the 1880s, from remote places such as Kei. Around the same time, Johann Riedel[78] mentioned that Eli and Elat were "populated by people who fled from Banda in 1621." In the eighteenth-century Dutch narrative, however, the rebellious Bandanese escaped to Rarakit, a pirates' nest in East Seram, "where, or around which, they have mostly held to themselves after their escape."[79]

The Bandanese who migrated to eastern Maluku were difficult to pin down because they did not form a discrete community. Their political challenge to Dutch rule did not consist of a territorial struggle. Instead, the Bandanese survived by virtue of a system known in Maluku and Western New Guinea as *sosolots*, localized "trade franchises" led by resident middlemen who belonged to the regional mercantile community.[80] It is likely that this system also facilitated the settlement of the Bandanese in the Kei Islands. As late as the 1960s, people of Banda Eli exercised trading rights among their old allies on the New Guinea coast.

Until the late nineteenth century, the VOC's main concern in Maluku was its spice monopoly. In the late nineteenth century, the colonial gaze turned to the problem of governing indigenous populations. The interest in early colonial events among the historians writing in the 1880s reflects the imperial sentiment of the time, but it is also an effort to find precedents for the emerging geography of power. Van Hoëvell sought in vain the mythical geography of the Bandanese because it was expressed in narrative songs about the sea voyages of ancestral figures. Their destinations included Mecca, Ambon, Banda, and a number of islands between central Maluku and the Kei Islands. I have argued elsewhere[81] that these songs are part of a larger complex of cultural motivations related to seaborne travel: they encourage young men to look for wealth and self-knowledge by visiting other places. Present-day Bandanese still regard the experience of overseas travel as part of men's initiation into full adult status: men who speak in public meetings are expected to have some experience from migrant work elsewhere.

The songs maintain a view of the Bandanese as a social network rather than a localized group. They underline that the Bandanese are strangers in the Kei Islands society. Keiese mythology revolves around powerful strangers—men or women—who give autochthonous people the knowledge of cooking, marriage exchange, and political authority. The people of Banda Eli claim that their whole village consists of strangers, intensely connected to the inter-island trade network that connects Kei to other places. Whereas the status of other chiefly groups in Kei was based on their ability to control reproductive exchange and the circulation of valuable objects within society, the Bandanese avoided marriage with the Keiese. Marriage in Kei binds persons into domestic hierarchies and long-term relations of exchange. It creates what the Keiese call *inan lifan,* a lifelong debt toward one's in-laws and the ancestors buried in Keiese soil. The Bandanese, on the other hand, imagine that their ancestors are present in faraway places that are accessible only for individual travelers. Their kinship is not limited to localized social relations but flows[82] toward the world of interisland trade.

This cosmological perspective turns the politics of exile on its head. I have suggested that Dutch colonizers used exile as a means of turning people into colonial subjects who would populate and expand the space under their control. Exile deprived these people of the social and political conditions to which they desired to belong. In their place of exile, they were expected to learn new desires and subject themselves to new social classifications, such as the colonial constructs of race. The Bandanese, however, slipped away from this territorializing project. In central Maluku and Sulawesi, they were happy to merge into larger ethnic categories and political orders that stood for opposition against the Dutch. At the same time, particularly in Kei, they remained strangers in the place where they lived.

Van Hoëvell's oral historical concerns were not purely academic. As a proponent of the Dutch ethical policy, he wanted to define groups with a stable cultural identity and develop their legal institutions. The colonial state could extend its legal order to remote areas only by creating systems of customary law. Paradoxically, the Bandanese stood in the way of this project because they had assumed the role of legal experts among their Keiese hosts. The uncomfortable presence of Bandanese and other outsiders was the occasion for the nineteenth-century use of punitive exile, discussed in the next section.

IMAM BUDIMAN'S EXILE

In the 1860s, the Dutch administration began to expand its presence to areas in which the people of Maluku had effectively governed themselves. One of these areas was the Kei Islands, an archipelago that lies due west from Aru and some one hundred kilometers from the New Guinean coast. Due to the "blood-thirsty nature of the natives," as Robert Townsend Farquhar put it,[83] the free traders of Banda avoided visiting the islands. Even so, Banda depended on the areas farther east for its food supplies, and indigenous traders from Great Kei sailed to Banda every year with their own boats, bringing oil, sago, coconuts, and earthen pots.[84] The export of pots is evidence that Banda Eli had a major role in this trade: pot manufacture in Great Kei is limited to this village.

It is safe to say that the Bandanese living in Kei were informed of the events that changed the colonies of the VOC into a modern colonial state. Eastern Indonesia was in British hands for two short periods during and after the Napoleonic Wars, and the VOC declared bankruptcy in 1799. When Dutch rule in Ambon was restored in 1817, people in Ambon revolted against the renewed policy of suppressing the indigenous clove trade.[85] It was only in faraway places, such as Aru and the Southwestern Islands, that the Dutch could pretend they were simply carrying on the colonial presence started by the VOC. When the Dutch Captain Dirk Hendrik Kolff sailed around southeast Maluku in a warship, he focused on such areas and passed, but did not stop in, Banda Eli—even though he noted that it was regarded as the most important place in Kei.[86]

Dutch reports from half a century later present a very different picture of the same area. In 1862, a Dutch official called H. C. Eijbergen made a thorough inspection of northern Great Kei, with the orders to "put an end to the lawlessness and irregularities which had taken place in recent years."[87] The administration's concern with law and order would have been based on the reports of traders and disaffected villagers because there had been no Dutch visits to the area in more than a decade.[88] Local people were not aware of the Dutch ship that had visited in 1850; they remembered only that two ships had called at a nearby village some thirty years before—a visit that Eijbergen dates to 1833.[89]

In the mid-nineteenth century, an increasing commercial interest in Kei Island forests produced resource conflicts, and the Bandanese took the role of mediators toward their Keiese neighbors.[90] Their traditional legal interventions were an obvious nuisance to outside traders, who asked the Dutch administration for help. On his first trip, Eijbergen took the side of Ismael, an ally of the Bandanese, who told him in confidence that Budiman, the imam of Banda Eli, demanded that he should pay an annual fine for eloping with a slave of the imam's family.

Eijbergen visited the Kei Islands again in 1864. On this trip he began to pay more attention to people who in his view resided in the wrong place. The first person he took away was Abdullah, a man who introduced himself as the imam of Kataloka, an island near the east coast of Seram. Abdullah had stayed in Aru as the home instructor of a Buginese man's children for four years. Then he had eloped with the wife of his Buginese host.[91] Eijbergen told Abdullah that he had no right to stay in Aru and put him on his ship, to be brought to the custody of the governor at Banda, where he would be sent home to Kataloka.[92]

As a Muslim from East Seram, Abdullah was part of the same Islamic trade diaspora that Eijbergen suspected for breeding unrest in other places he visited.[93] Eijbergen was already suspicious of such people after hearing the complaints against Imam Budiman two years earlier.[94] When he reached Great Kei on his second trip, Budiman came to meet him with a large entourage and sat down smoking a cigar.[95] Hiding his annoyance, Eijbergen went on to another village, where he had summoned all village heads from northern Great Kei. Budiman had assured Eijbergen he had sent word to chiefs who were in dispute with him, but when these did not show up in the meeting, Eijbergen decided to arrest Budiman.[96] He sent the imam to his boat under the guard of two soldiers in order to give a separate hearing to other Banda Eli chiefs. They revealed that Budiman had imposed a large fine on a chief who disputed his land rights and attacked his village when all was not paid.[97]

Budiman's arrest marks a turning point in the relations between the Kei Islands and the colonial state. During Eijbergen's visit, Banda Eli and other Muslim trading communities were not resisting state authority but appropriated it by turning Dutch flags and other insignia of the government into signs of their own power. Recently they had sent a *hongi*—a fleet of war canoes modeled after the punitive expeditions of the VOC—to punish the village of the killers of an alleged witch.[98] In order to limit such activities, the Dutch established a governing post in the Kei Islands in 1882.

There is no information about Budiman's fate after he was exiled from Kei. Budiman's relatives, however, have kept his memory alive. Both of his sons served as imams in different Banda Eli mosques. Wahab, the elder son, became imam of the prestigious Friday mosque, while the younger, Ismail, became imam of the mosque in Futelu, the southern end of the village. During my fieldwork in 1994–1996, the imam of the Friday mosque was Haji Jeilani Salamun, Budiman's direct descendant in the male line.[99]

Haji Jeilani's story did not give many details about the circumstances of Budiman's exile. Instead of suggesting that Budiman resisted Dutch power, Jeilani stressed his conviction that Budiman was his absent relative. According to a story that Jeilani repeated to me many times, he had met a very familiar-looking person from the central Javanese city of Semarang on a visit to Ambon. The man told him that he was descended from a man who had moved there from Banda Eli. Jeilani was convinced that this person was indeed his kinsman, another great-great-grandson of Budiman.[100]

Jeilani's story follows a line similar to those of the traditional songs of Banda Eli. The most profound, self-revealing encounters with kinsmen happen in a distant place, where one never expects strangers to show affection and kindness similar to what one receives from relatives. This case, as well as myths of exiled ancestral figures, shows kinship in an expansive mode, as a source of personal identity and distinction.

I have already suggested that Dutch officials were interested in stabilizing cultural institutions that stood for legal order and helped manage the diverse population of the expanding colonial state. Transporting people away from areas where they did not belong is consistent with this policy. Budiman's punishment, however, is more reminiscent of the VOC practice of royal exile. Not knowing where to "return" him, the Dutch officials moved him to the colonial space, presumably to a prison in Ambon or Java.

Clare Anderson and Carol Liston, in chapters 1 and 8, respectively, in this volume, argue that in some circumstances punitive exile can be perceived as having beneficial results, for instance, when it points to new possibilities of access to the colonial domain. Although Budiman's exile was intended as a politically repressive gesture, it had unintended consequences similar to those that concerned the British authorities in the case of Maharaj Singh, discussed in Anand Yang's chapter (chapter 3 in this volume). Budiman's family has held its claim to the most influential chiefly office in the village and still thinks of him as one of the ancestors whose overseas travels underlie the Bandanese kinship with faraway places. Because of Eijbergen's published account of Budiman's arrest, he is probably the only nineteenth-century Bandanese who stands out as an individual in the historical record. For Budiman's relatives, the forced relocation of their ancestor extended their imagined ethnic space to locations identified with education and bureaucratic power—two aspects of Indonesian modernity that many Bandanese have successfully pursued from the 1960s onward.

EXILE AND THE FORMATION OF COLONIAL SPACE

The VOC's monopolistic practices and violence were in conflict with contemporary Dutch sensibilities as much as with indigenous notions of legitimate power in Maluku. This is why the early stages of colonization have far less to do with state building than with its opposite: what Deleuze and Guattari[101] have called the war machine. It is difficult to not see the VOC's *hongi* fleets as a "tribal" organization, which almost spontaneously gathered to raid neighboring tribes a few hundred kilometers away.

Royal exile was an obvious means for depriving the indigenous polity of order and turning it into a war machine. François Valentyn and other contemporary writers hardly ever noted this because of their commitment to a state-like legitimacy of the VOC. Colonial writings refuse to see massacres and deprivations of indigenous people as contingent, tragic events and represent them as the outcomes of deliberate decisions and policies. The depopulation of Hoamoal and the conquest of Banda are represented as sovereign actions that restore, rather than displace, existing political and legal order. Royal exile, however, reveals the ambiguity of this state-oriented narrative. Even if exile was sometimes dressed as a benevolent way of inculcating modern statecraft in indigenous aristocrats, it confronted them with the colonizer's coercive, punishing power—something the exile was expected to internalize and apply. Sultan Hamzah's exile to Manila, for instance, familiarized him with absolute monarchy exemplified by Philip II but deprived him of sensibility toward the way legitimate authority was understood among his subjects in Maluku. In his case, exile created an unexpected void of state power quite near to the VOC base in Ambon, forcing the company into a troublesome military campaign that it probably had wanted to avoid.

What I have called colonial space was created by such unpredictable events. Space should not be confused with territory, the geographic distribution of specific social forms and relations. The VOC conquest of Banda and Hoamoal displaced their inhabitants and turned many of them into slaves and soldiers. Colonial space in central Maluku arose from such deterritorializing events. This space was not simply the "modern" counterpart of the indigenous states in the VOC sphere of influence. We might call it a "haeccic" space[102] because it did not draw in people so much by offering them an alternative ideological horizon and identity, but simply by depriving them of their former home, personal status, and relationships.

Fort Victoria, the Dutch garrison in Ambon, in the eighteenth century. The VOC's indigenous subjects were settled in the area to the left of this view. (Valentyn: *Beschryvinge van Amboina*, 1724.)

These qualities of colonial space may explain the many unexpected outcomes of exiling colonized people, as well as the fact that they often associated exile with new economic, cultural, and political possibilities. The indigenous traders' ability to challenge the VOC's monopoly was based on earlier historical patterns, but the migration of the Bandanese to East Seram and Kei also created a new connection between local trading sites and markets around the world. The new territoriality of the Bandanese put them in a position of power relative to more sedentary societies: through their commercial activities, they participated in the system created by the Dutch. At the same time, they were aware that full involvement in the colonial system would deprive them of the special deterritorialized ethnicity that they expressed as kinship with faraway relatives. Dutch attempts to put them into their place in the late nineteenth century did not erase their sense of kinship with other places: paradoxically, Imam Budiman's arrest and exile connected his family to yet another, distant site where they expect to feel welcome.

The fact that the development of colonial space did not follow a predictable historical logic also means that the qualities and meanings of exile kept shifting throughout the colonial period. In the context discussed in this chapter, colonial practices of exile shifted between an affirmative and a punitive regime. Exile was used to transform indigenous political authority but also to demonstrate the VOC's exceptional power toward people holding it. In the late nineteenth century, exile had become obsolete as a tool for managing indigenous states, but it reemerged as a central figure of historical imagination, driven by the pride about the Dutch Empire, the guilt about its violent past, and the need to put the colonial population on the map.

It is not clear if the Malay word *asing* (alien) ever had the same connotation as the word exile (*pengasingan*) before the firming of Indonesia's national boundaries. The colonial state was always able to send people away, but its subjects created new, socially meaningful identities for those arriving in a new place. The Bandanese memory practices are remarkable for their power to turn the alienating, depersonalizing effect of displacement into its opposite: a peculiar intimacy with ancestral relatives and homelands and with figures of religious and political power.

NOTES

1. Timothy Barnard, *Multiple Centres of Authority. Society and Environment in Siak and Eastern Sumatra, 1674–1827* (Leiden: KITLV Press, 2003).

2. Eric Tagliacozzo, "Smuggling in Southeast Asia: History and Its Contemporary Vectors in an Unbounded Region," *Critical Asian Studies* 34, no. 2 (2002): 193–220.

3. Roy Ellen, *On the Edge of the Banda Zone: Past and Present in the Social Organization of a Moluccan Trading Network* (Honolulu: University of Hawai'i Press, 2003), 120.

4. Gilles Deleuze and Felix Guattari, *A Thousand Plateaus: Capitalism and Schizophrenia* (London: Athlone Press, 1988), 131.

5. Leonard Andaya, *The World of Maluku: Eastern Indonesia in the Modern Period* (Honolulu: University of Hawai'i Press, 1993), 111; Ellen, *On the Edge of the Banda Zone*, 84.

6. See M. A. P. Meilink-Roelofsz, *Asian Trade and European Influence in the Indonesian Archipelago* (The Hague: Martinus Nijhoff, 1962), 173–206, for an overview on VOC competition with other European powers.

7. The role of the indigenous navy in controlling the periphery of VOC-held Ambon has been described in G. J. Knaap, *Kruidnagelen en Christenen: De Verenigde Oost-Indische Compagnie en de bevolking van Ambon 1956–1696*, Verhandelingen van het Koninklijk Instituut voor Taal-, Land- en Volkenkunde 125 (Dordrecht: Foris Publications, 2004), 67–76; and in Meilink-Roelofsz, *Asian Trade*, 217. Dutch archival and historical records contain precise accounts of the number of war canoes in each VOC-allied village; see, e.g., G. J. Knaap, ed., *Memories van Overgave van gouverneurs van Ambon in de zeventiende en achttiende eeuw* (The Hague: Martinus Nijhoff, 1987), 177, 224–228, and François Valentyn, *Beschryvinge van Amboina*. vol. 2, pt. 1 of *Oud en nieuw Oost-Indiën* (Dordrecht: Joannes van Braam; Amsterdam: Gerard Onder de Linden, 1724), 185–189.

8. Andaya, *World of Maluku*, 152.

9. Meilink-Roelofsz, *Asian Trade*, 212; Knaap, *Memories van overgave*, 8–9.

10. Andaya, *World of Maluku*, 153.

11. Ibid., 171.

12. Ibid., 84.

13. François Valentyn, *Ambonsche zaaken*, vol. 2, pt. 2 of *Oud en nieuw Oost Indiën* (Dordrecht: Joannes van Braam; Amsterdam: Gerard Onder de Linden, 1724), 11, 32.

14. Ibid., 37.

15. Ibid., 80. *Hukum* translates as "magistrate," a title used in the sultan's court at Ternate; see Andaya, *World of Maluku*, 70. Hitu is a village on the north coast of Ambon Island. It originated as a Javanese trading settlement, but *hukum* and other courtly titles suggest that it modeled itself after an Islamic polity.

16. Andaya, *World of Maluku*, 83.

17. Knaap, *Memories van Overgave*, 119–120.

18. J. E. Heeres, "Eene engelsche lezing ontrent de verovering van Banda en Ambon in 1796 en omtrent den toestand dier eilanden groepen op het eind der achttiende eeuw, uitgegeven en toegelicht door J. E. H," *Bijdragen tot de Taal-, Land- en Volkenkunde van Nederlandsch-Indië* 60, nos. 3–4 (1908): 325.

19. Andaya, *World of Maluku*, 161.

20. Heeres, "Eene engelsche lezing," 342.

21. Kerry Ward, "Blood Ties: Exile, Family, and Inheritance across the Indian Ocean in the Early Nineteenth Century," *Journal of Social History* 45, no. 2 (2011): 445.

22. Knaap, *Memories van Overgave*, 279.

23. James T. Collins, "Language Death in Maluku: The Impact of the VOC," *Bijdragen tot de Taal-, Land- en Volkenkunde* 159, nos. 2–3 (2003): 251.

24. See Collins, "Language Death," 252, and Valentyn, *Beschryvinge van Amboina*, 204, for an account of these events. Batu Merah and Merdeka, two neighborhoods north of the VOC fort in Ambon, are living reminders of the city's exiled slave populations. Valentyn, *Beschryvinge van Amboina*, 134, calls Batu Merah "Roodenberg," or "Redhill," in

Dutch, and mentions a stone bridge connecting the company fort area to Mardyker Street. *Mardyker* was originally used for indigenous Christians affiliated to the former, Portuguese occupants of the fort in Ambon. On page 256 Valentyn describes them as "Black Freemen," free-bought or manumitted slaves occupied with sailing, fishing, and trade.

25. Valentyn, *Ambonsche zaaken*, 205.

26. Collins, "Language Death," 251; Knaap, *Kruidnagelen en Christenen*, 353n19.

27. Knaap, *Kruidnagelen en Christenen*, 369.

28. Ibid., 163.

29. Ibid., 163.

30. Leonard Andaya, *The Heritage of Arung Palakka* (Leiden: KITLV Press, 1981), 137.

31. G. J. Knaap, "A City of Migrants: Kota Ambon at the End of the Seventeenth Century," *Indonesia* 51 (1991): 112; Phillip Winn, "Slavery and Cultural Creativity in the Banda Islands," *Journal of Southeast Asian Studies* 41, no. 3 (2010): 371.

32. Gert Oostindie and Bert Paasman, "Dutch Attitudes towards Colonial Empires, Indigenous Cultures, and Slaves," *Eighteenth-Century Studies* 31, no. 3 (1998): 352.

33. Heeres, "Eene engelsche lezing," 349.

34. Winn, "Slavery and Cultural Creativity," 371.

35. Anthony Reid, "Introduction: Slavery and Bondage in Southeast Asian History," in *Slavery, Bondage and Dependency in South-East Asia*, ed. Anthony Reid (University of Queensland Press, 1983), 1–43.

36. Eric Jones, "Fugitive Women: Slavery and Social Change in Early Modern Southeast Asia," *Journal of Southeast Asian Studies* 38, no. 2 (2007): 215–245.

37. Deleuze and Guattari, *A Thousand Plateaus*, 389.

38. Ricci, in chapter 4 in this volume, stresses that exile was not simply about isolating people but about moving them within a single imperial realm. The geographic distance covered by this movement varied in proportion to the severity of the exile's crime and the colonizer's ability to punish it. I would suggest that the commensurability of crime and punishment was key to turning the exile from a member of a conquered local society into an imperial subject.

39. Karl Zemanek, "Was Hugo Grotius Really in Favour of the Freedom of the Seas?" *Journal of the History of International Law* 1 (1999): 54.

40. Ibid., 56.

41. Ibid., 53.

42. Deleuze and Guattari, *A Thousand Plateaus*, 394.

43. Andaya, *World of Maluku*, 158.

44. Ibid., 160.

45. Ibid., 161.

46. Collins, "Language Death," 251.

47. Ward, "Blood Ties," 441.

48. Andaya, *World of Maluku*, 219, 228.

49. "Junior king," an office created by the company to prevent a succession dispute; ibid., 217.

50. Ibid., 219.

51. Ibid., 231; Heeres, "Eene engelsche lezing," 279–280; Muridan Widjojo, *The Revolt of Prince Nuku: Cross-Cultural Alliance-Making in Maluku, c. 1780–1810* (Leiden: Brill, 2009).

52. Widjojo, *Revolt of Prince Nuku*, 174.

53. Anand Yang, "Indian Convict Workers in Southeast Asia in the Late Eighteenth and Early Nineteenth Centuries," *Journal of World History* 14, no. 2 (2003): 191.

54. Andaya, *World of Maluku*, 23.

55. P. A. Tiele, *Bouwstoffen voor de geschiedenis der Nederlanders in den Maleischen archipel*, 2nd ser., vol. 1 (The Hague: Martinus Nijhoff, 1886), 280.

56. J. A. van der Chijs, *De vestiging van het Nederlandsche gezag over de Banda-Eilanden (1599–1621)* (The Hague: Martinus Nijhoff, 1886), 161; Collins, "Language Death," 249.

57. Tiele, *Bouwstoffen*, vol. 1, 291.

58. Chijs, *De vestiging*, 162.

59. Timo Kaartinen, *Songs of Travel, Stories of Place: Poetics of Absence in an Eastern Indonesian Society.* Folklore Fellows' Communications 299 (Helsinki: Academia Scientarium Fennica, 2010).

60. Ibid., 101; Timo Kaartinen, "Handing Down and Writing Down: Metadiscourses of Tradition among the Bandanese of Eastern Indonesia," *Journal of American Folklore* 126 (2013): 400; Timo Kaartinen, "Perceptions of Justice in the Making: Rescaling of Customary Law in Maluku, Eastern Indonesia," *Asia-Pacific Journal of Anthropology* 15, no. 4 (2014): 333.

61. In Bandanese oral traditions, gusting, "five-faced" wind (*anin pancarupa*) regularly appears as a counterforce to a boat's directed movement at sea.

62. Cecile Barraud, "Wife-Givers as Ancestors and Ultimate Values in the Kei Islands," *Bijdragen tot de Taal-, Land-en Volkenkunde* (1990): 199, 201, notes that people of the Kei Islands use *marvotun* as the opposite of people who "belong" to the village community and as an attribute of a woman who will become a "stranger" at her marriage.

63. Kaartinen, *Songs of Travel*, 67, 82.

64. Chijs, *De vestiging*, 39.

65. Ibid., 158.

66. Ibid., 162.

67. Andaya, *World of Maluku*, 164, notes that historical literature usually identifies the Bandanese who continued their commercial activities in Maluku during the VOC time as "Makassarese." This category also includes Malays who relocated to Makassar after the Portuguese conquest of Malacca in 1511. See Andaya, *Heritage of Arung Palakka*, for a detailed account of the role of VOC's indigenous allies in this war.

68. Knaap, *Kruidnagelen en Christenen*, 68; Pamela Swadling, *Plumes from Paradise: Trade Cycles in Outer Southeast Asia and Their Impact on New Guinea and Nearby Islands until 1920* (Boroko: Papua New Guinea National Museum, in association with Robert Brown & Associates, 1996), 137.

69. Ellen, *On the Edge of the Banda Zone*, 84.

70. P. A. Tiele, *Bouwstoffen voor de geschiedenis der Nederlanders in den Maleischen archipel*, 2nd ser., vol. 2 (The Hague: Martinus Nijhoff, 1890), 165; J. E. Heeres, "Dokumenten betreffende de ontdekkingstochten van Adriaan Doortsman 1645–1646," *Tijdschrift voor de Indische Taal-, Land- en Volkenkunde* 6, no. 2 (1896): 246–279; 608–619; 635–662.

71. James Collins and Timo Kaartinen, "Preliminary Notes on Bandanese: Language Development and Change in Kei," *Bijdragen tot de Taal-, Land- en Volkenkunde* 154, no. 4 (1998): 521–570.

72. C. A. Gregory, *Savage Money* (Amsterdam: Harwood Academic Publishers, 1997), 165.

73. Jonathan Friedman, *Cultural Identity and Global Process* (London: Sage Publications, 1994), 33.

74. Ibid., 32.

75. M. C. A. Ricklefs, *A History of Modern Indonesia, c. 1300 to the Present*, 2nd ed. (London: MacMillan Press, 1993), 151.

76. Bruce Kapferer, *The Feast of the Sorcerer: Practices of Consciousness and Power* (Chicago: University of Chicago Press, 1997), 284.

77. C. W. W. C. van Hoëvell, "De Kei-eilanden," *Tijdschrift voor Indische Taal-, Land- en Volkenkunde* 33 (1890): 158.

78. J. G. F. Riedel, *De sluik- en kroesharige rassen tusschen Selebes en Papua* (The Hague: Martinus Nijhoff, 1888), 217.

79. Valentyn, *Beschryvinge van Amboina,* 57.

80. Ibid., 126; Thomas Goodman, "The Sosolot: An Eighteenth Century East Indonesian Trade Network" (PhD diss., University of Hawai'i, 2006).

81. Timo Kaartinen, "How a Travelling Society Totalizes Itself: Hybrid Polities and Values in Eastern Indonesia," *Anthropological Theory* 14, no. 2 (2014): 241.

82. Deleuze and Guattari, *A Thousand Plateaus,* 216.

83. W. G. Miller, "An Account of Trade Patterns in the Banda Sea in 1797, from an Unpublished Manuscript in the India Office Library," *Indonesia Circle* 23 (1980): 50.

84. Ibid., 52.

85. Richard Chauvel, *Nationalists, Soldiers, and Separatists: The Ambonese Islands from Colonialism to Revolt, 1880–1950,* Verhandelingen van het Koninklijk Instituut tot de Taal-, Land- en Volkenkunde 143 (Leiden: KITLV Press, 1990), 21–22.

86. Dirk Hendrik Kolff, *Voyages of the Dutch Brig of War Dourga through the Southern and Little-Known Parts of the Moluccan Archipelago and the Previously Unknown Southern Coast of New Guinea Performed during the Years 1825 & 1826* (London: James Madden & Co., 1840), 344.

87. H. C. Eijbergen, "Verslag eener reis naar de Aroe- en Key- Eilanden," *Tijdschrift voor Taal-, Land- en Volkenkunde* 15 (1866): 252.

88. Ibid., 338.

89. Ibid., 253.

90. Ibid., 256.

91. Ibid., 305.

92. Ibid., 307.

93. Ibid., 320, 324, 326.

94. Ibid., 336.

95. Ibid., 338.

96. Ibid., 341.

97. Ibid., 344.

98. Ibid., 340.

99. Jeilani's father, Muhammad, was Budiman's great-grandson through Budiman's son Wahab.

100. Kaartinen, *Songs of Travel,* 174.

101. Deleuze and Guattari, *A Thousand Plateaus,* 354.

102. Ibid., 261.

BIBLIOGRAPHY

Andaya, Leonard. *The Heritage of Arung Palakka.* Leiden: KITLV Press, 1981.

———. *The World of Maluku: Eastern Indonesia in the Modern Period.* Honolulu: University of Hawai'i Press, 1993.

Barnard, Timothy. *Multiple Centres of Authority: Society and Environment in Siak and Eastern Sumatra, 1674–1827.* Leiden: KITLV Press, 2003.

Barraud, Cecile. "Kei Society and the Person: An Approach through Childbirth and Funerary Rituals." *Ethnos* 55, nos. 3–4 (1990): 214–231.

————. "Wife-Givers as Ancestors and Ultimate Values in the Kei Islands." *Bijdragen tot de Taal-, Land-en Volkenkunde* (1990): 193–225.

Chauvel, Richard. *Nationalists, Soldiers, and Separatists: The Ambonese Islands from Colonialism to Revolt, 1880–1950.* Verhandelingen van het Koninklijk Instituut tot de Taal-, Land- en Volkenkunde 143. Leiden: KITLV Press, 1990.

Chijs, J. A. van der. *De vestiging van het Nederlandsche gezag over de Banda-Eilanden (1599–1621).* The Hague: Martinus Nijhoff, 1886.

Collins, James T. "Language Death in Maluku. The Impact of the VOC." *Bijdragen tot de Taal-, Land- en Volkenkunde* 159, nos. 2–3 (2003): 247–289.

Collins, James, and Timo Kaartinen. "Preliminary Notes on Bandanese: Language Development and Change in Kei." *Bijdragen tot de Taal-, Land- en Volkenkunde* 154, no. 4 (1998): 521–570.

Deleuze, Gilles, and Felix Guattari. *A Thousand Plateaus: Capitalism & Schizophrenia.* London: Athlone Press, 1988.

Eijbergen, H. C. "Verslag eener reis naar de Aroe- en Key- Eilanden." *Tijdschrift voor Taal-, Land- en Volkenkunde* 15 (1866): 220–272, 293–361.

Ellen, Roy. *On the Edge of the Banda Zone: Past and Present in the Social Organization of a Moluccan Trading Network.* Honolulu: University of Hawai'i Press, 2003.

Friedman, Jonathan. *Cultural Identity and Global Process.* London: Sage Publications, 1994.

Goodman, Thomas. "The Sosolot: An Eighteenth Century East Indonesian Trade Network." PhD diss., University of Hawai'i, 2006.

Gregory, C. A. *Savage Money.* Amsterdam: Harwood Academic Publishers, 1997.

Heeres, J. E. "Dokumenten betreffende de ontdekkingstochten van Adriaan Doortsman 1645–1646." *Tijdschrift voor de Indische Taal-, Land- en Volkenkunde* 6, no. 2 (1896): 246–279, 608–619, 635–662.

————. "Eene engelsche lezing ontrent de verovering van Banda en Ambon in 1796 en omtrent den toestand dier eilanden groepen op het eind der achttiende eeuw, uitgegeven en toegelicht door J. E. H." *Bijdragen tot de Taal-, Land- en Volkenkunde van Nederlandsch-Indië* 60, nos. 3–4 (1908): 249–368.

Hoëvell, C. W. W. C. van. "De Kei-eilanden." *Tijdschrift voor Indische Taal-, Land- en Volkenkunde* 33 (1890): 102–159.

Jones, Eric. "Fugitive Women: Slavery and Social Change in Early Modern Southeast Asia." *Journal of Southeast Asian Studies* 38, no. 2 (2007): 215–245.

Kaartinen, Timo. "Handing Down and Writing Down: Metadiscourses of Tradition among the Bandanese of Eastern Indonesia." *Journal of American Folklore* 126 (2013): 385–406.

————. "How a Travelling Society Totalizes Itself: Hybrid Polities and Values in Eastern Indonesia." *Anthropological Theory* 14, no. 2 (2014): 231–248.

————. "Perceptions of Justice in the Making: Rescaling of Customary Law in Maluku, Eastern Indonesia." *Asia-Pacific Journal of Anthropology* 15, no. 4 (2014): 319–338.

————. *Songs of Travel, Stories of Place: Poetics of Absence in an Eastern Indonesian Society.* Folklore Fellows' Communications 299. Helsinki: Academia Scientarium Fennica, 2010.

Kapferer, Bruce. *The Feast of the Sorcerer: Practices of Consciousness and Power.* Chicago: University of Chicago Press, 1997.

Knaap, G. J. "A City of Migrants: Kota Ambon at the End of the Seventeenth Century." *Indonesia* 51 (1991): 105–128.

————. *Kruidnagelen en Christenen. De Verenigde Oost-Indische Compagnie en de bevolking van Ambon 1956–1696.* Verhandelingen van het Koninklijk Instituut voor Taal-, Land- en Volkenkunde 125. Dordrecht: Foris Publications, 2004.

————, ed. *Memories van Overgave van gouverneurs van Ambon in de zeventiende en achttiende eeuw.* The Hague: Martinus Nijhoff, 1987.

Knaap, Gerrit, and Heather Sutherland. *Monsoon Traders: Ships, Skippers and Commodities in 18th Century Makassar.* Leiden: KITLV Press, 2004.

Kolff, Dirk Hendrik. *Voyages of the Dutch Brig of War Dourga through the Southern and Little-Known Parts of the Moluccan Archipelago and the Previously Unknown Southern Coast of New Guinea Performed during the Years 1825 & 1826.* London: James Madden & Co., 1840.

Meilink-Roelofsz, M. A. P. *Asian Trade and European Influence in the Indonesian Archipelago.* The Hague: Martinus Nijhoff, 1962.

Miller, W. G. "An Account of Trade Patterns in the Banda Sea in 1797, from an Unpublished Manuscript in the India Office Library." *Indonesia Circle* 23 (1980): 41–57.

Oostindie, Gert, and Bert Paasman. "Dutch Attitudes towards Colonial Empires, Indigenous Cultures, and Slaves." *Eighteenth-Century Studies* 31, no. 3 (1998): 349–355.

Overgekomen Brieven en Papieren in het jaar 1622, tweede boek (boek V), ongefolieerd. Bijlage I t/m IX. Algemeen Rijksarchief. National Archives of the Netherlands, The Hague, 267–285.

Pires, Tome. *Suma Oriental: An Account of the East, from the Red Sea to Japan, Written in Malacca and India in 1512–1515.* Vol. 1. Hakluyt Society New Series, vol. 89. London: Hakluyt Society, 1944.

Reid, Anthony. "Introduction: Slavery and Bondage in Southeast Asian History." In *Slavery, Bondage and Dependency in South-East Asia,* edited by Anthony Reid, 1–43. University of Queensland Press, 1983.

————. *Southeast Asia in the Age of Commerce, 1450–1680.* Vol. 2, *Expansion and Crisis.* New Haven, CT: Yale University Press, 1993.

Ricklefs, M. C. *A History of Modern Indonesia, c. 1300 to the Present.* 2nd ed. London: MacMillan Press, 1993.

Riedel, J. G. F. *De sluik- en kroesharige rassen tusschen Selebes en Papua.* The Hague: Martinus Nijhoff, 1888.

Swadling, Pamela. *Plumes from Paradise: Trade Cycles in Outer Southeast Asia and Their Impact on New Guinea and Nearby Islands until 1920.* Boroko: Papua New Guinea National Museum, in association with Robert Brown & Associates, 1996.

Tagliacozzo, Eric. "Smuggling in Southeast Asia: History and Its Contemporary Vectors in an Unbounded Region." *Critical Asian Studies* 34, no. 2 (2002): 193–220.

Tiele, P. A. *Bouwstoffen voor de geschiedenis der Nederlanders in den Maleischen archipel.* 2nd ser., vol. 1. The Hague: Martinus Nijhoff, 1886.

————. *Bouwstoffen voor de geschiedenis der Nederlanders in den Maleischen archipel.* 2nd ser., vol. 2. The Hague: Martinus Nijhoff, 1890.

Valentyn, François. *Ambonsche zaaken.* Vol. 2, pt. 2 of *Oud en nieuw Oost Indiën.* Dordrecht: Joannes van Braam; Amsterdam: Gerard Onder de Linden, 1724.

————. *Beschryvinge van Amboina.* Vol. 2, pt. 1 of *Oud en nieuw Oost-Indiën.* Dordrecht: Joannes van Braam; Amsterdam: Gerard Onder de Linden, 1724.

Ward, Kerry. "Blood Ties: Exile, Family, and Inheritance across the Indian Ocean in the Early Nineteenth Century." *Journal of Social History* 45, no. 2 (2011): 436–452.

Widjojo, Muridan. *The Revolt of Prince Nuku: Cross-Cultural Alliance-Making in Maluku, c. 1780–1810.* Leiden: Brill, 2009.

Winn, Phillip. "Slavery and Cultural Creativity in the Banda Islands." *Journal of Southeast Asian Studies* 41, no. 3 (2010): 365–389.

Yang, Anand. "Indian Convict Workers in Southeast Asia in the Late Eighteenth and Early Nineteenth Centuries." *Journal of World History* 14, no. 2 (2003): 179–208.

Zemanek, Karl. "Was Hugo Grotius Really in Favour of the Freedom of the Seas?" *Journal of the History of International Law* 1 (1999): 48–60.

Seven

Belongings and Belonging
Indonesian Histories in Inventories from the Cape of Good Hope

Jean Gelman Taylor

This chapter is a case study of peoples transported to the Cape of Good Hope from ports in the Indonesian archipelago that were controlled by the Netherlands' United East Indies Company (VOC).[1] They were slaves, men and some women, mostly non-Muslims, who had been captured by Muslim slavers and sold to the Dutch. This case study is a record of a search for them and their descendants in documents created by officials of the Cape's Orphan Chamber. Here are to be found words spoken by slaves and lists of goods owned by freed slaves. In oral testimony and material culture we discover something of the lives and lifestyles of peoples from the Indonesian archipelago for whom the southern tip of Africa became workplace and home.

My intention is to animate the long lists of people and objects in VOC records and to draw from the formulaic inventory perspectives of the slaves themselves. Piecing together the contours of individuals' lives allows placing slaves and the emancipated within the universal phenomenon of forced migration, enabling comparisons to be made with other categories of migrants, such as transported convicts. There are hardships and cruelties peculiar to the enslaved status. Nevertheless, my findings parallel results of studies of transported convicts in this book. In new environments some individuals, detached from birthplace by slavery or penal transportation, adjusted to their situations, developed skills, launched careers, formed families, and improved the social and economic standing of their children.

On the other hand, it is difficult to distinguish such adaptive skills and resourcefulness among the third category of forced migrants considered in this volume, the exiles. Princely contenders for Asian thrones and charismatic religious leaders who mocked indigenous rulers or challenged European powers—these men did not prosper in their places of banishment. There was the confinement of close guard, diminished importance, even irrelevance. The exiles' aim was to return home to the known and reclaim lost privilege. Slaves adapted. They attempted to improve their immediate living conditions where they were. Perhaps freed slaves harbored resentment of former rulers who had sold them off for textiles and guns, and looked on the Cape as home.

The Cape settlement, founded by Jan van Riebeeck in 1652, was initially intended to supply passing ocean traffic with fresh food and water. It was also to be a brief recuperative stop on the long sea journey between Europe and Asia. An immediate problem for VOC administrators was securing a workforce to build fortified headquarters, church, hospital, and warehouses, and finding laborers for market gardening and farming in the arable areas of the hinterland. For the new settlement had been planted in a landscape of mobile peoples. It was on the fringe of pasturelands of indigenous cattle herders; its wooded hills were home to hunter-gatherers. Wage laborers were not to be found locally.

VOC personnel were mobile people too. Soldiers, sailors, and merchant-administrators were regularly transferred between VOC hubs on the coasts of Asia. Settlers from Europe, called free burghers, never solved the Cape's labor shortage. They numbered only nine in 1657 when van Riebeeck sent a slave-purchasing mission to Madagascar.[2] Slavery was to be the VOC's solution for supplying labor for Company works and private businesses throughout its expansion into southern Africa. The Company recruited workers who would be bound to their urban workplace or inland farm by their difference. Distinctive in language and appearance, imported slaves would be unable to melt into surrounding Khoisan[3] populations as runaways. Slaves were the dominant category of people forcibly transported to the Cape, and the largest group of immigrants in the history of the VOC in the Cape region.[4]

At least 63,000 slaves were imported from Asia and Africa to the Cape between 1657 and 1808.[5] In the first century of Cape slavery, the "overwhelming majority" of slaves were from India, Ceylon, and the Indonesian archipelago.[6] African slaves were imported from Madagascar, Mauritius, and Mozambique. Around 22.7 percent, or 14,300, of all the slaves imported in the VOC period had Indonesian origins. Between 20 and 30 percent of them were women.[7] Records on slaves include Cape government decrees, judicial sentences, and auction rolls. Cape burghers and VOC personnel appear in official documents too, but they also figure in records of their own making, such as letters. Sometimes we see their likenesses in portraits. Mostly, the voices of slaves are missing, so that the personal has to be teased from the impersonal official record.[8]

Inventories of the Orphan Chamber

The documents scrutinized for this study are inventories of possessions of individuals who died without having made a will.[9] Trustees of the Orphan Chamber assumed executive responsibility on behalf of the heirs and had oversight of the inheritances of minor children.[10] These inventories are a major source for the development of Afrikaner society in South Africa, but among them are inventories of the possessions of freed people whose origins were in present-day Indonesia. Their histories and those of Indonesian slave personnel lurk in many records created by the Orphan trustees. For this survey, I have drawn information about 1,318 slaves from 226 inventories and sixty-two public auctions, which were also conducted by the Orphan trustees.[11] The inventories examined here were compiled between 1703 and 1799.

Inventories are documents of people who settle, acquire property, and develop a commitment to the future of their descendants. Material culture generates a history of people. Objects often outlive those who acquired them; they have a life of their own through bequest. Objects tell us about a society's technology, jobs, and fashions, about goods circulating across sea and land networks, about an individual's degree of wealth and lifestyle. People who own things leave them to named individuals, so inventories are also a source for relationships, the tangle of life with spouse, children, and siblings.

The Cape inventories also list human beings as possessions of the testators.[12] Slaves are entered by name and sometimes by occupation. Inventories record if a slave was infirm or a runaway. They record the transfer of slaves by bequest to an heir, or a slave's passage to a new legal and social status through manumission. Inventories of freed slaves list what they had accumulated in material goods and slaves. Former slaves appear in auction results as purchasers, and they are found in the sections of the inventory that recorded the discharging of debts to an estate or monies owed to it.

Some slaves were consulted by testators as to where and with whom they wished to live after the testators' death. Here we find the voices and personal wishes of slaves, for the Orphan trustees recorded slaves' choice of manumission or of which household they wanted to join. Orphan officials itemized possessions and took statements in the presence of witnesses. Relatives who could not sign their own names did so with a cross. In inventories, then, we have a form of oral history, words uttered by a cross section of Cape society in the 1700s.

Inventories chart the passing of Indonesian words for personal effects into Cape Dutch vocabulary. But the identity of individual Indonesians is sometimes ambiguous on account of Dutch naming practices. Europeans identify themselves in these inventories by names given them by parents at baptism and by father's surname. Slaves, on the contrary, are identified by names given them by those owning them at the time the inventories were made. Each such person had a name before enslavement, a name known to the individual slave, but possibly not known to the purchaser at the Cape.

Slaves were given first names that might be classical or biblical. Other slave names indicate the month when a slave was purchased or represent something of the slave's personality. Some names were derogatory. Slave surnames were formed by *van* (from, of) and place of origin. Examples include Titus van Java, Isak van Timor, Augustus van Maccassar, Mattroos (sailor) van Batavia, Fortuijn van Bougies, and Pasop (watch out!) van Samboua.[13] A place name may indicate the port to which slavers brought their human cargo for sale to the Dutch rather than the home region of the enslaved, so it may not always be a reliable indicator of ethnicity and origin. However, VOC documents confirm what slave surnames indicate, that most slaves originated in the eastern archipelago or Nias.[14]

These documents are written in eighteenth-century Dutch. Indonesia's slaves must have been speakers of many languages. Communication among themselves may therefore have been in forms of Malay used in archipelago ports. A pidgin Dutch replaced Malay and Portuguese among Asian slaves at the Cape in the eighteenth century[15] and was the language in which they communicated with African slaves and with their slaveholders. Gwyn Campbell notes the universal incentive for slaves to forge links with slaveholders, since only they could ameliorate the slaves' condition.[16] It is impossible to ascertain how well slaves understood the legalese of the inventory, but clearly those given the opportunity to choose among their deceased owners' heirs were able to communicate this important decision to the VOC officials responsible for taking their statements.

Children born at the Cape to imported slaves were surnamed van de Caab by their mothers' owners, and they inherited their mothers' slave status.[17] For example, the female slave Candase van Nias is listed in an inventory along with her baby, Clarinde van de Caab.[18] Here is evidence of reproduction within a social group, but as a result of this naming practice, knowledge of the ethnic and religio-cultural origins of forebears of succeeding generations of slaves and freed slaves is lost.

MARRIAGE AND INHERITANCE

Cape law codes were derived from Dutch-Roman law.[19] Possessions brought to marriage by husband and wife became joint property. On the death of a spouse the surviving partner inherited one-half of the estate, with the other half divided equally between legitimate male and female children, whether adults or minors, and including all legitimate children born to either partner from previous marriages. Illegitimate children had no claim on the father's estate. On the death of spouses, Orphan Chamber staff made a written record of the couple's joint possessions. They arranged sale of the property by public auction, certified the payment of debts, and distributed remaining funds among the heirs. Inventories list personal effects, household goods, and tools by the room or workplace in which they were found; they enumerate farm animals and wagons. They also list the slaves. Some inventories include monetary appraisals by Orphan staff of each object and person. Auction rolls list each item, material and human, the name of the purchaser, and the amount paid.

Slaves were not permitted to marry.[20] The Dutch Reformed Church restricted marriage to free Christians, so slave families had no officially acknowledged existence.[21] Children issuing from such unions were illegitimate and therefore could not inherit from the father, whether he were a free man or a slave. Slave families could be split up by sale or transfer of members to another worksite. Children of slave mothers were recorded by maternal parentage. It is rare to find cases where a slave or European father of illegitimate children is documented in the inventories.

The inventory record shows some slaves purchased their own manumission. It registers confirmation in cases where testators had nominated specified slaves to be freed on their death. At times, Orphan trustees itemizing the possessions of deceased freed slaves did record relationships between the deceased, a de facto spouse, children, and friends. Because slave marriages did not exist in law, slaves' inventories do not have the same generational depth or complexity of those of Europeans.

There were always more male slaves imported than female, so the possibility for slaves and former slaves of forming families was limited. Men were more numerous among the burgher population too.[22] Accordingly, slave and freed men competed with European men for female partners. Temporary relationships, rather than family formation, were the recourse for many slaves. Nevertheless, the inventory record suggests de facto relationships and family formation within and outside church-conducted marriage. According to Antonia Malan, the preferred marriage for an emancipated woman was with a European settler, so her children might prosper as part of the burgher class.[23]

Freed slaves who were not indigenous to Africa were labeled *vrijswart* (free black male) or *vrijswartin* (free black female).[24] "Free black" denoted slaves whose origins were in India, Ceylon, and the Indonesian archipelago. In the eighteenth century, less than 1 percent of free blacks were of African origin.[25] "Free black" was a status term. It was not heritable. Children born to free blacks were free. Boys confirmed this status by taking the burgher oath at adulthood. Transition from free black to burgher was accomplished in the VOC era in one generation.[26]

It is impossible to ascertain the ethnic origins of individual free blacks surnamed van de Caab from the inventories, as they do not include parents' names. What the inventories do show is relationships, including marriage, between slaves and former slaves from India, Ceylon, and Indonesia, but rarely between them and slaves or freed slaves whose origins were African. The inventories provide evidence of the formation of a free segment of society whose members' homelands were in Asia and whose descendants merged into the European community or the group today known as Cape Malay.

SLAVES' LIVES: THE VIEW FROM ABOVE

Most Cape inventories are documents compiled by Europeans for Europeans in VOC Africa.[27] We view slaves from the perspective of testators and Orphan trustees. We find that an individual purchased slaves from a variety of places as ships arrived from different slave-supplying ports.[28] A partial list of the workforce of burgher Hans Casper Gerringer, for example, shows his slaves came from both Asia and Africa:

> Daris van Bengalen
> Jan van Batavia
> Coridon van Ceijlon
> Jan van Madagascar.[29]

Orphanage officials sometimes entered their estimation of the value of an estate, as in the following list of two male and two female slaves:

Abraham van Batavia	100 rds [rixdollars]
Fortuijn van Madagascar	115
Rockea van Boegis	100
Candase van Madagascar	100[30]

In the example following, the estimate was for the slaves as a group:

> Slammat van Boegies
> Coridon van Bengalen
> Spadielle van Batavia
> Pedro van Bengalen

Diena van Maccassar, with her three children named Eva van de
Caab, David van de Caab, and Simpson van de Caab
The above slaves being estimated at 800 Rds[31]

The occupations of male slaves from Indonesia are given in this example from one of the properties owned by Petronella Catharina Leever
and Matthiam le Roes:

Achilles van Bougies, carpenter
Junij van Bougies, bricklayer
Panaij van Sambawa, bricklayer
Damon van Macassar, bricklayer
Joumat van Macassar, smith
Fortuijn van Bougies, cart driver[32]

Auction sheets record prices paid for slaves when humans and material possessions were sold in order to divide an estate between heirs. Slaves in the
estate of Elisabeth Richard, for instance, were sold in 1740 to five different
purchasers as follows:

Baatjoe van Boegis	[to] Pieter Hugot	160 [rds]
Haman van Boegis	Michiel Groos	76.4
Thoebara van Boegis	Nicolaas Walters	54.2
Adam van Boegis	Anthonij Lombart	207
Julij van Boegis	François Jubert	126[33]

By contrast, Fhortuijn van Macasser and his daughter, Sara van de Caab,
embarked on a new destiny when Godfried Heijdenrijk bought them together
for 403 rixdollars.[34] This is a rare instance in the inventory and auction records
of a slave father's paternity being acknowledged and a family bond preserved
when slaves were sold at public auction.

Testators sometimes bequeathed designated slaves to their heirs. Orphan
officials made a sworn statement that they had carried out such wishes, for
example, on behalf of Barbara de Savoije. She left a slave to each of her
sons and two of her daughters, along with clothing and household goods.
Her other daughter's share included two slaves, one of whom was Alida van
Java.[35] Sometimes Orphan officials took the initiative in assigning slaves among
heirs of the deceased. For example, when the widowed Maria de Leeuw died,
they selected some of her slaves to remain unsold to care for her three young
children. It is noteworthy that those chosen were a slave family, described in
these terms: "an old slave named Slammat van Bougies, his wife, the elderly

slave Martha van Bengalen, and their four small children, named Deborah, Camonie, Slammat and Martha, all [surnamed] van de Caab."[36]

From inventories we learn of fugitive slaves. Cupido van Batavia's name comes at the end of price estimates for the slaves owned by Caspar Hendrik Batenhorst with the note "in chains at the arsenal, [so] no valuation."[37] I found four other cases of Indonesian slaves who had fled servitude. Manus van Boegis, Herodus van Banda, and Arontus van Bogies are described simply as runaways; Meij van Boegies is recorded as having been missing for eighteen months when the estate of Geertruy Bockelenberg was wound up.[38]

Orphan officials sometimes entered personal descriptions of slaves. Caatje van Java is recorded as blind. A note attached to Spadillie van Bougies advises he has leprosy and therefore will not be sold.[39] Ten slave women, three of whom were surnamed van Boegies, are described as "robust girls."[40] Julij van Batavia and Soentie van Bogies must have reached the end of their working lives, being characterized by the Orphan scribes as old and infirm.[41] Another inventory lists "an old female slave Sanna van Batavia, now worn out," and values her at ten guilders.[42]

Examples of the ambiguity of slaves' origins can be found in the naming practices of certain slave owners. A slave named Javan van Bombaije is entered in the auction sheet for the estate of Ernst Fredrik de Swart; Bengalen van Batavia belonged to the estate of Andries du Toit.[43] Only seven of the 1,318 Indonesian slaves in the inventories and auctions I surveyed have Islamic names. They are Abbas van Maccassar, Abbas van Boegis, Mansoer van Boegies, Alij van Batavia, Aly van Sambava, Ismael van Timor, and Antonij Moor van Japare.[44] Does this signify that they were Muslim and, in naming them, the slaveholders acknowledged their religion?

The literature on Cape slavery often assumes that all inhabitants of the Indonesian archipelago were Muslim by the eighteenth century and that therefore slaves brought to the Cape were Muslim too.[45] But the extent of conversion is not fully known, and Muslim slavers who supplied Batavia sought their human supplies in non-Muslim villages of the archipelago. The VOC deliberately settled charismatic Muslim exiles at remote locations to prevent them from spreading Islam among slaves at the Cape.[46] It is unlikely that slaveholders would have allowed their slaves to leave off work and walk for days into the hinterland to study Islam from men whom the VOC considered seditious. Slaves absenting themselves without permission faced chained labor when apprehended.

Ward argues that there was a consciousness of Islam among Southeast Asian slaves and convicts at the Cape, but her example of actual propagation of Islam by a time-served Indonesian exile comes from the end of the eighteenth century.[47] The institutional presence of Islam at the Cape dates from the mid-nineteenth century with establishment of the first mosque and its attendant religious professionals. In VOC times and territory, incentives to convert were to Christianity. Christian baptism was a condition for manumission. The rare surviving writings by Cape slaves were the work of devout Christians.[48] The inventory records I consulted identify baptized slaves but do not contain any references to adherents of Islam among the slaves.[49]

Inventory takers recorded bequests made to slaves. Joachim Nicolaus van Dessin's estate comprised the numerous contents of two houses, including paintings, furniture, bed linens, clothing, silver cutlery and ornaments, 3,856 books and manuscripts, mathematical and astrological instruments, a packet of Japanese rice, and thirteen slaves. He prescribed that his stocks of workers' clothing should not be sold, but divided up among his slaves. For three he made additional provisions. Two male slaves, Fortuijn van Mallabaar and Leander van de Cust, were to receive six blue and six white shirts each, while one of his female slaves, Liesje van Bougies, was to receive lengths of plain and striped calico and gingham. The secretary of the Orphan Chamber also recorded that the considerable sum of three hundred guilders had been paid out to each of these three slaves "to help [them] stabilize."[50] In another case, landlord Dirk Coetzee declared to the Orphan trustees that his tenant, Emanuel Warner, had set free two of his slaves before his death. One of the manumitted men had Indonesian origins. This was Zacharias van Batavia, who thereby gained his personal liberty.[51]

SLAVES' LIVES: GLIMPSES FROM BELOW

Would slaves choose emancipation if given that choice? It seems some would not. Employment agencies did not exist at the Cape in the eighteenth century; slave and indentured labor were the norm.[52] Evidence from the inventories is that Indonesian slaves often opted for food, clothing, and shelter; they took up the offer to choose among their deceased owner's heirs which household they would join. In the case of the male slave Paccar van Sumbawa and female slave Carmona van Boogies, we have the Orphan officials' confirmation that they exercised this choice, which came with a guarantee of never being re-sold.[53]

In some inventories the slave's choice is explicit. For example, Mentor van Boegies exercised the choice given him by Johannes Fischer and opted to go to the married daughter Anna Jacomina Fischer; Fortuyn van Batavia and the female slave Soentier van Boegies chose the eldest son, Johannes Henricus Fischer; Alet van Boegies chose another daughter, Johanna Elizabeth Fischer.[54] Aletta van Cheribon, given the choice among the seven adult heirs of Frederik Kirsten, selected the son in employ of the VOC. Perhaps she felt her status enhanced by moving into the household of the Cape governor's secretary.[55] In another deposition, Forthuijn de klijne (the younger) van Ternaten "requests the widow [Catharina Hatting] that, because each of her married children has already received a slave, he should be allowed by the estate to remain unsold, which [request] was orally agreed to by the heirs."[56]

Some slaves acquired special provisions in testamentary dispositions. Mina van Macasser and Ontong van Batavia were perhaps reassured by a precautionary stipulation of Elizabeth Mostert in assigning them to her daughter Sophia Hendrina van der Heijde. If, "contrary to expectation," they were mistreated by Sophia, "then they shall be free to go live with another of her children."[57] Abram van Ternate and his son Adolf van de Caab chose to remain within the Berg family, with the guarantee that they would never again be sold.[58]

Auctions of large estates took place over several days. They were busy affairs. In the absence of department stores, people furnished their rooms and equipped their kitchens cheaply by buying secondhand goods at public sales. Slaves stood among the chests, bedsteads, and farm animals during the bidding. From this perspective, slaves may have valued the guarantee of never being sold again. After a working life grounded in dependency, some perhaps felt lacking in the entrepreneurial skills required for the life of a freelancer. For them a future as free men and women might seem the freedom to be indigent.[59] The few possessions left by former slave Cupido van Bougies seem to validate this hypothesis. His worldly goods were in a chest containing a blue jacket, seven old shirts, two blue singlets, three pairs of trousers, two golden buttons, a straw mattress, a pillow, and a blanket.[60] Manuel van Macasser's estate amounted to "odds and ends" or "rubbish" that raised a mere 15.7 rixdollars at auction. His sole "possession" of any value was a slave, Joseph van Batavia, who was sold separately for 81 rixdollars. After small charges had been deducted, 76.5 rixdollars went to his estate for Manuel's as then unidentified heirs.[61]

Tobias Christian Rönnenkamp evidently discussed other arrangements for the future of several of his slave personnel on his decease. Damon van Bougies chose to leave and board with the freed Amelia van Boegies. Through the legalese of the inventory we can still hear the eagerness of the freed slave, Geduld van Mandhaar, when another of Rönnenkamp's slaves, Camonia van Mandhaar, was given the opportunity to join her husband. Geduld declared himself "willing and offered and promised to pay the requisite costs of her emancipation at the first possible opportunity."[62] Two others, Tamerlang van Macasser and his wife, Marcina van Mandhaar, sought and were given permission to live out their days with the free black Anthonij van Bengalen.[63]

This Anthonij van Bengalen must have boarded newly freed slaves. He discharged the manumission taxes for the "old and worn out male slave Maart van Coromandel" on 31 May 1793 and for Tamerlang and Marcina on 30 September 1793, paying 45 rixdollars for the three. The free black Jacob van Amboina turned to Pieter van Bengalen for a loan to support his wife, Dorothea van de Caab, and their six children aged between eighteen months and fourteen years. When Jacob died, his possessions amounted to not much more than a teapot, a few plates, a rice block, five old chairs, and some bedding, and he still owed Pieter three hundred guilders.[64]

Here we see a web of social relationships at the Cape between slaves and ex-slaves from the Indonesian archipelago and India that must have helped the newly manumitted survive. The evidence of inventories is that slaves did form families and that some owners acknowledged affective relationships among their slaves. Pieter Willem Regnault, for example, stipulated that Julij van Macassar and Mina van Samboua were to be sold together "and may not be separated by the purchaser."[65]

Inventories and auction statements show us emancipated slaves who struck out on their own going about their daily lives in Cape Town.[66] Perhaps they had run small businesses for their slaveholders while enslaved, and so had the necessary work experience and confidence to take up the offer of manumission.[67] We find former slaves renting accommodations, taking out small loans, paying off debts, going to public sales, buying household goods and slaves, intermarrying across Indonesian ethnic groups, finding partners who had South Asian or European origins, caring for grandchildren, and ultimately leaving a glimpse of their work lives and personal tastes through the material objects they accumulated in life after slavery. Inventories of their estates were mostly modest, but some former slaves evidently prospered. Through the lists of chafing dishes, European cutlery, Asian rice blocks and pounders, Japanese ceramic plates, gloves, and cuspidors, we find evidence of participation in and contribution to a distinctive local culture that South Africa's scholars call Creole.[68]

We can begin with Susanna van Batavia, who affirmed an inventory to be a true record of the possessions of her partner, the *vrijswart* Jan van Macasser, who passed away in 1709.[69] The household and business of Jan and Susanna depended on the labor of three male slaves, Dammon, Bolij (written as Olij in the auction record made a month later), and Baetje. No place-surname is recorded for them. Among the couple's household goods were a bedstead, a mattress, blankets and four pillows, a small table, three chairs, plate racks, a teapot, a copper kettle, twenty-four small china plates (called by the Indonesian word *piering*), a gridiron, and a lamp. Evidence of their income-producing work is the six fish vats, buckets, casks, two horses, and a saddle and bridle. Two rixdollars were deposited with Frans Guito.

Perhaps Jan and Susanna were fishmongers, delivering to customers by horse. They appear to have modified their sleeping habits in the temperate climate of the Cape, sleeping in a bed seated upright against pillows as the Dutch did. They also appear to have taken their meals seated on chairs at a table rather than sitting on a mat on the floor. Although of modest means, the couple had chinaware, rather than tin plates, and had, at the Cape, become tea drinkers. Susanna maintained these habits, for she bought from the estate the pillows and chairs, as well as an iron pot, an empty cask, and the slave Olij. Her total purchases from Jan's estate amounted to 173.2 rixdollars.[70] Of this sum, 8.2 rixdollars were spent on the household items and 165 rixdollars on the slave, suggesting that Susanna had accumulated savings or working capital.[71] There were eighteen other successful bidders, fifteen with European names, one with a Chinese name, and another Indonesian purchaser, Titus van Macasser, who bought household items.

Jan's estate was liquidated for 519 rixdollars. Had the relationship been legally recognized, Susanna would have been named his sole inheritor. Instead, the estate was regarded as having no legatees, so the proceeds of the sale would have gone to the Church Poor Fund. Perhaps it was the same Susanna van Batavia who, nine years later, purchased two tin basins and six tin plates for 2.9 rixdollars from the estate of Adam Leendert van Nieuwenbroek, two racks and a scale with weights from the estate of Zimon Faassen, and odds and ends worth 1.1½ rixdollars the following year.[72] These purchases, made a decade after Jan's death, suggest reduced circumstances.

September van Boegis left behind far more than Jan van Macasser but had no acknowledged companions or heirs. His inventory tells us he rented three rooms of a house owned by the burgher Pieter Broeders.[73] September had slept in a curtained bed with bolster, pillows, bed linen, a woolen blanket, and a bedspread of Indian chintz. He left white and colored shirts, two pairs of trousers, two pairs of black wool socks, one pair of shoes, caps, and a loose gown (*moorse rok*).[74] He had also owned five chairs, twenty-eight large and small porcelain plates, three porcelain bowls, a milk jug and kettle, a mortar and pestle, a pipe rack, and a copper candlestick. The shoes may be noted, for shod feet were a sign of upward mobility, distinguishing free from slave.

Inventories of goods belonging to women lead us further into the social lives of former slaves at the Cape.[75] The widowed Susanna van Bougis had married a free black, Philip van Boeton.[76] They had a daughter, Pieternella, who married a man with the European name Paul Hertog, and grandsons, Philip and Johannes Hertog, who were aged fifteen and twelve at the time of Susanna's death. Pieternella had predeceased her parents, so her boys were named as heirs to the estate. Susanna had done well in worldly possessions. Her inventory lists numerous items in her own house in Table Valley, including Dutch bedding, twenty-six kerchiefs, gold and silver jewelry, a mirror, porcelain, and iron and earthenware cooking equipment. Also listed are a male slave, Assar van Maccasser, and a female slave, Isabella van de Caab, with her child Adriana (so, in this case, a second-generation Cape-born slave).[77] Susanna's estate owed interest on 250 guilders to the Orphan Chamber and 35 rixdollars to Paul Hertog. Susanna's son-in-law witnessed the inventory with his own signature.

Here we have a narrative of imported slaves converting to Christianity, being manumitted, contracting a legal marriage, earning a living, marrying their daughter into the European burgher segment of Cape society, and endowing the next generation. The boys' surname of Hertog conceals from future records their mixed Asian and European ancestry. Paul Hertog bought a copper casserole with lid and a few other household items at the public auction of his mother-in-law's possessions, and his name appears as a purchaser at other auctions too.[78]

Hanna van Boegies "married out." Her husband was Lucas van Bengalen. Their inventory shows a successful couple who had amassed a considerable number and range of personal possessions.[79] They rented a four-room house in town (foyer, front room, store room, and kitchen). The kitchen was well stocked with clay, tin, iron, pewter, and copper cookware. The couple ate from both china and tin plates with spoons and forks, and had a china tea service, teapots, and a coffeepot and mill. They ate rice (a rice block and pounder were listed), sat on chairs at a dining table, and slept in a red-curtained bed. Perhaps they chewed betel, because they owned two copper cuspidors. Candlesticks and a lantern lighted their house; ten paintings and a mirror hung on its walls. Slaves from Indonesia, India, and Mozambique served the household and family businesses.

Hanna and Lucas must have sold household supplies, for they left quantities of textiles, including chintzes, cambric, taffeta, velvet, wool, and linen. Numerous bottles and casks suggest they may also have retailed wine. They also apparently supplied builders, for they had stocks of brushes, buckets, and ladders, and they sold artists' supplies, including pencils and brushes, linseed oil, and paints such as yellow ochre and Persian red. They sold to Europeans on credit. A VOC surgeon and five other male customers owed them small amounts, but the widow of another European man had run up a debt of 101.6 rixdollars. The Orphan officials found the considerable sum of 1,445:18 rixdollars on the premises. In the absence of banks and credit unions, Hanna and Lucas also put their earnings into savings in the form of gold and silver ornaments.[80] The inventory lists silver buttons and buckles, gold bracelets, gold earrings, two diamonds, four rubies, and a three-string coral necklace with gold clasps.

Among the couple's personal apparel were skirts, blouses, frocks, shirts, trousers, shoes and stockings, caps and bonnets, handkerchiefs, and two pairs of women's white gloves. The blouses, skirts, trousers, and shirts tell us that Hanna and Lucas covered their entire bodies in tailored clothes, whereas they would have worn body wraps in their homelands. The wearing of shoes encouraged sitting on chairs, rather than on the floor. The footwear, headgear, gloves, and handkerchiefs indicate upward mobility in the adoption of European-style clothing and modes of decorum. Wool socks and the curtained bed show adaptation to European norms, as well as a response to the cooler Cape climate. The women's gloves may suggest churchgoing. They were a feature of Ambonese Christian dress and appear not to have been worn on other ceremonial occasions. At least, surviving portraits of VOC elite women do not show them wearing gloves.[81]

In 1781 Hanna and Lucas had drawn up their wills, and here we find evidence of their family ties and social relationships at the Cape. Having no children of their own, they designated as heirs Abraham and Sara, the two children of Hanna's sister Sietera van Boegies by a man named Jammel van Java. Abraham and Sara were illegitimate and so bore the surname van de Caab, but, according to the testimony of Hanna and Lucas, their grandchildren had been baptized and emancipated. In asking the free black David van Ceilon to become guardian of the children, rather than their father, Jammel (who may have still been a slave), we find evidence of relationships among the free black community of former slaves imported from Asia.

Christian orphans left without designated guardians and inheritances became a charge on the Church Poor Fund. Eleven-year-old Sara spoke through the trustees, requesting that the family's "old" slave Maria van Mosambicque be allowed to stay on as her nursemaid. Presumably the other five slaves listed in the inventory were sold along with assets of the estate not specifically left to the children. Through their removal by sale they contributed to the funds that supported the children while Abraham remained a minor and before Sara came to marry.

Some slaves accompanied their employers on journeys within the VOC world. Perhaps Aron van Makassar, Dorinde van Macasser, and Amaril van Mannaar felt a general sense of homecoming when they accompanied the widow of Councilor Extraordinary Abraham Cranendonk from the Cape to Java.[82] Other slaves traveled to the Netherlands itself as attendants for repatriating officials and burghers. For these slaves it was a journey of both novel experience and personal transformation, for, by Batavia ordinance of 9 October 1714, they made the return journey as free persons.[83] Patiencie van Balij,

Sara van Batavia, Roselijn van Bougis, Anthonia van Batavia, and Dupa van Turatja (Toraja, Sulawesi) were authorized to sail for the Netherlands in 1733, on the condition that their employers paid in full the costs of their round-trip journey.[84]

What did they make of wintry Holland in the time spent waiting for the next Indies fleet to sail for the Cape? Two inventories convey something for Aurora van Sambouna, who accompanied her mistress, Sara Duijm, to the Netherlands in 1763. In Amsterdam in January 1764 Aurora gave birth to a daughter, Catharina. For the return journey with her baby, Aurora packed baby clothes and diapers, a cake of Spanish soap, coins in various currencies, silver earrings set with small stones, a gold ring, other ornaments, and clothing. But Aurora did not live to make something of her status of manumitted woman and mother of a free child, for she died on board the *Scholtenburg* in November before it anchored at the Cape. Catharina seems to have been placed in the care of Anna Kleijns, widow of Cornelis Doesen, for Orphan staff recorded Anna as having Aurora's worldly goods in her keeping "for the deceased's child."[85]

Other Cape families that were founded in slavery leave tantalizing glimpses of their social and work lives, as the following examples show. Aagje van Java read from a Bible that had a silver clasp. We can picture her going to church, after first checking her appearance in one of her two mirrors, dressed in a silk gown, wearing silver earrings, gloves, shoes, and stockings. Perhaps she carried one of her three fans and a handkerchief.[86] Freed men conducted business arrangements with European burghers. Arcat van Boegies, for example, rented one of Albert Meyburgh's slaves, August van Boegies, for five rixdollars a month, and requested Meyburgh's executors to be allowed to continue this business arrangement with his heirs.[87] In the list of persons to whom money was owing at the time of Arnoldus Kruijsman's death is the entry: "Jacob Maccassar: 21.17.8 guilders."[88] Jacob van Maccasser Senior and Jacob van Maccasser Junior were foremen on Arnoldus Willemsz Basson's farm. At the time of Basson's death they were owed 172:2.8 and 103:10 guilders in wages.[89] In the absence of banks at the Cape, ex-slaves borrowed sums from wealthy Europeans (as did burghers). Maij van Soping (southern Sulawesi) and Aurora van Terra de Natal owed J. N. Dessin the balance on a loan taken out in 1755 and interest accruing since 1760, amounting to 160 guilders at the time of his death. Another couple, Sara van Batavia and Radin Mascar, owed the Dessin estate 210 guilders.[90]

Unlike Sara, Radin Mascar was not a former slave. He is called Radeen Mascaretta and "the Javanese prince" in other VOC documents[91] and had been banished to the Cape with a small suite in 1751. He had petitioned to be allowed early return to Indonesia in 1756 because of his impoverished circumstances. References in Council of Policy documents to his always be-having "quietly and with decorum" suggest Radin Mascar was allowed a large degree of personal freedom at the Cape, extending to forming a household with ex-slave Sara. Perhaps they were in business together or simply unable to live within their means, hence the loan from Dessin in 1761. Radin Mascar renewed his request for repatriation in 1765, which the Council of Policy "graciously" agreed to support. Sara must have perceived her status enhanced through her relationship with the prince. Perhaps she anticipated a return to Java with pride.

Unlike time-served convicts and exiles, emancipated slaves could not realistically think of returning to their home communities in Indonesia. Yet some did. Sampoerne van Boegies petitioned the Cape authorities for per-mission to travel free of charge on a Company ship with his wife and two young children to Batavia "so as subsequently to take up with his friends in Makassar."[92] Sampoerne's request suggests a continuing attachment to home, perhaps contact with folk in his natal village. What is striking is Sampoerne's confidence in his right as a freed person to address the Cape government and make demands on it.

CONVICTS AND EXILES

Convicts were individuals from VOC-controlled ports who had been brought before Councils of Justice by Asian or European accusers and on whom the sentence of deportation and labor for a fixed term had been imposed. Con-victs sent to the Cape labored on public works. They could not be sold to bur-ghers. Having the right to repatriation upon completion of their sentence, convicts do not show up in inventory records. I found only one inventory recording the possessions of a convict. This was the *vrij bandit* (time-served convict) Anna Codalilla van de West Cust Padang, who had borne a daughter at the Cape. Perhaps she felt unable to take up her former life on account of her poverty. All she had to leave Alima was two empty ordinary chests, one lot of odds and ends, one slave, Silon van Nias, and eight and a half *schelling*.[93]

Exile was a strategy used by both the Company and Indonesian sul-tans to remove men (plus their retinues) who had challenged the authority of the VOC or threatened royal power.[94] The latter might be rival claimants to the thrones of reigning sultans, or they were religious leaders who de-nounced royals and their Dutch backers. One inventory of an exile's posses-sions survives in the Orphan archives.[95] It lists the handful of belongings of Radeen Djoerit, "former regent of Madura," who died in the Cape fort in 1748. This was Cakraningrat IV (r. 1718–1745), whose lineage had ruled Bangkalan (West Madura) as a vassal of the Javanese kingdom of Mataram for generations. In 1743 Cakraningrat had switched allegiance to the VOC but later turned against the Company. He was declared a rebel and exiled, first to Banjermasin, then to Cape Town in 1746.[96] There Djoerit-Cakraningrat had been reduced to a household containing a bedstead, a bedspread and pillows, a table, four chairs, and a few copper and iron cooking utensils. He ate off clay and ceramic dishes, apparently with his fingers, Indonesian-style, for no cutlery is listed in the inventory. His personal effects amounted to a few articles of clothing, including a black dress coat, camisole, and breeches with worked silver buttons and buttonholes. Bedding, furniture, and kitchenware had been loaned to him from the Cape governor's household and were to be returned.

From this inventory we discover the former ruler's reduced and humbled state. No mattress or bed curtains are listed, and there were no paintings to beautify his quarters. Radeen Djoerit left behind a sum of twenty-eight rixdollars and eighteen stuivers (accruing from his VOC living allowance) and two male slaves, Datan van Aroe and Njasrie van Madura. According to the inventory the two latter were not to be sold until further orders from the governor. This inventory makes a valuable comparison with that of Hanna van Boegies and Lucas van Bengalen. Clearly, ex-slaves, by their entrepreneurial exertions, were able to attain a much more comfortable lifestyle than the prince of Bangkalan, who lived as a prisoner in the Cape fortress.[97]

The inventory is more than a list. It is a mini-biography, a record of belongings and of belonging. Its key elements—names and possessions—provide a research methodology for discovering a surprising amount and range of data. Names give us the individual and the individual's connections to others and relationship to society. Possessions reveal how a life was lived. The goods in inventories of emancipated slaves were not *pusaka* (ritual objects of spiritual significance or magical powers), such as Java's Amangkurat III spirited off to Ceylon when forced into exile in 1708, discussed by Ricci in chapter 4 in this volume. They were household goods acquired at the Cape. Little luxuries—a fan, a mirror, silver buttons—were small elegancies that lifted the individual above the daily grind.

The inventory is not a static document of a dead person's things. The several parts of the eighteenth-century Cape inventory allow us to see individuals in various settings, acting, being spoken for, and speaking for themselves. The inventory cautions us against transferring a contemporary horror of slavery onto the eighteenth century. Law court records show that house and farm slaves informed on their fellows and assisted the authorities in their capture of runaways.[98] Former slaves bought slaves. Personal experience of slavery did not cause ex-slaves to reject this mode of securing workers. Campbell argues that, in becoming slaveholders, ex-slaves aligned themselves with the values and practices of the slaveholding society in which they lived.[99] But we must also remember that ex-slaves came from Indonesian communities where slavery was a given. Shell gives no evidence to support his view that slaves imported to the Cape had been wrenched from happy, intact families.[100]

Emancipated men and women sold off their own slaves, splitting up families in the process. In some cases they failed to identify their own slaves by name. This point introduces a caution into the methodology. The inventory works as a research tool for people with names. There are 20,386 entries for slaves in the MOOC inventories. In numerous cases, slaves are entered in numbered batches only. In other cases slaves' names lack the geographic marker that formed their surnames. Considering the random survival of documents as well, we have to acknowledge that sampling cannot yield a wholly reliable picture of the history of Indonesians in Africa.

The primary source obviously shapes perception. If I had used criminal court cases, as Margaret Lenta has done, the findings of occasional benevolence in the inventories would be countered by the gruesome forms of execution to which slaves convicted of killing their owners were condemned.[101] One slave was publicly executed every month at the Cape between 1680 and 1775. What Lenta calls a judicial strategy of "spectacular violence" was employed in Cape Town to control the slave majority, and paralleled in the countryside by the private violence of burgher farmers against slaves.[102]

Nevertheless, the inventory is a significant source on Indonesians caught up in the universal phenomenon of forced migration in the eighteenth century. They do not figure in histories of Indonesia. And yet their history is of more than antiquarian interest. The inventory, with its peculiar devotion to names, allows us to draw tentative conclusions from actual lives.

The inventories show us that in too many cases human beings were considered by slaveholders to be assets with a monetary value. For most men and women whose life stories began in the Indonesian archipelago, inventories provide evidence only of labor in other peoples' homes, in workshops, and on farms. Their skills as builders, cart drivers, fishermen, cooks, and nannies contributed to the survival of a Company settlement on the southernmost fringe of Africa. But the inventory allows us to go beyond such basic data about societies based on slave labor. Slavery and slaveholders did not extinguish the humanity of the enslaved. Some slaves managed to impose an acknowledgment of their personal qualities. Cesar van Macassar and Catrijn van Mallabar, for example, were "on account of their many years of faithful service" given the option to go where they wished. In consequence, the Orphan officials recorded "the two slaves have remained with one of the [Roes] children and live there."[103] The individual personhood of the emancipated shines through in their preference for dining off porcelain rather than coarser pewter, in decorating their home with paintings, and in building up their own businesses.

Through names in inventories we grasp that most basic of human relationships: mother and child. Enslaved women passed on their condition of slavery to their children. They knew who the fathers were, but that information has not survived the legal constraints of the slave condition and time. The many children surnamed van de Caab tell us of both temporary and lasting relationships, forced or voluntary, across ethnic group and class. By the middle of the eighteenth century, slaves born at the Cape outnumber imported slaves in many inventory slave lists. This is evidence of a self-reproducing segment of society. It is also proof of personal relationships and roots in a new homeland.

The inventories tell us a little more: of the meaning of home to slaves; of spiritual change through conversion; of the dignity of recognized marriage; of the protection inheritance rights to family property gave wives and children. Malan cautions against seeing an embrace of Dutch culture in entries of things such as tart pans, water carafes, and candlesticks in inventories of ex-slaves. She argues that none came "naked" to the Cape, that acculturation was not one-way.[104] Everything had to be imported, whether from Europe or Asia, so the burgher and the emancipated owned similar types of goods. In her analysis, the difference the inventories show is that of wealth and therefore class.

But we *can* see lifestyle changes by former slaves. Coffee drinking did not become common among Indonesians until the nineteenth century, yet freed slaves were coffee drinkers at the Cape in the eighteenth to judge by the coffeepots and coffee grinders in their inventories. Buttons tell us their owners had worn shirts and blouses, in other words, had a covered upper body, which indicates both moral and fashion values. Shoes and wool socks may have been a response to winters at the Cape, but they were also marks of difference between slave and free, indigenous and immigrant. Former slaves no longer ate with their fingers. In porcelain dishes, silver tableware, and paintings we see cases where freed slaves had attained a standard of living that allowed for refinements and indulgence of an aesthetic sense.

The mirror (imported from Europe) allowed its owner scrutiny of self, and so suggests the emerging of a modern consciousness among former slaves at the Cape. Perhaps Wilhelmina van Macassar, gazing at her reflection in one of her mirrors, pondered with satisfaction her journey from slave market to mistress of a rented four-room house stocked with goods. They were to become the property of her only child, who bore the burgher-like name of Adolph Anthonysz.[105]

Freed slaves had a working knowledge of Dutch. If they owned a book, the inventory records that it was the Bible. When they named their own children, as opposed to naming by owners, former slaves chose names that were common among Dutch people of the age; they did not hark back to names remembered from their home villages.

Liston's study (chapter 8 in this volume) of nineteenth-century convicts transported to Australia is based on a wealth of data. By comparison, the inventory is not much to go on. But it does allow us to establish that ex-slaves, like ex-convicts, found opportunity in foreign environments and capacity in themselves to rise above miserable circumstances and succeed in ways they could never have done in the lands of their birth. The inventory fosters appreciation of the accomplishments of individuals whose life span encompassed a home village in Indonesia, transport to Africa, labor for others, establishment of small businesses for themselves, and provision for the next generation, whose future and identity were locally based.

NOTES

My appreciative thanks to Nigel Worden and Kerry Ward for comments on an earlier version of this chapter.

1. De Vereenigde Oost-Indische Compagnie controlled settlements along the coasts of Asia between 1602 and 1799. Its Asian headquarters was Batavia (present-day Jakarta).

2. Kerry Ward, *Networks of Empire: Forced Migration in the Dutch East India Company* (Cambridge: Cambridge University Press, 2009), 152. By 1700 the burgher population was 1,334. It had grown to 15,000 when the British took over the Cape in 1795.

3. "Khoisan" designates the indigenous herder and hunter populations in the Cape region.

4. The slave population outstripped the burgher community by the 1720s; Nigel Worden, *Slavery in Dutch South Africa* (Cambridge: Cambridge University Press, 1985), 11.

5. Robert C.-H. Shell, *Children of Bondage: A Social History of the Slave Society at the Cape of Good Hope, 1652–1838* (Hanover, NH: Wesleyan University Press, 1994), 40. Import of slaves ceased under British interim rule during the Napoleonic Wars (1795–1802). The British retook the Cape in 1806. Cape slaves were emancipated in 1834.

6. Shell, *Children of Bondage*, 64.

7. Ward, *Networks of Empire*, 146.

8. A rare notebook and letters written by VOC slaves are discussed in chapters 7 and 8 of Nigel Worden, ed., *Cape Town between East and West: Social Identities in a Dutch Colonial Town* (Sunnyside, South Africa: Jacana Media; Hilversum, the Netherlands: Uitgeverij Verloren, 2012). Voices of slaves giving testimony are also to be found in criminal cases heard by the Council of Justice. Nigel Worden and Gerald Groenewald, eds., *Trials of Slavery: Selected Documents Concerning Slaves from the Criminal Records of the Council of Justice at the Cape of Good Hope, 1705–1794* (Cape Town: Van Riebeeck Society, 2005), presents eighty-seven criminal cases in their original Dutch (with English translation).

9. Master of the Orphan Chamber (MOOC) of the Cape of Good Hope, series MOOC/8, inventories, and MOOC/10, auction results, http://databases.tanap.inet /vocrecords/. All translations from the original Dutch are mine.

10. The VOC established the Orphan Chamber at the Cape in 1673; Vertrees C. Malherbe, "Illegitimacy and Family Formation in Colonial Cape Town, to c. 1850," *Journal of Social History* 39, no. 4 (2006): 1154. It did not house orphans. The Cape's first orphanage was not founded until 1815. Shell, *Children of Bondage*, 128.

11. The inventories also provide data on slaves from India, Sri Lanka, Madagascar, Mozambique, and Mauritius. For a rich picture of Cape society in the seventeenth and eighteenth centuries, see the writings (in Afrikaans) of Karel Schoeman. Gerrit Schutte has analyzed his oeuvre in Gerrit Schutte, "Review Article: Karel Schoeman's Cape Colony," *African Historical Review* 44, no. 2 (2012): 119–139.

12. Slave labor was not universal at the Cape. Johan Fourie has estimated that 526 households between 1700 and 1790 had no slaves; Johan Fourie, "The Quantitative Cape: A Review of the New Historiography of the Dutch Cape Colony," *South African Historical Journal* 66, no. 1 (2014): 157. From inventory lists it appears that most slaveholders had between two and ten slaves. The very wealthy Tobias Rönnenkamp, owner of several properties, had twenty-nine, plus five children born to four of the women; MOOC8/46.28, 16 May 1793.

13. "Bougies," "Bougis," and "Bogies" refer to Bugis lands in southern Sulawesi (Celebes) and the Buginese ethnic group. "Samboua," "Sambouwa," and "Sambouna" are variant spellings for the island of Sumbawa. I have not standardized spelling of place names that form the surnames of slaves in VOC records.

14. Heather Sutherland, "Slavery and the Slave Trade in South Sulawesi, 1660s–1800s," in *Slavery, Bondage and Dependency in Southeast Asia,* ed. Anthony Reid (St. Lucia: University of Queensland Press, 2003), 266.

15. Robert Ross and Alicia Schrikker, "The VOC Official Elite," in *Cape Town between East and West: Social Identities in a Dutch Colonial Town,* ed. Nigel Worden (Sunnyside, South Africa: Jacana Media; Hilversum, the Netherlands: Uitgeverij Verloren, 2012), 36.

16. Gwyn Campbell, "Slave Trade and the Indian Ocean World," in *India in Africa, Africa in India: Indian Ocean Cosmopolitanisms,* ed. John C. Hawley (Bloomington: Indiana University Press, 2008), 36. Shell stresses that manumission was not a right offered to slaves by the Cape government, but a favor granted by slaveholders; Shell, *Children of Bondage*, 394.

17. The child of a slave father and Khoisan mother was free, because the indigenous population was not enslaved.

18. MOOC8/6.25, 16 February 1738.

19. Wayne Dooling, "The Making of a Colonial Elite: Property, Family and Landed Stability in the Cape Colony, c. 1750–1834," *Journal of Southern African Studies* 31, no. 1 (2005): 147–162.

20. Gerald Groenewald, "'A Mother Makes No Bastard': Family Law, Sexual Relations and Illegitimacy in Dutch Colonial Cape Town, c. 1652–1795," *African Historical Review* 39, no. 2 (2007): 58–90.

21. Only burghers and VOC employees above the rank of soldier and sailor were accorded official recognition of their marital status; Nicole Ulrich, "Time, Space and the Political Economy of Merchant Colonialism in the Cape of Good Hope and VOC World," *South African Historical Journal* 62, no. 3 (2010): 571–588. However, clerks recording inventories and testimony in law courts do sometimes note emotional and sexual relationships between slaves. See, for example, MOOC8/46.28, where it is recorded that the slave Mentor

van de Westcust was manumitted and went to live with "his wife [*wyf*] the free woman Aemelia van Boegis." (*Wyf* has the sense of "mate." The wife of a burgher is designated by the higher-status term *huijsvrouw* in the inventories.)

22. The proportion of women in the burgher segment remained at 40 percent through most of the eighteenth century. Nigel Worden, *Slavery in Dutch South Africa* (Cambridge: Cambridge University Press, 1985), 52.

23. Antonia Malan, "Chattels or Colonists? 'Freeblack' Women and Their Households," *Kronos* 25 (1998–1999): 66. From their investigation of the Cape VOC elite, Ross and Schrikker conclude that slave descent was no hindrance to advancement in the Company's service or in the burgher class for men born to mothers who were emancipated and married. Ross and Schrikker, "VOC Official Elite," 30.

24. There were different terms for children by slave or European fathers and Khoisan mothers. Ward, *Networks of Empire*, 249.

25. Malherbe, "Illegitimacy and Family Formation," 1163.

26. Teun Baartman, "Protest and Dutch Burgher Identity," in *Cape Town between East and West: Social Identities in a Dutch Colonial Town*, ed. Nigel Worden (Cape Town: Jacana Media; Hilversum, the Netherlands: Ultgeverij Verloren, 2012), 74–75. Male free blacks could engage in the same jobs as burghers, but they could not be elected to public office and they did not have representation on the Council of Justice. These were rights accorded to their burgher sons.

27. It is important to note Robert Ross' categorization of Cape Europeans in the eighteenth century as the "community defined by baptism," because it included free blacks and their descendants. Robert Ross, *Beyond the Pale: Essays on the History of Colonial South Africa* (Middletown, CT: Wesleyan University Press, 1993), 126. Ross always encloses "white" in quotation marks when discussing the Cape's burgher population.

28. Nearly all slaves brought to the Cape from the Indonesian archipelago were bought in private transactions. VOC ordinances of 1700 and 1713 permitted men repatriating to the Netherlands from Batavia to take with them up to three slaves for sale during the stopover at the Cape. J. Fox, "'For Good and Sufficient Reasons': An Examination of Early Dutch East India Company Ordinances on Slaves and Slavery," in *Slavery, Bondage and Dependency in Southeast Asia*, ed. Anthony Reid (St. Lucia: University of Queensland Press, 2003), 260.

29. MOOC8/3.95, 18 February 1719.

30. MOOC8/7.29 1/2, 12 February 1753. One rixdollar was the equivalent of three Cape guilders.

31. MOOC8/15.28, 8 March 1775. Estimates consistently show that most funds were invested in laborers. In this case, for comparison, while Martha Hendrina van Aarde and Johannes Mattheus Hertzog's slaves were valued at eight hundred rixdollars, their four paintings were estimated at only eight rixdollars.

32. MOOC8/16.53, 18 January 1774. VOC-era inventories do not show occupations for female slaves.

33. MOOC10/5.35, 28 November 1740.

34. MOOC10/5.31, 26 April 1740.

35. MOOC8/2.22c, 16 February 1729.

36. MOOC8/19.48a, 16 April 1789.

37. MOOC8/6.55, 21 May 1742. Cupido had to serve out his sentence for absconding before being sold for the benefit of the heirs: Batenhorst's widow and five children.

38. MOOC8/6.25, 16 February 1738; MOOC8/4.61, 7 December 1720; MOOC 8/21.35, 25 April 1796; MOOC8/50.70, 15 October 1790, respectively.

39. MOOC8/12.59, 10 March 1766; MOOC8/16.53, 16 January 1774.

40. MOOC8/75.4, 3 December 1796.

41. MOOC8/22.4, 1 August 1796.

42. MOOC8/16.9, 5 May 1776.

43. MOOC10/3.75, 28 February 1729; MOOC8/10.64a, 20 January 1764.

44. MOOC8/6.25, 19 February 1738; MOOC8/6.79, 22 April 1745; MOOC8/20.2, 1790; MOOC8/18.26, 17 May 1780; MOOC8/18.16, 24 December 1779; MOOC8/5.127, 23 June 1734; and MOOC8/1.63, 1 March 1701, respectively. "Moor" in VOC usage meant a Muslim originating from outside the Indonesian archipelago, especially an Arab. Armstrong makes a case for Muslims among Chinese convicts serving their sentences at the Cape. From VOC records he cites "Carim *anders* [otherwise] Toy Engo" and "Lijmsieuko, also known as Kiaij Moeda." James C. Armstrong, "The Chinese Exiles," in *Cape Town between East and West: Social Identities in a Dutch Colonial Town*, ed. Nigel Worden (Cape Town: Jacana Media; Hilversum, the Netherlands: UItgeverij Verloren, 2012), 104. (He also found Christian converts among the Cape's tiny Chinese community.)

45. For example, Saarah Jappie, "*Jawi dari Jauh:* 'Malays' in South Africa through Text," *Indonesia and the Malay World* 40, no. 117 (2012): 143–159; Sirtjo Koolhof and Robert Ross, "Upas, September and the Bugis at the Cape of Good Hope: The Content of a Slave's Letter," *Archipelago* 70 (2005): 281–308.

46. See, for example, Resolution of the Council of Policy (the Cape's governing body), C127, 11 November 1749, to settle three recently arrived Banten exiles away from Cape Town, http://databases.tanap.net/cgh/.

47. Ward, *Networks of Empire*, 231–237. In Kerry Ward, "Monitoring Death at the Cape of Good Hope," *South African Historical Journal* 59, no. 1 (2007): 169, she notes a consensus of historians on the attractions of Islamic rituals and amulets, and possibilities for social mobility within the Muslim community. The attraction of Hindu rituals for Indians and the broader slave population at the Cape could be explored in further research.

48. Susan Newton-King, "Family, Friendship and Survival among Freed Slaves," in *Cape Town between East and West: Social Identities in a Dutch Colonial Town*, ed. Nigel Worden (Sunnyside, South Africa: Jacana Media; Hilversum, the Netherlands: Uitgeverij Verloren, 2012), 153–175; Robert Shell and Archie Dick, "Jan Smiesing, Slave Lodge Schoolmaster and Healer, 1697–1734," in *Cape Town between East and West: Social Identities in a Dutch Colonial Town*, ed. Nigel Worden (Sunnyside, South Africa: Jacana Media; Hilversum, the Netherlands: Uitgeverij Verloren, 2012), 128–152.

49. For example, Sophia Christina Wilhelmina van de Caab is described in MOOC8/46.28, 16 May 1793, as "a baptized slave girl [. . .] not yet emancipated."

50. MOOC8/10.76, 23 September 1761.

51. MOOC8/22.31, 20 February 1799.

52. Indigenous laborers were bound by indentures because they could not be enslaved.

53. MOOC8/15.26, 14 July 1774.

54. MOOC8/21.29, 28 February 1795.

55. MOOC8/18.52, 28 April 1783.

56. MOOC8/15.25, 27 September 1774.

57. MOOC8/17.23, 18 August 1777.

58. MOOC8/5.143a, 2 November 1736.

59. Slaveholders offering manumission to slaves were required, under a VOC law of 1708, to deposit funds with the Church's Poor Relief to support them when ill or in old age; Malherbe, "Illegitimacy and Family Formation," 1155.

60. MOOC8/18.72, 13 June 1785.

61. MOOC10/2.5 1/2, 5 October 1718, and MOOC10/2.6, 14 November 1718.

62. MOOC8/46.28, 15 May 1793. The emancipation fee could be paid in installments. The freed slave Catharina van de Caab paid twenty-five rixdollars every four months into the estate of Anna Heuning; MOOC8/16.51 1/2, 7 May 1777.

63. MOOC8/46.28, 16 May 1793.

64. MOOC8/5.70, 5 November 1734.

65. MOOC8/11.42, 2 January 1765. Regnault also stipulated that their child Simareij van de Caab was to be freed.

66. Few free blacks took up farming. Most lived and worked in Cape Town; Worden, *Slavery in Dutch South Africa*, 145.

67. Slaves who worked in town or were hired out as farmhands had to pay their slaveholders a monthly fee from their earnings. Indonesian exiles at the Cape also sent their slaves out to work, thereby supplementing their VOC subvention. See documents from the trial of Doulat van Balij [Bali] in 1718. He justified charges of breaking and entering by the burden of having to pay five rixdollars every month to his slaveholder, Daeng Mamoetje, a Ternate prince. Worden and Groenewald, *Trials of Slavery*, 60–65.

68. For example, Antonia Malan, "Beneath the Surface—Behind the Doors: Historical Archaeology of Households in Mid-Eighteenth Century Cape Town," *Social Dynamics: A Journal of African Studies* 24, no. 1 (1998): 88; Shell, *Children of Bondage*, chap. 2; Robert Shell, "The Tower of Babel: The Slave Trade and Creolization at the Cape, 1652–1834," in *Slavery in South Africa: Captive Labor on the Dutch Frontier*, ed. Elizabeth A. Eldredge and Fred Morton (Boulder, CO: Westview Press; Pietermaritzburg, South Africa: University of Natal Press, 1994), 11–39. Shell and Dick argue that creolization was most advanced among slaves owned by the VOC and housed at the Slave Lodge, founded in 1679, where they were taught Dutch and received vocational training and religious instruction leading to baptism. Shell and Dick, "Jan Smiesing," 133. The inventories suggest that the creolization process was also occurring among ex-slaves in the burgher category.

69. MOOC8/2.36, 4 September 1709. Susanna made a cross beside her name on the inventory.

70. MOOC10/1.54, 9 October 1709.

71. Susanna might have opted to pay by installments. The VOC, which administered auctions, allowed buyers up to six months to pay the purchase price with interest. Shell, *Children of Bondage*, 99.

72. MOOC10/2.5, 22 August 1718; MOOC10/2.8, 16 November 1718; MOOC10/2.20, 29 April 1719.

73. MOOC8/16.23, 23 April 1776.

74. "Moorish" to describe the garment indicates a tailored gown, not the Indonesian unstitched wrap worn by men and women.

75. Gender offers new insights into studies of exile. See chapters 8 and 9, by Liston and Paterson, respectively, in this volume.

76. Buton Island lies off Southeast Sulawesi.

77. MOOC8/5.144, 5 January 1737.

78. MOOC10/4.162.

79. MOOC8/19.8, 1 March 1786.

80. The Cape's first bank was not established until 1792. Shell, *Children of Bondage*, 109.

81. Jean Gelman Taylor, "Painted Ladies of the VOC," *South African Historical Journal* 59, no. 1 (2007): 47–78.

82. Council of Policy, C59, 14 April 1722.

83. Fox, "'For Good and Sufficient Reason,'" 260.

84. Council of Policy, C91, 11 February 1733.

85. Council of Policy, C141, 25 May 1763; MOOC8/11.32a and 8/11.32b, 11 January 1765.

86. MOOC8/18.68, 5 February 1785. She was the widow of Francis van der Westcust [Sumatra].

87. MOOC8/17.58, 8 January 1779.

88. MOOC8/4.48, 5 December 1722.

89. MOOC8/4.120, 3 October 1724.

90. MOOC8/10.76, 23 September 1761.

91. Council of Policy C134, 11 September 1756, and C143, 28 January 1765.

92. The council granted permission and free travel but required Sampoerne to work on board during the voyage, C28, 3 April 1711.

93. One *schelling* was the equivalent of three Cape guilders or one rixdollar; MOOC 8/4.79, 21 May 1726.

94. Sri Margana and Ronit Ricci (chapters 5 and 4, respectively, in this volume) draw on Javanese-language accounts of exile that reveal perspectives of the exiled and of the royal exiling authority.

95. MOOC8/6.131, 17 June 1748.

96. Heather Sutherland, "Notes on Java's Regent Families, Part II," *Indonesia* 17 (April 1974): 1–42; Kerry Ward, "Blood Ties: Exile, Family, and Inheritance across the Indian Ocean in the Early Nineteenth Century," *Journal of Social History* 45, no. 2 (2011): 436–452.

97. Cape-born descendants of some royal exiles can be traced through inventory records. For example, a son born to Abulbas, exiled raja of Tambora [Sumbawa], converted to Christianity in 1721. He married Helena Valentijn, who was the daughter of free blacks. MOOC8/13.11 renders his name as Abraham à de Haan and shows that their two daughters had married burghers with European names. Baartman notes that Raja Tambora's grandson, named Abraham after his father, took the burgher's oath in 1750. This à de Haan signaled his Cape identity by signing the burghers' petition of 1779 that demanded for Cape burghers equal rights with burghers in the Netherlands. Tambora's grandson married the Dutch immigrant Christina Alesia Eversdijk of Amsterdam. Baartman, "Protest and the Dutch Burgher Identity," 75–76.

98. See, for example, court documents on Alexander van Maccasser, who was held down by fellow slaves after he had threatened his slaveholder and fellow slaves with a knife; Worden and Groenewald, *Trials of Slavery*, 169–175.

99. Campbell, "Slave Trade," 39.

100. Shell, *Children of Bondage*, 103.

101. Margaret Lenta, "Sentencing Slaves: Verdicts of the Cape Courts, 1705–1794," *English in Africa* 35, no. 2 (2008): 35–51. The article gives a single example of an Indonesian slave condemned to death. Lenta does not classify convicted slaves by their ethnic group, so it is impossible to estimate the percentage of Indonesian slaves who had criminal convictions. Cases in *Trials of Slavery* show that a number of male slaves, aged between twenty and thirty, from eastern Indonesia, were tried and condemned. While the transcripts reveal much about the daily lives of slaves, editors Worden and Groenewald remind us that court documents are records of the extraordinary rather than the everyday.

102. Worden, *Slavery in Dutch South Africa*, 4.

103. MOOC8/15.25, 27 September 1744.

104. Malan, "Chattels or Colonists?" 53.
105. MOOC8/18.33, 11 May 1787.

BIBLIOGRAPHY

Armstrong, James C. "The Chinese Exiles." In *Cape Town between East and West: Social Identities in a Dutch Colonial Town*, edited by Nigel Worden, 101–127. Cape Town: Jacana Media; Hilversum, the Netherlands: Uitgeverij Verloren, 2012.

Baartman, Teun. "Protest and Dutch Burgher Identity." In *Cape Town between East and West: Social Identities in a Dutch Colonial Town*, edited by Nigel Worden, 65–83. Cape Town: Jacana Media; Hilversum, the Netherlands: Uitgeverij Verloren, 2012.

Campbell, Gwyn. "Slave Trade and the Indian Ocean World." In *India in Africa, Africa in India: Indian Ocean Cosmopolitanisms*, edited by John C. Hawley, 17–51. Bloomington: Indiana University Press, 2008.

Dooling, Wayne. "The Making of a Colonial Elite: Property, Family and Landed Stability in the Cape Colony, c. 1750–1834." *Journal of Southern African Studies* 31, no. 1 (2005): 147–162.

Fourie, Johan. "The Quantitative Cape: A Review of the New Historiography of the Dutch Cape Colony." *South African Historical Journal* 66, no. 1 (2014): 142–168.

Fox, J. "'For Good and Sufficient Reasons': An Examination of Early Dutch East India Company Ordinances on Slaves and Slavery." In *Slavery, Bondage and Dependency in Southeast Asia*, edited by Anthony Reid, 246–262. St. Lucia: University of Queensland Press, 2003.

Groenewald, Gerald. "*Een Dienstig Inwoonder*: Entrepreneurs, Social Capital and Identity in Cape Town, c. 1720–1750." *South African Historical Journal* 59 (2007): 126–152.

———. "'A Mother Makes No Bastard': Family Law, Sexual Relations and Illegitimacy in Dutch Colonial Cape Town, c. 1652–1795." *African Historical Review* 39, no. 2 (2007): 58–90.

Hall, Martin. "The Secret Lives of Houses: Women and Gables in the Eighteenth-Century Cape." *Social Dynamics* 20, no. 1 (1994): 1–48.

Jappie, Saarah. "*Jawi dari Jauh*: 'Malays' in South Africa through Text." *Indonesia and the Malay World* 40, no. 117 (2012): 143–159.

Koolhof, Sirtjo, and Robert Ross. "Upas, September and the Bugis at the Cape of Good Hope: The Content of a Slave's Letter." *Archipelago* 70 (2005): 281–308.

Kritzinger, M. S. B., et al. *Groot woordeboek Afrikaans-Engels, Engels-Afrikaans*, 4th rev. ed. Pretoria: J. L. Schalk, 1940.

Lenta, Margaret. "Sentencing Slaves: Verdicts of the Cape Courts, 1705–1794." *English in Africa* 35, no. 2 (2008): 35–51.

Malan, Antonia. "The Archaeology of Probate Inventories." *Social Dynamics: A Journal of African Studies* 16, no. 1 (1990): 1–10.

———. "Beneath the Surface—Behind the Doors: Historical Archaeology of Households in Mid-Eighteenth Century Cape Town." *Social Dynamics: A Journal of African Studies* 24, no. 1 (1998): 88–118.

———. "Chattels or Colonists? 'Freeblack' Women and Their Households." *Kronos* 25 (1998–1999): 50–71.

Malherbe, Vertrees C. "Illegitimacy and Family Formation in Colonial Cape Town, to c. 1850." *Journal of Social History* 39, no. 4 (2006): 1153–1176.

Master of the Orphan Chamber (MOOC) of the Cape of Good Hope. Series MOOC/8, inventories, and MOOC/10, auction results. databases.tanap.net/mooc.

Mitchell, Laura J. *Belongings: Property, Family, and Identity in Colonial South Africa (An Exploration of Frontiers, 1725–c. 1830)*. New York: Columbia University Press, 2009.

Murray, Jennifer. "Gender and Violence in Cape Slave Narratives and Post-Narratives." *South African Historical Journal* 62, no. 3 (2010): 444–462.

Newton-King, Susan. "Family, Friendship and Survival among Freed Slaves." In *Cape Town between East and West: Social Identities in a Dutch Colonial Town*, edited by Nigel Worden, 153–175. Sunnyside, South Africa: Jacana Media; Hilversum, the Netherlands: Uitgeverij Verloren, 2012.

Penn, Nigel. "The Wife, the Farmer and the Farmer's Slaves: Adultery and Murder on a Frontier Farm in the Early Eighteenth Century Cape." *Kronos* 28 (2002): 1–21.

Resolutions of the Council of Policy. C series. http://databases.tanap.net/cgh/.

Ross, Robert. *Beyond the Pale: Essays on the History of Colonial South Africa*. Middletown, CT: Wesleyan University Press, 1993.

———. "The Last Years of the Slave Trade to the Cape Colony." *Slavery and Abolition: A Journal of Slave and Post-Slave Studies* 9, no. 3 (1988): 209–219.

Ross, Robert, and Alicia Schrikker. "The VOC Official Elite." In *Cape Town between East and West: Social Identities in a Dutch Colonial Town*, edited by Nigel Worden, 26–44. Sunnyside, South Africa: Jacana Media; Hilversum, the Netherlands: Uitgeverij Verloren, 2012.

Schutte, Gerrit. "Review Article: Karel Schoeman's Cape Colony." *African Historical Review* 44, no. 2 (2012): 119–139.

Shell, Robert. "The Short Life and Personal Belongings of One Slave: Rangton of Bali, 1673–1720." *Kronos, Southern African Histories* 18 (1991): 1–6.

Shell, Robert C. *Children of Bondage: A Social History of the Slave Society at the Cape of Good Hope, 1652–1838*. Hanover, NH: Wesleyan University Press, 1994.

———. "The Tower of Babel: The Slave Trade and Creolization at the Cape, 1652–1834." In *Slavery in South Africa: Captive Labor on the Dutch Frontier*, edited by Elizabeth A. Eldredge and Fred Morton, 11–39. Boulder, CO: Westview Press; Pietermaritzburg, South Africa: University of Natal Press, 1994.

Shell, Robert, and Archie Dick. "Jan Smiesing, Slave Lodge Schoolmaster and Healer, 1697–1734." In *Cape Town between East and West: Social Identities in a Dutch Colonial Town*, edited by Nigel Worden, 128–152. Sunnyside, South Africa: Jacana Media; Hilversum, the Netherlands: Uitgeverij Verloren, 2012.

Spuy, Patricia van der. "Slave Women and the Family in Nineteenth-Century Cape Town." *South African Historical Journal* 27 (2009): 50–74.

Sutherland, Heather. "Notes on Java's Regent Families, Part II." *Indonesia* 17 (April 1974): 1–42.

———. "Slavery and the Slave Trade in South Sulawesi, 1660s–1800s." In *Slavery, Bondage and Dependency in Southeast Asia*, edited by Anthony Reid, 263–285. St. Lucia: University of Queensland Press, 2003.

Taylor, Jean Gelman. "Painted Ladies of the VOC." *South African Historical Journal* 59, no. 1 (2007): 47–78.

Ulrich, Nicole. "Time, Space and the Political Economy of Merchant Colonialism in the Cape of Good Hope and VOC World." *South African Historical Journal* 62, no. 3 (2010): 571–588.

Villiers, M. de, J. Smuts, and L. C. Eksteen. *Kernwoordeboek van Afrikaans*. Cape Town: Nasou, 1967.

Ward, Kerry. "Blood Ties: Exile, Family, and Inheritance across the Indian Ocean in the Early Nineteenth Century." *Journal of Social History* 45, no. 2 (2011): 436–452.

———. "Monitoring Death at the Cape of Good Hope." *South African Historical Journal* 59, no. 1 (2007): 153–170.

———. *Networks of Empire: Forced Migration in the Dutch East India Company*. Cambridge: Cambridge University Press, 2009.

Worden, Nigel, ed. *Cape Town between East and West: Social Identities in a Dutch Colonial Town*. Sunnyside, South Africa: Jacana Media; Hilversum, the Netherlands: Uitgeverij Verloren, 2012.

———. "New Approaches to VOC History in South Africa." *South African Historical Journal* 59, no. 1 (2007): 2–18.

———. *Slavery in Dutch South Africa*. Cambridge: Cambridge University Press, 1985.

Worden, Nigel, and Gerald Groenewald, eds. *Trials of Slavery: Selected Documents Concerning Slaves from the Criminal Records of the Council of Justice at the Cape of Good Hope, 1705–1794*. Cape Town: Van Riebeeck Society, 2005.

EIGHT

An Exile's Lamentations?
The Convict Experience in New South Wales, Australia, 1788–1840

Carol Liston

Transportation to New South Wales was punishment and exile. But it was exile to a settlement in a largely homogenous society. For those who could deal with the emotional impact of separation and who were perhaps able to communicate with loved ones left behind, was the opportunity it provided greater than the intended punishment?

AN EMBARRASSING HISTORY

Until the 1960s, most Australians had little interest in their history and avoided reference to the country's European foundations as a penal settlement. No questions were asked about a national past that might reveal too close a personal link with those who had left Old England "for their country's good." Only a handful of convicts were known by name. Access to the official records of the convict system in New South Wales was restricted to those who could acquire a Mitchell Library reader's ticket (requiring signatures of university lecturers, justices of the peace, or clergymen) and sign an undertaking not to use information to embarrass any living person. Applications to publish academic works based on archival records that named individual convicts were rejected by library authorities.[1] Records of the British side of the convict system required expensive travel to overseas archives or painstaking trawling through unindexed microfilmed British records.

Celebrations in 1970 of the bicentenary of Captain Cook's voyage, followed by the bicentenary of European settlement in 1988, stimulated curiosity. Australia's population now included immigrants from non-English-speaking countries—immigrants who were aware of their own cultural heritage and origins. Indigenous Australians were more assertive about the inclusion of their stories of dispossession in the national narrative. Among Australian descendants of colonial families who had no knowledge of their family roots, there was a surge of popular interest in family history that pushed archives and libraries to open their doors to community researchers. For a generation who was more open about de facto relationships, children born outside marriage, the Protestant/Catholic religious divide, and the impact of poverty, convicts were acceptable ancestors. Academic interest from the 1970s in the social history of ordinary people provided a context to understand this past.

The convicts in New South Wales had passed through the British legal system, most sentenced to transportation for theft. Their punishment was physical removal from their homes and families, but the vocabulary they themselves used to describe their experiences rarely invoked words like "exile" or "banishment." While aspects of the convict system were brutal, this chapter suggests that for many, transportation provided opportunities for greater material prosperity, though the price was an emotional exile.

Twentieth-century descendants had much to be proud about when the achievements of the convict and emancipist generations were examined. Convict transportation to New South Wales ended in 1840 and as early as 1843 an ex-convict took his seat as an elected member of Parliament. In 1858 all adult men gained the right to vote in elections, regardless of wealth, social origins, or place of residence. The silence of the immediate descendants of the convicts implied shame, but did it conceal confusion over whether transportation had been a punishment or an opportunity for the family?

HISTORIOGRAPHICAL OVERVIEW

Uniquely for a continent of colonial settlement, Australians have access to a vast archive of records from the foundation of the colony, including lists of the people (convict and free) who sailed on the First Fleet in 1788. Edited administrative records of the settlement of Australia were published before the First World War as *Historical Records of New South Wales* and *Historical Records of Australia*. Archival work from the 1960s by Lloyd Robson, *The Convict Settlers of Australia,* and A. G. L. Shaw, *Convicts and the Colonies,* provided a detailed understanding of the penal system, but there were few insights into the personal stories of the convicts who comprised that population.[2]

In 1920 George Arnold Wood wrote that the convicts were more victims than criminals—the products of an unjust British legal system. In the 1950s C. M. H. Clark contradicted this comfortable view by suggesting they were part of a criminal underclass of British society. The work of George

Rudé in *Protest and Punishment* countered with evidence of "respectable" convict founders who had been transported as political protestors.[3]

A generation later, Stephen Nicholas and Peter Shergold conducted a massive statistical project and concluded that the convicts were part of a global system of forced labor migration. The convicts brought useful work skills, had reasonable levels of literacy, and were well looked after once they arrived, being provided with adequate food and health care.[4]

And what about the female convicts? Were Australia's founding mothers "damned whores"? The widely held assumption that convict women were prostitutes was overturned from the 1980s with work as varied as Portia Robinson's *The Hatch and Brood of Time,* suggesting that the majority of women were in stable colonial relationships and were good mothers, and Deborah Oxley's *Convict Maids,* which proposed that the women, like the men, brought useful working skills to the colony. Kay Daniels in *Convict Women* looked at the intersections of official control and personal choice to investigate the ways women managed their experiences.[5]

Drawing on extensive archival records, family historians and local history groups have produced many volumes documenting the stories of the convicts on particular ships, registers of convicts who lived in local areas, and many individual biographies of convict lives. Collectively, these community histories argue that for many convicts and their families, despite trauma and misadventure, transportation to New South Wales ultimately had a positive outcome.[6]

THE PHASES OF CONVICT TRANSPORTATION

Convicts were sent to Australia, mostly from Britain, between 1788 and 1868. The political and economic need for a "convict dumping ground" is still the main acknowledged reason for the British settlement at Botany Bay (New South Wales) in 1788 and its expansion to penal settlements on Norfolk Island and in Van Diemen's Land (Tasmania) and Moreton Bay (Queensland). Western Australia requested convicts from 1850 until 1868. The last convict was pardoned in 1906 and the last Western Australian convict died about 1940.[7]

Overall about 168,000 people were transported, including 25,000 women. About 80,000 convicts arrived in New South Wales between 1788 and 1840. The convicts were young (with a mean age of twenty-six) and mostly single, with about half transported for the minimum period of seven years. Young thieves from urban areas predominated, many having prior convictions. More than 70 percent were tried in England, and just 22 percent

Transported for Sedition: Thomas Muir, Maurice Margarot, Thomas Fyshe Palmer, William Skirving, and Joseph Gerrald were transported to New South Wales for supporting the ideals of the French Revolution. They were political radicals who publicly argued for parliamentary reform in Britain, 1793 (Mitchell Library, State Library of New South Wales).

in Ireland. Women formed 15 percent of convicts transported to Australia, and 12,460 were landed in New South Wales, mostly after 1825.[8]

Convicts transported to New South Wales had been sentenced by criminal courts. Often they were sentenced for lesser offenses than those for which they had been found guilty, because of the severity of the British legal system, which required the death penalty for so many offenses, especially crimes against property. Others had a death sentence commuted to transportation, usually for life.

Acts of political protest, such as membership in illegal organizations or sabotage of property and livestock, were treated as criminal acts. A small proportion of convicts were explicitly transported for political activism from

England and Scotland and particularly from Ireland under the Insurrection Act. Simple acts such as being out at night could trigger the penalties of the Insurrection Act, particularly after 1822.[9]

Exile and banishment in some form had been practiced by many societies from the earliest times.[10] Transportation to New South Wales was based on a British legal model established in 1718 when British convicts were sent to the North American colonies. Until the law of transportation was modified in 1824, the common understanding retained an eighteenth-century view that transportation (or exile) constituted the punishment and should not include bonded labor or imprisonment at the destination. Convict accounts referred to transportation as the punishment—not imprisonment. Convict women particularly resented confinement. Riots often marked overcrowding in jail or attempts to limit the women's freedom to come and go from the institution. Implicit in this view was that their punishment by transportation was exile from family and community but not imprisonment.[11]

From the mid-1820s the British authorities increasingly saw transportation as a continuum of punishment including both exile from home and forced labor for the length of the sentence.[12] Other chapters in this volume discuss convict servitude, and their consistent theme is convict labor on public works. The early experience in New South Wales was somewhat different.

ADMINISTERING THE CONVICT COLONY

The convict experience varied greatly over time and place. The "tyranny of distance" is a common phrase used to describe the Australian experience. Criminals were sent so far away from their homes that it was impossible for them to return—or so the authorities believed. Distances within the colony acted as a further impediment, as lengthy and difficult overland journeys limited mobility and embryonic mail services made contact with family in Britain uncertain.

Those who arrived in New South Wales between 1788 and 1810 came to a place with little physical or social infrastructure. The local indigenous people lived a nomadic existence determined by the seasonal environment and had few material resources of immediate use to the occupying Europeans. The settlement concentrated on a narrow plain between the sea and a mountain range sixty kilometers to the west. This was a pioneering environment, where the practical skills, adaptability, and resourcefulness of both convict and jailer were essential for survival. Food was the most desperate need in the first few years, and Governor Arthur Phillip, the first governor (1788–1792), used convicts to work on public farms. Following his departure, the military favored private farming and the convict labor force was dispersed among the settlers, permitting private enterprises by ex-convict as well as free settler.

After the Napoleonic Wars ended in 1815, the number of convicts rose rapidly as postwar social stresses in Britain led to crime and political unrest. With little advance notice, almost ten thousand convicts arrived over the four years from 1815 to 1819.[13] In the 1830s convict numbers escalated again, with more than thirty thousand transported to New South Wales in that decade. Such numbers created difficulties for the colonial administration, which had to feed, house, clothe, and employ them.

The governor requested assistance to manage the distribution of convicts. Nicholas Divine, a former superintendent of the British hulks, was appointed as superintendent of convicts in 1790 and held the position until 1808. His successors—Isaac Nichols and William Hutchinson—had themselves arrived as convicts and were appointed by Governor Lachlan Macquarie, the fifth governor. The British government viewed their backgrounds as undesirable and appointed Irish public servant Frederick Augustus Hely in 1823. Following Hely's death, Captain John McLean was appointed by the secretary of state in 1837 and held the position until it was abolished with responsible government in 1856.[14] With only five superintendents between 1790 and 1856, the administration of the convict system in New South Wales was stable and consistent.

Initially the records that accompanied the convicts noted only their names, the dates and places of their trials, and their sentences. The governor had the authority to pardon any sentence except those imposed for sedition or treason. However, the record of a convict's crime was not sent to the colony, so punishment was never linked to the seriousness of the crime. When Governor Thomas Brisbane (1821–1825) gave an absolute pardon to a convict servant of a colonial official who wanted to take his servant to England, the governor was not aware that the servant had been transported for sedition.[15] After 1826 the record sent to New South Wales included a convict's crime and additional information such as physical description, occupation, marital status, and family.

Convicts could be distributed to free settlers or officials in the towns or rural areas to work as assigned servants. Alternatively they were retained to work for the government in roles as diverse as clerk and laborer. Many of these tasks, both skilled and menial, were little different from those listed by Yang in his account of the work of Indian convicts in Penang in the 1820s. In New South Wales, convicts who worked on major road-building projects often received pardons.[16]

From the earliest years, a convict's good behavior was rewarded with permission to work independently. This evolved into a system of tickets of leave, or parole, whereby after a certain period of good behavior a convict could work to support himself and his family. The ultimate reward for good behavior was a pardon. A conditional pardon meant freedom in the colony or anywhere else, except a return home. If the convict was found back in Britain, the original sentence was reimposed. Those whose sentence had expired or who obtained an absolute pardon could return home—at their own expense.

Misbehavior was punished by time in a government work gang, or from the mid-1820s by removal to places of secondary punishment, isolated from the settled districts. By the 1830s, as the British government sought to make transportation more severe, these places were brutal, and even those sentenced to government work gangs now found themselves laboring on public works in remote areas and working in chains.

For the first thirty years, convicts arriving in Sydney had to find their own accommodations, as there were no jails or barracks to house them. Government work ceased at three p.m. so that convicts could find alternative employment to pay for their private accommodations. Free people with assigned convict servants were required to feed and house them.

Hyde Park Barracks, Sydney, was completed in 1819. Its dormitories housed six hundred men sleeping in hammocks and double that number on some occasions. The men worked in street-cleaning and construction gangs and returned to the barracks for meals and to sleep. In 1820 a Female Factory was completed to provide accommodations, a workplace, a hospital, and a place for punishment for female convicts at Parramatta, some twenty-five kilometers west of Sydney. Male convict barracks were also constructed at Parramatta. As convict work gangs moved into the countryside in the 1830s, barracks were built at central work sites. Portable housing was also used in remote areas where the gangs needed to be mobile.[17]

The British government conducted one major investigation into the convict system in New South Wales. In 1819 John Thomas Bigge, previously chief justice of Trinidad, investigated the convict system, the administration of justice, and the state of agriculture and trade in the colony. As part of his inquiry he interviewed convicts and ex-convicts, their jailers and their masters, gathering a vast archive of firsthand accounts, which were deposited with the Colonial Office in London.[18]

TRUE EXILES

Only a small number of convicts in New South Wales were truly exiles who had made a formal agreement with the British government to go into exile rather than face trial and sentencing. United Irishman rebel leader General Joseph Holt surrendered to the English in 1798 on condition of exile without trial in Botany Bay. He brought his family with him, made a success of farming, and received a free pardon that enabled him to return to Ireland in 1812.[19] Similarly, seven of those transported from Ireland on the *Minerva* in 1799 had surrendered for "self-transportation."[20] The Tellicherry Five arrived from Ireland in 1806. Michael Dwyer, rebel leader from 1797 until he surrendered in 1803, was deported from Ireland to New South Wales as an unsentenced exile. With him on the *Tellicherry* were his family and four other rebel leaders—Hugh Byrne, John Mernagh, Arthur Devlin, and Martin Burke. The five men received one-hundred-acre farms near Liverpool to support their families.[21] For such men, their "exile" offered new lives in the colony.

In 1847 the British government attempted to revive transportation to New South Wales by sending out "exiles"—men who had already served most of their sentences in English prisons and were to serve the rest of their sentences on parole in Australia. This move was energetically opposed in New South Wales, where the population had been diluted by more than a decade of assisted free immigration. Perhaps surprisingly, those who supported it included former convict Dr. William Bland and William Charles Wentworth, son of the exiled D'Arcy Wentworth. Several ships were dispatched, but protests prevented the scheme from continuing in Sydney. About three thousand men arrived. Some of these men received tickets of leave in rural New South Wales, but most of the exiles went to Moreton Bay or Port Phillip, where they were called "Pentonvillians."[22]

British legislation halting transportation to New South Wales had an unforeseen consequence, as the colonial authorities had regularly transported prisoners to Norfolk Island or Van Diemen's Land. In 1847 the New South Wales legislature passed "An Act to Substitute Other Punishments for Transportation beyond the Seas." The act allowed the courts to give sentences of hard labor on public works in irons and gave the governor the power to grant pardons on condition of exile after two years of hard labor, usually at Cockatoo Island penal institution in Sydney Harbour.[23] Exile was now a formal punishment. Best known of these exiles was the bushranger Frank Gardiner, who was exiled to China in 1874 and subsequently went to the United States. Less well-known were a number of colonial-born young men who took their exile in New Zealand, Asia, or the Pacific, often requesting and receiving permission to return to New South Wales after a certain number of years. Those who were not colonial-born were exiled to their place of origin (effectively pardoned and deported rather than sentenced, as there was no process to trace them).[24]

SOCIAL RANK, RELIGION, AND ETHNICITY IN CONVICT NEW SOUTH WALES

Transportation to New South Wales removed people from their families and communities. Yet this exile to the antipodes was neither as remote nor as foreign as it might seem at first sight. The convicts came to a settlement where the ethnicity, religion, and trades of the population were not greatly different from those of their communities at home.

The majority of convicts transported to Australia came from Britain. Most were English, with smaller numbers of Irish, Scots, and Welsh. Most spoke English, though some Irish spoke only Gaelic. Most were Protestants, with a smaller proportion of Roman Catholics. Though Catholic worship was subject to legal penalties in Britain, this was only notionally enforced in New South Wales. Socially the convict settlement was probably as homogeneous as the convicts' home communities. The majority of convicts came from the laboring classes of urban and rural populations. There were some tradesmen and craftsmen, along with a small number of professionals and men of education, such as clergymen, solicitors, and doctors.

As chapters 4, 9, and 2, by Ricci, Paterson, and Aldrich, respectively, in this volume reveal, the exile population in colonial Asia included members of royalty and others of high social caste. This was not the case in New South Wales. No member of the British aristocracy was transported, and members of the gentry were notably absent, with the colorful exception of Sir Henry Browne Hayes (1762–1832).[25] Members of Asian royal families were sent into exile to other British colonies in the region, but none was exiled to New South Wales. This is despite regular transport links provided by the transfer of British regiments between New South Wales, India, and Ceylon.

British families with social or political influence appealed for clemency for relatives whose activities had brought them before the court. Such appeals included the request to be sent into voluntary exile rather than be formally punished. Best known of the settlers whose family had sufficient influence to seek such clemency was D'Arcy Wentworth, who was related to the powerful Whig politician Earl Fitzwilliam. D'Arcy's exploits as a highwayman while a medical student ended with his family negotiating his removal to Botany Bay as a surgeon. He had a spectacularly successful colonial career as police administrator, doctor, and landowner.[26]

Benjamin Carver was also convicted of highway robbery and sentenced to death. His family and local members of Parliament petitioned for him to go into voluntary exile on Prince Edward Island, Canada. Instead his sentence was commuted to transportation for life to New South Wales in 1792. However, the family appeal was sufficiently successful to allow his fiancée to accompany him, and they were married three days after their arrival in Sydney.[27]

Clergymen were transported, but not for religious activities. The Reverend Henry Fulton, a well-educated Englishman, was caught up in the Irish rebellion of 1798. Convicted of sedition, he was transported for life. Pardoned in 1800, he served as a colonial Protestant chaplain.[28] Roman Catholic priests Father James Dixon, Father James Harold, and Father Peter O'Neil were also caught up in the rebellion and transported to New South Wales. Only Dixon was granted formal permission to minister privately in the colony.[29]

Although the majority of convicts were transported from Britain and Ireland, at least thirty-two hundred were tried in other places, such as British North America, the West Indies, Bermuda, Gibraltar, Cyprus, the Cape of Good Hope, Mauritius, India, Ceylon, and the Straits Settlements.[30] Most of these convicts were British soldiers who were tried by court-martial and sentenced to transportation to Australia. Criminal courts in these countries occasionally transported civilian prisoners to New South Wales, though as early as 1802 the British government had decided not to transport Indians to New South Wales.[31] As many of these convicts had European names, it is difficult to assess their ethnicity without knowledge of their physical descriptions.

Clara Ward, one of the few women to be transported from India, was tried at Fort William, Bengal, and transported for seven years. She arrived in Sydney in 1812 on the *Campbell Macquarie,* a local vessel returning with a trade investment. Details of her crime were not provided, but she immediately received a ticket of leave. Governor Macquarie described her as a native of India when he appointed her the court translator for a group of Indian indentured servants who had been mistreated by their master. Her sentence expired in 1819 and she advertised her intention to return to Bengal, but from 1822 until at least 1828 she was a householder residing in Sydney, suggesting that she remained in New South Wales and had acquired some property.[32]

In 1834 the ship *Dart* brought four convicts from Mauritius to Sydney. Two were young girls—Elizabeth, aged twelve, and Constance, aged nine. They were black slaves convicted of attempting to poison their mistress and transported for life, but not to the usual destination for Mauritian convicts. In place of Robben Island, Cape Town, the girls were sent to New South Wales. They were child servants in Mauritius and convict servants in Sydney, but in New South Wales their lives achieved a degree of freedom. Both married in 1841. Elizabeth's husband was a freeman from Mauritius. While her life in Sydney may not have been prosperous, her three surviving sons were freemen. Constance married a former convict and they lived on their own pastoral property near Wellington, assisted by their eleven children.[33]

The exile experiences of Clara, Elizabeth, and Constance were largely positive. The exile of two young men from the Cape of Good Hope in the 1830s was quite different. Described as a native of the Cape of Good Hope, ruddy and freckled nineteen-year-old James Ward was charged with warehouse breaking and sentenced to seven years' transportation to New South Wales. He arrived on the *Jane* in 1831 and in the following seven years seemed unable to turn his exile to advantage. Involved in a robbery in 1834, he served twelve months in an iron gang, but he committed a further robbery in 1835, so his sentence was increased by two years, to be worked in irons, followed by one hundred lashes for absconding from the iron gang. His appeal for clemency to the governor in 1838 was rejected with the note that he was not considered worthy of the smallest indulgence and would be free in less than two years. His certificate of freedom was issued in May 1840.[34]

Also nineteen was Adonis, another native of Cape Town, with a black complexion, black woolly hair, and black eyes, sentenced to fourteen years' transportation for housebreaking with intent to steal. He arrived in Sydney on the *Eden* in 1837. Shortly after his arrival, Charles Younger applied for Adonis to be assigned to him, as he had been a Cape resident for twelve years and could speak the language. This was refused and within a few months Adonis was accused of stealing from his new master. For a decade, Adonis slipped from public view, but from 1846, now known as Peter Adonis, he had repeated convictions for theft and assault, receiving six terms of imprisonment with hard labor. In July 1860 he received a ticket of leave but died six months later.[35]

CONVICTS AT WORK—OR WORKING FOR THEMSELVES

Chapters 1 and 9 in this volume, by Anderson and Paterson, respectively, document how convicts in most of colonial Asia were transported to work as laborers on government public works. From 1824 Britain also transported European convicts to work on imperial infrastructure, such as building the naval docks in Bermuda. However, for most of the first forty years in New South Wales, the British government did not want convict labor used to construct public infrastructure. This was a cost-cutting measure. Convicts in private assignment were fed and clothed by their masters, but convicts retained by the government had to be fed and clothed by the government.

In New South Wales before 1820, the small number of settlers could not absorb the available convict labor. Governor Macquarie embarked on a program of public works using convict labor but was rebuked by the Colonial Office because this added to the cost of the convict settlement. Macquarie circumvented this restriction by using local funds derived from customs

The Costume of the Australasians: Convicts, overseers, and the military were distinguished by their clothing. The two men carrying loads were convicts, as was the short man on the far right. They were wearing short jackets colored yellow, brown, or blue and a leather cap. (New South Wales Sketchbook: Sea Voyage, Sydney, Illawarra, Newcastle, Morpeth. Creator: Edward Charles Close. Date: c. 1817–1840. Mitchell Library, State Library of New South Wales.)

duties and fines to pay for many public projects. Private contractors, using their own convict or ex-convict labor, carried out major government works, such as Sydney's public hospital, the Rum Hospital, so called for the monopoly on rum imports granted to the contractors. Other projects, such as the construction of convict barracks, had to await British Treasury approval for funds to support government convict labor.

Expansion of settlement in New South Wales from the mid-1820s coincided with the new British policy favoring the use of convict labor on public projects under the supervision of military engineers. From 1831, a board managed the distribution of assigned convict servants and a commissioner replaced the board from 1836. By the end of 1838, the "luxury" of private assigned convict servants ended and all male convicts were retained by the government for public labor. From 1841, the declining number of convicts still under sentence labored on public works.[36]

Free immigration in the 1830s provided an alternative source of servants in New South Wales. This particularly affected female convicts, who found their services as assigned servants less in demand. They were returned to the government and accommodated in the Female Factory at Parramatta, where overcrowding led to riots.

Punishment or Opportunity?

Academic historians have explored many aspects of the convict experience, though too often the demands of general histories merge the distinctive regimes in New South Wales, Van Diemen's Land, and Norfolk Island into a single "Australian" experience of hardship and cruelty. Community historians seeking the specific experience of their ancestors or their local areas have energetically embraced open access to convict records and have uncovered a different picture. In many instances transportation offered opportunities that far outweighed the intended punishment.

There was a high degree of literacy among the convicts, possibly higher than that of the average British population.[37] Did this enable them to take advantage of their situation? The archive contains many letters by male and female convicts, either in their own hand or written by scribes. These letters comment on their backgrounds and their fortunes in the colony and articulate hopes for their future.

Convicts did not hesitate to use the colonial courts to argue for their rights. A convict's right to own personal property was upheld as soon as the First Fleet arrived in 1788. The child of two convicts, Henry Kable and his wife, Susannah née Holmes, was born in jail prior to their transportation, and the jailer gave them clothes for the baby. When they arrived in Sydney, the ship's captain would not give them the parcel because convicts could not own property. Kable protested to Judge Advocate Collins, who heard the case and upheld their right to the property, even though they were convicts attaint, their sentences of death having been commuted to transportation.

Governor Phillip was given the authority to grant land to emancipated convicts. The first land grant was issued in 1791 to James Ruse, an English convict who showed he could support himself on a small farm at Parramatta. Convicts brought with them goods, including money. After 1821, their money was put in a savings bank until they were free. In a colony where everything had to be imported or manufactured from local resources, convicts with agricultural or trade skills could advance, while those with organizational skills that could be applied to commerce and retail found opportunities, either working for military and civil officials or on their own account.

Colonial practice ignored the fact that some convicts were subject to felony attaint. Under common law, those who had been sentenced to death and then respited with a sentence of transportation for life forfeited the right to own property or give evidence in court. Felony attaint was not removed by a pardon in the colony. However, from the beginning of settlement, emancipated convicts and convicts on tickets of leave bought and sold property. It was only in 1820 that the legality of this was challenged. Emancipists in 1821 petitioned the Crown to approve their pardons and confirm their rights as property owners. The New South Wales Act of 1824 validated their situation but did not clarify the rights of convicts subsequently transported. In the colony, free and convict turned a blind eye to these legal complications.[38]

Heritage studies and archaeological investigations of places settled in the convict period provide physical evidence that the opportunities for a comfortable life in the convict period were significant, especially in New South Wales. Grace Karskens has written extensively on life in the Rocks, the residential part of Sydney most densely occupied by convicts and former convicts. Drawing on historical, genealogical, and archaeological evidence, she revealed a comfortable, consumer-oriented society that had access to a variety of sophisticated material goods.[39] Her analysis reinforced the earlier conclusion of John Hirst that New South Wales was almost a free society in its early decades, but became more penal in the late 1820s and 1830s.[40]

A Strange Land with Familiar People

Exile removed the person from his or her home and family, but New South Wales was as much a colony as a prison, so there was no barrier to the formation of new social and personal relationships. Convict women were assigned as housekeepers and servants to military and civil officials and to emancipated convicts. This was, essentially, an official condoning of the prostitution of the women and is characterized as this in the historiography of convict New South Wales.[41] This interpretation has been offset by the family stories of those women and their children, revealing many instances of stable relationships formed in the colony. These relationships were rarely formalized by marriage, partly because of the lack of clergymen in the colony, though Governor Macquarie sought to change this situation with an edict urging marriage.[42]

Even after convict barracks were built, there were never sufficient accommodations for all convicts, so many enjoyed a considerable degree of autonomy in their private lives. Physical freedom to move about the towns and districts meant that new relationships were formed. Convicts could apply to marry with their masters' permission. Many did not, having families in Britain, though the lack of records meant that bigamous unions were inevitable when couples did marry. Colonial families with one or both partners still convicts under sentence were common. Their colonial-born children were called "currency," in a local parlance intended to disparage their origins (being not as pure as "sterling," like the children of free parents). However, unlike slave colonies, where the status of the parent was inherited, these "native-born" white children were free citizens.[43] Like the Andaman example in Anderson's chapter 1 in this volume or the Vietnamese in New Caledonia documented by Paterson in chapter 9, these children had a future in the land where their parents had been exiled. Their opportunities were documented in requests for land and other benefits.

Because this was a place of new European settlement, there were no extended families to care for people in sickness or misfortune. Informal arrangements proliferated as neighbors and strangers offered care. A female orphan institution was established in Sydney by Governor Philip Gidley King in 1802 to provide care for girls whose families were unable to do so. Macquarie built a larger institution at Parramatta and the girls who found refuge there came from all parts of colonial society—convict, free, military, and indigenous. A male orphan school was established in 1819. The government, through the clergy, provided free schools for children, regardless of their parents' social status. Would these children have received an education in Britain?

A surprising number of convicts had strong personal networks in the colony. In the early years, there were opportunities for the wives of convicts to go with their husbands on the transport ships. Families followed partners, parents, or children to New South Wales at their own expense, and from 1815 there was a formal scheme to bring out at government expense the wives and children of well-behaved convicts who had tickets of leave. The advantage for the convict was the prospect of assignment to a free family member (spouse or adult child) and the opportunities to establish family businesses.[44]

Female transports usually included a number of children of the convict women. Johanna Cunningham was a babe in arms when she came with her mother, Honora Leary, from Ireland on the *Mariner* in 1825. Johanna was placed in the Female Orphan School and her mother was sent into assignment as a servant. By 1829 Honora had a ticket of leave and in 1832 married a freeman and successfully applied for the return of her child.[45]

While most children on the convict transports were under twelve, there are instances of older daughters accompanying their mothers. Mary Boulton was transported on the *Grenada*, arriving in 1822. She brought her four daughters. The younger two were placed in the orphan school and the older two found work and husbands, after which they retrieved their siblings from the orphan school. Their mother joined them when she received her certificate of freedom in 1831.[46]

Reunification of wives (or, rarely, husbands) and children of convicts relied on a British bureaucracy able to track the families at home and a willingness on the part of those families to leave home.[47] Free passages were provided for women like Peggy Cooper and her two small children, who in 1822 traveled to New South Wales to join her husband, who had just been transported.[48] Many women applied to join their husbands in exile, but the government would send only those who were sent for by the colonial authorities.[49] For the British government, reconnecting families avoided the burden of impoverished families relying on local parish welfare and provided more women in the colony, where the imbalance of the sexes was a constant moral fear.

Not all reunions went to plan. Isabella Wiles was the wife of James Wiles, who was transported on the *Countess of Harcourt* in 1824. The government paid the expenses so that she and her five children could join him in New South Wales in 1828. Her husband was an assigned servant working for a tailor, but within a few years he had disappeared, leaving her to appeal for her youngest son to be placed in the Male Orphan School, as she could not support him. Thrown upon her own resources, Isabella Wiles, like many other women, turned to small business to provide a precarious existence, running a boardinghouse in the Rocks until her death at age seventy-four in 1850.[50]

Sometimes many years passed before the family arrived, though few separations were as drawn out as that of the family of John Tighe. He arrived on the *Parmelia* in 1834 with a sentence of transportation for seven years. He went to the Illawarra District as an assigned servant and made several requests for his wife and children to be sent out to join him. In 1853 he paid a deposit toward his wife's passage. Meanwhile, she had moved to the United States and was living in New York with her son-in-law. In 1858 she decided to join her husband in New South Wales at her own expense, bringing with her their son and grandchildren.[51]

Some reunions involved more than the immediate family. James Taafe was transported from Ireland on the *Regalia* in 1825. His wife, Jane Taafe, was transported on the *Brothers* in 1827, bringing with her their son William, who was placed in the orphan school. In order to retrieve the boy from the orphan school in 1833, they had to prove that the child was theirs. Two women who had attended the child's baptism in Dublin and had also been transported to Sydney were able to provide testimony.[52] Historians have yet to assess these extended transported communities.

Emotional Exile—The Impact of Transportation

Who was punished by transportation? The emotional impact was not simply on the criminal who was sent away but also on the family left behind to deal with emotional and economic hardship.

Elderly parents petitioned the Home Office for pardons for their children to return to care for them in old age. Yet returning home was not always possible, even when a sentence had expired, unless someone paid the fare, as the father of Jane Curtis discovered. In 1822 he wrote to the Colonial Office requesting a free passage home for his daughter, who had been transported for seven years in 1806 but who was still in the colony. He was told that the government did not have ships returning on which a passage could be provided. Convict ships were usually private vessels chartered for the voyage out but never for a voyage back to Britain.[53] Jane made her future in the colony, becoming the housekeeper and common-law wife of David Neal of Windsor in 1823; at age forty-one, in 1828, she was still with him.[54]

Some convicts accepted the separation from home philosophically, but for others it was an emotional trauma that endured for the terms of their natural lives. In her analysis of the women on the *Princess Royal*, which arrived in 1829, Babette Smith calculated that a little over half adjusted to the new opportunities that transportation had brought through marriage and financial security. For the others, she documented a sad trajectory of alcohol abuse, poverty, an inability to cope by themselves, and a return to crime.[55]

Convict letters home reveal people caught between interest in the new opportunities and sorrow at the loss of family and friends. Josiah Godber, a fifty-four-year-old laborer transported for fourteen years for participation in the Pentrich Rebellion in 1817, wrote to his wife that he was "quite at home except for the loss of you," and wondered if she would come to join him. With no news from home, he wrote of his despair: "If I could but once more enjoy your company, all the powers on earth should not part us. Oh my dear, to think that we have lived together so many years and then torn asunder at last. It almost distracts me when I think of it my dear."[56] Godber died in 1822 without seeing his wife again.

A more extreme strategy for family reunification was for a family member to commit a crime in the expectation of a sentence of transportation so he or she could follow the convict to the colony. Colonial musters of convict arrivals routinely indicated newly arrived convicts coming to join family members who had been transported some years earlier. In 1831 John Clark, a nineteen-year-old from Gloucestershire, was transported for seven years for stealing clothes and joined his sister who was already in New South Wales.

James Waddington, a married cotton weaver, was transported for life and joined his brother who had been sent out eighteen months earlier.[57]

Jane Jones, otherwise Lindbeck, was tried at Lancaster Quarter Assizes and transported for seven years on the *Providence* in 1822. She brought with her two children, Margaret, aged eight, and Charles Edward, aged three. Margaret was placed in the Female Orphan School. Her mother with young Charles remained at the Female Factory until she was assigned, taking the boy with her into private assignment. In 1825 her husband, Charles Lindbeck, a Swedish sailor, was tried at Lancaster Quarter Assizes and transported for life, arriving in Sydney in 1826 aboard the *Sesostris*. He was assigned in Sydney but was able to locate his family, and in their petition to be reunited under the same master, the couple explained that Charles had

> willfully made himself amenable to transportation with the hopes of getting to a country where the only treasures of his heart was an affectionate wife and two dear children more dearer to him than life itself.

As both of their masters supported the application, Jane was transferred to the same master as her husband (and soon became pregnant with their third child).

Jane received her certificate of freedom in 1827 and in May 1828 requested that her husband be exempted from government labor so that he could help support her and the children, "finding her constant exertions are very unequal to the task of providing for three children, one of whom is blind." Her request was granted and in the census of 1828 the family was together at Parramatta. Charles was a carpenter and able to support the family. He gained a ticket of leave in 1837 and a conditional pardon in 1840 and the family successfully settled at Braidwood, some 285 kilometers from Sydney.[58]

While some convicts did not have the resources (or the desire?) to return to England, other emancipists arranged for their children to go to England and live with grandparents or returned to see family and seek relatives to migrate and help in their colonial enterprises.

Mary Hyde arrived as a convict with a seven-year sentence in 1798 and married successful emancipist merchant Simeon Lord in 1814. Like many convict women, she had two children prior to her marriage. Despite having an absolute pardon, Mary did not return home. She sent her older daughter, Mary Ann, to England to live with her paternal grandfather in 1807. The child's father had been a freeman and his family was willing to accept his illegitimate daughter. When her grandfather died, Mary Ann returned to Australia in 1814. A colonial-born woman with an English education and a substantial dowry, she was a suitable marriage partner for a free-man willing to overlook her parents' origins.[59]

William Hayes, a convict from Ireland, was appointed manager of the farming estates of Governor King's family. A successful farmer on his own account, he raised cattle and purchased land. He was wealthy enough to return to Ireland, see his family, and recruit his nephew to go back to New South Wales to assist him, as he had no children.[60]

RETURNING FROM TRANSPORTATION

Transportation was a one-way ticket to Australia, but pardons or completion of the original sentence meant that the exile was not always permanent. Descendants tracing their family history have compiled the biographies of many who remained in the colony. But what of those who did not stay? Historians have generally assumed that most convicts remained in the colony, but as sources become more accessible and more aspects of colonial life are explored, evidence is emerging that many convicts did return home.

Investigation of the convicts associated with one small rural property at Appin, south of Sydney, revealed that as many as five returned to Ireland. More extraordinary was their willingness to abandon farm and colonial prosperity to return to their homeland. Connor Bryan was convicted at Clonmel and transported for life aboard the *Atlas (2)* in 1802. He received a conditional pardon in 1809 and an absolute pardon in 1812. As early as 1810 Bryan had stated his desire to return home, "being an aged man who left [in Ireland] a wife and six children to bewail his absence." In 1814 he was permitted to become a settler. A forty-acre farm was measured for him at Appin in 1816 and Bryan successfully tendered to supply the government with fresh meat. The paperwork for his land grant had not been processed, but in 1817 Bryan made out a power of attorney in favor of two other Irish convicts and sailed from Sydney on the *Harriet,* never to return. Another convict on the *Atlas* similarly named, Connor Ryan, also returned to Ireland to his wife and seven children, in 1821, after he received his absolute pardon earlier that year.

One of those holding Bryan's power of attorney was his assigned convict servant, Connor Boland, a native of Clare, who was transported for life on the *Three Bees,* arriving in 1814. Boland occupied the grant issued to his master until he could collect the grant documents, in mid-1824. Meanwhile, Boland had successfully applied for land in his own name. He received a conditional pardon in 1820 and built a profitable business raising and selling cattle. Documents for his land grants were delivered in 1832, and three years later his absolute pardon was confirmed. The land was put up for sale and

Connor Boland sailed for Ireland in 1837. He died in Limerick in March 1839, leaving significant sums of money to his sisters and nephew.

At least three other convicts who worked with Boland in the 1820s also returned to Ireland in the 1830s. Absolute pardons by this period had to be confirmed by the British government. As the only practical advantage offered by an absolute pardon over a conditional pardon was the right to return home, it must be assumed that a significant proportion of applications for absolute pardons were made by convicts intending to return from their exile.[61]

The Forgotten Exiles

The end of transportation to New South Wales in 1840 did not mean that convicts disappeared from the colony. In 1855 the duties of the superintendent of convicts were transferred to a convict branch within the police department. Tickets of leave, certificates of freedom, and pardons continued to be issued. Elderly, infirm, sick, and insane convicts were moved into health and welfare institutions, while recidivist convicts were confined in prisons. The British government paid for the costs of imperial convicts held in asylums and jails until the end of the nineteenth century. As the colonial population swelled with free immigrants, convict families were absorbed into the larger population. The important documents of freedom—pardons, tickets of leave, and certificates of freedom—disappeared as the detritus of a time best forgotten. Stories of arrival in the colony became muddled with indistinct references to home in England or Ireland, and vagueness about when the family arrived in New South Wales. It was not surprising that their descendants knew little of their origins.

Notes

Thomas Cook, *The Exile's Lamentations* (North Sydney: Library of Australian History, 1978). Cook was transported for fourteen years in 1831. He served in places of secondary punishment, being retransported to Norfolk Island, where he wrote his account of convict life and reformation before disappearing, possibly back to Britain.

1. B. Smith, *Australia's Birthstain: The Startling Legacy of the Convict Era* (Sydney: Allen and Unwin, 2008), 39–41. For an account of Van Diemen's Land, see A. Alexander, *Tasmania's Convicts: How Felons Built a Free Society* (Crows Nest, NSW: Allen and Unwin, 2010).

2. F. M. Bladen, ed. *Historical Records of New South Wales*, 8 vols. (Sydney: Government Printer, 1892–1901); F. Watson, ed. *Historical Records of Australia*, 34 vols. (Sydney: Library Committee of the Commonwealth Parliament, 1914–1925); L. L. Robson, *The Convict Settlers of Australia: An Enquiry into the Origin and Character of the Convicts Transported to NSW and VDL 1787–1852* (Melbourne: Melbourne University Press, 1965); A. G. L. Shaw, *Convicts and the Colonies: A Study of Penal Transportation from Great Britain and Ireland*

to Australia and Other Parts of the British Empire (Melbourne: Melbourne University Press, 1977).

3. G. A. Wood, "Convict Origins," *Journal of the Royal Australian Historical Society* 8, pt. 4 (1922): 177–208; C. M. H. (Manning) Clark, "The Origins of Convicts Transported to Eastern Australia 1787–1851," *Historical Studies: Australia and New Zealand* 7, no. 26 (May 1956): 121–135; 7, no. 27 (November 1956): 314–327; G. Rudé, *Protest and Punishment: The Story of the Social and Political Protesters Transported to Australia 1788–1868* (Melbourne: Oxford University Press, 1978). See also D. Kent and N. Townsend, *The Convicts of the Eleanor: Protest in Rural England, New Lives in Australia* (London: Merlin Press, 2002).

4. S. Nicholas, ed. *Convict Workers: Reinterpreting Australia's Past* (Cambridge: Cambridge University Press, 1988).

5. P. Robinson, *The Hatch and Brood of Time: A Study of the First Generation of Native-Born White Australians 1788–1828* (Melbourne: Oxford University Press, 1985); D. Oxley, *Convict Maids: The Forced Migration of Women to Australia* (Melbourne: Cambridge University Press, 1996); K. Daniels, *Convict Women* (St. Leonards, NSW: Allen and Unwin, 1998). Other works include M. Sturma, "Eye of the Beholder: The Stereotype of Women Convicts 1788–1852," *Labour History* 34 (1978): 3–10; and Joy Damousi, *Depraved and Disorderly: Female Convicts, Sexuality and Gender in Colonial Australia* (Cambridge: Cambridge University Press, 1997).

6. For example Barbara Hall, *A Nimble Fingered Tribe: The Convicts of the Sugar Cane, Ireland to Botany Bay 1793* (Sydney: author, 2002); Ralph Hawkins, *The Convict Timbergetters of Pennant Hills: A History and Biographical Register* (Hornsby, NSW: Hornsby Shire Historical Society, 1994); June Reeks, ed., *They Were Here: The Convicts of Raymond Terrace*, 2 vols. (Raymond Terrace, NSW: Raymond Terrace and District Historical Society, 2006); Ian Webb, *Convict Road Gangs 1826–1836* (Wahroonga, NSW: Convict Trail Project, 2003); Anthony Watson, "The Story of John Breen: A Convict Reunited with His Family," *Descent: The Journal of the Society of Australian Genealogists* 42, pt. 2 (June 2012): 58–63.

7. Smith, *Australia's Birthstain*, 285.

8. Robson, *Convict Settlers*, 74, 170–171.

9. Rudé, *Protest and Punishment*, 104.

10. For a list of international places of transportation, see Michael Bogle, *Convicts* (Sydney: Historic Houses Trust, 1999), 5–19.

11. Carol Liston, "Convict Women in the Female Factories of New South Wales," in *Women Transported: Life in Australia's Convict Female Factories*, ed. Gay Hendriksen and Carol Liston (Parramatta, NSW: Parramatta Heritage Centre, 2008), 44.

12. Alan Atkinson, "The Free-Born Englishman Transported: Convict Rights as a Measure of Eighteenth Century Empire," *Past and Present* 144 (1994), 88; Bruce Kercher, "Perish or Prosper: The Law and Convict Transportation in the British Empire 1700–1850," *Law and History Review* 21, no. 3 (2003): 527–584.

13. Robson, *Convict Settlers*, 170.

14. State Records of NSW, *Administrative Note—Superintendent of Convicts, Later Principal Superintendent of Convicts*, accessed 6 December 2014, http://investigator.records .nsw.gov.au/Entity.aspx?Path=\Agency\1650.

15. Carol Liston, "New South Wales under Sir Thomas Brisbane 1821–1825" (PhD diss., University of Sydney, 1980), 149–150.

16. A. Yang, "Indian Convict Workers in Southeast Asia in the Late Eighteenth and Early Nineteenth Centuries," *Journal of World History* 14, no. 2 (June 2003): 200–201. The convicts who worked for William Cox on the construction of the road over the Blue

Mountains in 1813 received pardons and land grants at the end of the project. Anne-Maree Whitaker, *William Cox and Cox's Road: A Bicentenary Souvenir* (Blackheath, NSW: Write-Light, 2014), 111–114.

17. J. S. Kerr, *Design for Convicts: An Account of Design for Convict Establishments in the Australian Colonies during the Transportation Era* (Sydney: Library of Australian History in association with the National Trust and ASHA, 1984).

18. John Ritchie, *Punishment and Profit* (Melbourne: Heinemann, 1970).

19. G. C. Bolton, "Holt, Joseph (1756–1826)," in *Australian Dictionary of Biography*, National Centre of Biography, Australian National University, accessed July 20, 2013, http://adb.anu.edu.au/biography/holt-joseph-2194/text2831.

20. Quoted by K. J. Cable, "Fulton, Henry (1761–1840)," in *Australian Dictionary of Biography*, accessed February 10, 2014, http://adb.anu.edu.au/biography/fulton-henry -2074/text2593.

21. Carol Liston, *Pictorial History of Liverpool and District* (Sydney: Kingsclear Books, 2009).

22. State Records of NSW, *On-line Index to Convict Exiles 1846–1850*, accessed 10 February 2014, http://www.records.nsw.gov.au/state-archives/indexes-online/indexes -online; B. Walsh, *Toil and Trouble from Maitland to Moreton Bay: John Eales' Convicts* (Paterson, NSW: Paterson Historical Society, 2014), 75–77.

23. Helen V. Lloyd, *Exiled: Colonial Prisoners Banished from NSW* (Panania, NSW: author, 2004), 2–3.

24. Ibid., 47.

25. N. S. Lynravn, "Hayes, Sir Henry Browne (1762–1832)," in *Australian Dictionary of Biography*, accessed 10 February 2014, http://adb.anu.edu.au/biography/hayes-sir-henry -browne-2172/text2787.

26. J. J. Auchmuty, "Wentworth, D'Arcy (1762–1827)," in *Australian Dictionary of Biography*, accessed 10 February 2014, http://adb.anu.edu.au/biography/wentworth-darcy -1545/text3917.

27. Greg McCarry, "Sarah Dibbs: A Mystery Solved," *Descent: The Journal of the Society of Australian Genealogists* 43, no. 2 (June 2013): 94–95.

28. Cable, "Fulton."

29. Vivienne Parsons, "O'Neil, Peter (1757–1835)," in *Australian Dictionary of Biography*, accessed 11 February 2014, http://adb.anu.edu.au/biography/oneil-peter-2524/text3419; Vivienne Parsons, "Dixon, James (1758–1840)," in *Australian Dictionary of Biography*, accessed 11 February 2014, http://adb.anu.edu.au/biography/dixon-james-1980/text2401; Harold Perkins, "Harold, James (1744–1830)," in *Australian Dictionary of Biography*, accessed 11 February 2014, http://adb.anu.edu.au/biography/harold-james-2156/text2755.

30. Marie Jones, ed. *From Places Now Forgotten: An Index of Convicts Whose Places of Trial Were outside the UK and Ireland* (Cardiff, NSW: author, 2005).

31. Yang, "Indian Convict Workers," 191.

32. Biographical Database of Australia, biographical report for Clara Ward, accessed 11 February 2014, http://www.bda-online.org.au.

33. J. Bradley and C. Pybus, "From Slavery to Servitude: The Australian Exile of Elizabeth and Constance," *Journal of Australian Colonial History* 9 (2007).

34. Research provided by Joy Hughes, Sydney, from her project on convicts from the Cape of Good Hope, June 2014.

35. Research provided by Joy Hughes, Sydney.

36. State Records of NSW, *Administrative Note—Commissioner for the Assignment of Convict Servants*, accessed 6 December 2014, http://investigator.records.nsw.gov.au/Entity .aspx?Path=\Agency\3173.

37. Nicholas, *Convict Workers*, 74–78.

38. Kercher, "Perish or Prosper," 548–552.

39. Grace Karskens, *Inside the Rocks: The Archaeology of a Neighbourhood* (Alexandria, NSW: Hale and Iremonger, 1999), 48–74.

40. J. B. Hirst, *Convict Society and Its Enemies: A History of Early New South Wales* (Sydney: George Allen and Unwin, 1983).

41. For example, see Anne Summers, *Damned Whores and God's Police: The Colonization of Women in Australia* (Ringwood, Vic: Penguin, 1975); Miriam Dixson, *The Real Matilda: Women and Identity in Australia 1788–1975* (Ringwood, Vic: Penguin, 1978); Damousi, *Depraved and Disorderly*.

42. Carol Liston, "Colonial Society under Macquarie," in *The Age of Macquarie*, ed. J. Broadbent and J. Hughes (Melbourne: Melbourne University Press, 1992).

43. Robinson, *Hatch and Brood of Time*; John Molony, *The Native Born: The First White Australians* (Melbourne: Melbourne University Press, 2000).

44. Perry McIntyre, *Free Passage: The Reunion of Irish Convicts and Their Families in Australia 1788–1852* (Dublin: Irish Academic Press, 2011).

45. State Records of NSW, *NRS 793 Female Orphan School Admission Books 1817–1832*, 4/350, 4/351 Reel 2777; State Records of NSW, *NRS 783 Applications for Children out of the Orphan Schools 1825–1833*, 4/334, Reel 4777, 551.

46. State Records of NSW, *NRS 783 Applications for Children out of the Orphan Schools 1825–1833*, 4/333 Reel 2776, 243; 4/334 Reel 4777, 277.

47. McIntyre, *Free Passage*.

48. National Archives of the UK, *Colonial Office CO 324/144*, f. 118.

49. For example, see National Archives of the UK, *Privy Council PC 1/81*.

50. State Records of NSW, *NRS 782 Applications for Admission into the Orphan Schools 1825–1833*, 4/330, Reel 2776, 325.

51. McIntyre, *Free Passage*, 59.

52. State Records of NSW, *NRS 783 Applications for Children out of the Orphan Schools 1825–1833*, 4/335, Reel 2777, 115.

53. National Archives of the UK, *Colonial Office CO 324/144*, f. 72.

54. Biographical Database of Australia, biographical report for Jane Curtis, accessed 11 February 2014, http://www.bda-online.org.au.

55. B. Smith, *A Cargo of Women: Susannah Watson and the Convicts of the Princess Royal* (Kensington: University of New South Wales Press, 1988), 140–150.

56. Josiah Godber to Rebecca Godber, 21 August 1820, transcription, the Pentrich Rebellion, "Letters from Australia," accessed 18 December 2013, http://www.pentrich rebellion.co.uk/html/letters_from_australia.html.

57. State Records of NSW, *NRS 12188 Convict Indents*, Printed Indent of the York, 1831 X633, Reel 907.

58. State Records of NSW, *NRS 905 Colonial Secretary's Correspondence*, 26/3443 in 4/1893, 28/3583 in 4/1977.

59. Mary Hyde and Simeon Lord Collection, Powerhouse Museum Sydney, accessed 18 December 2013. http://www.powerhousemuseum.com/collection/database/collection =Simeon_Lord_and_Mary_Hyde; "Mary Hyde," *Wikipedia*, accessed 18 December 2013,

http://en.wikipedia.org/wiki/Mary_Hyde; D. R. Hainsworth, "Lord, Simeon (1771–1840),"
Australian Dictionary of Bibliography, accessed 2 July 2013, http://adb.anu.edu.au/biography
/lord-simeon-2371/text3115.

60. Dorothy Walsh, ed. *The Admiral's Wife: Mrs Phillip Parker King—A Selection of Letters 1817–56* (Melbourne: Hawthorn Press, 1967).

61. Megan Martin and Carol Liston, "Beulah, Appin—Insights into Early Irish Australia" (conference paper, Irish-Australian Conference, National Museum of Australia, July 2011).

BIBLIOGRAPHY

Alexander, A. *Tasmania's Convicts: How Felons Built a Free Society.* Crows Nest, NSW: Allen and Unwin, 2010.

Atkinson, Alan. "The Free-Born Englishman Transported: Convict Rights as a Measure of Eighteenth Century Empire." *Past and Present* 144 (1994).

Auchmuty, J. J. "Wentworth, D'Arcy (1762–1827)." In *Australian Dictionary of Biography*. National Centre of Biography. Australian National University. Accessed 10 February 2014. http://adb.anu.edu.au/biography/wentworth-darcy-1545/text3917.

Biographical Database of Australia. Accessed 11 February 2014. http://www.bda-online.org.au.

Bladen, F. M., ed. *Historical Records of New South Wales.* 8 vols. Sydney: Government Printer, 1892–1901.

Bogle, Michael. *Convicts.* Sydney: Historic Houses Trust, 1999.

Bolton, G. C. "Holt, Joseph (1756–1826)." In *Australian Dictionary of Biography*. Accessed 20 July 2013. http://adb.anu.edu.au/biography/holt-joseph-2194/text2831.

Bradley, J., and C. Pybus. "From Slavery to Servitude: The Australian Exile of Elizabeth and Constance." *Journal of Australian Colonial History* 9 (2007).

Cable, K. J. "Fulton, Henry (1761–1840)." *Australian Dictionary of Biography*. Accessed 10 February 2014. http://adb.anu.edu.au/biography/fulton-henry-2074/text2593.

Clark, C. M. H. (Manning). "The Origins of Convicts Transported to Eastern Australia 1787–1851." *Historical Studies: Australia and New Zealand* 7, no. 26 (May 1956): 121–135; 7, no. 27 (November 1956): 314–327.

Cook, Thomas. *The Exile's Lamentations.* North Sydney: Library of Australian History, 1978.

Damousi, Joy. *Depraved and Disorderly: Female Convicts, Sexuality and Gender in Colonial Australia.* Cambridge: Cambridge University Press, 1997.

Daniels, K. *Convict Women.* St. Leonards, NSW: Allen and Unwin, 1998.

Dixson, Miriam. *The Real Matilda: Women and Identity in Australia 1788–1975.* Ringwood, Vic: Penguin, 1978.

Hainsworth, D. R. "Lord, Simeon (1771–1840)." In *Australian Dictionary of Biography*. Accessed 2 July 2013. http://adb.anu.edu.au/biography/lord-simeon-2371/text3115.

Hall, Barbara. *A Nimble Fingered Tribe: The Convicts of the Sugar Cane, Ireland to Botany Bay 1793.* Sydney: author, 2002.

Hawkins, Ralph. *The Convict Timbergetters of Pennant Hills: A History and Biographical Register.* Hornsby, NSW: Hornsby Shire Historical Society, 1994.

Hirst, J. B. *Convict Society and Its Enemies: A History of Early New South Wales.* Sydney: George Allen and Unwin, 1983.

Jones, Marie, ed. *From Places Now Forgotten: An Index of Convicts Whose Places of Trial Were outside the UK and Ireland.* Cardiff, NSW: author, 2005.

Karskens, Grace. *Inside the Rocks: The Archaeology of a Neighbourhood.* Alexandria, NSW: Hale and Iremonger, 1999.

Kent, D., and N. Townsend. *The Convicts of the Eleanor: Protest in Rural England, New Lives in Australia.* London: Merlin Press, 2002.

Kercher, Bruce. "Perish or Prosper: The Law and Convict Transportation in the British Empire 1700–1850." *Law and History Review* 21, no. 3 (2003): 527–584.

Kerr, J. S. *Design for Convicts. An Account of Design for Convict Establishments in the Australian Colonies during the Transportation Era.* Sydney: Library of Australian History in association with the National Trust and ASHA, 1984.

Liston, Carol. "Colonial Society under Macquarie." In *The Age of Macquarie*, edited by J. Broadbent and J. Hughes. Melbourne: Melbourne University Press, 1992.

———. "Convict Women in the Female Factories of New South Wales." In *Women Transported: Life in Australia's Convict Female Factories,* edited by Gay Hendriksen and Carol Liston, 29–52. Parramatta, NSW: Parramatta Heritage Centre, 2008.

———. "New South Wales under Sir Thomas Brisbane 1821–1825." PhD diss., University of Sydney, 1980.

———. *Pictorial History of Liverpool and District.* Sydney: Kingsclear Books, 2009.

Lloyd, Helen V. *Exiled: Colonial Prisoners Banished from NSW.* Panania, NSW: author, 2004.

Lynravn, N. S. "Hayes, Sir Henry Browne (1762–1832)." In *Australian Dictionary of Biography.* Accessed 10 February 2014. http://adb.anu.edu.au/biography/hayes-sir-henry-browne-2172/text2787.

Martin, Megan, and Carol Liston. "Beulah, Appin—Insights into Early Irish Australia." Conference paper, Irish-Australian Conference, National Museum of Australia, July 2011.

"Mary Hyde." *Wikipedia.* Accessed 18 December 2013. http://en.wikipedia.org/wiki/Mary_Hyde.

Mary Hyde and Simeon Lord Collection. Powerhouse Museum Sydney. Accessed 18 December 2013. http://www.powerhousemuseum.com/collection/database/collection=Simeon_Lord_and_Mary_Hyde.

McCarry, Greg. "Sarah Dibbs: A Mystery Solved." *Descent: The Journal of the Society of Australian Genealogists* 43, no. 2 (June 2013).

McIntyre, Perry. *Free Passage: The Reunion of Irish Convicts and Their Families in Australia 1788–1852.* Dublin: Irish Academic Press, 2011.

Molony, John. *The Native Born: The First White Australians.* Melbourne: Melbourne University Press, 2000.

National Archives of the UK. *Colonial Office CO 324/144.*

———. *Privy Council PC 1/81.*

Nicholas, S., ed. *Convict Workers: Reinterpreting Australia's Past.* Cambridge: Cambridge University Press, 1988.

Oxley, D. *Convict Maids: The Forced Migration of Women to Australia.* Melbourne: Cambridge University Press, 1996.

Parsons, Vivienne. "Dixon, James (1758–1840)." In *Australian Dictionary of Biography.* Accessed 11 February 2014. http://adb.anu.edu.au/biography/dixon-james-1980/text2401.

———. "O'Neil, Peter (1757–1835)." In *Australian Dictionary of Biography.* Accessed 11 February 2014. http://adb.anu.edu.au/biography/oneil-peter-2524/text3419.

Pentrich Rebellion. "Letters from Australia." Accessed 18 December 2013. http://www
.pentrichrebellion.co.uk/html/letters_from_australia.html.

Perkins, Harold. "Harold, James (1744–1830)." In *Australian Dictionary of Biography*. Accessed
11 February 2014. http://adb.anu.edu.au/biography/harold-james-2156/text2755.

Reeks, June, ed. *They Were Here: The Convicts of Raymond Terrace.* 2 vols. Raymond Terrace,
NSW: Raymond Terrace and District Historical Society, 2006.

Ritchie, John. *Punishment and Profit.* Melbourne: Heinemann, 1970.

Robinson, P. *The Hatch and Brood of Time: A Study of the First Generation of Native-Born
White Australians 1788–1828.* Melbourne: Oxford University Press, 1985.

Robson, L. L. *The Convict Settlers of Australia: An Enquiry into the Origin and Character of
the Convicts Transported to NSW and VDL 1787–1852.* Melbourne: Melbourne University Press, 1965.

Rudé, G. *Protest and Punishment: The Story of the Social and Political Protesters Transported to
Australia 1788–1868.* Melbourne: Oxford University Press, 1978.

Shaw, A. G. L. *Convicts and the Colonies: A Study of Penal Transportation from Great Britain
and Ireland to Australia and Other Parts of the British Empire.* Melbourne: Melbourne
University Press, 1977.

Smith, B. *Australia's Birthstain: The Startling Legacy of the Convict Era.* Sydney: Allen and
Unwin, 2008.

———. *A Cargo of Women: Susannah Watson and the Convicts of the Princess Royal.* Kensington: University of New South Wales Press, 1988.

State Records of NSW. *Administrative Note—Commissioner for the Assignment of Convict
Servants.* Accessed 6 December 2014. http://investigator.records.nsw.gov.au/Entity
.aspx?Path=\Agency\3173.

———. *Administrative Note—Superintendent of Convicts, Later Principal Superintendent of
Convicts.* Accessed 6 December 2014. http://investigator.records.nsw.gov.au/Entity
.aspx?Path=\Agency\1650.

———. *NRS 782 Applications for Admission into the Orphan Schools 1825–1833.*

———. *NRS 783 Applications for Children out of the Orphan Schools 1825–1833.*

———. *NRS 793 Female Orphan School Admission Books 1817–1832.*

———. *NRS 905 Colonial Secretary's Correspondence.*

———. *NRS 12188 Convict Indents.*

———. *On-line Index to Convict Exiles 1846–1850.* Accessed 6 December 2014. http://
www.records.nsw.gov.au/state-archives/indexes-online/indexes-online.

Sturma, M. "Eye of the Beholder: The Stereotype of Women Convicts 1788–1852." *Labour
History* 34 (1978): 3–10.

Summers, Anne. *Damned Whores and God's Police: The Colonization of Women in Australia.*
Ringwood, Vic: Penguin, 1975.

Walsh, B. *Toil and Trouble from Maitland to Moreton Bay: John Eales' Convicts.* Paterson,
NSW: Paterson Historical Society, 2014.

Walsh, Dorothy, ed. *The Admiral's Wife: Mrs Phillip Parker King—A Selection of Letters
1817–56.* Melbourne: Hawthorn Press, 1967.

Watson, Anthony. "The Story of John Breen: A Convict Reunited with His Family." *Descent: The Journal of the Society of Australian Genealogists* 42, pt. 2 (June 2012): 58–63.

Watson, F., ed. *Historical Records of Australia.* 34 vols. Sydney: Library Committee of the
Commonwealth Parliament, 1914–1925.

Webb, Ian. *Convict Road Gangs 1826–1836.* Wahroonga, NSW: Convict Trail Project,
2003.

Whitaker, Anne-Maree. *William Cox and Cox's Road: A Bicentenary Souvenir.* Blackheath, NSW: WriteLight, 2014.

Wood, G. A. "Convict Origins." *Journal of the Royal Australian Historical Society* 8, pt. 4 (1922): 177–208.

Yang, A. "Indian Convict Workers in Southeast Asia in the Late Eighteenth and Early Nineteenth Centuries." *Journal of World History* 14, no. 2 (June 2003): 179–208.

NINE

Prisoners from Indochina in the Nineteenth-Century French Colonial World

Lorraine M. Paterson

In a contemporary suburb of Libreville, the capital of Gabon, on the west coast of Africa, there is a hilly neighborhood colloquially referred to as "Derrière l'Hôpital" (Behind the Hospital). It is known across the city as an area of intensive vegetable cultivation; its irrigation canals have been dug, and tomatoes and other vegetables planted, since the 1880s. Although the contemporary inhabitants of this neighborhood are Gabonese, the original cultivators were from central Vietnam, tending the soil a world away from their natal landscapes. Erased from the community of Libreville itself, traces of these exiles remain only in the contours of the cultivation plots.

During her travels in West Africa in the 1890s, Mary Henrietta Kingsley, English traveler and early anthropologist, came upon this network of irrigation canals while walking in a suburb of Libreville. Kingsley was surprised that the farmers were "Anamese [*sic*] convicts."[1] She commented in her travel account, "[T]hose who conduct themselves well, and survive, have grants of garden ground given them, which they cultivate in this tidy, carefully minute way, so entirely different from the slummacky African methods of doing things."[2] The "slummacky" African way may have been swidden cultivation systems, yet they appeared to Kingsley only as African disorder compared to Asian precision. Sparse traces of these exiles remain; Kingsley's use of "survive" is tragically appropriate. Out of the original group of eighty-seven Vietnamese prisoners (including six women) who arrived in Gabon in May 1888, forty-eight were dead within thirteen months. The remaining prisoners were suffering from tuberculosis and various debilitating fevers.[3] This was anecdotally corroborated by a French priest, who noted, "[W]hen the Annamites were deported to Libreville, they dropped like flies."[4]

Although the odds were against them, if prisoners did survive the hard labor of their punishment and reach the two-year mark, they might then be granted a concession of land regardless of the original length of their sentence. Local authorities needed them; Vietnamese were generally acknowledged for their ability to cultivate, and those who worked the African terrain were no exception. American missionaries reported that "Annamite farmers" had won agricultural prizes in Libreville in 1891; some were even promoted to judge the competitions in which their vegetables had proved so successful.[5] Judging Gabonese vegetables was one of the more unusual tasks that Vietnamese prisoners ended up performing in a global penal context, but it shows the unexpected twists and turns of lives forced to move across transcolonial landscapes.

Between the years 1885 and 1893, approximately six hundred prisoners from Indochina were transported to Gabon and Congo.[6] Some prisoners arrived before Gabon was designated the official location for all prisoners of Vietnamese and Chinese descent. By a decree of 22 October 1887, Gabon became an official penal colony in the French system of penal settlements, but only for Vietnamese and Chinese prisoners. This decree was followed two months later by a decree also designating Brazzaville, French Congo, as a site for forced labor for Vietnamese prisoners.

Historian of Gabon Jeremy Rich suggests that this initial group of eighty-seven prisoners was transported for involvement in the Cần Vương (Save the King) movement, an uprising against the French colonial administration led in 1885 by advisers to the recently installed Vietnamese emperor, Hàm Nghi.[7] However, many of the prisoners sent to Gabon were from Cochinchina, and not from the areas most affected by the Save the King movement.[8] Some of these prisoners were transported for "criminal association," which could denote a multitude of activities.[9] What is clear, however, is that as these prisoners arrived in Gabon, Hàm Nghi himself was hiding in the mountains of central Vietnam before capture and subsequent exile to Algiers—his perpetual exile documented in meticulous detail in the French colonial archives in Aix-en-Provence. These potentially interwoven cases indicate the territorial expanse used by the French colonial administration in order to both contain threat and utilize Vietnamese labor. These exilic traces show that from Libreville to Algiers, the French administration of Indochina used various territories within the global expanse of the French colonial empire as locales for prisoners from Indochina of differing backgrounds between 1863 and 1941.[10] This chapter initially gives a broad overview of French policies regarding exile from Indochina and then examines specific cases of the use of deportation and exile from Indochina in the nineteenth century.

Prisoners from Indochina

Hàm Nghi was just one of the casualties of the French colonization of the territories that comprise contemporary Vietnam, and the uprising he participated in occurred as French forces were in the process of consolidating power. The fact that these territories were colonized over a forty-year period meant significant legal differences existed across the various territorial areas.

Southern Vietnam (Cochinchina) was ceded to the French by treaty beginning in 1863 under great military pressure on the Vietnamese emperor, Tự Đức. By 1867, with Cochinchina completely ceded to France, French attacks began on Annam (central Vietnam) and Tonkin (northern Vietnam). A protectorate treaty was imposed on the Huế court in 1884—an event that sparked Hàm Nghi's flight and eventual capture. Widespread uprisings followed, but by the late 1880s the French military controlled virtually all the important lowland regions. The Union of French Indochina was announced in 1887, and six years later, Laos became the fifth territory under the rubric of the union (under duress, the royal kingdom of Cambodia had become its first member in 1863).

France's staggered takeover of the three territories that comprise modern-day Vietnam meant that its three regions—Annam, Tonkin, and Cochinchina—came under separate administrations. Cochinchina became a colony under direct French control and subject to French law, and Tonkin and Annam were technically "protectorates," and legally, no decree issued in a colony could contradict metropolitan French law. Although this distinction made no difference in many realms of law, it affected the smooth enactment of sending prisoners overseas. For example, in the protectorate of Annam the only person technically allowed to exile an individual was the emperor himself. Exile as a punishment had precedence in the Vietnamese territories prior to French arrival and was generally applied in cases too serious for hard labor but not requiring the death penalty. The legal code used by the Nguyễn dynasty in the nineteenth century, known as the Lê code, was adapted from Chinese law. It used the Chinese measurement of *ly* as a unit of exilic distance, which was largely metaphorical given the smaller possible distances.[11] Exiles were sent two thousand *ly*, which would ensure expulsion from the home province, or three thousand *ly*, which would "cause expulsion from the Middle Kingdom."[12] Again, Vietnam's territory was much smaller than China's; therefore, exile in precolonial Vietnam used "nearby region," "outlying region," and "distant region," and the exact location of these areas changed with dynastic shifts.[13] In precolonial Vietnamese territories, the usual practice was for convicts to be exiled from the north to the south and vice versa.[14] This circulation of convicts, especially from north to south, was not only to rid an area of potential troublemakers but also to supply labor.[15] However, separation from the home village and ancestral graves was also meant to impose a profound spiritual disjuncture in a society in which filial piety played a central role.

One of the first priorities of the French administration was a prison system. Even before Cochinchina had officially been ceded, Admiral Louis-Adolphe Bonard had designated the island of Poulo Condore, 180 kilometers off the coast of southern Vietnam, as a penal island.[16] As historian Peter Zinoman points out, "[T]he intensity of the Vietnamese resistance [against the French] generated demands for fortified camps where anticolonial leaders and prisoners of war could be locked away."[17] Zinoman also notes that the legal definition of political prisoners was unclear in Indochina during the early stages of the prison system; the line between so-called prisoners of war and those incarcerated for common crimes was blurred. Indeed, it was not until the 1890s that a new law in Indochina titled Article 91 allowed for some leeway and not until after tax protests in 1908 that officially designated political prisoners were given special dispensations and treatment.[18] Prior to the 1890s, anticolonial rebels could not be charged with political acts—the crime committed came under the rubric "banditry" or "piracy."[19]

Given the extensive prison system emerging within Indochina, exile would seem imperative only for individuals for whom containment and distance from Indochina were absolutely necessary. However, similar to the British context, other considerations were present—like colonial labor needs— and these should be understood along with the role transportation played in the wider French penal system.

The impetus for penal transportation of French prisoners from metropolitan France survived from the eighteenth century. After being moved from their initial penal servitude as oarsmen on ships, prisoners worked in naval dockyards, or *bagnes,* eventually considered sites that engendered criminal activities. Inspired by British models of deportation to Australia, transportation was "a way of ridding the body politic of these troublemakers, but it was also deemed a way to rehabilitate wrongdoers through hard work under the eye of warders and soldiers."[20] The rhetoric of rehabilitation— and regeneration—was central to French prisoners being deported. Arguably this was merely rhetoric, but even as a rhetorical stance it differed from the version applied to Indochina, where no discourse of rehabilitation existed, just containment or extraction of labor, or both.

Once transportation was decided for these dockyard French prisoners, a suitable location had to be found. Initially that locale was French Guiana, with its establishment as a penal colony in 1863, although its efficacy was quickly questioned because of endemic disease and high mortality rates.

Within ten years the penal colony of New Caledonia was established as a healthier alternative, especially for French prisoners. Indeed, New Caledonia's proximity to Australia positioned it as the French answer to Botany Bay, just as transportation to the latter was being phased out.[21] French Guiana received seventy-four thousand French convicts of all sentencing categories from 1852 to 1946, and New Caledonia, thirty thousand from 1864 to 1897.[22] Once a decree to transport overseas was issued for a specific individual or group, the decision about the exilic location would be based on various (sometimes arbitrary) factors. These included the legal category of the prisoner, whether the exile needed special surveillance (or, more rarely, special privilege, like Hàm Nghi), the penal colonies in operation, and which French territories submitted requests for hard labor workers for specific colonial projects. At different periods, prisoners from Indochina could be sent to the following exilic locales: Gabon, Congo (both incorporated into French Equatorial Africa in 1910), Obock (later part of French Somaliland), French Guiana, New Caledonia, Madagascar, Réunion, Martinique, Guadeloupe, Algeria, and French Oceania (both Tahiti and the Marquesas). Some locations—Algeria, Tahiti, and the Marquesas—were used only for high-level political prisoners. Indeed, there were three key categories of prisoners: exiles, deported prisoners, and transported prisoners. Although, as Clare Anderson argues for the South Asian context (chapter 1 in this volume), there are many ways in which such categories blurred and overlapped.

Exiles were considered the most dangerous, "political," prisoners. The term "exile" itself, which implies estrangement and distance from the home territory, is necessary for political containment (and perhaps punishment). Exiles required a specific exile decree, which had to stipulate the grounds of exile and a selected locale; additionally, a tribunal or trial might take place, but the decree itself was sufficient. They might also be able to bring along family members or, in certain cases, whole entourages.

The governor-general of Indochina made a tentative decision about exilic location, often in consultation with regional French officials. However, the minister of colonies could change the destination based on a broader metropolitan perspective, or arguably based on transportation schedules, so that prisoners could end up in exilic locations more rapidly. Marseille acted as the intermediary point for exiles being shipped from Indochina to exilic locales, and onward travel could take various routes. Exiles might be sent anywhere that metropolitan and local French authorities could agree upon: a location in which solitary, isolated exile could be structured in its borders, and individual exiles managed in a way meant to preclude or constrain contact with others. In the 1890s, Algeria operated as a place of strategic seclusion for political exiles from around the French Empire, including

Indochina. Locales selected could be fairly cosmopolitan, like Algiers, where Hàm Nghi could socialize with other exiled royals (he compared his exile stipend with that of Queen Ranavalo from Madagascar and found it unsatisfactory),[23] to the desolate town of Djelfa on the edge of the Sahara desert, where Prince Duong Chakr, son of King Norodom I of Cambodia, died of the combined effects of "climate, boredom and alcoholism" in 1897 at the tender age of thirty-three.[24]

Duong Chakr was assigned one of the worst possible exilic locales. It is tempting to say this reflects the French conception of Cambodia being of lesser import in the colonial hierarchy than the Vietnamese territories, but it may also be because his father, King Norodom, had declared him persona non grata after the French informed him that Duong Chakr had attempted patricide.[25] However, keeping different colonial exiles in separate locales was difficult and very expensive. In 1903, a site of exile in Algeria was requested in an exile decree issued for a Vietnamese prisoner, Vi Van Duyet, and his wife, from Bắc Giang Province in northern Vietnam. (He was accused of having "relations with armed Chinese bands and of the fabrication of opium," which was a lucrative French monopoly.) The Minister of Colonies cast some doubt on whether Algeria was a feasible suggestion; his letter began by stating that Algeria was not available as a site of exile anymore because of the difficulty of finding different locations for multiple deportees from Indochina.[26] Instead the Minister wrote, "I ask: is it not easier to find the means to put Vi Van Duyet somewhere in isolation in Indochina? Could you perhaps find a fishing village on an island off the coast?"[27]

The expense and complications of exile arrangements meant that it was advantageous to designate prisoners as *déportés* (deported prisoners) rather than exiles, as they entered a particular legal stream with designated locales attached. Deported prisoners contrasted with *transportés* (common-law prisoners, or transported prisoners) and were accused of some kind of "political" crime, a category that encompassed a wide group of individuals—from those who positioned themselves in direct challenge to French colonial authorities to those who destabilized French colonial monopolies like opium, thereby undermining a key economic component of colonial Indochina. In Vietnamese the same word was used to denote both exile and deportation, whether near or far: *đày*. On occasion a more literary term, *lưu vong*, which implies separation from one's natal land in a way that *đày* does not, was used, but it was not common.

Prisoners may have resided in prison in Vietnam for some time before a decision to move them overseas was taken. In other words, their sentencing was not predicated on removal from Indochina to "a place far from Indochina" (which was the terminology used on an exile decree before the governor-general of Indochina wrote in the location). Peter Zinoman's seminal work on colonial imprisonment in Vietnam, *The Colonial Bastille*,[28] illustrates that many political prisoners were imprisoned in the aforementioned penal island of Poulo Condore; therefore, there was a certain logic as to when prisoners should be sent abroad. Laws designated different levels of deportation, from those requiring "an enclosed location" to those in which a hard labor sentence could be passed. Lower-category deportees could—like common-law prisoners—be assigned "TF," meaning *travaux forcé*, in other words, hard labor. Indeed, the exilic trajectories of deportees often overlapped with those of common-law prisoners sent overseas after being convicted of anything from petty crimes to murder. The same convoys would carry exiles, deportees, and common-law transported prisoners to various intermediary points.

Common-law prisoners were often sent overseas for labor purposes, and it is impossible to write about transportation from Indochina without also exploring colonial labor, which was needed for an expanding empire. This was not just punishment for the sake of it, but strategic use of laborers whom the French considered to be efficient workers for developing colonial enterprises. Indeed, balancing demands from other parts of the French empire (and from private companies) for these allegedly useful prisoners was quite problematic. Quite apart from the labor projects of the two penal colonies, there were constant applications from Madagascar, Gabon, and Congo, to name just three French colonies, which wanted prisoners from Indochina as "exemplary" agricultural workers. However, unlike other colonial contexts, there was not a surplus population in Vietnam. This contrasts with what Robert Cribb has argued regarding the Dutch East Indies, where in Java, "the Dutch had abundant access to labor by other [i.e., nonpenal] means."[29] French officials in Indochina were constantly trying to retain workers of all kinds in Vietnam, who were usually in short supply. For example, in 1899, the governor of Madagascar asked for two thousand "Asiatics" as deported laborers.[30] When this request was relayed to Indochina, Governor-General Paul Beau responded that "there are 53 detained in Poulo Condore of the correct category and I do not possess exactly the number of the condemned of Asiatic origins detained in New Caledonia and Guiana."[31] Failing to acquire convicts, the colonial government of Madagascar attempted to contract laborers through Chinese communities in Vietnam, due to a perceived reluctance of Vietnamese nonpenal workers to travel overseas.

Typographies of Exile in Other Contexts

While migrants and diasporic communities have received special attention as exemplary illustrations of the transnational or transcolonial moment, little scholarship has explicitly examined prisoners sent from colonial sites whose lives became entwined in a web of interconnected cultural and economic links across continents.

Anand Yang's scholarship on convict labor exiled from South Asia to Southeast Asia illustrates many of the ways it impacted local communities, from labor disputes to intermarriage.[32] The Dutch East India Company's use of the Cape Colony is another parallel to the ways the French used their empire to designate far-flung sites of exile. Kerry Ward's seminal work on exile from the Dutch East Indies demonstrates that to a large extent there was no coherent policy or overarching strategy that governed the use of exile. There are several differences, however, between exile from the Dutch East Indies and exile from Indochina. The difference is not just temporal, with the former having established exilic communities by the seventeenth century, but also political: indigenous allies of the Dutch East India Company could petition for the exile of their enemies. The financing of exile also operated differently, as Ward points out: "The [Dutch East India] Company often paid the subsistence expenses of exiled nobles and . . . extracted these expenses from their remaining relatives or rulers," which was not the case in Indochina, where exile expenses were charged to the protectorate or colony issuing the exile decree.[33] Yet as Ward points out, "Although forced migration limited agency by imposing legal categories of bondage, it could not limit agency through control of communication within indigenous networks of communication."[34] For Vietnamese exiles, especially political ones, these "indigenous networks" could sometimes be based on a broader sense of race, one that encompassed Chinese communities. Indeed, being able to speak Chinese and "pass" as Chinese were often the greatest assets an exile could possess, because everywhere the French could exile, even to the farthest reaches of their own empire or within their own penal colonies, Chinese communities existed.

Examining the different locales, different temporal periods, and different streams of prisoners is quite complex. However, throughout the complicated and multilocational history of exile from French Indochina, two penal sites stand apart: Réunion, as the first site of transportation, and one that undoubtedly received the first wave of political deportees (even if they were not officially designated as such), and New Caledonia, which has experienced three distinct types of prisoners from Indochina—political exiles, prisoners forced to stay in New Caledonia and settle as owners of agricultural concessions, and common-law prisoners sent to labor for colonial projects and private companies. The rest of this chapter examines these different types of prisoners from Indochina in order to explore what transportation to Réunion and New Caledonia illuminates about the limits—and opportunities—of certain transcolonial penal contexts.

Nguyễn Hữu Huân: the First Political Exile

The first Vietnamese prisoner to be deported as an (unofficial) political prisoner from Vietnam was Nguyễn Hữu Huân, a classically trained scholar who participated in fighting against the French near his hometown of Mỹ Tho in Cochinchina after the Treaty of Saigon was signed in 1862.[35] In 1864, Huân was captured and sentenced to five years' exile. Although many secondary biographical materials state that his exile was to French Guiana or New Caledonia, it seems clear, based on French transportation patterns, that Réunion was his eventual destination.[36] Between 1863 and 1868, 1,287 prisoners were sent from Indochina to Réunion, many of them connected to the first wave of anticolonial activities in Cochinchina.[37] Of Huân's time there, and the conditions under which he labored, very little is known. However, two poems are attributed to Huân's time in exile, and they circulated among literary circles in Vietnam during the late 1860s. These poems were written in classical Chinese and reflect the alienation of an exile from Cochinchina, evoking traditional idioms of estrangement. The first is a fairly straightforward poem evoking images of departure and grief at the moment of departure from his home village:

> As I distance myself from my Emperor,
> And leave my father and mother,
> Clustered around the village,
> Bamboo glistens with tears of parting.
> My hair quivers, although I am not afraid;
> But my cap flinches and not from the winter wind.[38]

The line "bamboo glistens with tears of parting" uses the landscape to reflect his sorrow in traditional idioms of estrangement. Nguyễn Hữu Huân's other poem attributed to his time in exile draws on allusions to a classical Chinese text. Given his educational background, it is not surprising he drew on these metaphors to illustrate alienation in this radically different environment. Two lines of this second poem draw on historical allusions to times of societal rupture in Chinese history, when scholars of the Jin were suffering under oppression by the Chu dynasty. The lines of Huân's poem read:

> How can we speak of drinking with wineglasses at the New Pavilion?
> For poetic verses of my ancestral country, I am at a loss for words.

This reference to the "New Pavilion" has specific cultural connotations, known to those trained within the classical Vietnamese education system. It alludes to a story in which "officials of the Eastern Jin dynasty (317–730) who had fled from the north to the south [from the Chu dynasty] often met at the New Pavilion in Nanjing to weep together."[39] Although they drank wine together, the scholars could not ignore their utterly changed landscape, and consequently looked at one another and sobbed.[40] The phrase "facing each other and sobbing at the New Pavilion" subsequently became a reference in both Chinese and Vietnamese classical poetry to evoke powerlessness in the face of adversity, and also loyalty to dynasty, or homeland. Huân's use of the "New Pavilion" suggests that the extremity of deportation left him unable to describe those landscapes he left behind and from which he felt utterly estranged.[41] Even the oft-used allusion to the "New Pavilion" from this classical canon was not able to convey the anguish he felt. The ways in which Huân drew on traditional idioms to explore the devastation of exile are echoed in Ronit Ricci's examination of how Javanese historical chronicles (*babads*) depicted the plight of prominent Javanese exiled to Ceylon by the Dutch East India Company (chapter 4 in this volume). Although Huân's poems were reputedly penned in situ, both the poems and the fragments of *babads* examined by Ricci are infused with loss and the difficulties of the "emotional state of exilic life," even if rendered in different idiomatic forms. Huân's poetry is illustrative of how a traditional intellectual would poetically convey the estrangement of exile and also shows the limits of colonial cultural legibility, given its supposed circulation back to Vietnam during his exile.

In both the penal colonies and sites of convict labor, the French bureaucracy relied on a system of interpreters to assist in communicating with deported prisoners, who were usually not conversant in French. Many issues are evoked when considering these individuals who played a key role in facilitating exile.

An ability to communicate instructions to prisoners was of paramount importance to French colonial officials. An interpreter able to converse in both French and Vietnamese could serve that purpose. However, competent translation of the correspondence of literate deportees was also of vital importance; this proved to be problematic. Technically, exiles were allowed to write only once a month to immediate family members.[42] Letters written in *quốc ngữ* (romanized Vietnamese) did not pose a problem for the authorities, as interpreters were trained in it, but letters in *chữ nôm* (the Vietnamese-based character system) or classical Chinese, like Huân's, could prove very difficult to translate. This difficulty operated on two levels; first, whether the interpreter had knowledge of a character-based script, and second, whether the interpreter was competent in his comprehension of the metaphors or allusions that might be drawn upon. Interpreters, especially in this early period, were often Catholic and unschooled in the allusions inculcated in exiles who had participated in the traditional examination system in Vietnam. Exiles conversant with classical Chinese texts could use opaque idioms, which potentially confounded a translator uneducated in such a tradition. Even if compelled to write in romanized Vietnamese, these exiles could draw upon these allusions, which could prove difficult to translate. The content of letters that passed the colonial censor's eye is impossible to know; however, unsent letters—withheld by the censor—make translation difficulties apparent.[43] This difficulty was often compounded overseas, where the penal administration might have only one interpreter on whom to rely.[44] Interpreters sometimes allowed material to pass, presumably because they did not want to reveal linguistic limitations to the Interpretation Service of Indigenous Affairs. If exile is in one sense the ultimate exercise of colonial power—capable of moving physical bodies to distant places—then the fact that Huân's poems may have managed to slip the censor's net, so to speak, also makes clear that colonial power was fragmentary, arbitrary, and incomplete in its ability to constrain cultural and political flows.

Vietnamese historical accounts narrate that after he left Réunion, Huân's sentence still kept him under house arrest in Cochinchina for another five years, although the terms of this "house arrest" remain vague in the sources cited.[45] On his release, Huân once again joined anti-French forces and was subsequently arrested and executed.[46]

TRANSPORTED INTO MARRIAGE

Four years after Nguyễn Hữu Huân's arrival in Réunion, the first group of prisoners from Indochina was transported to New Caledonia, in 1868. These sixteen prisoners arrived in New Caledonia from Saigon via Marseille with sentences ranging from ten to twenty years for a variety of crimes in the nascent colony of Cochinchina.[47] On their release, the prisoners were not returned to Vietnam under any form of house arrest. Instead they were obliged to remain in New Caledonia and encouraged to marry female French prisoners with whom they would work on agricultural concessions. This administrative directive to marry and settle did not just prevent return to Vietnam, but was part of a wider policy to try to establish a settler colony in New Caledonia under the direction of the governor-general of New Caledonia, Charles Guillain.[48] It was Guillain who argued in 1869 that all female French prisoners should not be sent to French Guiana but rather to New Caledonia.[49] His attitudes are reflected in a report from the directory of the penitentiary administration in 1872, which emphasized, "This is the most serious hour; let us put women on the farm and children in the house. We can have no more illusions: women or no colonization."[50] This concern with the need to—and difficulty of—acquiring women is reflected in other penal contexts, as Robert Cribb has argued in reference to the Karimun Jawa islands.[51]

As historian Matt Matsuda points out, "Capitalizing on the island's status as a penal colony, colonial ministers mandated liaisons, partnerships and marriages to convicts and ex-convicts, seeking to create families and thereby engender paternal, maternal, and domestic affection and solidarity in the name of *patrie* and empire."[52] However, what is surprising is the emphasis on the *métis*—interracial—nature of that settlement community. This reflects a pragmatic approach to a dearth of women in a multiethnic settler community.[53] Indeed, it should be noted that the Vietnamese "competed" for the few brides available along with white French prisoners. For the Vietnamese prisoners, this practice contrasted strongly with interracial policies in Indochina itself, where fears about *métis*, or mixed-race children—the girls would become prostitutes and the boys would become anti-French—reflected a very different attitude.[54] As Anne Stoler argues for the Dutch East Indies and Indochina itself, "Métissage emerged as a powerful trope for internal contamination and for challenges to rule that were morally, politically and sexually conceived."[55] Under Guillain's tenure as governor, *métissage* had precisely the opposite connotation in New Caledonia.

There was a great dearth of French women in New Caledonia because transportation to a penal colony was largely optional on the part of convict women. Under French law, women convicted of certain crimes were given a choice of where to spend their sentences, and only 2 percent of women opted to leave France.[56] This differed from other penal contexts, for example, sentencing under British or Portuguese transportation regulations. As Colin Forster points out, "Critics of Australia said that the gender imbalance was too great (15% were women) however this was nothing compared to French penal colonies."[57]

On arrival in New Caledonia, female prisoners were placed under the supervision of the Catholic sisters in the convent of Saint Joseph of Cluny.[58] While in the convent, women would sew, assist with laundry, and repair the clothes of the penal administrators.[59] The procedure for the selection of a wife was highly regulated. Freed men wanting to find a wife would go to the convent with a group of other ex-prisoners. After being introduced to the available women, they would state a preference. If the woman also expressed interest, a meeting would be arranged in a kiosk structure, built between the convent and the prison. Under strict supervision, the couples were allowed to converse and discuss a potential union. Common questions

The courtship kiosk where convicts used to meet potential spouses at the convent of Saint Joseph of Cluny. (Taken from Jean Carol, *Le bagne à la Nouvelle-Calédonie*, Paris: Ollendorf, 1903.)

included whether either of them had any assets (e.g., animals or mosquito nets).[60] The desire for a healthy spouse was also of central importance, as syphilis and tuberculosis were rampant among the prison population of New Caledonia. Once a marriage was decided on, group weddings would be held in the courtship kiosk.[61]

On their release, several of these Vietnamese prisoners were taken to the convent of Saint Joseph and introduced to female French prisoners. In terms of communication issues between these couples, some form of French must have sufficed; the men had spent several years in the penal colony and would have learned some French in their penal assignments.

These ex-prisoners and their spouses were given land concessions near the town of Bourail on the Grand Terre (largest island) in New Caledonia and the center of the penitentiary service. The ceding of land to these couples was key to the success of colonial goals. After all, "appropriate marriage statuses and domestic sensibilities were a dominant part of colonial planning in New Caledonia, but they could not be effective without land concessions to grant new households."[62]

One of the Vietnamese prisoners deported in 1868 was a young man called Tchong Winki (probably Tchong Vinh Ky originally). Similar to half of his group, Tchong had actually been born in Canton, China, and it is not clear how long he resided in Cochinchina prior to his arrest.[63] After serving his ten-year sentence he married a Frenchwoman from the Bourail convent, Marie Poirier, in November 1884.[64] Although her crime is unknown, most female deportees at this time were convicted for murder (infanticide being most prevalent).[65]

After Marie died, Tchong married the widow of a recently deceased ex-Vietnamese prisoner (Trân Van Huong).[66] Their first child, known as Thion "Winsky," was born in Bourail on 5 August 1887. This change in the rendering of "Winki" was probably to make pronunciation easier; however, it makes the name even less Vietnamese than its original (and subsequent) renderings. Marriage and remarriage in the agricultural concessions of Bourail were quite common. Given early deaths and illness, and the disproportionate ratio of men to women, it was not unusual for women to marry several times.[67] What is interesting is that once married within the Vietnamese community, Trân Van Huong's widow remarried within it too.

Also among this first group of prisoners was Nguyễn Vân Xứng. He was sentenced in Saigon to ten years' hard labor for having taken part in anti-French activities. Despite a sentence of ten years, he was permitted to marry Catherine Benjoux in 1874, after six years of exemplary conduct. The couple married and settled on a concession in Bourail, eventually having three children.[68] Another prisoner, Trân Vân Hap, became a concession holder in Bourail in March 1886. He had originally been a stallholder in Saigon and received a twenty-year sentence connected to anti-French activities in 1866. On his death, Trân bequeathed his concession to Catherine Benjoux, widow of Nguyễn Vân Xứng, for her and her three half-Vietnamese children, thus extending the concessionary land of the Benjoux-Nguyễn family.[69]

It is not clear that Trân and Xứng knew each other in Vietnam. They were both sentenced in Saigon but at different tribunals on different days, and for different crimes. However, their prisoner numbers are consecutive, so they would have been in prison together from the very beginning.[70]

One British colonial traveler observed that Bourail should be named the "Arcadia of the Redeemed Criminal."[71] This theme of redemption should be noted because the racially based orientations of French criminology usually meant that non-European prisoners were assumed to be incapable of change. This attempt to rehabilitate prisoners—through their concessions—contradicted how Vietnamese prisoners had previously been (and subsequently were) positioned as unalterable Asians. As mentioned earlier, the rehabilitation of Vietnamese prisoners was not part of the agenda of the French colonial government. Peter Zinoman argues in *The Colonial Bastille* that Vietnamese were considered "dulled to the inducements and disincentives that had long shaped behavior in the West."[72] The experiment of Bourail contradicted such an assessment and offered incentives for the ex-Vietnamese prisoners to become members of the settled landholding colonial community.[73] Bourail was also the site of numerous concessions of Arab and Berber convicts as well.

Concessions were assessed after five years for efficiency and profitability and if not deemed sufficiently profitable could be repossessed from the concession holder. By 1910, there were only 130 concession holders in New Caledonia, as the authorities reclaimed several concessions.[74]

If exile is first and foremost a constraint, we can also see the ways in which the exilic experience created new societal opportunities and potentially new narratives of self. In this case, through interracial marriage, which was essentially banned in Indochina, this group of prisoners was encouraged, or indeed somewhat pressured, to marry, and was given concessionary land in New Caledonia. For prisoners in the prisons of Vietnam, the idea of being married to French women and being given land by the French government on completion of their sentences would have seemed utterly fantastical. Within Indochina itself, the allocation of concessions was an agricultural opportunity permitted to only French citizens and those with close and favorable connections to the colonial regime.[75] By the same token, for a Vietnamese man to marry a Frenchwoman was virtually unheard of in nineteenth-century Indochina, let alone occurring with state endorsement.[76] The French-Vietnamese families of Bourail were the first such interracial community in the French colonial world.

The First "Contract" Prisoners

In 1891, a group of 791 Vietnamese penal and contract workers arrived by the ship the *Chéribon* at the small quarantine island, Île Freycinet, off the New Caledonian coast close to Nouméa. This was the largest group of prisoners shipped from Indochina to any exilic locale at one time.

By the end of the nineteenth century there was an acute need for colonial labor in the expanding nickel mines and other colonial commercial enterprises in New Caledonia. Nickel, which had been discovered in 1875, changed the landscape of New Caledonia, and the development of the island illustrates how the use of overseas convict labor was constantly at the center of competing local and international concerns. In examining New Caledonia it becomes apparent that boundaries between contract and penal labor were artificially constructed; in 1891 this first group of 791 Vietnamese "workers" contained 750 prisoners, including two female prisoners.[77] Do Thi Ngan had been condemned for theft in Hanoi and given a five-year sentence. Le Thi Cam had a ten-year sentence for murder and ended up working in the shop of Mademoiselle Le Riche in Nouméa, apparently a better fate than befell her male compatriots.[78] Out of the forty-one family members (who actually had signed work contracts), twenty were women accompanying prisoner husbands.

Although on the surface it might appear that these prisoners were being shipped under the auspices of the colonial regime, closer examination shows that the transportation of these prisoners to New Caledonia was not the idea of the prison authorities of Indochina, nor the local authorities in New Caledonia, nor even the ministry of colonies itself. Instead it was the idea of a Bordeaux-based private company. Private companies in New Caledonia explicitly asked if they could have prisoners from Indochina put at their disposal.[79] The company that initially lobbied for the export of prisoners to New Caledonia was the Oceania branch of the Ballande company, run by André Ballande, scion of the company with an extensive overseas commercial network. It should also be emphasized that although some prisoners would be designated for Ballande company enterprises, the intention was that the majority would be "resold" to other businesses for a fee. One of André Ballande's most lucrative trades was in cheap labor. He imported various kinds of indentured labor into New Caledonia from the 1890s to the 1930s: Melanesians from Vanuatu and the Solomon Islands, as well as Vietnamese, Javanese, and Japanese. This "enabled him to become a broker in cheap labor to employers in the colony as well as ensuring a labor supply for his own enterprises."[80] For Ballande, placing colonial French prisoners in what was essentially a private system of indenture seemed like the logical next step.

Indeed, exporting penal labor was not a new phenomenon. In 1890, all prisoners in Indochina sentenced to jail terms longer than ten years were systematically and permanently sent to French Guiana.[81] The Vietnamese of Gabon described in the opening paragraphs of this chapter built roads as a punitive measure—labor that created colonial infrastructure in order to punish the miscreant. However, as the description of Ballande's company should make clear, what was different in this case was the overt emphasis on penal labor for commercial purposes as opposed to punitive uses of labor. Originally, Ballande wanted to export labor from Guangdong, China; however, this endeavor ultimately failed due to conditions imposed by the Chinese viceroy of the province.[82]

Both the governor of Cochinchina and the resident superior in Tonkin strongly objected to Ballande's proposal. Indochina's most senior legal officer, the chief prosecutor, also supported opposition to it.[83] Objections were framed from various angles. The governor of Cochinchina and the resident superior in Tonkin were of the view that many of the prisoners serving sentences of ten years and longer were political prisoners. They claimed that many of them were men who had not committed any crimes themselves but were jailed on the basis of acts of piracy committed in areas under their jurisdictions.[84] They therefore feared that political instability might ensue from sending them overseas.

Also, the Ballande company was interested in transporting prisoners sentenced to as little as three years' imprisonment, technically illegal under colonial law.[85] Ballande tried to counter these claims of illegality by suggesting that prisoners originally sentenced to between three and five years would become contract workers on completion of their sentences. However, this transition to contract worker would not be optional and the newly minted "workers" would be forced to remain in the penal colony for at least ten years.[86] Quite apart from legal issues as to who could be deported and how, colonial officials within Indochina itself did not consider Indochina to have a surplus population; they were very reluctant to permit the export of potential workers.

Ultimately, any debates or objections within Indochina itself were overruled. As well as his own commercial influence, André Ballande had the backing of the Paris-based Colonial Union, which lobbied the minister of colonies. The directive came from the minister of colonies to the governor-general of Indochina on 23 January 1891. The governor-general was advised to issue instructions for the embarkation of "all prisoners serving sentences of between 4 and 10 years without distinction on the nature of the sentence or the political or common law character of the sentence."[87]

The clash between the ministerial level and authorities in Tonkin on the export of prisoners continued right up to the moment of departure; the local authorities refused to assist with the transportation of the prisoners.[88] The prisoners were privately organized and shipped.[89] Ever the entrepreneur, along with the prisoners themselves, Ballande exported items they would need that could be profitably sold to their employers: rice, clothing, "Annamite hats," and "Annamite pipes."[90]

The prisoners endured a painfully slow trip to New Caledonia (which usually lasted between 80 and 140 days); as soon as the prisoners disembarked they were transferred to quarantine. Unfortunately, a group of six hundred Japanese contract workers arrived at precisely the same time, adding to the scarcity of water and vegetables under an unusually hot Nouméan sun.[91] According to doctors who initially examined them, many were in terrible health due to malnutrition. Indeed, from this first group of convicts and workers in 1891, two hundred contracted beriberi, seventy of whom died.[92] Beriberi was a thiamine deficiency, and although these deportees believed it was unknown in their homeland, in reality it was endemic in colonial prisons in Vietnam throughout the 1880s and 1890s.[93]

Ballande's role as labor broker roused voracious reproach in the French and Indochinese press, and not surprisingly, he was accused of trafficking in humans. One contemporaneous French critic of transportation, Yves Joleaud-Barral, readily compared the contracting, or "selling," of the Annamites to the buying and selling of slaves.[94] In discussing this initial shipment of 791 prisoners to New Caledonia, Joleaud-Barral explained that on arrival the prisoners were taken in groups of 20 to 30 at a time by the colonial employers, emphasizing that they were being used by private companies, which selected them as if in a market.[95] He also claimed that there were cases in which the working conditions were so appalling that pardons were given. For example, he referred to "Mguyen," condemned to twelve years of exile in 1890, who was pardoned after only two because of "atrocious conditions." Although Joleaud-Barral does not expand on what these conditions were, a pardon based on poor working or living conditions seems unlikely and he may have fabricated this incident to underline his argument.[96] At the time, Ballande was generally considered a benevolent employer of penal or contract laborers.[97] For those contracted to his own businesses, he was the only employer to provide leisure activities.

After the *Chéribon* prisoners left Vietnam in 1891, colonial authorities in Indochina were constantly fielding inquiries (often impassioned entreaties) from their relatives, eager for information as to their fate.[98] Requests for information from the authorities in Indochina went unanswered on the part of the governor of New Caledonia. Instead the governor argued that the shipment had proved problematic because there had been difficulty placing some prisoners due to the high fee charged per prisoner.[99]

Despite all these issues, prisoners were still shipped to New Caledonia—increasingly in tandem with the export of workers from Vietnam who had signed five-year work contracts. (This export of contract workers peaked in 1929 with 6,700 Vietnamese workers in New Caledonia.) A second prisoner contingent arrived in 1895, and all 150 prisoners were placed within three weeks. Among this group were 15 Vietnamese Catholics whom Ballande assured the Bishop of Nouméa he had specifically asked his agents to seek out, presumably because Ballande considered them to be specifically compliant workers.[100]

Prisoners were also sometimes transported between French Guiana and New Caledonia, depending on the latter's labor needs. This intercolonial transportation echoes what Clare Anderson discusses in chapter 1, referring to the South Asian case: the movement of people on intercolonial circuits. In 1896, an unusually large group of deportees arrived from French Guiana:

104 Tonkinese, 32 Cambodians, and 338 Cochinchinese.[101] Once they arrived in French Guiana, the group sent a special petition to the minister of colonies on 4 July 1897 raising concerns about their repatriation to Indochina on the completion of their sentences. The petition was written in *quốc ngữ* (romanized Vietnamese) and was signed on behalf of Annamites, Tonkinese, Cochinchinese, and Cambodians (Cao Mien).[102] Unusual for its evidence of solidarity between Cambodian and Vietnamese deportees, it arguably emerged from this instance of transcolonial deportation. For the most part, Cambodian and Vietnamese prisoners did not mix, nor were they placed together. This was largely because of language-based considerations, although a high proportion of exiled Cambodians were of Chinese descent and may have been able to communicate with Vietnamese of a similar southern Chinese linguistic background.[103]

Although the transport of French prisoners to New Caledonia ceased in 1897, penal convoys of political prisoners from Indochina continued to be sent to New Caledonia well into the twentieth century. A group of political deportees was even sent to a site of "secluded" deportation: the island of Maré in the Loyalty Islands in 1913.

CONCLUSION: EXILIC TRACES

The traces of these exilic experiences have shaped the societal contours of both the Socialist Republic of Vietnam and New Caledonia today, the latter still being a "special collectivity" of France and considered part of the extended French world. Although a very small Vietnamese community exists in Réunion today, in Vietnam, Nguyễn Hữu Huân's poetry of exile is repeatedly anthologized as patriotic poetry from prison, whether it actually slipped the eye of the censor or was written subsequent to his return.[104] Despite Huân's reference to estrangement from a natal locale that is embodied as an "Emperor," he is written into a communist narrative of anti-French heroism as a nationalistic hero of the people. A large statue of him is erected in his hometown of Mỹ Tho in the Mekong Delta, where he dominates the central square.

Not all of the Vietnamese Bourailian concessions of the 1880s proved to be successful agricultural enterprises. However, more than 150 years later, the Winsky family still lives in Bourail with the descendants of Tchong Vinh Ky and Marceline Gratienne, now a large interracial family of Vietnamese, French, and Kanak.[105]

The ways in which penal and contract labor overlapped in the export of the Vietnamese to New Caledonia allows for a particular history of the Vietnamese community to be written that occludes large shipments of prisoners.

In New Caledonia, contemporary renderings of the 1891 *Chéribon* group often position them as solely contract workers. Of course, some arrivals (forty-one relatives of prisoners) were under work contracts from the beginning, but for the vast majority of this group, and those prisoners who followed, the connection to the colonial prisons of Indochina is largely erased. The concept of exploitative contract labor overwrites the hint of any form of criminality (even criminality in the name of nationalism) in the history of this community.[106] The large numbers of contract workers subsequently recruited enable a further blurring of the line between penal and contract labor. Indeed, the use of "matricule" numbers to designate Vietnamese contract workers (because of the difficulty in pronouncing their names) echoes that of the penal system, which also used "matricules" for all nationalities of convicts. Therefore, there tends to be only one history of the Vietnamese in New Caledonia, that of the so-called *chân dang*, the Vietnamese contract workers.[107] The preeminent Vietnamese intellectual of New Caledonia, Jean Vanmai, both historian and novelist, encapsulates this view in his writing. In his various historical and fictional depictions of the Vietnamese community in New Caledonia, he generally occludes the circumstances of penal labor from Indochina being used on a large scale.[108] In discussing his novels *Chân dang* and *Fils de chân dang* (Sons of *chân dang*), Tess Do narrates how "the majority of Caledo-Viets are descendants of the voluntary workers who were recruited as early as 1891 who signed a five-year contract with the French Ministry of Indigenous Affairs."[109] Do also states that Vanmai's purpose in writing "is to remind the Vietnamese community of the dignity and respect inherent in their tales of migration and settlement."[110]

This selective historical memory is also reflected in how the Vietnamese community, through the auspices of the Amicale Vietnamienne de Nouvelle Calédonie, portrayed itself in a year-long exhibit at the Musée de Nouvelle Calédonie from May 2012 to February 2013, titled "When the Bamboo Is Old, the Shoots Grow."[111] The exhibit consisted of dioramas of the Vietnamese community and a panel explaining the history of the community titled, "Les chân dang de Nouvelle Calédonie, 1891–1946." It began by recounting the history of the "the first group of more than 700 Indochinese workers" who arrived on the *Chéribon* in 1891. Nowhere in the exhibit were the penal roots of the community alluded to. Ironically enough, the coercion that accompanied the passage of the *Chéribon* to New Caledonia has largely been occluded, an omission not by French historians wishing to tread lightly on the use of forced penal labor by commercial interests and for colonial projects, but rather by a Vietnamese community wishing to distance itself from potential connection to a penal past.

The exile, deportation, and transportation of Vietnamese prisoners in the nineteenth century thus illustrates many seminal issues attached to the penal expulsion of colonial subjects to other colonial territories as a policy of political containment or extraction of labor, or both. Seen through the prism of prisoners' lives, the individual rupture, physical suffering, and social displacement such sentences produced are often, quite rightly, foregrounded. Yet, these coerced transcolonial contexts also engendered a diversity of unforeseen personal, economic, and societal repercussions. Examining Indochina's penal connections within a wider French world of transcolonial constraint—but also mobility—adds historical and cultural depth to the idea that flow and connection have long been elements of empire, but in ways that are uneven, often unpredictable, and relatively underexamined. Scholarship concerned with colonial projects has tended to focus on links between the metropole and its colonies as opposed to intercolony connections. However, by lifting exilic itineraries out of the footnotes and margins of colonial and national histories, we can foreground the societal and economic repercussions of these transcolonial penal networks, along with exploring the lived experiences of those deported from—and to—the "distant possessions" of the French colonial world.

NOTES

1. Mary Kingsley, *Travels in West Africa: Congo Français, Corisco and Cameroons* (London: Macmillan, 1897), 120. Annam was used by the French to designate central Vietnam, and the term Annamites became used for all residents of the Vietnamese territories of Indochina.

2. Ibid.

3. The report of Inspector Hoarau-Desruisseaux, 16 May 1893. As quoted in Patrick Ceillier, "Déportés Annamites: Le Pénitencier de Libreville," *Gabon Magazine* 5 (September 2008): 13. The full citation is not given in the article.

4. As quoted by Jeremy Rich and Larissa Petrillo, *A Workman Is Worthy of His Meat: Food and Colonialism in the Gabon Estuary* (Lincoln: University of Nebraska Press, 2007), 57. Many of the prisoners may have died of malaria.

5. Jeremy Rich, "Where Every Language Is Heard: Atlantic Commerce, West African and Rich Asian Migrants, and Town Society in Libreville, ca. 1860–1914," in *African Urban Spaces in Historical Perspective*, ed. Steven J. Slam and Toyin Falola (Rochester, NY: University of Rochester Press, 2005), 202.

6. Details of the transportation of prisoners are found in CAOM: GGI-22776, CAOM: NF-77, CAOM H: 2662, and CAOM: 2026. Prisoners from Indochina often moved between Congo and Gabon.

7. Rich, *Workman Is Worthy of His Meat*, 190.

8. CAOM H: 2662.

9. "Piracy" and "criminal association" were the two of the most commonly cited crimes for transported prisoners.

10. The first prisoners from Indochina went to the island of Réunion in 1863 and the last group to Madagascar in 1941.

11. The legal code came into use under Lê Thánh Tông (1442–1497).

12. One *ly* is about 576 meters, or about a third of a mile. The *ly* is still occasionally used on Vietnamese maps but not in contemporary Vietnamese usage.

13. Nguyễn Ngọc Huy and Tạ Văn Tài, *The Lê Code: Law in Traditional Vietnam—A Comparative Sino-Vietnamese Legal Study with Historical-Juridical Analysis and Annotations*, vol. 2 (Athens: Ohio University Press, 1987), 14.

14. Byung Wook Choi, *Southern Vietnam under the Reign of Minh Mang (1820–1841): Central Policies and Local Response* (Ithaca, NY: Southeast Asia Program Publications, Cornell University, 2004), 66.

15. Ibid. In China, exiles were sent to a specific province, Xinjiang. See Johanna Whaley-Cohen, *Exile in Mid-Qing China, 1785–1820* (New Haven, CT: Yale University Press, 1991).

16. Peter Zinoman, *The Colonial Bastille: A Social History of Imprisonment in Colonial Viet Nam 1862–1940* (Berkeley: University of California Press, 2001), 29.

17. Ibid., 29.

18. Ibid., 108.

19. Ibid., 109.

20. Robert Aldrich, *The French Presence in the South Pacific, 1842–1940* (Honolulu: University of Hawai'i Press, 1990), 144.

21. Colin Forster, *France and Botany Bay: The Lure of a Penal Colony* (Melbourne: Melbourne University Press, 1996). This book gives an excellent background to France's desire for a penal colony of its own.

22. Colin Forster, "Unwilling Migrants from Britain and France," in *Coerced and Free Migration: Global Perspectives*, ed. David Eltis (Stanford, CA: Stanford University Press, 2002), 259, lists the figure 103,000. Isabelle Merle, *Expériences coloniales: La Nouvelle Calédonie (1895–1920)* (Paris: Belin, 1995), breaks down the figures as shown in the text. I estimate between 6,600 and 7,000 prisoners of all categories were sent to other French colonies from Indochina (this figure includes all sites of exile, not just designated penal colonies).

23. CAOM: GGI-957, Dossier on the Life Pension of Prince Ung Lịch, 21 June 1899.

24. See Pierre L. Lamant, "L'Affaire Duong Chakr," *Revue Française d'Histoire d'Outre Mer* 67, nos. 246–247 (1980): 123–150.

25. It is unclear whether this was substantiated or not. Duong Chakr, previously Norodom's chosen heir, had always been viewed with suspicion by colonial French authorities.

26. Governor-General Paul Beau originally suggested exile for Doc Xuyet to Constantine, which was already "hosting" a political exile from Tonkin.

27. CAOM: Indo/NF-303.

28. Zinoman, *Colonial Bastille*, 284.

29. Robert Cribb, "Penal Exile in the Netherlands Indies" (unpublished paper, 2013).

30. CAOM: Indo/NF 2222. Note from the Minister of Colonies, 5 April 1899. This is an interesting use of the term "Asiatics."

31. CAOM: Indo/NF 2222, 31 July 1899.

32. Anand Yang, "Indian Convict Workers in Southeast Asia in the Late Eighteenth and Early Nineteenth Centuries," *Journal of World History* 14, no. 2 (2003): 179–208.

33. Kerry Ward, *Networks of Empire: Forced Migration in the Dutch East India Company* (Cambridge: Cambridge University Press, 2009), 188.

34. Ibid., 236.

35. Nguyễn Hữu Huân is often referred to as "Thư Khoa Huân," which indicated that he was the best candidate of the regional (second tier) exams. David G. Marr, *Vietnamese Anticolonialism 1885–1925* (Berkeley: University of California Press, 1971), 34, 36.

36. Given that Réunion was the site of the first prisoners shipped, and the only location receiving prisoners from Indochina in 1864, it seems logical that it was his site of exile. Nguyễn Q. Thắng and Nguyễn Bá Thế, *Từ Điển Nhân Vật Lịch Sử Việt Nam Sử* [A dictionary of Vietnamese historical figures], 2nd ed. (Hanoi: Nhà Xuất Bản Văn Hóa, 1997), 551, also lists his exile locale as Réunion. Historian Truong Buu Lam states that Huân was exiled to an unnamed Pacific island; Truong Buu Lam, *Patterns of Vietnamese Response to Foreign Intervention, 1858–1900* (New Haven, CT: Yale University, 1967), 149. Presumably he is referring to New Caledonia, or perhaps even Tahiti. Thomas Hodgkin discusses Huân's poetry during a seven-year exile in Réunion in Thomas Hodgkin, *Vietnam: The Revolutionary Path* (New York: Macmillan, 1981), 148.

37. Daniel Varga has compiled a chart of yearly statistics of prisoners for each of these years. See Daniel Varga, "Les Vietnamiens à La Réunion, de la déportation à l'émigration volontaire (1859–1910)," *Revue Outre-Mers* 100, nos. 374–375 (2012): 254. Correspondence regarding some of the backgrounds of the prisoners and transportation details are in CAOM: REU 316/1913, 1914, and 1916.

38. Both poems can be found in Phạm Thiều, *Nguyễn Hữu Huân nhà yêu nước kiên cường nhà thơ bất khuất* [Nguyễn Hữu Huân: A resilient patriot and an indomitable poet] (Ho Chi Minh City: Nhà Xuất Bản Trẻ, 2001), 44–45. These poems, and their allusions, were translated with the assistance of Trần Khải Hoài. Along with many other Vietnamese scholars, Phạm Thiều cites Huân's site of exile as Cayenne, French Guiana, 44.

39. Kang-I-Sun Chang and Stephen Owen, eds., *The Cambridge History of Chinese Literature*, vol. 1 (Cambridge: Cambridge University Press, 2010), 551. Also, John Minford and John S. M. Lau, eds., *Classical Chinese Literature: An Anthology of Translations* (Hong Kong: Chinese University Press, 2000), 479.

40. Ibid.

41. Phạm Thiều, *Nguyễn Hữu Huân*, 45, also examines these lines.

42. CAOM: NF-77, Regulations of the Penal Colony.

43. I have several examples of letters from political prisoners from Indochina held in New Caledonia in 1897–1898 in which the original letter and the translated version bear little resemblance to each other.

44. Just as prisoners were susceptible to illnesses, the interpreters were also prone to difficult illnesses. Personnel files of interpreters are full of requests for leave due to illness, although this was more problematic for French Guiana than for New Caledonia.

45. Phạm Thiều, *Nguyễn Hữu Huân*, 47.

46. Nationalistic accounts depict Huân biting off his tongue to commit suicide, which was a traditional form of honorable suicide in Vietnam. See Truong Buu Lam, *Patterns of Vietnamese Response*, 149.

47. The prisoners' files are found on microfilm in New Caledonia: SANC: 1 MI 38 22 and I MI 38 23. Some of their files are available at the CAOM but some have deteriorated too much to be studied.

48. Charles Guillain was governor-general of New Caledonia from 1862 to 1870.

49. Merle, *Expériences coloniales*, 63.

50. CAOM H-1834, 30 October 1872.

51. Cribb argues that the local official van Michalofsky had difficulty because "very few Javanese women" were willing to move to the island. Robert Cribb (unpublished paper, 2013).

52. Matt K. Matsuda, *Empire of Love: Histories of France and the Pacific* (Oxford: Oxford University Press, 2005), 119.

53. Ibid., 118, discusses more of Guillain's policies that would have "been impossible to realize back in France."

54. Anne Laura Stoler, *Carnal Knowledge and Imperial Power: Race and the Intimate in Colonial Rule* (Berkeley: University of California Press, 2010), 70.

55. Stoler, *Carnal Knowledge and Imperial Power*, 79.

56. Louis-José Barbançon, *L'Archipel des forçats: Historie du bagne du Nouvelle Calédonie (1863–1931)* (Nord–Pas de Calais: Presses Universitaires du Septentrion, 2003), 181. Barbançon's book is the most comprehensive overview of the penal colony of New Caledonia.

57. Colin Forster, *France and Botany Bay*, 175.

58. Odile Krakovitch, *Les femmes bagnardes* (Paris: Perrin, 1998), 115.

59. Ibid., 127.

60. Ibid.

61. Claudy Chêne, "Déportation Tonkinoise en terre Calédonienne," in *Île d'exile, terre d'asile: Les déportations politiques et les expulsions en temps de guerre en Nouvelle Calédonie* (Nouméa, New Caledonia: Ville de Nouméa, 2005), 49.

62. Matsuda, *Empire of Love*, 127.

63. SANC: 1 MI 38 22.

64. SANC: État Civile, 1853–1900.

65. Krakovitch, *Les femmes bagnardes*, 173.

66. SANC: État Civile, 1853–1900.

67. Krakovitch, *Les femmes bagnardes*, 107.

68. SANC: État Civile, 1853–1900.

69. SANC: État Civile, 1853–1900. Two of the children were named Augustin Jules and Theodore.

70. Each prisoner designated for New Caledonia was allocated a sequential number—a "matricule" number—that became the number (as opposed to the name) used to designate him.

71. George Griffith, *In an Unknown Prison Land: An Account of Convicts and Colonists in New Caledonia with Jottings Out and Home* (London: Hutchinson and Co., 1901), 168.

72. Zinoman, *Colonial Bastille*, 35.

73. Although the Vietnamese in Gabon were allowed to tend their vegetable gardens, this was not on the scale of the concessions of Bourail.

74. Krakovitch, *Les femmes bagnardes*, 166.

75. See Tạ Thi Thúy, *Les concessions agricoles françaises au Tonkin de 1884 à 1918* (Paris: Les Indes Savantes, 2009).

76. One caveat here is that this was the so-called criminal class marrying the so-called criminal class. In other words, they were not Vietnamese men marrying French women of supposedly unblemished pasts.

77. CAOM: 78/MIOM/852. Le Thi Cam was conditionally released in April 1897.

78. CAOM: 78/MIOM/852.

79. An example of this is in CAOM: GGI-23259, which lists nickel companies putting in their labor requests.

80. Dorothy Shineberg and Jean-Marie Kohler, "Church and Commerce in New Caledonia: Ballande and the Bishops, 1885–1935," *Journal of Pacific History* 25, no. 1 (June 1990): 3–21.

81. CAOM: GGI-23258, Resident Superior of Tonkin to the Governor General of Indochina, 14 August 1890.

82. CAOM: GGI-27652.

83. Ibid.

84. CAOM: GGI-23258, Resident Superior of Tonkin to the Governor General of Indochina, 4 August 1890.

85. CAOM: GGI-23269, 29 January 1891.

86. CAOM: GGI-23269. The salary was low.

87. CAOM: GGI-23259, Minister of Colonies to the Governor General of Indochina, 23 January 1891.

88. CAOM: GGI-23268.

89. Ibid.

90. Shineberg and Kohler, "Church and Commerce in New Caledonia," 11. It is not clear to me what "Annamite pipes" are. It would seem to suggest the use of opium, which would not be encouraged by Ballande.

91. CAOM: GGI-23268, "The Introduction of Emigrants to New Caledonia."

92. CAOM: GGI-23268. The article by Louis-José Barbançon and Véronique Devambez, "Les damnés du Chéribon," *Paroles Calédoniennes: De la Grand Terre et des Îles*, no. 1 (May 1992): 43–45, also discusses the health problems of the weakened transported prisoners.

93. Zinoman, *Colonial Bastille*, 94–95.

94. Yves Joleaud-Barral, *La colonisation française* (Paris: Plon, 1899), 212.

95. Ibid., 205.

96. Ibid., 213–214. Nor indeed does Joleaud-Barral give any more details about the individual concerned, although this name must have been Nguyễn, as opposed to "Mguyen," showing the problems with cataloging, names, and identification.

97. Shineberg and Kohler, "Church and Commerce in New Caledonia," 17.

98. CAOM: GGI-23270.

99. CAOM: GGI-23269, Governor of New Caledonia to Governor General of Indochina, 22 October 1894.

100. Shineberg and Kohler, "Church and Commerce in New Caledonia," 22. Ironically, this later caused problems for Ballande. He paid for a Vietnamese-speaking priest to be assigned to his Catholic workers and the priest took up their labor grievances against the Ballande company itself.

101. CAOM: GGI-7689.

102. CAOM: GGI-9421.

103. Based on the extant French and Cambodian archives, I estimate that approximately 80 percent of Cambodian prisoners were of Chinese descent.

104. Varga refers to the small Vietnamese community. See Varga, "Les Vietnamiens à La Réunion," 270. In 1916, Réunion was the also the site of exile for two deposed Vietnamese emperors, Duy Tân and Thành Thái, and their entourages.

105. The Kanaks were the indigenous inhabitants of New Caledonia. Louis-José Barbançon, interview with the author, Nouméa, June 2012. I am indebted to Louis-José Barbançon, who greatly assisted me in untangling the histories of Vietnamese families of Bourail.

106. This stands in marked contrast to the Vietnamese community of French Guiana. Without any contract laborers sent to French Guiana, the Vietnamese community generally embraces its penal past, with most interviewees claiming political-nationalistic crimes as the reasons their forebears were exiled.

107. The actual Vietnamese term would be spelled *chân đăng*, with *chân* meaning "foot" and *đăng* meaning "worth." The term indicates hired or contract labor.

108. An exception to this lacuna is in the official publication Jean Vanmai wrote, titled *Centenaire de la présence Vietnamienne en Nouvelle Calédonie, 1891–1991* (Nouméa, New Caledonia: Centre Territorial de Recherche et de Documentation Pédagogique, 1991). Here on 35 he mentions the penal roots of the first "workers."

109. Tess Do, "Exile: Rupture and Continuity in Jean Vanmai's *Chân Dang* and *Fils de Chân Dang*," in *Exile Cultures, Misplaced Identities,* ed. Paul Allatson and Jo McCormack (Amsterdam: Rodopi, 2008), 151.

110. Ibid.

111. The Amicale Vietnamienne de Nouvelle Calédonie was founded in Nouméa in 1974.

Bibliography

Archival Materials

Centre des Archives d'Outre Mer, Aix-en-Provence (CAOM)
    Fonds Gouvernement-Général d'Indochine (GGI)
    Indochine Noveau Fonds (Indo/NF)
    Bagne (Series H)
    REU (Réunion)
Service des Archives de Nouvelle Calédonie (SANC)
    État Civile, 1853–1900

Books and Journal Articles

Aldrich, Robert. *The French Presence in the South Pacific, 1842–1940.* Honolulu: University of Hawai'i Press, 1990.

Anderson, Clare. *Subaltern Lives: Biographies of Colonialism in the Indian Ocean World, 1790–1920.* Cambridge: Cambridge University Press, 2012.

Barbançon, Louis-José. *L'Archipel des forçats: Histoire du bagne de Nouvelle-Calédonie (1863–1931).* Nord–Pas de Calais: Presses Universitaires du Septentrion, 2003.

Barbançon, Louis-José, and Véronique Devambez. "Les damnés du Chéribon." *Paroles Calédoniennes: De la Grand Terre et des Îles,* no. 1 (May 1992): 43–45.

Bullard, Alice. *Exile to Paradise: Savagery and Civilization in Paris and the South Pacific, 1790–1900.* Stanford, CA: Stanford University Press, 2000.

Ceillier, Patrick. "Déportes Annamites: Le pénitencier de Libreville." *Gabon Magazine* 5 (September 2008): 12–18.

Chang, Kang-I-Sun, and Stephen Owen, eds. *The Cambridge History of Chinese Literature.* Vol. 1. Cambridge: Cambridge University Press, 2010.

Chêne, Claudy. "Déportation Tonkinoise en terre Calédonienne." In *Ile d'exil, terre d'asile: Les déportations politiques et les expulsions en terre de guerre en Nouvelle Calédonie,* 48–53. Nouméa, New Caledonia: Ville de Nouméa, 2005.

Choi, Byung Wook. *Southern Vietnam under the Reign of Minh Mang (1820–1841): Central Policies and Local Response.* Ithaca, NY: Southeast Asia Program Publications, Cornell University, 2004.

Cribb, Robert. "Penal Exile in the Netherlands Indies." Unpublished paper, 2013.

Do, Tess. "Exile: Rupture and Continuity in Jean Vanmai's *Chân Dang* and *Fils de Chân Dang.*" In *Exile Cultures, Misplaced Identities*, edited by Paul Allatson and Jo Mc-Cormack, 151–172. Amsterdam: Rodopi, 2008.

Forster, Colin. *France and Botany Bay: The Lure of a Penal Colony.* Melbourne: Melbourne University Press, 1996.

———. "French Penal Policy and the Origins of the French Presence in New Caledonia." *Journal of Pacific History* 26, no. 2 (1991): 135–150.

———. "Unwilling Migrants from Britain and France." In *Coerced and Free Migration: Global Perspectives*, edited by David Eltis, 259–291. Stanford, CA: Stanford University Press, 2002.

Griffith, George. *In an Unknown Prison Land: An Account of Convicts and Colonists in New Caledonia with Jottings Out and Home.* London: Hutchinson and Co., 1901.

Hodgkin, Thomas. *Vietnam: The Revolutionary Path.* New York: Macmillan, 1981.

Joleaud-Barral, Yves. *La colonisation française*, Paris: Plon, 1899.

Kalikiti, Webby S. "Indochina's Colonial Regime and the Export of Penal Labour to New Caledonia, 1890–1896." Unpublished seminar paper for presentation at the Asia Research Institute, National University of Singapore, 2011.

Kingsley, Mary. *Travels in West Africa: Congo Français, Corisco and Cameroons.* London: Macmillan, 1897.

Krakovitch, Odile. *Les femmes bagnardes.* Paris: Perrin, 1998.

Lamant, Pierre L. "L'Affaire Duong Chakr." *Revue Française d'Histoire d'Outre Mer* 67, nos. 246–247 (1980): 123–150.

Marr, David G. *Vietnamese Anticolonialism 1885–1925.* Berkeley: University of California Press, 1971.

Matsuda, Matt K. *Empire of Love: Histories of France and the Pacific.* Oxford: Oxford University Press, 2005.

Merle, Isabelle. *Expériences coloniales: La Nouvelle Calédonie (1895–1920).* Paris: Belin, 1995.

Minford, John, and John S. M. Lau, eds. *Classical Chinese Literature: An Anthology of Translations.* Hong Kong: Chinese University Press, 2000.

Nguyễn Ngọc Huy and Tạ Văn Tài. *The Lê Code: Law in Traditional Vietnam, A Comparative Sino-Vietnamese Legal Study with Historical-Juridical Analysis and Annotations.* Vol. 2. Athens: Ohio University Press, 1987.

Nguyễn Q. Thắng and Nguyễn Bá Thế. *Từ Điển nhân vật lịch sử Việt Nam sử* [A dictionary of Vietnamese historical figures]. 2nd ed. Hanoi: Nhà Xuất Bản Văn Hóa, 1997.

Phạm Thiều. *Nguyễn Hữu Huân nhà yêu nu ớc kiên cu ờng nhà thơ bất khuất* [Nguyễn Hữu Huân: A resilient patriot and an indomitable poet]. Ho Chi Minh City: Nhà Xuất Bản Trẻ, 2001.

Rich, Jeremy. "Where Every Language Is Heard: Atlantic Commerce, West African and Asian Migrants, and Town Society in Libreville, ca. 1860–1914." In *African Urban Spaces in Historical Perspective*, edited by Steven J. Slam and Toyin Falola, 191–212. Rochester, NY: University of Rochester Press, 2005.

Rich, Jeremy, and Larissa Petrillo. *A Workman Is Worthy of His Meat: Food and Colonialism in the Gabon Estuary.* Lincoln: University of Nebraska Press, 2007.

Sénes, Jacqueline. *En Nouvelle Calédonie de 1850 à nos jours.* Paris: Hachette, 1985.

Shineberg, Dorothy, and Jean-Marie Kohler. "Church and Commerce in New Caledonia: Ballande and the Bishops, 1885–1935." *Journal of Pacific History* 25, no. 1 (June 1990): 3–21.

Stoler, Ann Laura. *Carnal Knowledge and Imperial Power: Race and the Intimate in Colonial Rule*. Berkeley: University of California Press, 2010.

Tạ Thi Thúy. *Les concessions agricoles françaises au Tonkin de 1884 à 1918*. Paris: Les Indes Savantes, 2009.

Toth, Stephen A. *Beyond Papillon: The French Overseas Penal Colonies 1854–1952*. Lincoln: University of Nebraska Press, 2006.

Truong Buu Lam. *Patterns of Vietnamese Response to Foreign Intervention, 1858–1900*. New Haven, CT: Yale University, 1967.

Vanmai, Jean. *Centenaire de la présence Vietnamienne en Nouvelle Calédonie, 1891–1991*. Nouméa, New Caledonia: Centre Territorial de Recherche et de Documentation Pédagogique, 1991.

———. *Chân Đăng: Les Tonkinois de Calédonie au temps colonial*. Nouméa, New Caledonia: Publications de La Société d'Études Historiques de la Nouvelle-Calédonie, 1980.

Varga, Daniel. "Les Vietnamiens à La Réunion, de la déportation à l'émigration volontaire (1859–1910)." *Revue Outre-Mers* 100, nos. 374–375 (2012): 234–273.

Ward, Kerry. *Networks of Empire: Forced Migration in the Dutch East India Company*. Cambridge: Cambridge University Press, 2009.

Whaley-Cohen, Joanne. *Exile in Mid-Qing China, 1785–1820*. New Haven, CT: Yale University Press, 1991.

Yang, Anand. "Indian Convict Workers in Southeast Asia in the Late Eighteenth and Early Nineteenth Centuries." *Journal of World History* 14, no. 2 (2003): 179–208.

Zinoman, Peter. *The Colonial Bastille: A Social History of Imprisonment in Colonial Viet Nam 1862–1940*. Berkeley: University of California Press, 2001.

TEN

Watching the Detectives
The Elusive Exile of Prince Myngoon of Burma

Penny Edwards

> We are in a territory that lies beyond historical knowledge, and is inaccessible to it. But narrative processes act like magnetic fields: they provoke questions.
>
> Carlo Ginzburg

T his chapter interrogates the limits of colonial surveillance through an examination of the life in exile of Prince Myngoon-Min (hereafter Myngoon) of Burma, who jumped ship and sojourned across Rangoon, Benares, Chandernagore, Pondicherry, and Saigon from the 1860s to the 1920s. Myngoon (1844–1921) was doubly exiled, first from his father's kingdom in Upper Burma, when he sought refuge in the British colonial capital of Rangoon, and then from British Burma. For Myngoon, unlike Guru Bhai Maharaj Singh, the subject of Anand Yang's contribution to this volume (chapter 3), exile was no "momentary rupture" but a defining and terminal experience, in which he transitioned between British and French empires, commencing with his forced relocation from Burma to the Andaman Islands and ending with his death in Saigon.[1] Where scholarship by Eric Tagliacozzo has focused attention on the itinerant histories of such figures as smugglers and the porosity of borders in British and Dutch colonial Southeast Asia,[2] in what follows I explore the itinerant subject of Southeast Asian history through a solitary figure of exile.

In examining Myngoon's histories of subterfuge and evasion, the chapter questions the uniform applicability to colonial states of the Foucauldian trope of the panopticon and the Scottian notion of the colonial state as an entity that left its subjects nowhere to hide.[3] Rather, we see in some stages of Myngoon's story the "paradox" of Leviathan described by the colonial scholar-official J. S. Furnivall as being "least efficient where he is most effective"; for "Leviathan may be omnipresent and all powerful but he does not, like your neighbor, live next door."[4] The colonial states that surveilled Myngoon lacked peripheral vision and were frequently outwitted, and the police captains and detectives in their employ sometimes complained of the impossibility of their task.

Myngoon, conversely, saw states with the wide-angle lens of the stateless elite. Living in exile sharpened his notion of a geography sutured between and across colonial borders. As he crossed the boundaries of French and British empires, his connections to fellow exiles and European aristophiles linked him into regional and metropolitan networks that expanded his field of vision and sharpened his sense of a transcolonial geography. Similarly to others in exile, he lived in "a kind of subjunctive, especially the past subjunctive."[5] From the 1880s to 1910s he harbored genuine dreams of a return to Burma. Like Ali bin Yusuf, the prince from early modern Bijapur studied by Sanjay Subrahmanyam in the context of the "complex itineraries and processes of circulation" at play in his study of "marginal and liminal figures cast adrift from their traditional moorings into an unknown world," Myngoon experienced a "multiple displacement," which positions him as a case study at the gap between "micro-history and world history."[6] In global terms, his story plays out against the backdrop of strained Anglo-French relations, both countries entertaining designs on Upper Burma until Britain's annexation in 1885–1886, with tensions still simmering until the Entente Cordiale of 1904. Burma was governed as a province of British India until 1935, and in the French colonial imaginary, Myngoon's embrace of exile on French territory against claims of having been poorly treated in British India played to the deeper history of France's eighteenth-century loss of India to the British.

Myngoon's antics beguiled and confused colonial authorities, intelligence agents, and security personnel. Central to their anxiety was the figure of the trickster. This chapter considers three separate instances of colonial confusion where fraud or deception was suspected: two in British India and one in French Indochina. The first involves the carrier of a letter purported to be written by Myngoon; the second, Myngoon's own trajectory of disguise and subterfuge and his possible collaboration with a Sikh who was involved in a broader network tied to Dalip Singh; and the third involves a monk who appears to have been an imposter and seems to have become allied to Myngoon's cause through a possible revenue-raising scheme in Cambodia that fell awry. In addressing these cases, this chapter considers the narrative tracks of exile. Like Yang's contribution to this volume (chapter 3), it raises questions about what kinds of sources are generated by, and generative of, histories of exile, and what kinds of histories, to paraphrase Prasenjit Duara, exile rescues from the nation-state.[7]

There are many ways to read the paper trail that Myngoon penned and generated, from the writer Octave Mirbeau's *Lettres de l'Inde* to the prince's memorials and a commission of inquiry into Myngoon's escape. His exile involved entrepreneurial entanglements with a Chinese backer in Yunnan, a Burmese monk in Cambodia, forestry and gem-mining concessions in Cambodia and Laos, and various scripted roles—enfant terrible, assassin, agitator, pretender, and political exile. Myngoon entered into charismatic correspondence with a Cambodian king, European officials and sympathizers, and Chinese merchants.[8] His archival trail mixes court records, petitions to governments, and police reports. The narratives of exile, sacrifice, and return that Myngoon conjured for various audiences coexisted with narratives scripted by his supporters and detractors. Where Burmese histories cast him as the murderer of his uncle, his own account, printed in Calcutta in 1882, stated that he and his brother should "justly claim the meed of Patriots, and not be stigmatised as murderers!"[9] The same document accused the British of treating him like a "felon" on his voyage to the Andamans and keeping him "caged, under lock and key, as though he had been a Bengal tiger, instead of the Prince Royal of Ava."[10] Told through his letters and memorials, prepared by attorneys and private secretaries of Bengali, Eurasian, and British descent, and presented in English and French, occasionally in bilingual text with Burmese, Myngoon's narrative footprint also raises questions about the mediation of translation.[11] His epistolary trail evokes the "sense of doubleness at the heart of the narrator's identity, and the uneasy status of a life lived outside the anchoring 'truth' of a single cultural and geographic location" described by literary scholar Karl Britto in his study of Franco-Vietnamese writing, while also invoking the sense of the "proleptic nostalgia of a colonial subject always aware of the future in which his present will be past."[12] In Myngoon's case, that nostalgia is framed in terms of throne and nation, and yet his locus and status as an exile have largely excluded him from, or marginalized him in, histories of Burma.

In this chapter I consider three narrative frames from the colonial era, spanning more than four decades. The first relates to a letter purported to be written by Myngoon, the second relates to his series of escapes, and the third, to his liaisons with a Burmese monk named U Villasa, who appears to have been an imposter. While these narratives include letters from Myngoon and from the Burmese monk, whose letters are for the most part in French and English, my primary sources for this chapter are all drawn from colonial archives. The historical narratives on which I base my analysis are thus at once inflected by "the distribution of archival power" and "profoundly shaped by Western conventions and procedures": even the accounts penned by Myngoon and U Villasa reflected those conventions inasmuch as each was writing for European audiences enjoying a particular degree of power. Historian Michel-Rolf Trouillot describes archives as "institutionalized sites of mediation between the socio-historical process and the narrative about that process" that "help us select the stories that matter."[13] Despite the limitations of interpretation and the constraints of convention set by my reliance on the archive, I believe that the stories examined here do matter inasmuch as they shed light on both the complex dynamics of exile and the inadequacy of the nation-state as a unit of analysis for modern Southeast Asian history.[14]

Anand Yang's work situates Indian convicts as part of a larger traffic pattern in South and Southeast Asia that transported different people in different directions, including convicts from Ceylon and Burma to Singapore. The identities of these "Indian convict workers," Yang writes, "were shaped by their encounters with other groups."[15] In British India, transportation was developed as a particularly brutal "transgressive punishment," which "transgressed indigenous notions about the religious and cultural dangers of crossing the *kala pani,* or 'black waters.'"[16] The exile of royalty, examined in chapter 2 in this volume by Robert Aldrich in his study of the last King of Kandy, was a strategy first used by the British in Ceylon in 1816, where it proved a successful means of displacing possible rallying points of resistance. As Kerry Ward has shown, exile was no European invention.[17] And in T'ang dynasty China, as Edward Shafer shows us, the specter of banishment was used to terrifying effect, as reflected in the memoirs of one ninth-century minister who "was so obsessed by the idea that his career would end in banishment" that he "developed a phobia of looking at maps showing a southern land." Here, the southern perimeter functioned as a site for political "banishment" of disgraced mandarins and ostracized courtiers, who were banished to a distance proportional to their crime, even as far as the malarial and "nostalgia-plagued" lands of Hainan and Nam-Viet.[18] For Myngoon, however, exile afforded political opportunity, and his banishment, sealed by the British, would have conferred upon him a certain legitimacy in the eyes of the Karen, Shan, and Burmese leaders and laity who lent or pledged him their support for several planned campaigns for his return to Burma as a figure of resistance.

In November 1885, when an insurrection was raging in Cambodia as a result of French attempts to enforce a treaty dispossessing the king of all fiscal power, Britain dethroned the Burmese King Thibaw and Queen Supayalat and forced them into exile in western India, at Ratnagiri. Thereafter, the Myngoon Prince represented a double-edged threat to the British: as a rebel on French territory who was considered a French puppet, and as the embodiment of a monarchy the British had liquidated in bringing Burma under the reign of Queen Victoria.[19] The most potent phase of Myngoon's political career in exile runs from 1883, when the increasing unpopularity of

King Thibaw, and his subsequent eviction by the British, opened up the possibility of return, to the late 1890s. Unlike Bhai Maharaj Singh, Anand Yang's focus in chapter 3 of this volume, Myngoon enjoyed the ability to play the British and the French against each other. Myngoon had never successfully commanded an army against the British but was charged with an attempt to instigate an attack on Europeans in Rangoon and was kept under daily surveillance at home following his release from the Andaman Islands to Benares. In 1883, he escaped British territory for the French territory of Chandernagore, and from there he moved to Pondicherry and then Saigon. Settled for more than twenty years in Saigon, Myngoon might have come to experience what writer Michael Chabon describes as "the safety of exile."[20] In 1911, he wrote to the British renouncing his claim to the throne under certain conditions, which included being kept in comfort by the British in a French colony of his choice.[21] This temporary abandonment of the idea of a return to Burma resonates with what Subrahmanyam describes in the case of Nicolo Manuzzi, who died "as an alien in an Indian exile," and indicates that Myngoon, settled in Saigon, might have "crossed a threshold, and would have been no less an alien in [Burma] had he returned there after an absence" of four decades.[22] "It is not space alone," Subrahmanyam reminds us, "but time too that can make one a stranger."[23]

The three narrative trails considered here all involve instances of colonial confusion over identities where fraud was suspected or disguise adopted. The first involves the carriers of a letter purported to be written by Myngoon to his father in 1871; the second involves police frustration at attempts to track and survey Myngoon following his escape from British Benares to French Chandernagore; the third involves the self-professed monk U Villasa, who claimed to be acting for Myngoon in Cambodia in the 1910s. Linking all these cases are letters and their carriers. In all three cases, despite (or because of) voluminous correspondence and colonial records, we are never quite sure of the final outcome. We are left guessing. This uncertainty unhinges notions of the hermetic quality of the colonial state as judge and executioner. If Myngoon has failed in his claim to the throne, in his dream of return, he has succeeded as a trickster, a ghost in the archival machine who tantalizes us with a kaleidoscope of possibilities.

Duara has described the borderland as a kind of "liminal and indeterminate historical space often characterised by warfare, but also by opportunities for local elites who are able to play off one outside power against another."[24] This approach typifies the survival strategies of Myngoon. We might also think of Myngoon as a trickster figure, located in what Lewis Hyde describes as "the shadowy terrain between the wise and the witless, truth and falsity." "Just as he can slip a trap then make his own," writes Hyde, so the trickster can "debunk an illusion, then turn around and conjure up another," as a "great imitator" of "agile appetite" who can disguise his tracks as surely as he can disguise himself.[25]

Background

In 1866, as narrated in British records, the Myngoon Prince, a pretender to the Burmese throne, docked at the colonial capital of Rangoon in the steamer *Honesty*. He had commandeered the steamer from his father, King Mindon, in Mandalay, the royal capital of Upper Burma, which had as yet escaped British colonization, after joining his younger brother to mount an attack on his uncle, who was the heir apparent to the throne and who they alleged had mistreated them. After assassinating their uncle and one of his ministers, Myngoon, his brother Myngoondaine, and their supporters followed the king to the city palace, to which they laid siege. Driven out by the king's troops, they left Mandalay with some two hundred to three hundred armed followers on board *Honesty*. They continued south with the aim of raising revolt and for a while held the country from Magway to the frontier.

The "fierce and devastating civil war" that ensued continued until 2 November 1866, and as Colonel E. B. Sladen observed the following year, there were likely no "authorized or authentic records of the several events or incidents which make up the narrative of the civil war."[26] When the inspector general of police and the deputy commissioner of Prome District boarded the steamer, Myngoon told them that he was going to Rangoon, that he did not wish to fight the king, and that he had no intention of taking the throne. "All the power that I had is gone," Myngoon reportedly said, "and I look on the English as my protector." The inspector general of police offered Myngoon and his brother "safe refuge" in British territory. The princes were then accommodated in Rangoon, where expenses for hosting them included silk *putsoes* at their request, furniture, two gharries, and servant wages and charges for building repair, as well as items such as cooking oil and fuel for lamps.[27] King Mindon refused to allow Myngoon's wife and children to join him, or to make any allowance for him, but promised to spare the princes' lives should they return to Burma.[28] Colonel Sladen described Myngoon as "a plucky determined fellow with some idea of organization, but thoroughly unscrupulous," who "may be regarded as a source of danger, until removed beyond the reach of Burmese territory and Burmese influences."[29]

In February 1867, Myngoon escaped and fled Rangoon, with what the British saw as "the avowed intention of again attempting to foment disturbances and to raise a rebellion against his father." The chief commissioner wrote, presciently, that "this Prince . . . is of a restless disposition and not at all calculated to be satisfied with a quiet life, but would probably always be scheming to recover what he considers he has lost."[30] Following Myngoon's flight, Prince Myngoondaine was sent to the Andaman Islands as a state prisoner, to prevent him from joining up with his brother.[31] The India Office in London questioned the decision to send someone of his "rank and position" to a "convict station," and in early 1868 Myngoondaine was relocated to Bhaugulpore in Bengal.[32] The undersecretary to the government of India advised that Myngoondaine "should not be subjected to personal restraint further than is needed to prevent him from joining in any attempt on the tranquility of Burma."[33] In August 1868, after visiting Siam and other places, Myngoon returned to Rangoon in disguise,[34] "hoping to receive that hospitality ever extended by Great Britain to all political refugees and exiles."[35] He was arrested on the outskirts of Rangoon, charged and sentenced for "endeavouring to foment a rising," detained as a political prisoner under Regulation III of 1818, and exiled first to the Andamans and then on to Fort Chunar in Benares, where he was kept under close surveillance.[36] Among the other interns at Chunar were a number of Sikhs from Punjab.[37]

In 1869, Myngoondaine moved to Fort Chunar to live with Myngoon, under continued surveillance.[38] In 1870, Myngoon and his brother were moved to Benares, where Myngoon is described variously as being kept under "mild surveillance"[39] and as a "Burmese political detenu."[40] From Benares, Myngoon effected his escape to Chandernagore, a territory of les Indes françaises, and from there to Pondicherry, ending up in Saigon, where he remained until his death in 1921.

CASE ONE: AN INCENDIARY LETTER AND A BETEL BOX

In Benares, the British preoccupation with surveillance of Myngoon resulted in a prolonged exchange over a letter purportedly written by Myngoon that was ultimately found to bear no relation to him. I consider the letter here because of what its treatment reveals about the level of British concern about Myngoon, because of the clandestine way in which the letter moved, and because British interrogations failed to procure a singular convincing narrative about the genealogy of the letter.

On 22 May 1871, the officiating political agent in Mandalay forwarded to the chief commissioner of British Burma a copy of a letter purportedly written by the Myngoon Prince. The letter was of "an incendiary nature, and contained wild and absurd plans for subverting the power of the British in this country." It had been delivered by one Booja Singh, who described himself as a nephew of the "King of Jeyphoor."[41]

The British linkage of the letter to Myngoon continued despite the description of the author of the letter as variously Kumatta and Remeeter. Booja Singh said that he had been imprisoned "in the Bombay Presidency," and there met a Burman prince called Kumatta "who had entrusted to his care the letter to the King of Burmah."[42] On presenting themselves before the prime minister of the Burmese court, they were imprisoned and were released only on the intervention of the political agent.[43] The chief commissioner requested that the political agent either keep Booja Singh under guard on strict surveillance or send him to Rangoon.

In July 1871, A. Forbes, the officiating agent to the governor-general of Benares, reported that he had cross-examined the Myngoon Prince and that he was satisfied that Myngoon knew nothing of the man Booja Singh or of the letter addressed to the king of Burma. "He was satisfied on this point from the frank and open way in which the Prince answered all questions put to him and volunteered the communication that some few months since a man trading as a diamond merchant, had arrived from Burma and had told him that his [the prince's] father was now no longer angry with him for his past conduct." The prince told Forbes that to this he replied that he could trust to no such verbal message. Forbes continued that the police had watched the movements of the Armenian trader and took Myngoon's reference to him as proof of the honesty of his account and of his "distinct denial of all knowledge of Booja Singh and his letter."[44]

By August the colonial authorities had established that there was no proof of the letter having been written by Myngoon, and in October the chief commissioner suggested that the letter might have been prepared in Burma by the enemies of the Myngoon Prince "in order to raise a prejudice against him." A full statement from Booja Singh revealed that the letter was given to him by a Burmese prince "Remeeter" imprisoned somewhere in the Bombay Presidency.[45] Chuttra Singh, an unemployed Hindu also questioned about the letter, said he received it on board a steamer from Madras to Rangoon and that one Booja Singh made over the letter to him to give to the king of Burma, promising a good reward. The letter was given openly and then hidden beneath glass in the lid of the betel box, so that it "might not be lost or get wet."

There the paper trail stops, at least as it is preserved in the archive. Myngoon was cleared of any involvement by the colonial authorities.[46] We do not know who wrote the letter. But the chain of correspondence generated by the letter gives us insight into colonial surveillance patterns, as well as their limitations. The movement of the letter across British India and its presentation at the court show lines of communication outside colonial channels, and the passage of the letter gives insight into how messages traveled. We see how a clandestine letter is carried and concealed and changes hands along the way, and the confessions yielded by British interrogation of the carriers. We see that Myngoon was kept under a close watch of his household by the British in Benares, down to the visitations by an Armenian gem merchant. In the reverberations around the letter are ghost traces of Myngoon's exile and the nervousness of a colonial regime that expended considerable ink and paper on this case. Also evident is a degree of cooperation between the Burmese court and the British, who in the early 1870s shared common cause in wanting to suppress any planned uprising led by Myngoon.

Case Two: Watching the Detectives/Chance Glimpses

> Political prisoner, Burmese Prince Myngoon . . . disappeared last night; supposed to have gone to Calcutta for Burmah. Police communicated with.[47]

The second case I consider involves the escape of Myngoon from Benares to Chandernagore, from British India to l'Inde francaise and then onward to Saigon, and the frustration that his escape and subsequent instructions to keep him under close surveillance in French territory caused the British colonial police in the first instance. James Scott has written that compared to the states they replaced, colonial states "left few places to hide," as "nets of finer and finer official weave caught and recorded the status of each inhabitant."[48] For part of his time in exile, Myngoon managed to subvert that fine weave and to evade colonial surveillance by hiding at the interstices of British and French power lines.

In 1870, Myngoon and his brother moved from Fort Chunar to bungalows in an enclosure adjacent to the police inspector's house in Benares. In their first years there, reports were made of the prince's "drunken and dissolute" conduct, but in the 1880s his conduct was "free from suspicion and unremarkable." A special peon, considered trustworthy, was stationed on the premises from 1871, with the duty of watching the movements of the prince and his visitors, and reporting twice daily, beginning each day with an inquiry at the prince's bedroom door.[49]

Surveillance escalated when news was published of King Thibaw's insanity, and when the Burmese ambassadors visited India in 1885. Routine surveillance revealed that Myngoon kept as a concubine a Muslim prostitute and had a Burmese cook, a few other servants, and a Eurasian clerk named Cox who had on occasion traveled to Rangoon to sell jewelry and to attempt to borrow money. Since Cox traveled without the approval of the police commissioner, a police guard was placed over the prince as punishment for a couple of weeks, and then removed. The prince was greatly distressed about this and visited the commissioner, emphasizing his good behavior in the past decade.[50] In 1882, Myngoon—after seventeen years of imprisonment as "politically condemned"—escaped from British Benares to the French possession of Chandernagore "disguised as a beggar." According to Vivien Ba, the prince knew several Parsi merchants, who came to transact merchandise in precious stones with him. One of them helped the prince flee Benares by arriving with his coolie at the prince's residence and leaving with the prince disguised as his coolie.[51] This second reference to Myngoon's relations with gem merchants underscores the role of jewelry donors and traders as well as moneylenders in financing his movement.[52]

In his report of the prince's disappearance, the commissioner of Benares division stated that the prince was believed to have left his house after ten p.m. on Sunday, 3 December 1882, when he was last seen by his concubine, since when "nothing is at present known of him." His brother claimed complete ignorance.[53] Local police were in active search, and Calcutta, Rangoon, the North-Western provinces, Nagpore and Bombay police had all been alerted. "Every effort is being made to obtain some clue," wrote the commissioner. There followed detailed correspondence assessing the prince's likely movements, much of it threaded through with anxieties about his identification. The prince was first presumed to have fled to Calcutta. On 6 December 1882, orders were given to effect Myngoon's recapture.[54] Within a week of his flight, the deputy commissioner of police, Calcutta, reported that Myngoon had been identified by a Benares police officer in Chandernagore.[55] Following Myngoon's passage to French territory, correspondence between the chief commissioner of police in Calcutta and the government in Bengal escalated and gives us unusual insight into the mechanics of surveillance and police resentment at their mission. In Chandernagore, the detectives assigned to Myngoon complained of the difficulty of their task.[56] Wanting to ascertain the whereabouts of Myngoon, the agent of the governor-general in Benares asked the police, Calcutta, to "take action at railway stations, stopping prince." A description was given:

> aged forty-eight, short, thin, wheat colour, small moustache, wears long hair and white clothes like Mussalman, with usual tattoo marks on arms and legs.[57]

On 22 December Myngoon wrote to the British from Chandernagore that he had fled Benares in order to escape from the "unbearable" treatment he had received, and also asked for better treatment of his brother, a "refugee."[58] He was informed that any request he might wish to make would be considered if he left Chandernagore and surrendered to the British authorities.[59] It was later ascertained that Myngoon had taken refuge in the house of a ruby broker, Kyambway; the sale of jewelry would play a large part in financing his campaign from Chandernagore.[60] In January, a Mr. Bryce of the Bombay-Burmah Corporation reported that he had seen Myngoon at Chandernagore "dressed as an Englishman," leading Charles Bernard, governor of Burma, to state that "there is little chance of our recognising him on board the steamer here if he succeeds in getting away."[61] The British were eager to achieve his return to India, and the prince was much feared in Mandalay.[62] Among intelligence gleaned was that a monk from Rangoon visiting Chandernagore had divined that Myngoon would gain the throne of Burma; the monk was among one hundred people who had rallied to the prince.[63]

Mr. Peacock, officiating secretary to the government of Bengal, political department, reported that when the prince moved to Chandernagore, his surveillance placed a strain on the resources of the British police, who coordinated the watch from Calcutta. Peacock complained of the "harassing and unsatisfactory nature of the duties entailed on the Police in keeping a watch over" Myngoon, and that the limited surveillance took "a good deal of the time of several men."[64] On receipt of this complaint, the Bengal government concurred that "the duty of watching Myngoon . . . is a difficult one, as [the district superintendent of Hooghly] can exercise no real supervision, and is dependent on chance glimpses at the Prince."[65] The difficulties were compounded by the care that they had to take not to do anything that could be regarded by the French government as a "violation of their territory" in effecting the apprehension of the prince.[66]

Faced with this double bind, the police declared that it would be a great relief if the prince could be induced to return to British territory.[67] In January 1883, the inspector-general of police in Bengal reported that they had had to change the men watching Myngoon at Chandernagore, as "the French authorities got suspicious."[68] British concerns to keep Myngoon under tight surveillance were heightened by the prince's declared intentions to launch a campaign against King Thibaw. Great concern was expressed over fear of causing France offense; should the prince travel from Chandernagore to Pondicherry, caution was sounded that he must not be apprehended if on a French vessel.[69] Anxiety about his possible array of disguises continued. A telegram from British Burma pointed to the difficulty of recognizing him on board the steamer if he were disguised "as an Indian."[70] Bernard, commissioner of British Burma, worried that he could "disguise himself as a Bengali Babu, or as an up-country immigrant cooly," and added that the people of Mandalay feared Myngoon much more than they did the two other

Prince Myngoon's letterhead, Saigon, 1909.

pretender princes, Nyoung Yan or Nyoung Oke, as the Myngoon Prince "is said to be a man of much energy and force of character."[71]

In February 1883, S. J. Leslie, attorney-at-law, forwarded a petition from Myngoon complaining of his "unjust and illegal captivity" by the British, which alluded to the "right to offer an inviolable asylum to any and every political exile."[72] Police records kept track of followers who moved to join Myngoon in Chandernagore. But by April 1883, Peacock wrote repeatedly of police difficulties in maintaining a watch over Myngoon. In this correspondence we see the early frustration of police as Myngoon remains beyond their grasp. We also sense police disgruntlement with the mechanics of surveillance, especially as complicated by the need to watch Myngoon in French territory, for which purpose a team of detectives and police clerks from Calcutta were assigned to Chandernagore. In May 1883, we learn that "the Hooghly Police are sick of looking after [Myngoon]."[73] In November 1883, the Benares government approved the retention in Calcutta of a Benares chaprasi and policeman familiar with the prince's appearance, who would be better able to spot him in disguise than the Calcutta police.[74] The next month, the inspector general of police wrote that he had to change the spies continually and that he did not "personally believe much in the watch," and he complained of the difficulty of maintaining surveillance, as the French authorities are "very suspicious and very touchy."[75] French attempts at surveillance were also inadequate. For five days after Myngoon's escape from Chandernagore, daily police reports indicated that he was still at home.[76]

Surveillance cost money as well as manpower. A statement of expenditure on account of Myngoon, from 4 December 1882 to 11 July 1883, included several entries for surveillance: 120 rupees paid to two policemen for travel to Rangoon in January, to assist the local police; 122.8 rupees paid to a sub-inspector of police for a travel allowance to Calcutta in pursuit of Myngoon; and the pay of a Harprasad Chaprasi, sent to Calcutta, at 10 rupees per month.[77] Additional living allowances were also disbursed to the constables deputed to Burma and Calcutta, who had to board and search steamers two or three times a week and "[look] after" two train stations. His private secretary reported to the British that Myngoon was planning an escape in disguise to the Shan territories, hoping to gain the throne of Upper Burma. It is not clear from the records whether his secretary was informing on him with or without his knowledge.[78]

From Chandernagore, Myngoon dispatched his Calcutta agent, Baboo Nobo Coomar Mookerjee, to arrange meetings between his prime minister Achee Daw and the British and to carry a letter in which Myngoon pleaded for his liberty and pledged his allegiance to the British should he succeed to the throne, as their "staunch and faithful ally." In June 1883

Achee Daw met with the British and on Myngoon's behalf enumerated nine Shan and two Karenni chiefs who would join his standard, claiming that Myngoon had strong enough popular, financial, and military support to "make good his footing" in Upper Burma, and iterated that against French encroachments Myngoon would strive not to lose a single acre of land.[79] Myngoon subsequently wrote to thank Lieutenant Colonel Prideaux for the courtesy shown Achee Daw.[80]

The additional British police maintained in Chandernagore, and the French surveillance of his home, did not stop Myngoon from fleeing to Pondicherry. Three weeks after the French colonial lobbyist François Deloncle had filed his report, a commission of inquiry was launched in Chandernagore to investigate Myngoon's escape to Pondicherry via a plan elaborated in part by a French judge, Lhermitte. The seven interviewees included Lhermitte's servant; Myngoon's neighbor; a police agent, a scribe of the secretariat, and a court interpreter; a boatman; and the police chief. Lhermitte's Bengali servant Moungla claimed to have recognized the prince on the morning of his escape, "dressed as a poor man." Daily reports by Police Chief Pinot from 17 to 24 June declared the prince "present" and at home. The basis for this error was the sighting of someone he took to be the prince in his usual position (and usual dress) on the veranda. While Pinot's subordinate observed the prince's double on his veranda, Myngoon was carried out of his house in a large trunk and transported by carriage, boat, and cart to Garden Reach in Calcutta. Here, from a small walled garden, the Bengali servant Moungla saw Lhermitte emerge in the company of the prince, who was "dressed like a poor man."[81] The narratives contained in the inquiry point to the multiple involvement of people in support of his escape. In Calcutta, Myngoon boarded the *Tibre* with a third-class ticket arranged for him by Lhermitte. In the writer Octave Mirbeau's fictionalized account, Myngoon states, "I passed myself off as a coolie in 3rd class, and didn't show my face the whole journey."[82] During these escapades we can think of Myngoon as a trickster figure who transgresses boundaries and slips the trap, heightening governmental anxieties as he defied colonial control with his disguises.

In Pondicherry, Myngoon was placed under close surveillance by the French.[83] Visiting Pondicherry in 1884 as part of a grand colonial tour, Deloncle described Myngoon as absolutely incapable of toppling King Thibaw, "à moins de se déguiser habilement, de traverser seule sans suite, comme un couli, l'Inde et la Birmanie anglaise" (unless he disguises himself, and travels alone without an entourage, as a coolie, in India and British Burma), conditions the Myngoon Prince considered "too humiliating for his dignity."[84] Myngoon would prove Deloncle at least partially wrong, adopting disguises beneath his station.

Mirbeau subsequently rewrote excerpts of Deloncle's report of his visit as *Lettres de l'Inde*, an elegant work designed to woo public opinion to Deloncle's vision of an extended "empire of pacification," where France would "liberate" Indians and Burmese from "the British yoke," and where the Burmese government was "ready to accept French influence."[85] In her analysis of Mirbeau's publication, Ioanna Chatzidimitriou examines its potency in the context of colonial discourses, most notably Jules Ferry's imperialist program.[86] Here we see a semifictional narrative about Myngoon gaining traction as colonial propaganda.

Mirbeau described Myngoon as "a man of forty years, with fine features, doe eyes, and a thin face," dressed in a "turban of silk brocade over his long, glossy and perfumed hair, . . . a longyi . . . , slippers embroidered in gold," his hands glittering with rubies. In their reported conversation, when asked if there was any truth in English newspaper accounts that Myngoon was a prisoner of the French government in Pondicherry, Myngoon replied, "Nothing could be further from the truth. I am absolutely free here . . . and I am not the object of any surveillance."[87] Due to the semifictitious nature of *Lettres de l'Inde*, it is hard to know how far Mirbeau had tampered with the conversation recorded by Deloncle, to whom Myngoon had complained in Chandernagore, shortly before his departure for Pondicherry, of the "incessant surveillance by English spies who," Myngoon alleged, "come into his bedroom at night."[88]

Myngoon presented himself as motivated by love for his people, whom he regarded as his children.[89] In correspondence with the British Colonel Sladen, Myngoon asserted that he was "greatly afflicted to hear about the present miserable condition of the people of Burmah and the tottering throne of my ancestors and therefore eagerly desire for the peace and welfare of that nation."[90] While Myngoon continued to fashion his narrative in memorials and letters, in Burma, British troops and indigenous auxiliaries engaged in the "ritualistic destruction" of court records alongside the disestablishment of the Burmese monarchy with the exile of King Thibaw and Queen Supayalat to Ratnagiri in 1885.[91] From 1883 to 1885, some British officials still considered Myngoon a possible successor to Thibaw, but this possibility was foreclosed when Britain opted for "annexation, pure and simple."[92] In March 1886, Chief Commissioner Charles Bernard announced, "No Burma Prince will ever rule again in Burma. The Queen and Empress of India is sovereign throughout the whole country and all the people of Burma are now Her Majesty's subjects."[93] The Burmese were slow to accept that sovereignty, and until 1890, the Burmese army put up a guerrilla resistance to British troops.[94]

In Pondicherry, Myngoon again became the object of British surveillance, due to his relations with Sikh supporters of the Maharaja Dalip Singh, formerly exiled in England. As Yang notes in chapter 3 in this volume, Dalip Singh converted to Christianity at a young age. He returned to India, having announced that he wanted to return to the Sikh religion following the death of his mother, via Paris and Russia in the 1880s to lead a Sikh resistance movement against the British, with Russian support.[95] The "Pondicherry Sikhs" were a vital nexus in this plan, and central to a complex network of messages linking Sikh supporters of Dalip Singh in various states. Dalip Singh's cousin and the prime minister of his government in exile, Thakur Sandanwalliah Singh, moved to Pondicherry with his sons in the 1880s, where Thakur befriended Myngoon. Here we see possible indirect collaboration between two exiles of the British Empire. A British history of Myngoon compiled in 1907 wrote that the "Sikh Sadars" had dissuaded Myngoon from "having anything to do with the British government."[96] For several years Maharaja Dalip Singh operated offshore, communicating by letter from London and Paris and then Kiev, Russia, with Thakur Singh, whose visit to London in the 1880s had, British intelligence believed, persuaded Dalip Singh to return to India to reclaim Punjab.[97] Part of the plan involved emissaries from Dalip Singh and Thakur Singh sending men to coax Sikh and Rajput soldiers in the native army to join their cause, with a number of these men then journeying to Pondicherry to take an oath of allegiance.[98]

Thakur Singh was compared to Prince Myngoon by a British consular agent: "I hope you have no intention of making another Mingoon Prince of Thakur Singh," Colonel Fisher told the governor of Pondicherry, "or I assure you that it would not be worth the candle."[99] In March 1887, the chief secretary of Madras telegraphed that Myngoon and Thakur Singh had become "intimate" in Pondicherry and exchanged "visits and correspondence."[100] Thakur Singh would die in suspicious circumstances in Pondicherry in August 1887, rumored to have been poisoned by the British.[101] We can only speculate as to the substance of Myngoon and Thakur Singh's friendship. Like Nathalie Zemon-Davis in her biography of al-Hasan al-Wazzan, in thinking about Myngoon's journeys I have had to make use of the conditional and the speculative.[102]

Britain's annexation of Upper Burma, and the exile of King Thibaw, his queen, and a number of descendants to India, generated a new energy in Myngoon. Despite his continued surveillance, Myngoon managed to retain and galvanize support in Burma, and from February to June 1888, a resistance movement broke out in Lower Burma in his favor.[103] In the late 1880s, the ministry of marine and colonies in Paris tasked the newly appointed acting French governor of Pondicherry with ensuring that Myngoon was kept under serious surveillance, and requested "a daily and confidential" police report from the two agents stationed near Myngoon's home.[104] On 15 November 1889, Myngoon traveled from Pondicherry to Saigon with the help of French authorities. He dressed first "in the disguise of a Baboo [or Bengali man] and then, in order to evade the British at Colombo, disembarked dressed as a sailor.[105] The governor of France's establishments in India, M. Nouet, had advised the captain, "in the interests of the French government," to allow "this exile" to travel to Cochinchina under a pseudonym, in the third class.[106] When in transit via Singapore, he hid in the coal bunker for eight hours during a British search.[107] On 15 November 1889, the ministry of commerce of India and colonies cabled the governor general of Indochina, Hanoi: "Keep Myin Goon in Saigon provisionally, allowing him freedom, but placing him under active surveillance."[108]

A month after his arrival in Saigon, Myngoon wrote of his thankfulness, but also of the loneliness and pain of exile. "Words cannot express my gratitude for the kindness the French Government has shown me. But alone, with no-one who speaks my language, the pain of exile [*les douleurs de l'exil*] is unbearable. . . . I beg you to allow my family to come and join me."[109] In May, the political department of foreign affairs wrote to A. M. Etienne, under secretary of colonies, arguing against sending Prince Myngoon back to Pondicherry, and stating that "the Pretender will be the object of an effective surveillance on the part of our authorities, and . . . will not be allowed to go beyond the capital of Cochinchina."[110] In Saigon, Myngoon was kept under a detailed police watch.

In the early 1880s, some quarters of French opinion still saw a prospect of French influence in Upper Burma and regarded Myngoon as a powerful political pawn. Following Britain's annexation of Upper Burma, France's policy vis-à-vis Myngoon soon turned to one of cooperation with the British. In 1897, when Myngoon was detained on his attempted journey through northern Indochina to the Shan States, the British ambassador in India expressed the appreciation of the British government for France's friendly action in securing his arrest.[111] Myngoon would stay in Saigon until his death in 1921.

Myngoon's series of escapes, hideouts, and disguises speak to an exile shaped by subterfuge and surveillance. The frustration of the British police following his escape from Benares to Chandernagore points to blind spots in the panopticon, as does his successful stowaway from Chandernagore to Pondicherry and his later concealed transit through Colombo and Singapore. The narrative tracks of exile are here penned by a watchful surveillance apparatus that stretched from governors to police clerks, while a ship's captain and the governor of the French Indies connived in his concealed passage from the British. For his part, Myngoon wrote elaborately worded missives to the authorities whom he variously regarded as his captors, leaving his own narrative traces in a trail of diplomatic letters and memorials telling his story of unjust treatment by the British as the reason for his escape into French territory, and elaborating his desire to gain the Burmese throne.

CASE THREE: U VILLASA, THE MASQUERADING MONK

The third and final case I examine involves the intrigues of a possibly fraudulent monk, U Villasa, who attempted to gain a footing in the gem-mining town of Pailin, a small town in western Cambodia close to the border with Siam that counted several thousand Burmans, including migrant labor from the Shan States. This episode took place when Myngoon was some twenty years into his Saigon sojourn. The Cambodian Minister of Interior Sathavong, based on reports from a Cambodian district official in Pailin, wrote that U Villasa had lived "tranquilly" in Pailin since 1912, had gained the respect of the Burmese community, had correctly observed monastic rules, and was not a "monk in disguise."[112] In February 1914, U Villasa reentered Cambodia bearing a letter of introduction from Myngoon to the Resident Superieur of Cambodia (RSC), in which Myngoon asserted that he had known him for a very long time.[113] U Villasa reportedly visited Myngoon several times a year.[114] His escapade lasted several years and ended in failure, with U Villasa facing charges of theft. This episode sheds tangential light on the ambitions of the Myngoon prince and on French and British anxieties about his influence. We can only speculate as to the parameters of Myngoon and U Villasa's acquaintance, but the prince's trajectory of embracing entrepreneurial schemes, his letter of support for U Villasa, and reports of regular contact indicate possible shared plans. In 1897, Myngoon had asked to move to Phnom Penh, but his request was denied by the ministry of foreign affairs, which deemed it "dangerous."[115] Through support of U Villasa, he could live vicariously, extending his reach to this Burmese community along Cambodia's frontier with Siam.

This was not Myngoon's first attempt at economic enterprise. In 1902–1903, increasingly concerned about the upkeep of his family, Myngoon had located another potential source of revenue, a teak concession in Laos.[116] In 1905 he proposed bringing several hundred Burmese to work a forest concession in Cambodia where he hoped to find ruby mines.[117] This plan seems to have gone nowhere and is a reflection of the shifting and contracting of his sights from the possibility of return to Burma and more grandiose concerns about nation and sovereignty to quotidian questions of economies of exile. Reflecting a perceived decline in Myngoon's political capital in Burma, Governor-General of India Lord Curzon of Kedleston described him in 1903 as "wholly insignificant and quite harmless,"[118] but four years later the government of Burma noted that he still had "many adherents" and that his return to India was "desirable."[119] It was in the 1910s that Myngoon's sights shifted again to the Cambodian capital of Phnom Penh and the district of Pailin, whose Burmese and Shan inhabitants were treated as British subjects.[120] From 1912 to 1913, Myngoon's son Thaithinjyi rented a house in Phnom Penh, and then moved to Battambang, a large town close to Pailin, to work for a French company involved in phosphate mining. The protectorate funded part of his expenses.[121] The Burmese who first inhabited Pailin were miners from the Burmese gem-mining town of Mogok, who were encouraged to develop the land under a concession from the Siamese king in the late nineteenth century. British and French correspondence shows strong interest in the economic potential of the area and elevated awareness of its importance as a frontier region.[122]

In February 1914, U Villasa returned to Pailin from Saigon via Phnom Penh, carrying a letter from Myngoon to the RSC requesting assistance in his wish to rebuild the Preah Chetdey temple, for which approval had been granted by the Cambodian authorities.[123] The commissioner of Battambang gave U Villasa the status of head monk of Pailin, granting him the powers to ascertain whether the Burmese monks in the area were of good character and "real" monks, so that all those who were not should pay revenue tax.[124] This appointment of U Villasa by a French secular authority seems to have carried little weight in Pailin. Within months, these forays had galvanized opposition from the long-term secular leader of the community, Maung Swe, who was also the holder of a five-year gem-mining concession, alongside the monopolies for alcohol and opium.[125] Accounts about U Villasa conflicted. Some reported that he was held in high esteem and a bona fide monk, others that he was an imposter who ate at all hours of the day in violation of monastic precepts, and others that he was a petty thief. U Villasa's main misdemeanor, however, appeared to have been political and economic: his presence split the Burmese population of Pailin, polarizing the community into camps for and against Maung Swe. Maung Swe and his supporters blocked U Villasa's plans to rebuild the temple, cut off his supply lines, and, among other moves to evict him from Pailin, confiscated his key to the monastery.[126] U Villasa, some held, had the skills to make sapphires sparkle like diamonds and was highly knowledgeable in matters of the gem trade.[127] The colonial correspondence moves from an embrace of U Villasa to a rejection and voices suspicions that he was acting as an agent of Myngoon and fomenting anti-

British feeling in the area. In January 1915, RSC Outrey reported British concerns that U Villasa—a long-term acquaintance and regular visitor of the prince in Saigon—was Myngoon's political go-between.[128]

U Villasa wrote copious letters and petitions to the French authorities alleging criminal conduct of Maung Swe and asserting his own credentials.[129] Since France and Siam redrew the boundary lines in 1907 under a Franco-Siamese Treaty, Pailin was legally part of the French Protectorate, but this did not translate into French influence. Maung Swe had protection—his guards, who watched over the gem merchants, the bazaar, and the mines, were allegedly armed with two hundred rapid-fire rifles.[130] French authorities acknowledged that they possessed "no means of effective pressure on the Chief of the Burmese who is in effect the absolute master within the limits of his mining district."[131] In March 1914, an anonymous letter to the RSC, in a thin, spidery hand, reported a litany of complaints against Maung Swe: opium trade; siphoning off taxes for his personal gain; sending thieves, dacoits, and others out for plunder and banditry; and taking bribes for theft, rape, robbery, assault, and other cases. The letter, almost certainly written by U Villasa, recommended that Maung Swe be imprisoned and declared that the people of Pailin feared him like a king.[132] By December, U Villasa's battle was lost. The governor of Cochinchina wrote to the RSC requesting "any information you have that might shed light on the head monk, U Villasa of Pailin . . . touching on his relations, his conduct, his reputation. This monk, a Burmese subject, has been in truck with the Myngoon Prince for a very long time. He has been visiting Myngoon two or three times a year, and is suspected of acting as an intermediary between Myngoon and Burmese agitators." The RSC requested the commissaire délégué in Battambang to investigate U Villasa's "relations, conduct, and reputation."[133] A telegram from Hanoi asked for an investigation into a monk engaged in anti-English agitation among Burmans in Pailin.[134] In mid-February 1915, U Villasa informed the commissaire délégué in Battambang that he was leaving for Saigon, having been called by Prince Myngoon. The commissaire wrote to the RSC suggesting that he question U Villasa about his passage to Phnom Penh and his relations with the prince, "so as to provide intelligence to the British," and claimed that U Villasa had left Prome, in Burma, after a "semi-political" and "semi-judicial" affair, and had donned monk's robes only to gain immunity.[135] This correspondence reveals the tight network of surveillance on U Villasa and the collaboration between British and French authorities.

For his part, U Villasa claimed to be "a monk of Prince Myngoon" and stated that he dared not return to Burma, asking the RSC to take pity on him.[136] U Villasa was soon on trial for petty theft, charged by a Burmese doctor in Phnom Penh with stealing one hundred piastres.[137] Condemned to two months in prison, he demanded to appeal the sentence in Saigon and was accompanied by one of Myngoon's secretaries, who was fluent in French and Burmese.[138] The Resident of Battambang declared U Villasa a fraud who had nothing religious about him except his robes, and Myngoon claimed that he had no formal ties to U Villasa and that he had offered him assistance only out of the "respect that we hold for monks."[139]

The French and British interest in U Villasa hinged in large part on his relationship with Myngoon. We can thus read the colonial correspondence surrounding his venture in Pailin as part of broader narrative processes of exile. In the relationship between Myngoon and U Villasa, we see the figure of the trickster at large, with Myngoon in his spirit of entrepreneurship probably hoping for a footing in the lucrative gem-mining concession whose Burmese and Shan workers were prospective royal subjects and supporters. Here Myngoon's economic ambition may also be apparent, in a possible ruse to supplement his pension, which was insufficient to keep him and his sons in the lifestyle to which they aspired. The figure of the imposter monk acts as a symbol of the frustrated exile confined to Cochinchina. We see also the tempering of Myngoon's ambition as he began to rein in his own aspirations, shifting from a desire to return to Burma to gain the throne, as this became a more unrealistic goal, to a desire to live in better financial circumstances.

The ruling classes of Java, Burma, and other countries in Southeast Asia, writes historian Michael Adas, "believed that they were privileged and superior beings, and sought to emphasise the gulf that separated them from the mass of the population. Detailed sumptuary laws regarding housing, dress and even eating utensils, elaborated conventions to regulate encounters between superiors and inferiors." As Myngoon adapted to colonial housing and experimented with different attire, first through temporary disguises and then adopting European dress in Saigon and retaining only the Burmese headdress, these codes became retranslated in exile. In Southeast Asia, Adas continues, dependents were a marker of a man's power and status. If their numbers expanded, so did the belief that he was a man of "worth and ability." Conversely, "if he lost clients or was unable to maintain them properly . . . his status declined and his power was threatened."[140] In exile, Myngoon needed to generate wealth in order to finance his dependents at his offshore court and to retain the aura of power.

Where Pailin at least had offered the potential for a regal dimension and a convergence of political and economic opportunity, the teak concession gestured toward the prospect of links with the Shan States through Laos. Overall these schemes were unsuccessful. In 1919, Myngoon wrote that "my supporters, discouraged or placed under excessive surveillance, don't send me subsidies like before."[141] His earlier escapades offered a more exotic and dignified outlet to Myngoon's imaginings of region and his place in it than the crimping requests he wrote to the French in relation to his pension, against the growing shadow of his creditors.

What do these three episodes tell us about the life in exile of Prince Myngoon, about the narrative processes elaborated around exile, and about exile as a lens on microhistory? They give us a glimpse of the colonial mechanics and limitations of surveillance, of the networks with whom Myngoon liaised, and of Myngoon's possible attempt to establish a power base in Cambodia. The figure of the imposter monk galvanized colonial anxieties about Myngoon's reach. The first case illuminates the energies directed by colonial authorities toward Myngoon and points to the weaving of narrative threads around Myngoon in colonial record keeping. In all cases, details loomed large, as surveillance patterns created a web of minutiae and an armature of documentary "control." Historiographically, Myngoon's exile offers an alternate vista on Southeast Asian pasts, positioned as he was at the interstices of empires. To his supporters in Burma, he represented an alternate future to the society devoid of a monarchy imposed by colonial rule.

From the 1860s to the 1910s, Myngoon beguiled and confused colonial authorities and security personnel from French India, British India, and French Indochina. Various cases of disguise and subterfuge reveal, in the case of the Calcutta detectives, a sense of frustration at the impossibility of adequately policing Myngoon. In the case of the betel box with the hidden letter, we glean the suspicions of intrigue directed at Myngoon. In the case of Myngoon's purported connection with Dalip Singh's movement, we see the concern of British intelligence that exiles from different countries might combine causes. In the case of the monk U Villasa, colonial responses were confused, providing initial support, then querying his credentials and worrying that Myngoon was using him to stir up anti-British sentiment.

What do these narrative tracks tell us, and how might we read what Carlo Ginzburg calls the "threads and traces" of these accounts?[142] We sense a deep anxiety in colonial records exacerbated by Myngoon's role as a boundary-crossing trickster figure who played to both British and French audiences. Myngoon successfully evaded British police when transiting through Colombo and Singapore, escaped under their watch in Benares, and became an irritant to their surveillance system in Chandernagore, where he also flouted French surveillance. His antics reveal places to hide despite colonialism's long reach. His intermittent successes in raising support and resistance in Burma point to a system of communications outside colonial control. However, once Myngoon had entered French territory, he became financially dependent on the French, much as he had been on the British while in exile in British Burma and India. His own archival narrative tracks cast him as a national hero and an exile, ill-treated by the British, who was the rightful heir to the throne of Burma. As a pensioned prince whose range of movement was limited, he sought to expand his means of income through offshore schemes, but these did not materialize into wealth. The Myngoon Prince, whose motto alongside his peacock emblem on his stationery read, "The body dies, the plumage never," died deep in debt and heirless in exile in 1921.

Through the escapades explored in this chapter, we glean some of the avenues of enterprise open to exiles. As Hyde writes, all cultures have binary categories, such as true and false, to which we might add the watched and the watcher. "Trickster is the great shape shifter, which I take to mean not so much that he shifts the shape of his own body but that, given the materials of this world, he demonstrates the degree to which the way we have shaped them may be altered."[143] Myngoon tested the limits of colonial surveillance and the binary between the spies and the spied upon.

The history of the Myngoon Prince as refracted through these three diverse episodes reveals the power of exile to subvert dominant scripts. Myngoon's late-nineteenth-century missives to colonial authorities reveal how intimately he tied his identity to a royalist and national framework as the future king of Burma. On fleeing British India for French territory, he escaped his status as a state prisoner. Through disguise, enterprise, and subterfuge, he managed to outwit his colonial captors at decisive moments in his life in transit, and thus to exercise partial control over his life journey. At different times, Myngoon managed to retain a prime minister and private secretaries but was unable, in his increasingly penurious state as he lived beyond the confines of his pension and accumulated debts, to support an offshore court in the twilight of his life. The contrast between his capacious visions of his destiny as the future king and his growing dependency on colonial powers as a pensioned prince led to his attempts to carve out a space for himself that would give him some autonomy of movement, motivated by the ideal of return. Exile in both British and French territories expanded his horizons and his political capital, although the latter waned with the passage of time and as his own support base shrank and colonial interests changed. The narrative traces considered here reveal the life of a quixotic dreamer who was able to imagine his place in a world beyond the geographic confines of exile, in part due to his own journeys across diverse colonial places and cultural spaces. They also point to the paranoia of empire, as seen most conspicuously in the exaggerated British responses to a letter written by another hand, and the copious correspondence over Myngoon's surveillance.

NOTES

Epigraph. Ginzburg, 2011, 150.

1. His three sons and one adopted son had all died before him, leaving him with no male successor, but he was survived by two widows, two daughters, and five granddaughters, all totally bereft of resources. Archives d'Outre-Mer (hereafter cited as AOM), Indochine, Le Ministre des Pensions, des Primes et des Allocations de Guerre, Chargé de l'Interim du Ministère des Colonies, à Monsieur le President du Conseil, Ministre des Affaires Etrangères.

2. Eric Tagliacozzo, *Secret Trades, Porous Borders: Smuggling and States along a Southeast Asian Frontier, 1865–1915* (New Haven, CT: Yale University Press, 2005).

3. See Michel Foucault, *Discipline and Punish: The Birth of the Prison* (New York: Knopf Doubleday, 2012); John S. Furnivall, *The Fashioning of Leviathan: Beginnings of British Rule in Burma*, Occasional Paper of the Department of Anthropology, Research School of Pacific Studies, ed. Gehan Wijeyewardene (Canberra: Australian National University, 1991); and James Scott, *The Moral Economy of the Peasant* (New Haven, CT: Yale University Press, 1976).

4. Furnivall, *Fashioning of Leviathan*, 58.

5. Richard Holmes, *Shelley: The Pursuit* (New York: New York Review Books, 2003), 168.

6. Sanjay Subrahmanyam, *Three Ways to Be Alien: Travails and Encounters in the Early Modern World* (Waltham, MA: Brandeis University Press, 2011).

7. Prasenjit Duara, *Rescuing History from the Nation* (Chicago: University of Chicago Press, 1995).

8. AOM, FM 1, affpol 54, M. A. Filippini, Governor of Cochinchina, to M. le Ministre de le Marine et des Colonies, Paris, 12 June 1887. This letter contains a translation of a letter from Myngoon to King Norodom of Cambodia.

9. AOM, FM 1, affpol 54, "Notes Explanatory on the Brief Details Contained in the Genealogical Table Hereto Prefixed."

10. Ibid.

11. "What was the nature," asks Subrahmanyam, writing of Spanish soldiers in the markets of Tenochititlán, "of translation in the whole process, mediated as it was by one or perhaps more than one intervening social layer?" Subrahmanyam, *Three Ways to Be Alien*, 174.

12. Karl Britto, *Disorientation: France, Vietnam and the Ambivalence of Interculturality* (Hong Kong: Hong Kong University Press, 2004), 9, 118.

13. Michel-Rolph Trouillot, *Silencing the Past: Power and the Production of History* (Boston: Beacon Press, 1995), 52–55.

14. See Caroline S. Hau and Kasīan Tēchaphīra, eds., *Traveling Nation-Makers: Transnational Flows and Movements in the Making of Modern Southeast Asia* (Singapore: National University of Singapore Press, 2011), 5.

15. Anand Yang, "Exile Experiences: Indian 'Convicts' in Nineteenth Century Singapore" (paper presented at the Annual Meeting of the Association of Asian Studies, Philadelphia, 2010).

16. Ibid.

17. Kerry Ward, "Conceptualizing Center and Margin in Early Modern Dutch and Indonesian Banishment" (paper presented at the Annual Meeting of the Association of Asian Studies, Philadelphia, 2010).

18. Edward Shafer, *The Vermilion Bird: T'ang Images of the South* (Berkeley: University of California Press, 1967), 31.

19. Thant Myint U, *The Making of Modern Burma* (Cambridge: Cambridge University Press, 2000), 5, 130–131, 154, 177, 178, 194.

20. Michael Chabon, *The Amazing Adventures of Kavalier and Clay* (New York: Picador, 2000), 14.

21. AOM, FM 1, affpol 54, GGI, Saigon, to Minister of Colonies, Paris, 24 November 1911.

22. The British terms are outlined in British Library, India Office Records Collection (hereafter cited as IORC), Secretary to the Government of India in the Foreign Department to Prince Myngun Min, Simla, 7 August 1911. Myngoon's desired terms are outlined in AOM, FM 1, affpol 54, Myngoon Min, Copie de la 1ère Proposition.

23. Subrahmanyam, *Three Ways to Be Alien*, 178.

24. Prasenjit Duara, *Sovereignty and Authenticity: Manchukuo and the East Asian Modern* (Boulder, CO: Rowman and Littlefield, 2004), 49.

25. Lewis Hyde, *Trickster Makes This World: Mischief, Myth and Art* (New York: Northpoint Press, 2010), 39–54, 77–78.

26. IORC, L/PS/6 549 1867, "Narrative of Events Which Occurred in the Vicinity of Mandalay during the Civil War in Aug, Sep, Oct 1866," by Captain E. B. Sladen.

27. IORC, L/PS/6 549, Captain C. Hildebrand, Officiating Secretary to Chief Commissioner of Burma, to Secretary to Governor of India, Foreign Department, 12 January 1867.

28. IORC, L/PS/6/550, Fort William, Copy No. 194, 8 December 1866, Col. A. Phayre, Chief Commissioner British Burma, to the Secretary to the Government of India, Foreign Department, 15 October 1866.

29. IORC, L/PS 6/549, Sladen to Phayre, 8 November 1866.

30. IORC, L/PS/6/550, Fort William, Foreign Department, Political, No. 72, 9 April 1867.

31. National Archives of India, New Delhi (hereafter NAI), 1867, Foreign Department, Political—A, Prince Meng-gon-daing's Exile to the Andamans as a State Prisoner, K. W. Proceedings, March, No. 210.

32. IORC, L/PS/6/555, Coll 61, Pol. No. 120, India Office, London, to HE RH Governor-General of India, in Council, London, 29 June 1867; Foreign Department, Political, to HM Secretary of State for India, 4 February 1868.

33. IORC, L/PS 6/555, Under Secretary to Governor of India, Foreign Department, to Under Secretary to Government of Bengal.

34. NAI, Government of India, Foreign Department, 1883, Secret—E, April, No. 349, Government of India to Secretary of State for India, dated Simla, 16 April 1883.

35. NAI, Government of India, Foreign Department, 1883, Secret—E, April, No. 328, "The Memorial of Prince Myngoon, a Resident at Chandernagore."

36. IORC, L/PS/6/562, Government of India, Foreign Department, Political, to the Duke of Argyll, 22 January 1869; NAI, Government of India, Foreign Department, Précis-Docket, 1883, Secret—E, September, Nos. 195–221, 5, Prince Myngoon Mintha.

37. IORC, L/PS/6/566, 192, Maj. G. Weld, Commandant at Chunar, "Half Yearly Report of State Prisons under My Charge," 1 January 1869.

38. NAI, 1869, Foreign Department, Political—A, K. W. Proceedings, July, Nos. 67–68.

39. NAI, Government of India, Foreign Department, Précis-Docket, 1883, Secret—E, September, Nos. 195–221, 5, Prince Myngoon Mintha, from the Private Secretary to the Governor-General, 15 June 1883.

40. NAI, Government of India, Foreign Department, 1883, Secret—E, April, Nos. 285–349, Lieutenant Colonel Ridgeway to Commissioner of Police, Calcutta.

41. The Jaipur in either Orissa or the Madras Presidency.

42. NAI, Foreign Department, Political—A, July 1871, "Letter Said to Have Been Written by the Myngoon Prince to his Father the King of Burmah."

43. NAI, Foreign Department, Political—A, July 1871, "Letter Said to Have Been Written by the Myngun Prince to His Father the King of Burmah," from Mr. A. Forbes, Benares, to the Secretary to the Government of India, Benares, 24 July 1871.

44. NAI, Government of India, Foreign Department, No. 176 of 1871, From Mr. A. Forbes, Esq., C. B. Officiating Agent, GG, Benares, to the Secretary to Government of India, Foreign Department, India, Benares, 24 July 1871.

45. NAI, Government of India, Foreign Department, No. 148, Mandalay British Political Agency, 19 August 1871, Captain Strover Mandalay to the Secretary to the Chief Commissioner, British Burma.

46. NAI, Government of India, Foreign Department, 1871, Political—A, December, No. 123.

47. NAI, Foreign Department, 1871, telegram, 4 December, from Agent Governor General, Burma, to Foreign Department, Calcutta.

48. Scott, *Moral Economy*, 94–95.

49. NAI, 1883, Government of India, Foreign Department, Secret—E, April, Nos. 285–349, the Commissioner, Benares Division, to C. Grant, Secretary to the Government of India, Benares, 5 December 1882.

50. NAI, 1883, Government of India, Foreign Department, Secret—E, April, Nos. 285–349, Commissioner to Grant, 5 December 1882.

51. Vivien Ba, "Prince Myngoon's Odyssey," *Journal of the Burma Research Society* 54, nos. 1 and 2 (December 1971): 33.

52. NAI, 1883, Government of India, Foreign Department, Secret—E, April, H. G. Wilkins, Police Office, Calcutta, to C. Grant, 10 December 1882.

53. NAI, 1883, Government of India, Foreign Department, Secret—E, April, "Note on the Inquiry Made by the Police on the Escape of Burmese Prisoner, Prince Myngoon."

54. NAI, 1883, Government of India, Foreign Department, Secret—E, April, Lieutenant Colonel Ridgeway to Secretary to the Government of Bengal, 6 December 1882.

55. NAI, 1883, Government of India, Foreign Department, Secret—E, April, No. 297, Police Office, Calcutta, 10 December 1882, From H. G. Wilkins to C. Grant.

56. NAI, 1883, Government of India, Foreign Department, Secret—E, September 1883, Government of Bengal, 28 April 1883.

57. NAI, 1883, Government of India, Foreign Department, Secret—E, April, telegram, 4 December 1882, from Agent, Governor-General, Benares, to Police, Calcutta.

58. NAI, 1883, Government of India, Foreign Department, Secret—E, April, No. 315, Elder Prince of Burmah to HE the Viceroy and Governor-General of India, 22 December 1882.

59. NAI, 1883, Government of India, Foreign Department, K. W., Secret—E, April, Nos. 285–349, No. 316, C. Grant, Secretary to the Government of India, Foreign Department, to Myngoon, 9 January 1883.

60. NAI, 1883, Government of India, Foreign Department, K. W., Secret—E, April, Nos. 285–349, No. 337, Notes.

61. NAI, 1883, Government of India, Foreign Department, K. W., Secret—E, April, Nos. 285–349, No. 326, Extract from a demi-official from C. Bernard, 18 January 1883.

62. NAI, 1883, Government of India, Foreign Department, Secret—E, April, Nos. 285–349, No. 349, Simla, 16 April 1883, Government of India to Secretary of State for India.

63. NAI, 1883, Government of India, Foreign Department, Secret—E, April, Nos. 285–349, No. 344, 10 March 1883 (demi-official).

64. NAI, 1883, Government of India, Foreign Department, Secret—E, September, Nos. 195–221, Peacock to Grant, 28 April 1883.

65. NAI, 1883, Government of India, Foreign Department, Secret—E, September, Nos. 195–221, Lyall, Officiating Inspector General of Police, to Peacock, Secretary to the Government of Bengal, Political Department.

66. NAI, Government of India, Foreign Department, Précis-Docket, 1883, Secret—E, September, Nos. 195–221, H. W. Primrose, Private Secretary to the Governor-General, to C. Grant, 29 December 1882.

67. NAI, Government of India, Foreign Department, 1883, Secret—E, September, Peacock to Grant, 28 April 1883.

68. NAI, Government of India, Foreign Department, 1883, Secret—E, April, Nos. 285–349, 11 January 1883 (demi-official), from D. R. Lyall, Esq., Inspector General of Police, Bengal, to C. Grant, Esq., CSI.

69. Universities Historical Research Center (hereafter cited as UHRC), Yangon, Microfilm, Myngun Prince, Quai d'Orsay, M. D. Asie, Vol. 51 (Birmanie 3), 1883–1885, Simla, Foreign Department, Secret, 16 April 1883, Copy, Letter to HM Secretary of State for India.

70. NAI, Government of India, Foreign Department, 1883, Secret—E, April, Nos. 285–349, No. 324, telegram, 16 January 1883, from British Burmah, Rangoon, to Foreign, Calcutta.

71. NAI, Government of India, Foreign Department, 1883, Secret—E, April, Nos. 285–349, No. 326, C. Bernard, 18 January 1883.

72. NAI, Government of India, Foreign Department, 1883, Secret—E, April, Nos. 285–349, No. 327, S. J. Leslie to C. Grant, Calcutta, 14 February 1883, No. 328, the Memorial of Prince Myngoon, a resident at Chandernagore.

73. NAI, Government of India, Foreign Department, Précis-Docket, 1883, Secret—E, September, No. 200, Simla, 12 May 1883, J. Lambert to J. Wilkins.

74. NAI, Government of India, Foreign Department, 1883, Secret—E, December, Nos. 115–116.

75. NAI, Government of India, Foreign Department, 1883, Secret—E, December, D. N. Lyall to H. M. Durand, Hooghly, 24 December 1883.

76. AOM, FM 1, affpol 54, Chandernagore, Commission of Inquiry into the Escape by Prince Myngoon Min.

77. NAI, 1883, Government of India, Foreign Department, Précis-Docket, Secret—E, September, Nos. 29–45, No. 41, Statement Showing the Expenditure Incurred on Account of the Elder Prince of Burma.

78. NAI, Government of India, Foreign Department, K. W., Secret—E, April 1884, Nos. 47–56, No. 50, Chandernagore, 3 March 1884, C. S. Clark to Colonel W. F. Prideaux.

79. NAI, Government of India, Foreign Department, Précis-Docket, 1883, Secret—E, September, Nos. 195–221, Prince Myngoon Mintha, No. 210, Lieutenant Colonel W. F. Prideaux to Lieutenant Colonel J. W. Ridgeway.

80. NAI, Government of India, Foreign Department, Précis-Docket, 1883, Secret—E, September, Nos. 195–221, Prince Myngoon Mintha, No. 213, Prince Myngoon to Lieutenant Colonel W. F. Prideaux, 30 June 1883.

81. AOM, FM 1, affpol 54, Enquête Administrative, au Sujet de l'Evasion de Chandernagor du Prince Myn-Goon Mentha, 24 June 1884.

82. Octave Mirbeau, *Lettres de l'Inde*, ed. Pierre Michel and Jean-François Nivet (Paris: L'Echoppe, 1991), 106.

83. AOM, FM 1, affpol 54, Piquet to Ministre du Commerce, de l'Industrie et des Colonies, 30 November 1889.

84. UHRC, Microfilm of Quai d'Orsay, M. D. Asie, Vol. 51 (Birmanie 3), 1883–1885, François Deloncle, 2 June 1884, Chandernagore, to M. Jules Ferry, President of the Council and Minister of Foreign Affairs.

85. Mirbeau, *Lettres de l'Inde*, 61.

86. Ioanna Chatzidimitriou, "Lettres de l'Inde: Fictional Histories as Colonial Discourse," *Dalhousie French Studies* 84 (2008): 13.

87. Mirbeau, *Lettres de l'Inde*, 106.

88. UHRC, Microfilm, Deloncle, 2 June 1884, Chandernagor, to M. Jules Ferry, Minister of Foreign Affairs.

89. NAI, 1883, Secret—E, September, Memorial, Chandernagore, May 1883, from Myngoon to the Viceroy and Governor-General of India.

90. IORC, MSS Euro E 290/17, Myngoon to E. B. Sladen, Pondicherry, 1 October 1885.

91. Michael Charney, *Powerful Learning: Buddhist Literati and the Throne in Burma's Last Dynasty* (Ann Arbor: University of Michigan Press, 2006), 261.

92. IORC, MSS Eur E 290/17, Charles Bernard to E. B. Sladen, 12 June 1885.

93. Ni Ni Myint, *Burma's Struggle against British Imperialism 1885–1895* (Rangoon: Universities Press, 1983), 30.

94. J. S. Furnivall, *Colonial Policy and Practice: A Comparative Study of Burma and Netherlands India* (New York: New York University Press, 1948), 70–71.

95. IORC, L/PS/20/H38, Various; IORC, L PS 20 H 3 9, Various.

96. IORC, L/PS/10/232, "The Following Is a History of the Myngoon Mintha."

97. IORC, L/PJ/6/2006, No. 37 of 1887, Government of India, Home Department in Dublin, Confidential No. 113, Lahore, 8 February 1887.

98. Confidential Report, in Ganda Singh, ed. *History of the Freedom Movement in the Punjab*, vol. 3 (Patiala, India: Punjabi University, 1977), 457.

99. Ibid., 400.

100. Ibid.

101. Ibid., 557–558.

102. Nathalie Zemon Davis, *Trickster Travels: A Sixteenth Century Muslim between Worlds* (New York: Hill and Wang, 2006), 13.

103. Ni Ni Myint, *Burma's Struggle*, 79.

104. AOM, affpol 1/54, M. Mathivet, Gouverneur p.i. des Etablissements français dans l'Inde to M. le Ministre des Marines et Colonies, 1 September 1888.

105. UHRC, Yangon, "The Short Narrative of the Misfortunes and Hardships Encountered by Mingoon Min the Legitimate and Eldest Prince of Burma" (n.d.), 5.

106. AOM, FM 1, affpol 54, 21 October 1889, Captain of the *Tibre* to Directeur, Messageries et Maritimes, Calcutta, 1889.

107. AOM, FM 1, affpol 54, M. Piquet GGI à M. le Ministre du Commerce, de l'Industrie et des Colonies, 30 November 1889.

108. AOM, FM 1, affpol 54, Paris, 15 November 1889.

109. AOM, FM 1, affpol 54, 14 January 1890, Myngoon to Sous-Secretariat d'Etat des Colonies.

110. AOM, FM 1, affpol 54, 8 May 1890, Ministère des Affaires Etrangères Direction Politique sous-direction du Nord to A. M. Etienne, Sous-Secretaire d'Etat aux Colonies.

111. AOM, FM 1, affpol 54, British Ambassador in India to French Foreign Ministry, 22 March 1897.

112. National Archives of Cambodia (hereafter cited as NAC), Resident Supérieure du Cambodge (hereafter cited as RSC) 18235, Lettre du Ministre de l'Intérieur to RSC, 7 February 1914.

113. NAC, RSC 18235, Myngoon to RSC, Saigon, 5 February 1914.

114. Ibid.

115. AOM, FM 1, affpol 54, 12 March 1897, Ministre des Affaires Etrangères to M. Lebon, Ministre de Colonies.

116. AOM, GGI 42079, Demande d'exploitation de tecks au Laos (Prince M. M.), 1902–1903.

117. AOM 1, affpol 54, 18 September 1905, Riffault, Ministre de France à Bangkok, to M. Rouvier, Président du Conseil, Ministère des Affaires Etrangères.

118. IORC, Secret/Political Department, 1921, 843/12, Reg. No. 5112.

119. IORC, L/PS/10 232, Government of Burma, Chief Secretary's Office, No. 861-T, 3 July 1907.

120. IORC, MSS Euro F111/397, Report by Acting Vice-Consul Black, Siem Reap, 6 March 1895.

121. AOM, INDO GGI 42078, RSC to Governor of Cochinchina, n.d.

122. AOM, INDO GGI 2923. See, for example, M. Genevet, Battambang, 6 February 1909.

123. NAC, RSC 18235, Le Prince Myngoon Min to M. le Resident Supérieure au Cambodge à Phnom Penh, Saigon, 5 February 1914.

124. NAC, RSC 18235, RSC Baudoin to the Governor-General, Hanoi, 16 January 1915.

125. AOM, INDO GGI 2923, Protectorat du Cambodge, Territoire de Battambang, Entre M. Breucq . . . Commissaire Délegué du RSC pour le territoire de Battambang . . . d'une part; et M. Mang-Say . . . d'autre part. The lease ran from 1 April 1910 to 31 March 1915.

126. NAC, RSC 18235, Le Bonze U Vilassa . . . à M. Ernest Outrey RSC, 18 June 1914; NAC 18235 Note sur le conflit U Villassa–Mang-Say; Traduction le Bonze U Villassa à Outrey RSC, 12 March 1914.

127. NAC, RSC 18235, Resident Battambang à RSC Phnom Penh, 26 April 1915.

128. NAC, RSC 18235, telegram (date illegible), Phnom Penh de Hanoi—GGI to RSC. The suspicions had been relayed by the British chargé d'affaires in Bangkok.

129. AOM, INDO GGI 2923, to RSC from Rev U. Villasa, n.d.; RSC, 22 March 1914, 12 March 1914.

130. AOM, INDO GGI 2913, Battambang, 31 October 1911, Commissaire Délégué to RSC.

131. NAC, RSC 18235, Commissaire Délégué Battambang to RSC, 6 April 1914.

132. NAC, RSC 18235, Anonymous to RSC, 22 March 1914.

133. NAC, RSC 26147, RSC to Commissaire Délégué Battambang, 6 January 1915.

134. NAC, RSC 26147, telegram from Hanoi to Phnom Penh, 0431 646 19h30, RSC Phnom Penh.

135. NAC, RSC 18235, Resident of Battambang to RSC Phnom Penh, 26 April 1915.

136. NAC, RSC 18235, U Villasa to RSC, 18 June 1914.

137. NAC, RSC 18235, M. Dupuis, Commissaire Central de Police, to RSC Phnom Penh, 24 April 1915.

138. NAC, RSC 18235, telegram, Phnom Penh, 30 April 1915, RSC to Gouverneur Cochinchine, Saigon.

139. NAC, RSC 18235, Myngoon Min to RSC Phnom Penh, 1 May 1915.

140. Michael Adas, "'Moral Economy' or 'Contest State'? Elite Demands and the Origins of Peasant Protest in Southeast Asia," *Journal of Social History* 13, no. 4 (Summer 1980): 527–528.

141. AOM, INDO FM, affpol 1/54, Myngoon Min to Gouverneur de la Cochinchine, Saigon, 17 November 1919.

142. Carlo Ginzburg, *Threads and Traces: True, False, Fictive* (Berkeley: University of California Press, 2011).

143. Hyde, *Trickster Makes This World*, 91.

BIBLIOGRAPHY

Adas, Michael. "'Moral Economy' or 'Contest State'? Elite Demands and the Origins of Peasant Protest in Southeast Asia." *Journal of Social History* 13, no. 4 (Summer 1980): 521–546.

Ba, Vivien. "Prince Myngoon's Odyssey." *Journal of the Burma Research Society* 54, nos. 1 and 2 (December 1971).

Britto, Karl. *Disorientation: France, Vietnam and the Ambivalence of Interculturality.* Hong Kong: Hong Kong University Press, 2004.

Chabon, Michael. *The Amazing Adventures of Kavalier and Clay.* New York: Picador, 2000.

Charney, Michael. *Powerful Learning: Buddhist Literati and the Throne in Burma's Last Dynasty.* Ann Arbor: University of Michigan Press, 2006.

Chatzidimitriou, Ioanna. "Lettres de l'Inde: Fictional Histories as Colonial Discourse." *Dalhousie French Studies* 84 (2008): 13–21.

Duara, Prasenjit. *Rescuing History from the Nation.* Chicago: University of Chicago Press, 1995.

———. *Sovereignty and Authenticity: Manchukuo and the East Asian Modern.* Boulder, CO: Rowman and Littlefield, 2004.

Foucault, Michel. *Discipline and Punish: The Birth of the Prison.* New York: Knopf Doubleday, 2012.

Furnivall, J. S. *Colonial Policy and Practice: A Comparative Study of Burma and Netherlands India.* New York: New York University Press, 1948.

Furnivall, John S. *The Fashioning of Leviathan: Beginnings of British Rule in Burma.* Occasional Paper of the Department of Anthropology, Research School of Pacific Studies, edited by Gehan Wijeyewardene. Canberra: Australian National University, 1991.

Ginzburg, Carlo. *Threads and Traces: True, False, Fictive.* Berkeley: University of California Press, 2011.

Hau, Caroline S., and Kasīan Tēchaphīra, eds. *Traveling Nation-Makers: Transnational Flows and Movements in the Making of Modern Southeast Asia.* Singapore: National University of Singapore Press, 2011.

Holmes, Richard. *Shelley: The Pursuit.* New York: New York Review Books, 2003.

Hyde, Lewis. *Trickster Makes This World: Mischief, Myth and Art.* New York: Northpoint Press, 2010.

Mirbeau, Octave. *Lettres de l'Inde.* Edited by Pierre Michel and Jean-François Nivet. Paris: L'Echoppe, 1991.

Ni Ni Myint. *Burma's Struggle against British Imperialism 1885–1895.* Rangoon: Universities Press, 1983.

Scott, James. *The Moral Economy of the Peasant.* New Haven, CT: Yale University Press, 1976.

Shafer, Edward. *The Vermilion Bird: T'ang Images of the South.* Berkeley: University of California Press, 1967.

Singh, Ganda, ed. *History of the Freedom Movement in the Punjab.* Vol. 3. Patiala, India: Punjabi University, 1977.

Subrahmanyam, Sanjay. *Three Ways to Be Alien: Travails and Encounters in the Early Modern World.* Waltham, MA: Brandeis University Press, 2011.

Tagliacozzo, Eric. *Secret Trades, Porous Borders: Smuggling and States along a Southeast Asian Frontier, 1865–1915.* New Haven, CT: Yale University Press, 2005.

Thant Myint U. *The Making of Modern Burma.* Cambridge: Cambridge University Press, 2000.

Trouillot, Michel-Rolph. *Silencing the Past: Power and the Production of History.* Boston: Beacon Press, 1995.

Ward, Kerry. "Conceptualizing Center and Margin in Early Modern Dutch and Indonesian Banishment." Paper presented at the Annual Meeting of the Association of Asian Studies, Philadelphia, 2010.

Yang, Anand. "Exile Experiences: Indian 'Convicts' in Nineteenth Century Singapore." Paper presented at the Annual Meeting of the Association of Asian Studies, Philadelphia, 2010.

Zemon Davis, Nathalie. *Trickster Travels: A Sixteenth Century Muslim between Worlds.* New York: Hill and Wang, 2006.

Contributors

Robert Aldrich is professor of European history at the University of Sydney. Among his recent publications are *Vestiges of the Colonial Empire in France: Monuments, Museums and Colonial Memories* (Palgrave Macmillan, 2005) and *Cultural Encounters and Homoeroticism in Sri Lanka: Sex and Serendipity* (Routledge, 2014), as well as *The Routledge History of Western Empires* (coedited with Kirsten McKenzie). He is currently completing a book on indigenous rulers deposed and banished by British, French, and Dutch colonial authorities in the nineteenth and early twentieth centuries. He is a Fellow of the Australian Academy of the Humanities and of the Academy of the Social Sciences in Australia.

Clare Anderson is professor of history at the University of Leicester, England. She researches the history of incarceration and penal colonies and their intersections with other modes of confinement and coerced labor, with a focus on South and Southeast Asia, the Indian Ocean, and Australia. Her publications include *Convicts in the Indian Ocean* (Macmillan, 2000), *Legible Bodies* (Berg, 2004), *Subaltern Lives* (Cambridge University Press, 2012), and with Madhumita Mazumdar and Vishvajit Pandya, *New Histories of the Andaman Islands: Landscape, Place and Identity in the Bay of Bengal, 1790–2012* (Cambridge University Press, 2015). She is currently working on a global history of penal colonies, encompassing European and non-European empires from 1415 to the 1960s.

Penny Edwards is a cultural historian of nineteenth- to twentieth-century Cambodia and Burma. Her book, *Cambodge: The Cultivation of a Nation* (University of Hawai'i Press, 2007), received the Association of Asian Studies' Harry Benda Prize in 2009. She has coedited six volumes and special journal issues on subjects ranging from Aboriginal-Asian relations in Australia to Sino-Cambodian encounters, and has published widely on Cambodia and Burma from a range of angles including gender, dress, medicine, Buddhism, Gandhi, Chinese diaspora, graffiti, and heritage conservation. She is currently working on a political and cultural biography of the Myngoon Prince of Burma. She is associate professor of Southeast Asian Studies at the University of California, Berkeley.

Timo Kaartinen received his PhD in anthropology from the University of Chicago in 2001. He has taught anthropology at the University of Helsinki since 2001 and presently works at the Helsinki Collegium of Advanced Studies as Core Fellow. His former publications on Maluku history and culture include *Songs of Travel and Stories of Place: Poetics of Absence in an Eastern Indonesian Society*, a monograph published in 2010 by the Finnish Academy of Sciences. His latest fieldwork focuses on natural resource politics and perceptions of the environment in Indonesian Borneo.

Carol Liston is associate professor in Australian history, School of Humanities and Communication Arts, University of Western Sydney. She is an enthusiastic user of archival resources as the basis for historical research and writing. Her research and teaching cover early colonial history in New South Wales, with interests in people (convict, colonial-born, and free immigrant), local history, heritage, and the built environment. Her publications include histories of Campbelltown, Parramatta, and Liverpool; biographies of Sarah Wentworth and Thomas Brisbane and accounts of social life under Governor Macquarie; convict women at the Female Factory, Parramatta, and children in the Female Orphan School. Her current research project with Dr. Kathrine Reynolds is an investigation of convict women transported from Britain to New South Wales between 1818 and 1835.

Sri Margana obtained his PhD from Leiden University (2002). Since 1998 he has held a lecturer position at the History Department, Gadjah Mada University, Yogyakarta. His research interests include Javanese rural history, Javanese historiography, and social history. He is the author of articles and books on Javanese history, the latest of which is *Ujung Timor Jawa, 1763–1913: perebutan hegemoni Blambangan* (Yogyakarta: Ifada Pustaka, 2012).

Lorraine M. Paterson is a historian of Southeast Asia and a visiting scholar at Wolfson College, University of Oxford. She taught in the Department of Asian Studies at Cornell University for nine years and her research and publications have focused on both early-twentieth-century inter-Asian connections and political exile from Indochina to the wider French Empire.

Ronit Ricci is associate professor at the School of Culture, History and Language at the Australian National University. Her research interests include Javanese and Malay manuscript cultures, Islamic literary traditions in South and Southeast Asia, comparative literature, script histories, translation studies, and the history and writing of the Sri Lankan Malays. She has published articles and essays on these topics. She is the author of *Islam Translated: Literature, Conversion, and the Arabic Cosmopolis of South and Southeast Asia* (University of Chicago Press, 2011) and coeditor, with Jan van der Putten, of *Translation in Asia: Theories, Practices, Histories* (St. Jerome, 2011).

JEAN GELMAN TAYLOR taught Indonesian history at the University of New South Wales between 1992 and 2011. Her research focuses on the engagement of the Dutch East India Company in Indonesia and South Africa, and on the social history of colonialism. She is the author of *The Social World of Batavia: European and Eurasian in Colonial Indonesia* (University of Wisconsin Press, 1983; 2nd ed., 2009); *Indonesia: Peoples and Histories* (Yale University Press, 2003), and *Global Indonesia* (Routledge, 2013); coauthor of *The Emergence of Modern Southeast Asia: A New History* (University of Hawai'i Press, 2005); and coeditor and coauthor of *Cleanliness and Culture: Indonesian Histories* (University of Hawai'i Press, 2011).

ANAND A. YANG, Job and Gertrud Tamaki Endowed Professor, International Studies and History, University of Washington, Seattle, is the author of *The Limited Raj: Agrarian Relations in Colonial India* (University of California Press, 1990) and *Bazaar India: Peasants, Traders, Markets and the Colonial State* (University of California Press, 1999); and the editor of *Crime and Criminality in British India* (Association for Asian Studies, 1985) and *Interactions: Transregional Perspectives on World History* (University of Hawai'i Press, 2005). His forthcoming books are titled *Empire of Convicts* and *Thirteen Months in China*, a cotranslated work.

Index

Page numbers for figures are in bold face.

Indonesia. *See* Dutch East Indies (modern-day Indonesia)
infanticide, 233
Insurrection Act, 197
inventory records. *See* possession inventories
Ireland convicts, 197, 200, 207, 208
Islamic communities. *See* Muslims
Islamic manuscripts, 96
Ismail, Imam of Banda Eli, 154

Jaffna, Ceylon, 6, 50, 54, 98. *See also* Ceylon
Jagannath, India, 84–85
Jakarta, Indonesia. *See* Batavia, Dutch East Indies
Jaleka, Siti, 128, 130
Jaleka, Siti (junior), 130
Jamaluddin, Sultan of Tidore, 145
Japan, 24, 236
Java, Dutch East Indies: colonial administration of, 94–95, 100, 119, 128, 136n.14; naming practices of, 113n.31; penal colony on, 97; treaties of, 136n.29; wars in, 98, 119. *See also* Dutch East Indies (modern-day Indonesia)
Javanese historical texts. See *babad* genre
Javanese language, 96, 120
Jayakusuma, Pangéran, 104, 127
Jayawardene, Kumari, 57
Jeilani Salamun, Haji, 154
Jindan, Rani, 72–73
Johnston, Alexander, 59
Joleaud-Barral, Yves, 237
Jonge, Matelief de, 141
Juru, Pangéran, 106–7
Juru, Radèn Ayu, 106–7

Kaartinen, Timo, 139–61
kala pani, 23, 24, 44n.77
Kamaluddin Kaicili Asgar, 145
Kanaks, 238, 244n.105
Kandyan Convention, 56
Kandy and Kandyan politics, Ceylon, 26, 29–30, 51–58. *See also* Ceylon; Rajasinha, Sri Vikrama
Kanjeng Ratu Mas, 122, 125–26, 127
Kapferer, Bruce, 150

kapitan, 141–42
Karskens, Grace, 206
Kawi language, 120
Kei Islands, 146–47, 149–54, 160n.62
Kencana, Ratu, 127
Keppetipola, 57, 61, 63
Kerti, Mas, 110, 114n.39
Khan, Dost Mohammed, Emir of Afghanistan, 49
Khoisan people, Cape of Good Hope, 166, 184n.3
Khond prisoners, 26
King, Philip Gidley, 207
Kingsley, Mary Henrietta, 220
Kolff, Dirk Hendrik, 152
Kukas prisoners, 25
Kusuma Soco, Radèn, **99**

Labuan, Malaysia, 20
language: creolization of, 43n.59, 188n.68; of exile, 2–6, 17n.8; of French colonial exiles, 227, 229, 232, 238; in letters, 11–12, 82–83; of Malay literature, 95–96; official languages of India, 90n.20, 91n.45. See also *specific languages*
Laos, 222
Lembah, Radèn Ayu, **99**
Lenta, Margaret, 182, 189n.101
Leslie, S. J., 260
Le Thi Cam, 235
letters: by Australian convicts, 205; on dislocation, 33–35, 131; by Hamengkubuwana II, 124; as historical source, 11–12, 83; Myngoon and, 252, 254–56, **259**; from Singhs, 82–83; Vietnamese translation *vs.* original, 229–30, 242n.43
Lettres de l'Inde (Mirbeau), 249, 262
Lindsay, Jennifer, 135n.3
Liston, Carol, 193–216
literacy, 195, 205
Ludiyah, Dyah, 127
Luhu, Kaicili, 145
ly (unit of distance), 222, 241n.12

Maas, John Herman, 34
Macasser, Jan van, 175–76
Mackenzie, Colin, 123, 126, 136n.14

Macquarie, Lachlan, 198, 206
Madagascar, 25, 166, 224, 226, 240n.10
Makassar, Sulawesi, 97, 133, 143
Malabar, India, 25, 60
Malacca, Malaysia, 21, 51, 141
Malan, Antonio, 169
Malay language, 95–96, 120, 131, 168
Malays (group), 9, 17n.8, 110n.2, 160n.67
Malaysia. See *specific locations*
Maluku, Dutch East Indies, 140–41, 145.
　See also Bandanese people; *specific islands*
Mandela, Nelson, 8
Mangkudiningrat, Pangéran: as author
　of *babad*, 14, 120, 121, 130; death
　of, 130; description of, 121, 134;
　Hamengkubuwana II and, 125–28;
　petition for, 123; women and, 127, 131,
　132. See also *Babad Mangkudiningratan*
Mangkunagara, Pangéran, 104, 112n.24,
　113n.37
Mangkunagara, Pangéran Arya, 62,
　100–103, 104
Mangkuningrat, Pangéran, 104
Manipur political prisoners, 26
Manuzzi, Nicolo, 252
Mapilah prisoners, 25
maps, **ix**
Margana, Sri, 117–37
maritime law, 139, 143–44
marriage: in Cape law, 168–70, 185n.21; in
　New Caledonia, 231–34, **232**, 243n.76;
　in New South Wales, 206–7
martyrdom *vs.* exile, 8, 13, 25, 49, 76–77, 79
Mascar, Radin, 179–80
Mataram, House of, 110, 114n.38. See also
　specific persons
Matsuda, Matt, 231
Mauritius: British colonial administration
　in, 20, 119; convicts from, 202;
　creolization of, 43n.59; Kandyan
　prisoners in, 57; penal settlements
　and colonies in, 21, 26–27
McLean, John, 198
McNair, J. F. A., 80, 88
Mendis, Vernon L. B., 51
mental health. *See* psychological effects of
　exile
Mernagh, John, 200

Mertasana, 119, 128, 129, 135n.6
métissage, 230–31
Mindon, King of Burma, 253
miracle worker. *See* Singh, Nihal
Mirbeau, Octave, 249, 261–62
mirrors, 183
Mistree, Kunnuck, 34
money: in Cape of Good Hope, 179,
　186n.30, 189nn.92–93; children
　regarded as, 207; in New South Wales,
　205; requests for, 30, 42n.53
Mookerjee, Baboo Nobo Coomar, 260
Moor (term), 172, 187n.44, 188n.74
Moreton Bay, Australia, 195, 200
Mouat, F. J., 34
Moulmein prison, Burma, 26, 30, 43n.70
Muhammad, Sayid, 124
Muhammad Ja'far Thanesari, Maulana,
　25–26
Mul Raj, 73, 76, 78–79
Munsha Bin Baboosh, 35
Musa Ngidrus, Sayyid, 107–8
Musée de Nouvelle Calédonie, 239
Muslims: in Cape slave inventories,
　172–73, 187n.47; manuscripts by, 96;
　networks and rituals in exile, 107–8,
　113n.36, 131; in Punjab, 75; Wahabi
　prisoners, 25, 33
Muttusamy, 53, 54, 63
Myngoondaine, Prince of Burma, 253, 254
Myngoon-Min, Prince of Burma: death of,
　270; escape and surveillance of, 256–62,
　264–65; exile and political legitimacy,
　251; historical background of, 253–54;
　letters and, 249–50, 252, 254–56, **259**;
　Singh and, 263; summary of exile of, 3,
　16, 248–50, 252, 269–70; survived
　family of, 271n.1; as trickster, 16, 249,
　252–53, 261, 268–69; U Villasa and,
　250, 265–68

Naik Revolt (India, 1806–1816), 27
naming practices: of Javanese, 113n.31; of
　slaves in South Africa, 167–68, 172, 184,
　185n.13
Napier, Charles, 75
Natakusuma, Pangéran, 106–7, 120, 134
Nataningrat, 130

National Museum of Colombo, 61
Nayakkar Dynasty, Ceylon. *See under* Rajasinha
neem, 83, 84, 91n.48
Netherlands' United East Indies Company. *See* Dutch East India Company (VOC)
Networks of Empire (Ward), 95
New Caledonia penal colony: establishment of, 15, 224, 230–31; female convicts in, 230–31, 233, 235; land concessions, 232–33, 234, 238; marriages in, 231–34, **232**, 243n.76; penal and contract workers, 234–38; prisoner categories in, 227, 241n.22. *See also* French colonial administration
New South Wales, Australia: establishment of British settlement, 195; land and property rights in, 205–6; list of convicts, **196**; marriage in, 206–7; population statistics, 198; true exiles in colonial history of, 199–200; women in, 206. *See also* Australia
New South Wales Act of 1824, 206
ngungun, 103
Nguyễn Hữu Huân, 12, 228–30, 238, 242n.35, 242n. 46
Nguyễn Vân Xửng, 233
Nicholas, Stephen, 195
Nichols, Isaac, 198
nickel mining, 234, 243n.79
nomenclature, 2, 5–6, 9
Norfolk Island penal settlement, Australia, 195, 200, 205, 212. *See also* Australia
Nouet, M., 264
novelizations of exile, 51
Nuku, Prince of Tidore, 97, 145
nutmeg trade industry, 140–41, 143

Oberoi, Harjot, 74
O'Neil, Peter, 202
orphanages and orphan schools, 170, 185n.10, 207–8, 210
Orphan Chamber, Cape of Good Hope, 165, 167–69, 185n.10
Oxley, Deborah, 195

Pailin, Cambodia, 265–68
Pakualam dynasty, 130

Pakualam I. *See* Natakusuma, Pangéran
Pakubuwana I, Sunan of Kartasura, 98
Pakubuwana II, Sunan of Kartasura and Surakarta, 100, 103–4, 106, 113n.37
Pakubuwana III, Sunan of Surakarta, 106–7
Pakubuwana IV, Sunan of Surakarta, 120
Pakubuwana VI, Sunan of Surakarta, 97
Pakuningrat, Pangéran, 104, 113n.37
Panambangan III, Mas Ngabéhi Rangga, 102
Parramatta, Australia, 199, 205, 207
Paterson, Lorraine M., 220–45
Patimura rebellion (Ambon, 1817), 129, 132–33
peasant rebels: *vs.* political rebels, 21; tribal examples of, 26–27
penal settlements and colonies, 20–22, 27–29, 35–36. See also *specific locations*
penal transportation: to Australia, 195–97, 205; British legal codes on, 196–97, 200; disease and death from, 236, 240n.4, 244n.92; by Dutch East India Company, 24; emotional impact of, 209–11; of French colonies, 223; for Hindu Brahmins, 22, 23; intercolonial circuits, 237–38; to New Caledonia, 236; recollections on, 36; reconsideration of, 5, 20–21; of Singhs, 78–80; unintended consequences of, 31–33, 38. *See also* exile; punishment
Penang, Malaysia: description of, 131; exiles in, 11, 14, 50, 62, 91n.54, 117; penal settlement in, 21, 77, 87, 122
Persian language, 91n.45
petitions: by Cape freed slaves, 180; by elderly family members, 209; by Hamengkubuwana II, 123, 124, 126, 128; as historical source, 11; by Indian convicts, 28–29, 30, 33–38, 42n.53; by Mangkudiningrat, 123; by Rajasinha family, 60; by Singhs, 82–85
Phillip, Arthur, 197, 205
Pieter, Willem, 124
Pigeaud, Theodore, 135n.3
poems: of exile, 228–29, 238; by *pujangga*, 133; of resistance, 6, 12, 35–36; for royal glorification, 59

royal exile: examples of, 48–50; narrative on physical and cultural spaces, 130–34; possessions of, 180–81, 189n.97; purposes of, 141; repatriation of, 61–62, 103–6, 112n.21, 141, 153, 179–80; studies on, 2–3. *See also* exile; political prisoners; *specific persons*

royal regalia: of Kandyans, 56, 61, 62; repatriation of, 99, 100, 104, 105; symbolism of removal of, 3, 56. *See also* possession inventories

ruby mining, 265–68

Rudé, George, 194–95

runaway slaves, 166, 167, 172, 181

Ruse, James, 205

Said, Edward, 71, 72

Said, Radèn Mas, 101, 103, 112n.18

Saint Joseph of Cluny, New Caledonia, 231, **232**

Saktimulya, Sri Ratna, 135n.3

Saleh, Mohamed, 145

Saleh, Radèn, 122

sangha of Ceylon, 51–53, 55

Santal prisoners, 27

Scott, James, 256

secondary punishments, 27–28, 199, 203

sedition, **196,** 198, 202

Sen, Satadru, 23

Senapati, 123

Seneviratne, H. L., 51

Seram, Maluku, 142, 146, 148

Serang, Radèn Ayu, 122, 125

Serat Surya Raja (Hamengkubuwana II), 119

Shafer, Edward, 251

Shah Shuja, Emir of Afghanistan, 49

Shaw, A. G. L., 194

Shere Ali, 33

Shergold, Peter, 195

Shikohabadi, Mohammed Ismail Hussain, 12, 36

Sidhu, Choor Singh, 88

Sikh community: in Punjab, 72–75; in Singapore, 85–88, 91n.54

Silat Road Gurdwara Sahib, 88

Sing, Khurruck. *See* Singh, Kharak

Singapore: description of, 84; penal colony in, 21, 72, 80, 86, 91n.54; Silat Road Gurdwara Sahib in, 88

Singh, Bhai Bir, 73, 74

Singh, Bhai Maharaj. *See* Singh, Nihal

Singh, Booja, 254–55

Singh, Kharak: behavior as prisoner, 81–82; Christian conversion of, 85–86; experience of exile by, 30, 78–81; health of, 82; letters by, 71–72, 82–83, 84–86, 87

Singh, Maharaja Dalip, 50, 73, 263

Singh, Narain, 30, 34

Singh, Nihal: exile *vs.* death for, 76–79; experience of exile by, 13, 30, 71–72, 78–81; health of, 82, 84, 86; influence of, 8, 73–75; letter by, 82–84, 85; memorial of, 8, 87–88; as state prisoner, 72, 75–77, 79

Singh, Ranjit, 73

Singh, Thakur Sandanwalliah, 263

Sinhalese dynasty in Ceylon, 53, 55, 57–58, 61–62

Sivasundaram, Sujit, 58–60

Sladen, E. B., 253

slaves and slave trade: Bandanese people and, 142–43, 146, 158n.24; bequests of, 167, 169, 170, 171; bequests to, 173; in Ceylon, 57, 170; children of, 168, 169, 183, 185n.10, 186n.24; crimes of, 182, 189n.101; enculturation of, 183–84; fugitive, 98, 172; indentured labor, 173, 187n.52; manumission of, 167, 169, 173, 185n.16, 187n.59; mapping of, 7; marriage and, 168–70, 185n.21; naming practices of, 167–68, 172, 184, 185n.13; petitions for repatriation, 179–80; population in South Africa, 7, 14, 165–70, 184nn.4–5, 185n.10; religion and, 172–73, 177, 186n.27, 187n.47; runaways, 166, 167, 172, 181; valuation of, 170–71, 175, 186n.31. *See also* Cape of Good Hope, South Africa; Dutch East India Company (VOC); freed slaves

Sokur, Radèn, 122

South Africa. *See* Cape of Good Hope, South Africa; slaves and slave trade

Southern Vietnam. *See* Cochinchina, Vietnam
spice cultivation trade, 140–41, 143
Spice Islands. *See* Maluku, Dutch East Indies
Sri Lanka. *See* Ceylon
state prisoners. *See* political prisoners
Stewart, William, 30
Stoler, Anne, 231
Straits Settlements. See *specific territories*
stranger king, 60
Strathern, Alan, 60
Subrahmanyam, Sanjay, 252, 271n.11
Sujana, Mas, 112n.18
Sukra, Radèn, **99**
Sumekar, Encik, 125
sunan, 112n.26
Sunan Mas. *See* Amangkurat III, King of Mataram
Sundoro, Mas. *See* Hamengkubuwana II, Sultan of Yogyakarta
Supayalat, Queen of Burma, 26, 251, 262
Surapati, 98
Surojo, Pangéran, 121
surveillance, colonial: letters of Myngoon and, 254–55; metaphors of, 248; of Myngoon in exile, 256–62, 264–65; of U Villasa, 267
Suwija, Radèn Mas, 125
Swe, Maung, 266–67

Tagliacozzo, Eric, 248
Talawe, Pilima, 53–54, 55, 63
Tambiah, Stanley, 53
Tamil language, 96
Tan Jin Sing, 120, 121, 122, 125, 128, 134, 136n.8
Tasmania. *See* Van Diemen's Land penal settlement, Australia
Taylor, Jean Gelman, 134, 165–90
Tchong Winki (Tchong Vinh Ky), 233
teak concessions, 265, 268
Thibaw, King of Burma, 26, 49, 251–52, 256, 262
tickets of leave, 27, 200, 202, 203, 206, 207, 210
Tippu, Sultan, 49

Tonkin, Vietnam, 222, 238, 241n.26. *See also* Vietnam, French colonial
Tooth Relic Temple. *See* Dalada Maligawa (Tooth Relic Temple), Ceylon
trade industry: Bandanese networks, 150–53; spice cultivation and, 140–41, 143
transportation. *See* penal transportation
transported prisoner category, 224, 225, 240n.9
Trân Vân Hap, 233
Treaty of Amiens (1802), 54
Treaty of Giyanti (1755), 136n.29
Treaty of Saigon (1862), 228
trickster figure, 16, 249, 252–53, 261, 268–70
Trincomalee, Ceylon, 54
Trinidad, 43n.59
Trouillot, Michel-Rolf, 250–51
Tuan Sayid Ali, 123
Tự Đức, 222
Turwandan language, 147, 148

ulam, 113n.34
United Dutch East India Company. *See* Dutch East India Company (VOC)
Urdu language, 90n.20, 91n.45
U Villasa, 250, 265–68

Valentyn, François, 155
Van Batavia, Susanna, 175–76, 188n.71
Van Bengalen, Lucas, 177–78
Van Boegies, Hannah, 177–78
Van Boegies, Sampoerne, 180, 189n.92
Van Boegis, September, 176
Van Bougis, Susanna, 176–77
Van de Caab surname, 168, 170
Van Diemen's Land penal settlement, Australia, 28, 195, 200, 205. *See also* Australia
Van Java, Aagje, 179, 189n.86
Vanmai, Jean, 239
Van Riebeeck, Jan, 166
Van Sambouna, Aurora, 179
Vansittart, Henry, 73, 74–76
Vellore Fort, Madras, India, 49, 60
Verhoeven, Pieter, 147
Vibave, 57, 58